The English diaspora in North America

South·Tyneside
Libraries &
Information

The last date entered is the date by which the book should be returned or renewed. You can renew this book by telephoning the library or via the libraries website.

Telephone: 0191 427 1818
www.southtyneside.info/libraries/

Fines at the current rate will be charged if the book is kept after this date.

RFID

2718

MANCHESTER
1824

Manchester University Press

D1614715

The English diaspora in North America

Migration, ethnicity and association, 1730s–1950s

Tanja Bueltmann and
Donald M. MacRaild

Manchester University Press

Published by Manchester University Press
Altrincham Street, Manchester M1 7JA
www.manchesteruniversitypress.co.uk

British Library Cataloguing-in-Publication Data
A catalogue record for this book is available from the British Library

Library of Congress Cataloging-in-Publication Data applied for

ISBN 978 1 5261 0371 0 hardback

First published 2017

ISBN 978 1 5261 3959 7 paperback

First published 2019

The publisher has no responsibility for the persistence or accuracy of URLs for any external or third-party internet websites referred to in this book, and does not guarantee that any content on such websites is, or will remain, accurate or appropriate.

Typeset by
Servis Filmsetting Ltd, Stockport, Cheshire

For Sylvia Ellis:
our mutual friend

Contents

Maps

Figures

Tables

Acknowledgements

We have accumulated a host of debts throughout the preparation and writing of this book. First, we gratefully acknowledge the generosity of the Arts and Humanities Research Council (AHRC), which awarded a project grant (AH/I001042/1) that facilitated the research for this monograph. Without that grant we would not have been able to explore the history of English migration, ethnicity and association in North America as deeply, and in such rich and detailed ways, as we did.

Secondly, the material for this study has been collected from a large number of archives and repositories, all of which deserve our thanks. We were welcomed and assisted by staff at the Historical Society of Pennsylvania, Philadelphia; the New York Historical Society and the New York Public Library; the Maryland Historical Society, Baltimore; the South Carolina Historical Society, Charleston; the City of Toronto Archives; the Archives of Ontario, Toronto; Glenbow Archives, Calgary; Library and Archives Canada, Ottawa; the Anglican Diocese of Ontario Archives, Kingston; Moose Jaw Public Library, Archives Department; the National Archives of Australia and the National Library of Australia in Canberra; and the Turnbull Library and the National Archives of New Zealand in Wellington. In particular, we would like to extend our thanks to Julia Mitchell for her help with digitizing records held at Moose Jaw Public Library, and to the Royal Society of St George for giving us access to material held at its office in London. In the latter case, special thanks must be given to past chairman, Clifford Trowse; general secretary, Liz Lloyd; former chairman, John Clemence; and current chair, Joanna Cadman.

Thirdly, in the course of writing this book numerous colleagues and friends have also been liberal with their time and expertise, sharing their thoughts, offering suggestions and helping with some of the practical aspects of the research. We would like to thank the members of the AHRC project advisory team, particularly John Belchem and Jonathan

C.D. Clark, for their advice and support throughout the lifetime of the project. More than any other individual we are grateful to David Gleeson, who was our co-investigator on the AHRC project. His expertise in American history has been invaluable, and we learnt this well when he read the entire book in draft and made many invaluable comments. The AHRC project team also included our colleagues Dean Allen, Joe Hardwick, James McConnel, Monika Smialkowska and Mike Sutton, and our PhD students Lesley Robinson and Stephen Bowman, who shared their knowledge, time and companionship. For this, we thank them all. Fellow scholars of the English in North America have been unfailingly generous, but none more so than William Van Vugt, who has also been a great supporter of our work from the start. In particular, we would like to thank him for his helpful comments on our ideas about the 'invisible English', and for sharing material with us that has enriched our analysis in this book. Beyond the United States, Brad and Kay Patterson have been wonderful supporters, sharing their peerless knowledge of New Zealand archives and offering their unfaltering encouragement.

As we saw the book through the proposal and peer-review stages, Tom Dark of Manchester University Press earned especial admiration. Tom was thoughtful, challenging and professional from the first day. He simply 'got' the project straightaway and secured readers who, together with him, made searching but fair challenges to help us sharpen and modify aspects of what we had initially drafted. We hope the subsequent rewriting has improved the work; in any event, we are delighted to acknowledge the help provided. After that, Danielle Shepherd saw it through to print with an unerring professional care, and Alun Richards and Rob Byron oversaw the cover design process with great patience. Finally, we must acknowledge the work of our copy-editor, Fiona Little, whose professional skills are matchless.

Last but not least, Sylvia Ellis of Northumbria University deserves our deep appreciation not only as a friend and long-time supporter of the project, but also for her hands-on help with capturing some of the United States material drawn upon in this study, interrupting her own research to do so. It is for this and for so many other instances of support over the years and decades that we dedicate the book to her. It goes without saying, however, that neither Sylvia nor anyone else mentioned here is responsible for what follows.

Tanja Bueltmann and Don MacRaild
Christmas 2015
Newcastle upon Tyne and Coleraine

Abbreviations

ADOA	Anglican Diocese of Ontario Archives
BNA	British North America
CTA	City of Toronto Archives
GMA	Glenbow Museum Archive
GOH	German Order of Harugari
HSP	Historical Society of Pennsylvania
LAC	Library and Archives Canada
MdHS	Maryland Historical Society
NAStGU	North America St George's Union
OSH	Order of the Sons of Hermann
OSStG	Order of the Sons of St George
Record	Sons of England Record
RSStG	Royal Society of St George
SStG	Society of St George

Introduction:
ethnic associationalism and an English diaspora

In early 1953, a major storm hit parts of northern Europe, causing the North Sea to flood. Over 300 people died on land along the east coast of England, with a similar number also perishing at sea. The country's eastern coastline was devastated, properties were severely damaged, and thousands of people had to be evacuated from their homes.[1] At once, the tragedy activated powerful networks of English ethnic associationalism abroad. In New York, where the local St George's Society was gathering for its annual general meeting shortly after the flood, the response was immediate and well organized, with the Society's office becoming 'the centre for the assembling and packing of clothing for people in the devastated areas'. In total, the Society received 'about three tons' of clothes and other 'useful articles', airlifting them to England, specifically to the mayor of Lincoln and the Women's Voluntary Services in London, for distribution in the affected areas. The New York St George's Society was pleased to report that the dispatch of items to England proceeded 'with minimum delay and expense' thanks to the British Overseas Airways Corporation, which 'undertook to take large shipments free of charge'. In total, the Society estimated, about 2,000 families were supported.[2]

As the New York St George's Society reached across the Atlantic, scale and timeliness are highlighted in this directed and practical relief effort. Equally relevant is how the Society utilized a hundred-year-old tradition of English ethnic associational culture.[3] Since long before the American Revolution, Englishmen in the colonies had been helping their countrymen in distress. By the mid-nineteenth century, when mass migration propelled large numbers of English cross the Atlantic for a new life 'out west', English ethnic societies had also taken hold in Canada. These associations developed everywhere, with their spread intrinsically connected to the general settlement patterns of the English. Such was the proliferation and interest that, in 1881, one of the older organizations in the United States, the Sons of St George in Philadelphia,

1

had so many hundreds of members that its committee agreed that 'it was considered advisable to hold informal social meetings of members of the society for the express purpose of becoming better acquainted with each other'.[4]

Still, the elite nature of the St George's societies meant that they never secured mass participation. For this, we must turn to a much larger, initially distinctively lower-class type of English associational life – one built on mutualism and collective self-help – which flourished from the third quarter of the nineteenth century. In the United States this took the form of the Benevolent (sometimes called American) Order of the Sons of St George (OSStG); and in Canada it assumed the guise of the Sons of England Benevolent Society. These two associations became nationwide phenomena in their respective countries, and attracted thousands of members. Like other friendly societies, they adopted initiation rituals and ceremonial forms, and supported wider social and pastoral objectives. Both the OSStG and the Sons of England, as membership societies, dispensed not charity but mutual aid, paid for on a subscription basis.

These two types of English associations – the elite charities and the more working-class fraternities – pinpoint a common fault-line between those who gratefully accepted charity and those who sought robust independence from it through collective self-help. Culturally, the groups were similar. A love of England united them. Sometimes they would pray, play and feast together.

It is the purpose of this study to explore both elite and working-class English ethnic associationalism in North America from their first appearances in the 1730s until the 1950s, when their roles as friendly societies and charities declined in importance. We hope to show that the 'moment of Englishness', which Kumar notes in late nineteenth-century England, was fast established and robust in the United States and Canada long before the motherland awoke to its reasoning.[5]

The nature of English associational culture

While English associations characterized members' ethnic and national origins, they also typified what Alexis de Tocqueville viewed as a peculiarly American organizational culture. He marvelled at the extent of civic associationalism in nineteenth-century America, contrasting the richness and intensity of this participatory citizenship with the hierarchical nature of French and English life. Yet such communal connections were by no means alien to immigrants from the British Isles, since the English had, for centuries, formed diverse types of associations.[6] Civic organizations at home, however, did not have the same reach into the governance of members' lives. As de Tocqueville saw it, the considerable distance between citizen-subjects and the agencies that governed their lives characterized the European social order.

Across the Atlantic, things were different: 'Americans of all ages, all conditions, and all minds are constantly joining together in groups.' Putting political and industrial formations to one side, de Tocqueville marvelled at the dizzying range of things that brought Americans together, 'some grave, some trivial': fêtes, seminaries, inn-building, the erection of houses of worship, the distribution of books, or agencies 'to send missionaries to the Antipodes'. Americans joined together on the principle that enjoying the fruits of society required active participation for the common good. 'Wherever there is a new undertaking, at the head of which you expect to see in France the government and in England some great lord, in the United States you are sure to find an association.'[7] The English certainly expanded their associational reach in the eighteenth and nineteenth centuries, so that emigrants from England were hardly ignorant of the type of culture they would find in the United States. Still, de Tocqueville commented that 'the English were a long way from use of associations with anything like the same frequency or skill as the Americans'.[8]

While that may have been the case, the first societies in the United States, such as the Freemasons, planted in the colonies in the early eighteenth century, or the Manchester Unity of Oddfellows, which came in the early nineteenth, were imported directly from the old country.[9] Americans applied the principles of associational culture very widely to all manner of tasks and challenges, but the Englishmen's secret and ritual-bound societies, their charities and mutual aid associations, which interest us here, owe much to their long-standing European antecedents.[10] Therefore, while de Tocqueville saw associative forms as part of the American condition, there was in fact convergence with, not divergence from, the old country. English immigrants utilized their existing fraternal bonds, not least the masons, to establish 'contacts between English and American [business] members' and to act as 'convenient conduits for skilled English immigrants'.[11]

Once fraternity members had left the old country, the shape and intent of the associations developed and sometimes changed.[12] For one thing, in the United States all ethnic groups found a hothouse for such communal enterprises and so new arrivals quickly became integrated into American ways of associating. Indeed, it is hard to think of an immigrant nationality whose mostly non-political national societies did not play civic as well as ethnic roles. The present study describes a series of English associational structures that conform to these developments in the North American city.

Beito notices three fluid and overlapping, types of fraternal society in the United States: 'secret societies, sick and benefit societies, and life insurance societies'.[13] These correspond to the provision that the

English made available to their countrymen. Such societies emerged from ancient traditions, even though modern variations became less mystical and more practical.[14] Beito explains why people of the same class played the role of both beneficiaries and benefactors of funds. As he acutely puts it: 'today's recipient could be tomorrow's donor'.[15] In fact, this was a link-and-chain connection: the very thing that made relationships stronger. The limitations of state welfare in the nineteenth century also stimulated friendly societies – a development also facilitated, as Beito observes, by the stigma that ordinary people attached to receiving that welfare. There certainly were strong fault-lines between fraternal mutual aid and elite alms-giving, and immigrants thus shared strategies with millions of Americans and Canadians, who formed thousands of societies to provide collective protection. There was, however, a difference between the immigrant and the host. Generally, immigrants were likely to be more desperate than long-established and properly settled migrants, though they still bridled at charity when there was any prospect of an independent strategy. Within this wider context our study seeks answers to questions about the causes of mass mutualism among English immigrations in the United States and Canada, while also providing a test-bed for examining aspects of communal, civic and social interaction more broadly.

Immigrants – and, from an early point, African-Americans – were principal actors in the world of mutual aid, forming and joining fraternal societies in huge numbers.[16] Every imaginable ethnic and national group announced its order, fellowship or society to its new country. Associations with 'Polish', 'Czech', 'Greek', 'Irish', 'Scots', or 'Jewish' in their names were added to the plethora of non-ethnic fraternities, such the nationwide Modern Woodmen of America, or the regional Knights of the Maccabees.[17] Moreover, societies of American and Canadian provenance both aligned and blended with associations of European origins. For example, the Maccabees grew out of the Foresters in Ontario and spread mostly in neighbouring parts of the United States, such as Michigan.[18]

Those at most risk – recent arrivals, those lacking the security of well-established families and communities, people living in remote places and those whose European traditions involved guilds and fraternities – were quickest to form mutual aid societies. In England, those with a proclivity to joining fraternal orders demonstrated collectivism in response to Smilesian exhortations for self-help and thrift. 'Heaven helps those who help themselves', wrote Smiles at the head of his most famous book,[19] and countless societies followed just this stricture. Those joining together within formalized associational structures saw the advantages in unity: it shared risk, guaranteed benefits and came with a form of fraternity that was convivial and sociable, as well as simply financial.

Whether charities or mutual societies, ethnic associations always combined their commitment with strong functions of sociability. Most celebrated their national origins with a dinner on the national saint's day, reinforcing critical sites of national memory.[20] For mutual aid societies that exhibited some characteristics of secret societies, quasi-masonic rituals, passwords, the recitation of arcane-sounding text and the recognition of symbols and devices provided added adhesives for group identity. Not so for the charities: their determining identity was conviviality over dinner and fund-raising for English charities and monuments, not dressing up in aprons, collars and gloves. Yet if ritual separated, for example, the OSStG from the St George's societies, this was not true of religious services, which became increasingly popular foci for collective identification in the course of the nineteenth century. Both types of association also customarily invited members of other ethnic clubs to such dinners, a fact that is suggestive of the wider role of organizations in the social life of New World settlements. The English, then, were no different from other ethnic groups: they carried out the same types of ethnic activities, actively expressing their sense of Englishness through the formalized structures of associations.

Towards an English diaspora

From charity to mutual aid, whether open or secret, ritual-bound or not, the persistent activity of English ethnic associations provided a critical building block in what we believe constituted a functional diaspora, the foundations of which required sustained work by active agents. In conceptualizing the English as a diaspora, Brubaker's three-point typology is instructive. The English were widely dispersed, as peoples must be to be considered as a diaspora. Indeed, few European peoples were, in that sense, more widely spread. English emigrants also retained an orientation towards homeland, whether through concern for immigrants or in their celebrations of St George or the monarchy. We recognize, here, that the English formed a specific type of transnational entity, an imperial diaspora,[21] in the sense that their identity existed at both national and imperial levels and intertwined each unit of belonging in a formidable machine of colonial and imperial control. For the English, connections were maintained with the homeland through communication with the London-based Royal Society of St George (RSStG), which was set up in the 1890s in recognition of the work done in the diaspora to promote English culture and identity. Finally, the English actively fostered a distinctive identity, through their many clubs and societies, in their new places of settlement.[22]

With these considerations in mind, we argue here that there was an English diaspora. Such a view cuts against traditional scholarship, which has cast the English as non-ethnic – though the most recent works have increasingly questioned the idea of this invisible ethnicity of the English.[23] But why, then, have the English been overlooked as an ethnic diaspora? Three factors are crucial. First, in the broadest sense, core elements of United States society, from elites in the antebellum South or the post-war eastern cities, were naturally, at least culturally, Anglophile. Where they might bridle at English foreign policy, they did not demur at the perceived excellence of English intellectual and cultural contributions. As such, English immigrants were submerged under a flood of imported and assimilated English culture, from the schoolroom or theatre to the printed word.[24] Secondly, and more prosaically for ordinary English workers, the privileging of assimilationist narratives has placed the English at the forefront of those who were said to disappear quickly into the melting pot of American life. Thirdly, the celebratory notes of hyphenated Americanism, which became popular in the early twentieth century, had no real place for the English American who was the product of the first two variables. These elements together imposed a triple indemnity on the English: since the culture they established in North America was based on their own, they are assumed to have blended in and disappeared. Thus, for 'English American' read 'Anglo-American'. Equally, in Canada, a similar problem has been identified by scholars: 'the lack of recognition given to English settlement is remarkable ... [t]heir profile seems to have suffered from a perception that they were founding people rather than an ethnic group'.[25] The same traits of cultural synonymy, assimilation and invisible hybridity also were present there.

In general, historians have reflected these conditions in a culture of oversight. In the United States, Marcus Lee Hansen once wrote that 'the English who have contributed the most to American culture, have been studied the least by students of immigration'.[26] But Hansen died young and so did not rectify the weaknesses he observed. Bernard Bailyn consciously overlooked the English since they did not qualify as marginal in the first British Empire, while Carl Wittke chose to leave them out of his general account.[27] Oscar Handlin's classic, *The Uprooted*, which strongly favours the more miserable circumstances of the Irish, made no mention of the English whatsoever, though it discussed the British against whom the Irish migrant was partly defined.[28] Overall, for these ethnic historians, the putative ethnic culture of the English is ignored or downplayed, being considered too diffuse or amorphous for consideration, with little credit given to their ethnic roots.[29] While scholars such as David Hackett Fischer (on the colonial period) recognize the sheer weight of English immigrants, ethnicity is not considered in the multiplicity of elements within the regional-cultural folkways that he identifies as part of English migration to the American colonies.[30] Furthermore, Malcolm Gaskill's seminal study shows how the early English settlers clung on to their identity, as the surrounding environmental and cultural pressures inevitably changed them.[31] The process was not simple, quick or without moments of hybridity.

In spite of the large overall number of English arrivals in the United States and their importance to the growing American industrial economy, scholars of immigration to America generally have not matched recognition of the numbers of English arriving with appreciation of their ethnicity. Charlotte Erickson saw these English as 'invisible immigrants', who either blended in rapidly or else forged an Anglo-American culture that removed the need for ethnic self-expression.[32] Alan Kraut makes no mention of British or English immigrants in his survey of immigrants in industrial America.[33] John Bodnar refers to them only in the context of their role in industrialization.[34] And all the while specialists on the history of ethnicity, such as Kathleen Neils Conzen, David Gerber and Ewa Morowska, have largely concurred with this approach, arguing that immigrants themselves defined in an attempt to negotiate with 'the dominant [i.e. Anglo-American] ethno-culture'[35] – something the English are thought not to have engaged with. The assumed silence of the English is taken to mean a lack of ethnic self-ascription.

Part of the problem lies not in America but at home, where there has been a drifting interplay between the terms 'English' and 'British' with a resulting indeterminacy of the value of the former. Both Adrian Hastings and Krishan Kumar argued that 'England' remained a synonym for 'Britain' throughout the development of modern Britishness.[36] While classic works, such as Linda Colley's, were expressly concerned to explore how the components within the isles were knitted together to form this 'Britishness', Gerald Newman, who dated English nationalism to the eighteenth century, switched from 'British' to 'English' with impunity, as so many scholars have done.[37] If we avoid drifting between these identities there was some justification for favouring 'British' as a collective noun. Since Britain was partly the product of English imperial expansion through the 'Celtic fringe' of Wales, Scotland and Ireland, there had to be some core associations for the Celtic peoples to be co-opted to and 'British' fitted the bill.[38] It is small wonder, however, that the English, who have been subsumed on their own island to an identity, British, which they largely created, were thought to have no durable identity when they went to the colonies among another people whom their forefathers had shaped in cultural terms.

There is, however, a different view – one that points to the visibility of the English and their normative experience of the elements of settlement, adjustment and hardship that made other immigrants into ethnic groups.[39] Recently, for example, the principal scholar of English immigration to the United States has cautioned care in adopting the assimilationist anti-hyphenation approach for the English. Van Vugt writes that 'the cultural similarities between British immigrants and their American hosts must not be exaggerated, nor should their ease of assimilation be assumed'.[40] Van Vugt's warning points to an old, but less well integrated tradition in the scholarship which viewed the English as disillusioned returners – unlike the Irish or the Jews, they had something to return to if they failed in their new North American home, or did not like it. English disappointment at their American experiences was demonstrated by return migration and in the formation of trade unions to challenge American capitalism.[41] Even in Canada the English were far from immune to criticism, teasing and prejudice; they, too, could face enmity, opposition and some degree of prejudice.[42] Moreover, ordinary English unskilled agriculturalists, workers in pressed and dying handicrafts, political rebels and lesser commercialists often found United States capitalism no less severe than the system they had left behind. In fact, in some respects, it was considered worse. Struggles between capital and labour were more black and white in the United States, and violence was commonly resorted to on both sides. In the United States, unionization was fiercely resisted; in the United Kingdom, it was accommodated. In both countries, cartels could be formed to negate the power of workers, but nothing like the Pinkerton agency was resorted to by later Victorian industrial capitalism in the old country. Ethnic stratification also made accommodation with American capitalism difficult. While Britain had cheap Irish labour and landless rural migrants to break strikes and press down wages, the United States had many more such groups competing for survival.

Despite many early hardships and indignities, the New World undoubtedly eventually became a utopian class apart from life in the Irish countryside. In the United States, the English immigrant happened across a gradually more confident, and certainly much larger, group of Irish immigrants than they experienced at home. With long memories and growing political articulacy, the Irish filtered persistent Old World grievances through defiant forms of Irish nationalism, driven by a vigorous pro-independence press, in turn eliciting English hostility.[43] Whether in the workplace, around nationalism or in the face of anti-English hostility from Irish secret societies, there was at times severe conflict between the two nationalities in industrial and urban America. Furthermore, the Irish-American usage of the United States city as a springboard for attacks upon British rule in Ireland created further tensions.[44] In some ways, then, the tensions of Anglo-Irish relations had a further front between the English and the Irish in the United States city.

What this also highlights is that ethnicity was competitive; it was staged in synchronic sequence, one nation following the other in waves of migration; and while the Irish were largely poorer than the English who went to the United States and Canada, and stayed that way into the twentieth century, they nevertheless exerted ethnic power, not least politically. Conflict between the two peoples thus reflected considerable cleavages of history, consciousness and experience. Moreover, imperial propagandists, such as J.R. Seeley, spoke of the Empire as 'English' (including the pre-revolutionary American components).[45] If the Empire was English, then only others could be ethnic within it. The remorseless, purportedly 'civilizing', spread of the English language, which progressed as territorial acquisition increased, added to hegemony of the English in the Empire and colonies.[46] The language became so widespread that its perpetrators appeared invisible. Many middle-class English migrants did not advance their own cause by maintaining only a transient, partial and sometimes conditional relationship with the Empire and the colonies. While the Scots, Irish or Germans built ethnic pillars within the British World, many Englishmen saw themselves as sojourners, not emigrants.[47] Young makes this point trenchantly in his account of the English as a 'disappeared' ethnicity.[48] But did the English simply disappear into the host population? Were they so invisible? We are unconvinced. Our research suggests important alternative images of the English.

Ethnic associations as a measure of diaspora

While we accept the proposition of Erickson and others that some forms of organized Englishness – notably the St George's societies – were elite entities, we refute the resulting conclusion that this alienated such organizations from the English migrant population generally, making the associations weak and unrepresentative of the wider immigrant experience. Instead, we suggest that those elites were probably less aloof from their poorer countrymen than they would have been in the old country. We shall see in the relationship between elite and working class, in both the United States and Canada, a patrician connection of responsibility whereby acts of charity were utilized to benefit the wider English immigrant body rather than just that elite. In any case this charity was wide-ranging, handing out alms, tickets for food and lodgings or beds in hospitals, to name only a few of the provisions made. Labour historians bridle at such signs of hierarchical connection, but they were no less real for all that they drift away from the idea of an essentially class-bound agency among immigrants whose ethnic collectivism has often been read as a surrogate of class-consciousness. The English demonstrated class-consciousness in a broad-based and pioneering way: they were, after all, the progenitors of the American trade union movement in the factories of the mill districts of Massachusetts. Having sought out utopia and having found nascent capitalism, they confronted it. This does not mean that those who had the awareness to seek a passage home, or a few cents from the stewards of the local St George's society, were any less English. The question of whether such requests for alms at the house of their countrymen superiors were purely schematic or shaped by an ethnic awareness does not make those acts of connection any less relevant. The simple fact that an English widow turned to an English society for help means she knew its function well enough.

We contend that ethnic associations provide both a valid and a uniquely rich measurement of the English as a diaspora. Their formation – whether they were English, Scottish, Irish, German or derived from any other ethnic group – first occurred, naturally enough, in the ports of arrival and disembarkation. Charleston, Philadelphia and New York, three of America's only five urban settlements of more than 5,000 people in the 1770s, developed the earliest English associations. Boston also was registered in lists of English associational activity in the second half of the eighteenth century, while Baltimore was said to have a St George's organization in the 1790s. But these two cities were relatively quiet in comparison with New York and Philadelphia in the eighteenth century. Canadian cities followed suit in establishing English associational foundations only from the 1830s[49] – a trend in tune with the later urbanization and expansion of centres there, as well as the protracted arrival of larger numbers of English migrants. Often with little money to their names, without familial support and lacking intelligence about the labour and housing markets, the new arrivals making it to North America frequently needed help. It was here that middle-class men of the same nativity could see the travails of their countrymen, had those travails pointed out to them and so formed societies aiming to help and regulate not only relief for those already there but also, to some extent, the immigrant flows.

Below the bald overview statistics was another set of numbers that provides insights into the efforts made by English (and other) ethnic societies to care for their poor. The cities in question shared the experience of massive urban growth and economic development, but also the emergence of horribly overcrowded tenements, which in turn 'appalled middle-class observers and stimulated the settlement house and other reform movements'.[50] New York, as the principal point of entry for the famine Irish, was unique;[51] even so, we can expect that each port faced a proportion of pressure from those who arrived with little, or nothing, to their name and who required assistance. The New York emigration commissions reported that 2.7 million immigrants arriving between 1847 and 1860 received some form of relief; 129,644 received care at the Emigrant's Refuge and Hospital or the Marine Hospital; 333,136 received help with accommodation; and 129,148 were given employment. While the authorities were unable systematically to count the assets of those arriving, it was reckoned, from a partially successful count, that each immigrant carried an average of $68.[52] Civic authorities chivvied the better-off established immigrants to help their countrymen before the huge increases in numbers arriving precipitated by the famine and also by unemployment and hunger in Britain during the 1840s. The pressures of these middle decades coincided with a spate of ethnic associational developments: Albion societies and St George's societies, from Baltimore and inland to Illinois and Wisconsin, and northwards into Canada, where such pressures were also being felt. Small wonder that, with such numbers flowing in, and so many poor folk in the human traffic, that the English became further established in these ports and their environs. The growth in English ethnic associational culture, therefore, is no surprise.

Religious and national formations also provided cities with some of the earliest and strongest instances of ethnic associationalism. Certainly, the most significant organizational benevolence among English elite and middle-class immigrants can be found there.[53] Places such as Charleston, Baltimore, New York and Philadelphia were the major focal points and would be until the middle decades of the nineteenth century, when the English, like all others in the United States, pushed west and formed large towns and cities along the way. Canadian towns and cities in Ontario and Quebec followed suit from the 1840s because they were so closely connected to their American neighbours. Here, too, class and sectarian discontent shaped organizational structures. The Irish in Canada were significant, but unlike in the United States, Protestants from Ulster outnumbered the Irish Catholic population, ensuring that they were unable to exert the same communal power as was seen to the south. Many of these features were both blurred and blended by significant migrations from north to south. Canadians (British North Americans) were a sizeable grouping in the United States throughout the nineteenth century, and became more so as the twentieth century dawned. These Canadians allied closely with British and American Protestants and contributed further power to the anti-Catholic, anti-Irish and nativist impulses that shaped a significant element of British and Anglo-American ethnic associational culture.

Within this wider context, then, we are left wondering: while Irish, Scottish, Italian, African and many other diasporas now have their historians and major studies, even the most comprehensive general account of the development of diaspora studies makes no mention of the concept of an English diaspora. In large part this is a result of traditional scholarship casting the English as progenitors of an empire – hence as a group against which other groups defined themselves. But the English seemingly do not fit also because diasporas are frequently politicized – a focus intrinsically connected to the original Jewish experience of systematic victimization and the denial of a homeland.[54] For the most part, the best-known and most pervasive traditions of scholarly exploration and writing in a diasporic framework – chiefly those associated with Jews, the Armenians or the Africans of the Atlantic slave trade – share conceptions of victimhood, oppression, forced exile and reluctant migration as their driving meta-narratives. These narratives resonate too for the Irish and Scots through the experience of famine and removal from land held over generations – though, in the case of the Scots in particular, these narratives can easily distort reality, with the notion of an 'enforced diaspora' clearly at odds with contemporary evidence.[55] Within this wider context amnesia about English ethnicity – ethnicity being the key measure commonly used to capture a diaspora – is complicated by the tendency to focus on groups which suffered from imperial oppression. In a world of 'competitive victimhood', colonists and imperialists are the benchmark against which diaspora has often been measured.[56] This has meant, as a consequence, that diaspora has largely been considered weaker – at times non-existent – for migrant groups who have not experienced a fundamental rapture from the homeland by war or oppression. As we have argued elsewhere,

> If these experiences are key elements in the evocation of a diasporic consciousness, the English – oppressors rather than the oppressed, colonists not the colonized – do not fit the typology. In the modern period, England colonized more than any other nation; consequently, the English escape observation as progenitors of their own ethnic diaspora.[57]

We suggest an alternative conceptualization of diaspora, one that defines it as a conscious international community of people with shared ethnic-national roots and a heightened, potentially politicized, sense of common identity. By transcending the traditional meaning of diaspora (the dispersion of people across space), as well as the narrative of exile, this conception recognizes diaspora as actively maintained by its own members. As a result, diaspora is tangible through the migrants as historical agents, and the structures in which they operate. For our purpose, ethnic association-alism provides the key to such structure – a structure making possible the active use of fraternal networks and ethnicity – and one that, therefore, becomes a tool of enquiry into the nature of the relationship between homeland and diaspora, but also connections within the diaspora.

Records for many English associations are patchy at best, making us less certain of precise establishment dates for a significant number. That said, newspapers are a rich source of information concerning associational life; moreover, the digitization of newspapers enables us to sweep for news and knowledge of these societies as they spread, and how quickly, to other parts of the Anglo-world. Indeed, such knowledge would become important not only in encouraging Englishmen in other places to form their own such societies, but also to enable some degree of co-ordination. Though transnational organization was not a feature until the second half of the nineteenth century, the press quickly caught activities, plundering news from sister papers from much earlier times. Thus, the activities of the St George's Society of Toronto were being reported only a few days later by the press in places as far afield as Bermuda.[58] New York's business was captured in the Australian press. A year later, the activities of the Quebec St George's Society were similarly recorded, also in Bermuda.[59] Visits from politicians provided opportune hooks for such news dissemination. In addition to this dissemination through newspapers, British parliamentary papers, from the late 1830s, contain several references to Canadian St George's societies, which suggest that successive governments were made aware of the organizations' charitable work with poor English immigrants.[60] Invisible the English diaspora was not.

Themes

Our discussion opens with a general overview of English migration to North America, for this is the context of our study. It was from the earliest re-peopling of parts of North America that migration became critical to building Britain's Empire, driving forward territorial expansion and making colonies viable. We thus provide an assessment of the patterns and contexts of English migration across the Atlantic, commencing with a brief exploration of early colonial settlement and urbanization. In this we can see the types of patterns that were to become critical to the migrations and settlements of the long nineteenth century, which lie at the heart of our study. Importantly, it was these early settlements that established what we might call the English character of the colonial process more broadly, drawing fundamentally on English customs, law, religion and ideas for the founding of new settlements and the establishment of colonial society. The earlier emigrants carried with them cultural characteristics, habits and customs that were critical in shaping social and civic life and, thus, the notion of the English as foundational and invisible within American society. Hence, Chapter 1 examines English migration to the American colonies, the United States and Canada over the long run.

In the original thirteen colonies this base was challenged at different points – first, as a result of an increasingly diverse ethnic make-up in the colonies, and then, secondly, through that critical rupture – the American War of Independence – which altered the Anglo-world forever. Despite this rupture, however, North America was still a world of English cultural hegemony: a domination evident first and foremost in the very language spoken. Still, we problematize existing scholarship that concludes that this hegemony of language and immigrant culture gave English migrants some kind of permanent and unchanging advantage over other migrant groups by default. Ordinary English migrants faced the same challenges and hardships as any other group; working-class immigrants in particular dealt with many common economic pressures regardless of their origins. Ultimately, in four centuries of English immigration to North America, relatively little distinguishes the immigrants as an ethnic group, and they had much in common with those of other backgrounds. The English settled in all colonies, counties and states; they were loaded towards the urban and industrial areas, but the focus upon the north-east – in both the colonial and early republican periods, as well as north of the border in what was to become Canada – gradually gave way to greater diffusion. And this diffusion was in line with the spread of ethnic associations.

Chapter 2 turns attention to these associations and explores the development of elite English associations in North America, focusing on St George's societies. These earliest English societies were more than gentlemen's dining or drinking clubs, and extended beyond the cultural life of the colonial tavern where they often met.[61] Societies served diverse roles that encompassed social, cultural, civic and also emotional aspects of immigrant community life. Critically, the idea of charity underpinned them and provided the basis for all activities, with the societies established for the purpose of aiding fellow English migrants who were in distress. This associational anchor of benevolence that was put in place in the eighteenth century continues to be a mainstay for the St George's societies that are still active in North America today. And it was one that spread with the St George's tradition – first to the largest centres of the original colonies and then, in the 1830s, to British North America. All this was in tune with the patterns of English migration, as well as its overall volume, with a plethora of new societies being founded in the mid-nineteenth century to cater for the mass arrival of new migrants. Hence, while the associations' leaders were composed of the migrant elite, the work of St George's societies, particularly that channelled through charity, had much wider resonances. Importantly, it also signifies the extent to which the English diaspora was indeed an active diaspora: that is, one denoted both by the geographical range of its adherents and by transnational communication between them. The latter was fostered by the North America St George's Union (NAStGU), founded in the 1870s for the purpose of bringing closer together the St George's societies of the United States and Canada.

Critical though the St George's societies were in establishing the tradition of English ethnic associationalism, a second tier developed in the final quarter of the nineteenth century that catered specifically for working-class migrants, when, as we noted at the outset, the OSStG and the Sons of England were founded in the United States and Canada respectively. Clearly, working-class Englishmen and women in the United

States and Canada required a different type of organization – one whose fees they could afford and that provided them with support, while also enabling them to express their Englishness proudly in a crowded world of competitive ethnicity. It was an Englishness with a different practical function – one where benefit replaced charity, and where collective self-help was favoured over receipt of hand-outs. Supported by values of class solidarity, but also prompted by ethnic tension, both the OSStG and the Sons of England thus provided insurance rather than charity. Chapter 3 traces their development with a particular focus on the context in which they were founded, and where they were set up. The OSStG, for instance, came about in part as a co-ordinated response to a heightened ethnic consciousness as a result of the rise of the infamous Molly Maguires. Conflict was by no means uncommon in urban life for the English and Irish, Protestants and Catholics, and many of the existing divisions refor-mulated themselves in the New World, driving ethnic wedges between workers who otherwise shared sectional and class interests. Despite these concerns – or perhaps as effectively as a result of them – the OSStG grew significantly, as did the Sons of England, soon drawing support away from the St George's societies.

Additionally, all associations were united in their patriotism to England, which remained a constant. And despite their different social composition and emphases, the elite and middle-class St George's socie-ties still shared a number of characteristics with the more working-class organizations focused on providing collective self-help. Chapter 4 traces the inner workings and activities of the different organizations to explore these commonalities in terms of not only the internal organization and membership of the societies, but also the events and socio-cultural pur-suits they promoted. Anglo-Saxon roots and loyalty to the monarchy were critical for the latter, and were customarily expressed at St George's Day dinners and parades, but also at more directed activities, such as coronations and jubilees. War also played a significant role, heightening the sense of loyalty to the crown and shared roots even in the republican United States.

Chapter 5 examines charity and mutualism in detail as the two criti-cal pillars of English ethnic associationalism. It does so by analysing the charity dispensed by St George's societies throughout North America and the collective self-help offered by the Sons of England.[62] The chapter explores both the level of support provided over time and the regula-tory framework adopted by the associations. This will also bring to the fore, for the St George's societies in particular, the level of associational networking between organizations concerned with the provision of charity, and how this gave them a wider civic role in diverse places of settlement. The analysis of the Sons of England returns to questions con-cerning class and ethnicity, as the Sons were set up expressly to prevent

English working-class immigrants having to rely on charity: the founding members moved to action when they observed the superior attitude of poor law guardians as they distributed their 'Christmas Cheer' to the hard-up English of the city. The concern was not with the manner or activities of the St George's Society. Indeed, the constitution of the Sons of England praised their good work among the poor and unfortunate. What those keen to set up a new organization found problematic was that the English of Toronto 'were then the only people out of all the nationalities who had to parade their wants and sufferings to the gaze of others and be made recipients of charity in a public manner'.[63] Hence, those who founded the Sons of England established a mutual organization in keeping with the ethos of collective self-help and economic confraternity. What the examination of the two pillars of English ethnic associationalism highlights is that it has distinct layers, and layers that changed over time. These must be recognized fully to capture the breadth and significance of English associational culture in North America.

We have already noted that associational enterprise was characteristic of all immigrant groups in the United States, Canada and the wider English-speaking world. Indeed, as we have seen, European society more generally was known for the widest forms of collectivism. Unsurprisingly, therefore, the English were not alone in establishing ethnic societies soon after their arrival overseas; neither were they usually the first or the most prolific. Consequently, the English ethnic associationalism we describe here was not unique; indeed, it was part of a world of associations. Providing a comparative context is therefore critical in order to fully understand the English diaspora. Chapter 6 offers this context, charting the evolution and purpose of ethnic clubs and societies established in North America by other migrant groups. In this comparative endeavour we focus particularly on two groups, the Scots and the Germans. The Scots provide the most pertinent comparator – as a fellow group of the British Isles – given their similar cultural background and migratory trajectories. Examining the Scots is also valuable, however, because they were the most active in the early phase of settlement, also anchoring their associationalism in philanthropy. St Andrew's societies, much as those of St George, had an elite dimension, but catered for a broader migrant cohort. Similarities in the work of the two organizations even led to concrete co-operation, for instance in New York, where, for a time, the St Andrew's and St George's societies shared an almoner. From the mid-nineteenth century onwards, however, the Scots developed a second and distinct tier: an ethnic associational culture at the heart of which lay sport. This contributed to a significant proliferation in Scottish ethnic associational activity – though one that was trumped, in the early twentieth century, by the Scottish mutualist branches in both the United States and Canada (the Order of Scottish Clans and the Sons of Scotland

respectively). Developing non-British comparators through an examination of developments in the German immigrant community permits
consideration of the impact of group size – Germans being a significantly
larger group – but also of the role of language in immigrant adjustment.
Moreover, examining the Germans also permits consideration of how
external developments – in this case particularly the First and Second
World Wars – were watersheds that united migrants from the British
Isles, while casting out Germans.

By pointing out the importance of transnational connections and
communication of English ethnic societies within North America, and,
of course, the most fundamental remit of our study – that of mobility
and the crossing of borders – we have already highlighted the importance
of transnational connections. But these were by no means restricted to
the United States and Canada: English associational connections were
global. Consequently, we conclude our study in Chapter 7 by extending
the geographical focus, placing our North American research in wider
comparative context by examining the growth of English societies around
the world. In particular we investigate the spread of St George's societies
to locations beyond their first formation, investigating developments in
Africa and Australasia, and the role of the RSStG, which, from the late
nineteenth century, sought to facilitate the global spread or organized
Englishness and English culture. While Australasian St George's societies
developed at about the same time as those in the Mid-West of America,
and thus reflected the internal colonization of both British and American
worlds, they were not in any sense joined up. This did not occur until the
Royal Society of St George was founded and provided the adhesive to
bond all the Anglo-world's English societies. Celebrations of monarchy
and Empire were critical in this globalization, providing a communal
adhesive for English migrants wherever they were located. A similar
anchor – albeit for a very different reason – was war. Not only did it
heighten a sense of belonging among many, invigorating shared roots as
the common denominator, but it was, critically, a belonging often framed
by Britishness rather than Englishness, and one paramount among those
keen to stress the shared cultural characteristic of the English, British,
Americans, Canadians and other neo-Britons in Empire. Still Englishness
was employed within that wider identity to help the 'motherland'.
English associations around the world collected funds in support of the
war effort, or to help the widows and orphans of soldiers who had made
the ultimate sacrifice, during both world wars, and, more directly and
actively, the Toronto St George's Society provided homes for children
who had been sent over from England during the Second World War. All
of these actions and communications criss-crossed the world, connecting the English abroad not only with the old homeland but also with each
other. Associations, therefore, point not to an 'imagined community', but

to a practical and active transnational community, whose agency enabled real, not just psychic, connection.[64] It enabled an English diaspora.

Notes

1 Extensive reporting on various aspects of the flood in *The Times*, 2 February 1953. For a contemporary analysis see J.A. Steers, 'The East Coast Floods, January 31–February 1, 1953', *Geographical Journal*, 119 (1954), pp. 163–66.

2 Notice from the Society's almoner and reports in St George's Society of New York, *Annual Report for 1952* (New York, 1953), p. 9. See also St George's Society of New York, *Annual Report for 1953* (New York, 1954), p. 43.

3 Tanja Bueltmann and Donald M. MacRaild, 'Globalizing St George: English Associations in the Anglo-World to the 1930s', *Journal of Global History*, 7:1 (2012), pp. 79–105.

4 *Philadelphia Inquirer*, 4 March 1882.

5 Krishan Kumar, *The Making of English National Identity* (Cambridge, 2003), p. 176.

6 Peter Clark, *British Clubs and Societies 1580–1800: The Origins of an Associational World* (Oxford, 2000), passim.

7 Alexis de Tocqueville, *Democracy in America*, 2 vols (New York, 2004), vol. 2:2, p. 595.

8 Ibid., p. 596.

9 Robert Freke Gould, *The History of Freemasonry*, 3 vols (London, 1882–87); Jessica L. Harland-Jacobs, *Builders of Empire: Freemasonry and British Imperialism, 1717–1927* (Chapel Hill, NC, 2007), and Jessica L. Harland-Jacobs, '"Hands across the Sea": The Masonic Network, British Imperialism, and the North Atlantic World', *Geographical Review*, 89 (1999), pp. 237–53; R.W. Moffrey, *A Century of Oddfellowship: Being a Brief Record of the Rise and Progress of the Manchester Unity ...* (Manchester, 1910), an anniversary volume which notes the global reach.

10 See Bernard Harris and Paul Brigden (eds), *Charity and Mutual Aid in Europe and North America since 1800* (London, 2007), and the essays therein; see also P.H.J.H. Gosden, *The Friendly Societies in England, 1815–1875* (Manchester, 1961); Eric Hopkins, *Working-Class Self-Help in Nineteenth-Century England: Responses to Industrialization* (London, 1995); Simon Cordery, *British Friendly Societies, 1750–1914* (Basingstoke, 2003). For the early spread of mutual aid societies in England see Josef M. Barenreiter, *English Associations of Workingmen* (London, 1889).

11 W.E. Van Vugt, 'The Hidden English Diaspora in Nineteenth-Century America', in Tanja Bueltmann, David T. Gleeson, and Donald M. MacRaild (eds), *Locating the Hidden Diaspora, 1500–2010* (Liverpool, 2012); Roger Burt, 'Freemasonry and Business Networking during the Victorian Period', *Economic History Review*, 56 (November 2003), pp. 657–88.

12 Harris and Brigden (eds), *Charity and Mutual Aid*.

13 David T. Beito, *From Mutual Aid to the Welfare State: Fraternal Society and Social Services, 1890–1967* (Chapel Hill, NC, 2000), p. 1. Also see Mark

C. Carnes, *Secret Ritual and Manhood in Victorian America* (New Haven, CT, 1989); and Mary Ann Clawson, *Constructing Brotherhood: Class, Gender, and Fraternalism* (Princeton, NJ, 1989).

14 C.W. Heckethorn, *The Secret Societies of All Ages and Countries* 2 vols (London, 1897), vol. 1, introduction.

15 Beito, *Mutual Aid*, p. 3.

16 Ivan H. Light, *Ethnic Enterprise in America: Business and Welfare among Chinese, Japanese and Blacks* (Berkeley, CA, 1973) dates the development of black societies to the 1780s and black insurance enterprises to the 1810s; see ch. 8 (but detail at pp. 152–53). Also see Lisbeth Cohen, *Making a New Deal: Industrial Workers in Chicago, 1919–39* (New York, 1990).

17 Este E. Buffum and Charles E. Whelan, *Modern Woodmen of America: A History ... of the Society from its Inception in 1883 to and Including 1926* (Rock Island, IL, 1927); Nathan S. Boynton, *History of the Knights of the Maccabees: Book of the Ancient Maccabees and Biographical Sketches of the Executive Officers of the Order, 1881 to 1898* (Port Huron, MI, 1892).

18 B. Matthews and M. Cross, *Whispering Mountains: A History of Lewis, New York* (Honeoye Falls, NY, 2006), p. 58. Formed in 1878, it spread to the United States by the 1890s.

19 S. Smiles, *Self-Help; with Illustrations of Conduct and Perseverance* (London, 1886), p. 1. See also his *Thrift: A Book of Domestic Counsel* (London, 1875; London, 1908), p. 121. For a discussion in relation to self-help and mutual aid in Britain, see Donald M. MacRaild and David E. Martin, *Labour in British Society, 1830–1914* (Basingstoke, 2000), ch. 5, passim.

20 Pierre Nora, 'Between Memory and History: Les Lieux de Mémoire', *Representations*, 26 (1989), pp. 7–24.

21 Such a diaspora is conceptualized by Robin Cohen, *Global Diasporas: An Introduction* (revised edn, London, 2008), ch. 4; also p. 164; more specifically, see John Lambert, 'South African or British? Or Dominion South Africans? The Evolution of an Identity in the 1910s and 1920s', *South African Journal of History*, 43:1 (2000), pp. 197–222.

22 R. Brubaker, 'The "Diaspora" Diaspora', *Ethnic and Racial Studies*, 28:1 (2005), pp. 1–19.

23 See for instance Robert J.C. Young, 'The Disappearance of the English: Why is there no 'English Diaspora'?', in Tanja Bueltmann, David T. Gleeson and Donald M. MacRaild (eds), *Locating the English Diaspora, 1500–2010* (Liverpool, 2012).

24 The sheer depth of pre-Civil War English culture in America is revealingly discussed in Elisa Tamarkin, *Anglophilia: Deference, Devotion, and Antebellum America* (Chicago, 2008).

25 Marjory Harper and Stephen Constantine, *Migration and Empire* (Oxford, 2010), p. 14.

26 Marcus Lee Hansen, *The Immigrant in American History* (Cambridge, MA, 1940), p. 192. For examination of the dynamism of ethnic identity in the United States, see Timothy J. Meagher, *Inventing Irish America: Generation, Class and Ethnic Identity in a New England City, 1880–1928* (Notre Dame, IA, 2001).

27 Bernard Bailyn and Philip D. Morgan, 'Introduction', in Bernard Bailyn and Philip D. Morgan (eds), *Strangers in the Realm: Cultural Margins of the First British Empire* (Chapel Hill, NC, 1991), pp. 10–11; Carl Wittke, *We Who Built America* (New York, 1939).

28 Oscar Handlin, *The Uprooted: The Epic Story of the Great Migrations that Made the American People* (Boston, 1951).

29 C. Erickson, 'English', in S. Thernstrom, A. Orlov and O. Handlin (eds), *Harvard Encyclopaedia of American Ethnic Groups* (2nd edn Cambridge, MA, 1980), p. 320.

30 David Hackett Fischer, *Albion's Seed: Four British Folkways in America* (New York, 1989).

31 Malcolm Gaskill, *Between Two Worlds: How the English Became Americans* (Oxford, 2014).

32 The term 'invisible immigrants' is Charlotte Erickson's: *Invisible Immigrants: The Adaptation of English and Scottish Immigrants in Nineteenth-Century America* (Ithaca, NY, 1992). Erickson includes the Scots in this study. For Anglo-American culture, see W.E. Van Vugt, *British Immigration to the United States, 1776–1914* (London, 2009).

33 Alan Kraut, *The Huddled Masses: The Immigrant in American Society, 1880–1920* (2nd edn, Arlington Heights, IL, 2002).

34 John Bodnar, *The Transplanted: A History of Immigrants in Urban America* (Bloomington, IA,1985), pp. 60–61, 66–67, 111, 151–52, 154–55 and 186–89.

35 Kathleen Neils Conzen, David A. Gerber, Ewa Morawska, George E. Pozzetta and Rudolph J. Vecoli, 'The Invention of Ethnicity: A View from the U.S.A', *Journal of American Ethnic History*, 12 (Fall 1992), pp. 5–7.

36 Adrian Hastings, *The Construction of Nationhood: Ethnicity, Religion and Nationalism* (New York, 1997), pp. 61–65; Kumar, *English National Identity*.

37 Linda Colley, *Britons: Forging the Nation, 1707–1837* (New Haven, 1992); Gerald Newman, *The Rise of English Nationalism: A Cultural History, 1740–1830* (London, 1987). Kumar, *English National Identity*, pp. 176–78, takes firm exception to Newman's blurring of terminologies and dating of English nationalism to the eighteenth century.

38 The classic is Michael J. Hechter, *Internal Colonialism: The Celtic Fringe in British National Development, 1536–1966* (Berkeley, 1992).

39 The debate is most fully explored in Tanja Bueltmann, David T. Gleeson and Donald M. MacRaild, 'Invisible Diaspora? English Ethnicity in the United States before 1920', *Journal of American History*, 33:4 (Summer 2014), pp. 5–30.

40 W.E. Van Vugt, 'British and British Americans (English, Scots, Scots Irish, and Welsh), to 1870', in Elliott R. Barkan (ed.), *Immigrants in American History: Arrival, Adaptation, and Integration*, 4 vols (Santa Barbara, CA, 2013), vol. 1:1, p. 241.

41 See Wilbur S. Shepperson, *Emigration and Disenchantment: Portraits of Englishmen Repatriated from the United States* (Norman, OK, 1965) and his *British Emigration to North America* (Norman, OK, 1956). See also Stephen Fender, *Sea Changes: British Emigration and American Literature* (Cambridge, 1992).

42 Dirk Hoerder, *Creating Societies: Immigrant Lives in Canada* (Kingston, 2000), pp. 24, 111–12. See also Amy J. Lloyd, '"The Englishmen here are much disliked": Hostility towards English Immigrants in Early Twentieth-Century Toronto', in Bueltmann, Gleeson and MacRaild (eds), *Locating the English Diaspora*.

43 For the wider nationalist press, see William L. Joyce, *Editors and Ethnicity: A History of the Irish-American Press, 1848–1883* (New York, 1976).

44 David Sim, *A Union Forever: The Irish Question and US Foreign Relations in the Victorian Age* (Ithaca, NY, 2013); also see, on Fenians in America, Brian Jenkins, *The Fenian Problem: Insurgency and Terrorism in a Liberal State, 1858–1874* (Liverpool, 2009) and Niall Whelehan, *The Dynamiters: Irish Nationalism and Political Violence in the Wider World, 1867–1900* (Cambridge, 2012).

45 J.R. Seeley, *The Expansion of England: Two Courses of Lectures* (London, 1883; Chicago, 1971).

46 For a fascinating examination of the Australian dimensions of the enormous but shifting powers of certain types of English, see Joy Damousi, *Colonial Voices: A Cultural History of English in Australia, 1840–1940* (Cambridge, 2010).

47 Robert Bickers (ed.), *Settlers and Expatriates* (Oxford, 2010), introduction and passim.

48 Young, 'The Disappearance of the English', p. 235.

49 For example, list of associations enlisted to the British NAStGU: *Philadelphia Inquirer*, 10 September 1877.

50 Carol E. Heim, 'Structural Changes: Regional and Urban', in Stanley L. Engerman and Robert E. Gallman (eds), *The Cambridge Economic History of the United States* (Cambridge, 2000), p. 160.

51 Though of course we recognize the importance of other cities. Philadelphia's Irish immigrant experience, for example, is expertly analysed by Matthew Gallman, *Receiving Erin's Children: Philadelphia, Liverpool and the Irish Famine Migration, 1845–1855* (Raleigh, NC, 2000).

52 Bureau of Census, *Population of the United States in 1860: Compiled from the Original Returns of the Eighth Census under the Direction of the Secretary of the Interior* (Washington, DC, 1864), 'Introduction', p. xxiii.

53 Douglas Bradburn, *The Citizenship Revolution: Politics and the Creation of the American Union* (Charlottesville, VA, 2009), pp. 210ff.

54 For an introductory typology, see Cohen, *Global Diasporas*; also Kevin Kenny, 'Diaspora and Comparison: The Irish as a Case Study', *Journal of American History*, 90:1 (2003), pp. 134–62.

55 Marjory Harper, *Emigration from Scotland between the Wars: Opportunity or Exile?* (Manchester, 1998), p. 1.

56 Masi Noor, Rupert Brown and Gary Prentice, 'Prospects for Intergroup Conciliation: Social Psychological Indicators of Intergroup Forgiveness and Reparation in Northern Ireland and Chile', in Arie Nadler, Thomas E. Malloy and Jeffrey D. Fisher (eds), *The Social Psychology of Intergroup Reconciliation: From Violent Conflict to Peaceful Co-Existence* (New York, 2008), pp. 97–115, draws specifically on Irish examples.

57 Tanja Bueltmann, David T. Gleeson and Donald M. MacRaild, 'Introduction: Locating the English Diaspora: Problems, Perspectives and Approaches', in Bueltmann, Gleeson and MacRaild (eds), *Locating the English Diaspora*, p. 4.
58 *Royal Gazette*, 12 June 1838.
59 Ibid., 13 November 1839.
60 For example 1839 (3-II) *Appendix (A.) to report on the affairs of British North America, from the Earl of Durham, Her Majesty's High Commissioner ...*, p. 48; 1840 [211] [221] [222] [250] *Canada: Correspondence Relative to the Affairs of Canada*, part 1, p. 155.
61 Clark, *British Clubs and Societies*; Sharon Salinger, *Taverns and Drinking in Early America* (Baltimore, 2002).
62 Unfortunately there is no discrete manuscript archive for the Order of the Sons of St George, hence the focus exclusively on the Sons of England for the exploration of ethnic mutualism.
63 John S. King, *The Early History of the Sons of England Benevolent Society* (Toronto, 1891), p. 11.
64 Benedict Anderson, *Imagined Communities: Reflections on the Origins and Spread of Nationalism* (London, 1983).

1

The origins and development of the English diaspora in North America

The roots of the English diaspora lie in the sixteenth-century quest for an empire, which began processes of territorial settlement, first in the home islands, and then beyond the oceans. Mass plantations in 1580s Munster, for instance, signalled a new and more sustained phase of pacifying Ireland by English population settlement.[1] In 1609 this approach was further intensified via systematic, planned, popular migrations as the English joined the Scots of the pre-existing Hamilton-Montgomery settlement by undertaking the Plantation of Ulster.[2] Until that point, the northernmost province of Ireland was, as one London official said, 'heretofore as unknown to the English ... as the most inland parts of Virginia is yet unknown to the English colony there'.[3] Subjugating the 'Celtic fringe' was but one small step along the path of English imperial ambitions. Thereafter, as the Tudors and Stuarts began establishing colonies in the West Indies and North America, English expansions abroad were to become the foundations of the first British Empire.

Although the early plantations initiated a process of Anglicizing colonial possessions that was to become a key thread in English imperial history,[4] it would be too simplistic to see Scotland and Ireland as the first firm steps to re-peopling and exploiting the Americas. What we can say is that this was an age of English power and that the neighbouring countries within the British and Irish Isles were caught up in their larger neighbour's growing ambitions. Ireland, coastal North America and the islands of the Caribbean were each brought under the expansionist purview of the English, and were subjected to sustained but unevenly successful integration. As the English sought to rediscover an Arthurian sea-borne empire, their neighbours in the North Atlantic world suffered military aggression, colonial settlement and the prospect of sharing some of the benefits of imperial growth.[5] Monarchical unity and then political union with Scotland, and a long, bitter struggle to pacify the Irish element of the 'Celtic fringe': each of these developments comprised part of a larger process in which England expanded within the home archipelago and then across the Atlantic. It was as a consequence of this expansion that a new (or rather recycled) identity, Britishness, emerged to encompass the English, Welsh and Scots and some of the Irish. In turn, 'Englishness' receded as a much less useful term.

Continuing migration was critical to these political and imperial projects since territorial possession was made real only through the establishment of viable colonies. Many migrations in the early period were initially planned and driven by the state, but paid for by venture capital; some were gifted to individuals, companies and collectives who undoubtedly forced market interest with cheap and free land, systematic oceanic transportation, promises of military protection and infrastructure and propaganda flows. Yet, initially at least, English elites were slow to recognize the possibilities of exploitative colonization; or else they were disinclined to harbour such ideas, let alone act upon them. Whereas the Spanish and Portuguese, whose naval and technical prowess the English matched in the sixteenth century, had immediately applied themselves to task of adding settlement to commercial exploitation, the English were different. They focused, for almost all of that century, on exploring the world. Only Ireland was systematically settled at the time and even then only in parts of Munster.[6] Moreover, in the early 1600s, Ireland represented the summit of many English ambitions. In 1610 Arthur Chichester, Lord Deputy of Ireland and founder of modern Belfast, expressed contentment with the Ulster experiment, preferring not to stretch his interests to the Americas. 'I'd rather labour with my hands in the plantation of Ulster', Chichester opined, 'than dance or play in ... Virginia.'[7] Chichester may have sounded dismissive: in fact, he was expressing fear of competition. Besides, as Gaskill shows, Sir Walter Raleigh and his half-brother, Humphrey Gilbert, followed periods soldiering in Ireland with voyaging to plant the flag in Newfoundland and Virginia. In this way, these men connected Irish experiences of conquest to the other settings for colonization and expansion.[8]

Willing emigrants were crucial to English imperial designs, and here the circumstances of the age helped elites who harboured expansionist visions.[9] Indeed, attitudes to emigration changed as the turbulent seventeenth century progressed. A mind-set emerged that came to view the establishment of 'Englands out of England'[10] as both desirable and viable. Hence, England began to make a decisive contribution to a process that Bernard Bailyn described as 'the centrifugal *Völkerwanderung*',[11] with around half a million departing in the seventeenth century. Four-fifths of them went to the Americas, with the mainland colonies and the Caribbean being the principal destinations. But, as Hackett Fischer has argued, 'this exodus was not a movement of attraction. This great early migration was a flight from conditions which had grown intolerable at home.'[12] Monarchical tyranny saw England sliding into civil war; parallel economic hardship and disease contributed to disaffection with the old country.[13]

The notion of involving the Celtic peoples in these early ventures overseas was not on the minds of most proponents of imperial development and colonial settlement. With superior wherewithal and political control, the English, not the British, were the principal actors in the early colonization process.[14] Their traces remain strong. In a recent ancestry survey carried out in the United States, 27,658,000 people (of a total of 307,007,000 surveyed) identified their ancestry group as English – a figure putting the group in third place behind the Germans (50,708,00) and the Irish (36,915,000).[15] In Canada, a total of 6,570,015 people listed their ethnic origins as English, making it the largest ancestry group from the British and Irish Isles.[16] At the outset, we can say with certainty that the English were pervasive, both in reality and in collective memory. Set within this wider context, this chapter provides historical background to the aspects of English settlement in the Americas that we examine in this book,[17] focusing on migratory streams from the eighteenth century onwards. While we recognize the importance of earlier imperial endeavours, this time-frame is the most suitable for our work given that ethnic associations first developed in the eighteenth century, partly in unison with early urbanization patterns in North America, to which we also turn attention.

Colonial migration and early urbanization

Eighteenth-century migrations were different from the earliest transatlantic movements of the English,[18] not least because some contemporary commentators stressed the undesirability of poor and ill-conditioned English emigrants, singling out Scots or Ulster farmers as more independent and industrious migrants. Negative comments about the class composition of the English were common. 'Rogues, vagabonds, whores, cheats, and rabble of all descriptions raked from the gutter and kicked out of the country', A.E. Smith called the majority of indentured servants in the tobacco colonies.[19] Like some these English, Irish Catholics were also frequently scorned – a tendency dating to the earliest phases of transatlantic migration.

While the English were pervasively established across the Atlantic by 1700, migratory streams diversified greatly in the eighteenth century. For periods Irish Protestants and especially Germans dominated transatlantic emigrations to the American colonies, and we see the arrival of significant numbers of Swedes, Finns and Scots in what became an increasingly intense migration process. Principal among the eighteenth-century flows were as many as 150,000 people of primarily Scottish and English roots who left Ulster for colonial frontiers of New England, south-east Pennsylvania and the Upper South.[20] Having departed their original homelands for promises of land and opportunity within the context of a massive, planned plantation in Ulster, they reacted to violence, civil war, ethnic unrest, rising rents, agricultural modernization and religious restrictions to take their chances in the American colonies.

It is critical to understand that within the different migrant groups were sub-layers: northern Englishmen as opposed to southerners and Irish Catholics (initially a minority) as well as Ulster Protestants. No national group was a single indistinguishable body; from the offset the settlers were of different regional origins and religions, and therefore of varying cultures. And this brought with it additional complexities.[21] Where these people came from was one thing, but their overall effect was another. Along with high fertility rates, sustained and growing mass migration ensured that between 1700 and 1780 the colonies witnessed an eleven-fold population increase (Table 1.1).

While the eighteenth century saw the English generally eclipsed by other groups of immigrants, they still migrated in large and increasingly diverse numbers. Between 1718 and 1775, for example, the epoch most associated with Ulster-Scots, convicts totalling 50,000 in number became an important element of English and wider British migrations.[22] As well, towards the end of this period, migration was promoted by economic difficulties brought on by a series of poor harvests, which saw prices rise and hardship spread among the poor.[23] Richard Price speculated that England would be 'well-nigh depopulated within fifty years',[24] and questions were asked, both in parliament and beyond, about actions that might remedy the losses of particularly skilled people.[25]

Overall, in the eighteenth century, migration to the colonial Americas, particularly the Middle Colonies and New England, eclipsed the movement to Canada. In 1775, at the dawn of the American Revolution, the thirteen colonies contained about 2.5 million people, thus registering a ten-fold increase since 1700. In the same period, the Canadas and Newfoundland together were populated by perhaps 250,000 persons – a tenth of those found in the colonies to the south.[26] Critically, however, during the late eighteenth century, revolution provided a major spur to growth in the Canadas. In 1790, émigrés fleeing the revolution in America – the United Empire Loyalists – accounted for as many as 50,000 of the Canadian population. Their arrival boosted the population by as much as one-fifth. They settled in Nova Scotia, New Brunswick and parts of Quebec and, importantly, were among the first settlers in what became Ontario – a province created expressly in response to their migration.

These loyalist monarchists and Tories greatly affected the character of Canada. Their common value system confirmed and enhanced the

Table 1.1 *Populations of the American provinces in the colonial period, 1700–80*

	1700	1720	1740	1760	1780	X inc.[a]
New England	93,000	171,000	290,000	449,000	714,000	7.5,000
% white	98			97		
% black	2			3		
Middle Atlantic	51,000	98,000	201,000	395,000	678,000	13,000
% white	92			94		
% black	8			6		
Upper south	92,000	159,000	316,000	535,000	828,000	9,000
% white	77			63		
% black	23			37		
Lower south	17,000	38,000	99,000	214,000	506,000	30,000
% white	81			59		
% black	19			41		
West				17,000		
% white				83		
% black				17		
TOTAL	**251**	**466**	**906**	**1,954**	**2,780**	**11**

Note: [a]Multiple increase between 1700 and 1780.
Source: Adapted from James T. Lemon, 'Colonial America in the 18th Century', in Thomas F. McIlwraith and Edward K. Muller (eds), *North America: The Historical Geography of a Changing Continent* (Lanham, MD, 2000).

hegemony of English customs and ideas, and strongly underpinned Canada's long-living loyalty to Britain and the Empire. The United Empire Loyalists provided a population which generations later still called itself English. Moreover, some of their descendants were behind the formation of British and English associations, which wrapped together political identity with collective self-help for an identified ethnic group. It is very noticeable that they settled in numbers around the Great Lakes area of Ontario where most of the Canadian English societies were later established.

While this migration from the new Republic to British North America was critical, it was part of another wider shift in migration patterns in the later eighteenth century. Campbell states, for example, that the West Indies had lost their appeal, with 95 per cent of migrants now sailing for the North American colonies. In rank order, Maryland, Pennsylvania, Virginia and Nova Scotia were in the first group of destinations; New

Table 1.2 *Populations of the United States centres of English associational activity up to 1850*

City	1790	1800	1810	1820	1830	1840	1850
New York	33,131	60,515	96,373	123,706	202,589	312,710	515,547
Philadelphia	28,522	41,220	53,722	63,802	80,462	93,665	121,376
Boston	18,320	26,937	33,787	43,298	61,392	93,383	136,881
Charleston	16,359	18,824	24,711	24,780	30,289	29,261	42,985
Baltimore	13,503	26,514	45,555	62,738	80,620	102,313	169,054
Providence	6,380	7,614	10,071	11,767	16,833	23,171	41,513

Sources: Campbell Gibson, 'Population of the 100 Largest Cities and Other Urban Places in the United States, 1790–1990', Population Division, US Bureau of the Census, Washington, DC, Population Division Working Paper no. 27 (1998); Bureau of Census, *The Seventh Census of the United States, 1850, Embracing a Statistical View of Each of the States and Territories, Arrange by Counties, Towns, etc. ...* (Washington, DC, 1853), 'Population of States, Counties, etc.: Population of Places Included in the Census Volume of 1850', pp. cii–cxxvi.

York, Georgia, the Carolinas and Florida were in the second; and New England now lagged behind. Campbell suggests that the most popular destination, Maryland, was probably a site of significant onward migration; however, many of these migrants whom she identified probably settled in Baltimore at a time when it was rapidly climbing the league table of American cities (see Table 1.2).[27]

New York, which in 1664 passed from the Dutch to the British, was initially less English than these other colonies, though the balance was quickly redressed. Even when a minority the English enjoyed the powerful positions as merchant elites, political officials and so on. While they constituted less than 20 per cent of the population of New York City in 1680, the English made up half of the wealthiest merchants and 40 per cent of those eligible for taxation. Thus 'New York colony assumed a distinctly English character, even though only about 5% of England emigrants chose it as a destination.'[28] These settlers established key institutions, such as King's College (1754), the forerunner of Columbia, developed the legal system on English models and founded an array of social and cultural organizations, among them the St George's Society (1770).[29]

In 1785, Noah Webster, the Connecticut teacher and lexicographer, confidently asserted that in the American colonies, where country life predominated, the colonialist was 'a husbandman in the summer and mechanic in the winter'; then he tended fields and animals in the summer months, and fixed and made things in the winter.[30] Such self-sufficiency was an ideal for those who left the English countryside for the pastoral

America. It was a British plan. Whereas early colonists in the seventeenth century had imagined self-sufficiency in basic manufacturing, this had given way to an expectation, on the part of the British government, that the colonies would produce the raw materials and the home countries would manufacture those into goods. As relations dissolved during and after the revolution, the creation of a home-based manufacturing economy became a matter of patriotic pride.[31] Boycotts of British commodities politicized non-American products and gave impetus to the 'imagined community' of Americans that emerged through the experience of revolution.[32] Taken in combination, anti-British commercial rhetoric and the language of home production contributed importantly to sharp increases in production in the infant Republic that ensured a much more compressed development than was experienced by European nations. This was to change the balance, enabling America to lure the necessary labour for industrial growth from an economy in which substantial bodies of such workers were already long at their labours in textiles, machine-building, handicrafts and a plethora of other forms of production requiring manual and technical skill. Thus, before the revolution, and in close relationship with the development of a manufacturing ethos, the urban population was markedly growing. The immigrants we discuss here, and the ethnic associations they formed or benefited from, were almost entirely urban, far removed from Webster's independent farmer-artisan. While many immigrants dreamed of owning and farming land, the majority took up urban work when they arrived and never put together enough of a stake to leave it behind.

The major cities of colonial America and indeed of the early Republic were also the ports where immigrants first made landfall and to which would-be returners also found their way when the American dream went sour. Indeed the club culture of which we write here was massed in these same locations. Commercial elites from Britain, as well as the United States, Englishmen in addition to Americans, who were proud of their English roots, also appeared in dense formation in these same ports, and with them came culture expressions of civic togetherness. Capitalism, class, immigration, hardship and the determination to provide charity met and merged in these same entry-points. St George's societies were a response to these factors. But the share of the colonial population these early colonial centres held fell over the course of the eighteenth century, from around 9 per cent to a little under 5.

While the rise of lesser urban areas accounts for their declining share of the population, they retained immense importance, in terms of both trade and migration. In the 1760s, New York, Philadelphia and Boston were significant British World cities,[33] albeit a little smaller than comparable cities in Britain. On the eve of the American Revolution, Boston had a population of 16,500, Charleston 10,000 and New York and

Philadelphia each over 20,000. Subsequent growth rates were even more striking than those occurring in Britain. New York, for instance, doubled in size between 1790 and 1800, and then doubled again every two decades until 1880. With the exception of Charleston, which was restricted by natural barriers to growth beyond its original peninsula setting, and thus grew only gently, these cities expanded prodigiously (Table 1.2).

In Canada, French settlers, rather than the English, first initiated urban development. As the Anglo-French struggle for hegemony over the Canadas increased, urban planning was one visible manifestation of the growing imperial rivalry between the two powers, directly leading to the development of new urban centres. Halifax, for instance, was founded in 1749 specifically 'to subjugate and assimilate a hostile, non-urban local population ... the Acadian French'.[34] The American Revolution, and particularly the arrival of large contingents of the loyalists we discussed earlier, was a second critical trigger for increased urbanization as it was ultimately responsible for the establishment of a number of new towns, particularly in Nova Scotia. Elsewhere, St John, which had initially been a loyalist refugee camp, transformed into 'the commercial centre of a new province, New Brunswick'.[35] Overall, however, late eighteenth-century Canada did not match the trends of urban development of the United States. While Canada's York was founded at this time, serving as the new capital of the province of Upper Canada that had been established in 1791, even it began to grow in size on a more significant scale only in the 1830s, at which point it was incorporated and renamed Toronto. Despite these developments, Toronto remained a small population centre for some time when compared with cities in the United States.[36] In part the different growth patterns in Canada were simply a result of the fact that it was not yet attracting the same level of continuous settler migration as the United States. In fact, the fur trade – which was a critical business link between Canada and Britain and key motor to Canadian economic development – tended to show an 'antipathy to settlement'.[37]

On both sides of the Atlantic, the urban centres that developed were connected by trade and population flows; they were also, together, being shaped by the industrial revolution.[38] Importantly, at this time the growing population in North America was matched by further territorial expansion. By the 1770s, one-half to two-thirds of those living in the colonies in the 1770s were of English origins. In New England, the English share was 75 per cent, but the further south we look, the smaller the English cohort. In Pennsylvania, for example, the English accounted for one-fifth, the Germans one-third and the Scots and Irish a little more than two-fifths combined.[39] In 1776 approximately 50 per cent of white folk in New York colony were of English extraction.[40] It is estimated that natural population increase had become so much more significant than immigration that, in proportionate and actual terms, by the 1770s, 'perhaps only one white person in ten was born outside the colonies'.[41] Critically, it was this early settlement that established the English character of the wider colonial process, drawing heavily, as it did, upon English customs, law, religion and ideas. The changing ethnic balance of the colonies at the dawn of the young Republic challenged the certainties of this Anglo-American base, but did not fundamentally disrupt it.

The early nineteenth century

In the first decades of the young Republic, the port cities remained principal places of settlement and were the first sites of protean class-consciousness – a series of conditions comparable to those exercising the emergent working class in late eighteenth-century Britain, where wages, conditions, customary rights and political participation shaped public discourse. Like Liverpool, Glasgow and Manchester, these American cities developed considerable degrees of sectarian animosities as nativist and immigrant Protestants lined up against Catholic newcomers, especially the Irish, who themselves were capable of redoubtable acts of defensive and offensive aggression. British immigrants included fiercely anti-Catholic arrivals from Ulster, Wales, Scotland and England; indeed, uncompromising Protestantism and innate anti-Catholicism connected more of these colonial peoples than it separated.

Seaport and coastal centres were centres of early and advanced economic developments. As Peskin notes, '[A] disproportionate number of the late-eighteenth-century projects either were begun by immigrants or employed European mechanics as technical advisers.' Englishmen, Scots, Irish, Germans and Welsh were at the forefront in Baltimore, as potters, button-makers, stocking-makers, metal type founders for the printing trade and mechanics; Irish watch-makers, German glass-blowers and English sugar refiners were other specialists brought in. Much of the first machinery was imported from England, along with the workers to utilize it: this was true with, for example, stocking frames in 1830s Philadelphia.[42] Clearly, the towns of the interior could not compete with the ease of European labour and capital transfer that was enjoyed in the seaports,[43] though the coming transport revolution would bring a market economy to ever larger areas of the United States economy.

Philadelphia, the first city of the new Republic, held great appeal for English settlers well into the nineteenth century. The city's English community formed one of the earliest, and certainly the most active, English associations – the Society of the Sons of St George – which played a prominent part in the town's affairs. Philadelphia attracted merchants and professionals, tradesmen and labourers from England, though it was the former – men of influence and wealth – who sat at the heart of English life in the city. Philadelphia was, however, also the principal port for non-English immigrants, particularly the Scotch-Irish and the Germans. In the nineteenth century, like Baltimore, it lost out in the immigrant trade to New York. Whereas Philadelphia and Baltimore both developed their own systems of improved roads, railroads, canals and ferries to carry immigrants quickly towards the new opportunities of the Ohio region, New York had several advantages, from more clement winter weather at the waterside to the development of the Erie Canal connecting the Hudson River with Lake Erie. A combination of these factors saw Philadelphia's share of the immigration trade more than halved from 12 per cent in the 1820s to 5 per cent between 1830 and the American Civil War.[44]

Philadelphia and Baltimore were economically crucial to the exploitation of the Chesapeake and of Pennsylvania. By the 1830s, Baltimore had become the United States' second city, creeping ahead of Philadelphia (Table 1.2).[45] Baltimore did not outstrip Philadelphia for long, and its civic elites could not have predicted the rise of staggering competition in the form of Chicago, St Louis and other Mid-West towns. But from the beginning until the end of our period, Baltimore was a top-ten city and an important centre for English settlers. For decades after the westward road was improved in the 1810s, and long after the first rails were opened in 1828, construction and transport provided ready work for Irish, English and German unskilled labourers. Like all boom towns, the city had too little housing and a shortage of labour.[46]

Opinion-formers in the United States were, however, bullish about the conditions awaiting the immigrants. In a debate between William Cobbett and Hezekiah Niles in Baltimore in 1813, the latter denigrated English rates of pauperism, which were sixty times higher than those in the United States. American workers, he said, 'ate meat as they please', whereas 'fifty English workers would wrestle in the street to pick up butchers' scraps'. His newspaper, the *Niles' Weekly Register*, an influential organ of the day, banged this drum regularly, focusing on English misery as a prelude to emigration. In 1829, Niles told the tale of a Baltimore-bound ship's captain who 'found in Manchester "six or seven hundred persons all ready … to sell themselves into temporary slavery, in order to obtain the means of escaping to what they considered a better land."'[47]

One thing we argue most assuredly in this book is that not all English workers were sought-after skilled craftsmen operating in particular elevated niches. Those who fought for Niles's 'butchers' scraps' in England, or who fell on the mercy of the St George's societies were hardly well provisioned for life in America, even if they made it there. Among those who immigrated, some at least found that capitalism in the new country bore many of the hallmarks of its equivalents back home. But America was different in one respect: while Britain had cheap Irish labour, or landless rural migrants, to pressurize wage levels, the new country had cheap labour in profusion from diverse sources. In the 1830s, when Baltimore hat manufacturers sought to force down wages because of the pressures of competition, they looked to 'women and English and German immigrants, not freedmen or slaves' to suppress rates of pay.[48] The English who came to the United States and Canada did not therefore escape Irish competition; instead, they found many of them and other immigrant nationalities and African-American freedmen too.

As the English settled in cities such as Baltimore, they moved among Irish, Germans, and other Europeans. The Irish contingent in the city was not, however, solely composed of Catholics; it also included a 'vocal' body of Scots-Irish, who first descended on the city in the 1760s and continued to arrive throughout the nineteenth century. They found spiritual succour in Baltimore's role as the unofficial centre of American Methodism and seed-bed of the 'Second Great Awakening' – something Ulstermen, in the United States and at home, zealously adopted.[49] Irish Catholics also were beginning to rise in number in the years of the early Republic. The resulting mix created conditions for sectarianism, something that a strong and growing English presence did little to lessen. Between 1820 and 1850, Germans and Irish were the city's main immigrants, and by 1860, one-quarter of the city was German-born, a feature it shared with its nearby neighbour Philadelphia.[50]

Many hundreds of thousands of British and Irish emigrants crossed the Atlantic after 1815, following the final cessation of hostilities between Britain and France. Initially in this period, the passenger acts, which sought to curb the transfer of human capital to former colonies, ensured migration to British North America, which, as a result of cheaper fares, outstripped that to the United States into the 1830s. In fact, Canada accounted for more than 55 per cent of the emigrant traffic between 1815 and 1830 (Table 1.3), and the United States for 40 per cent. The Canadian timber trade also played its part, with timber ships 'hastily fitted' to transport people 'on the otherwise unprofitable journey west across the Atlantic'.[51] Quebec alone saw the arrival of about 10,000 settlers from ports in England in the decade after the Napoleonic Wars had concluded – though not all of them may have been English, and their number was certainly 'overshadowed' by those of the Scots and Irish.[52] The age of mass migration was coming, and it was coming with force.

An important factor was also the growing, and steadily improving, connections between Ontario and neighbouring states in America, since geographical proximity facilitated cross-border migrations and business links. Oswego, Rochester, Auburn, Syracuse, Oneida, Utica and Little Falls on the American side, and Hamilton, London, Toronto and Kingston on the Canadian, were all within striking distance of each other, highly connected via arterial transport systems, with migrants

Table 1.3 *Destinations of emigrants from Great Britain and Ireland, 1815–60*

	United States		British North America		Australasia		Other		Total per period	Total %
	Total	%	Total	%	Total	%	Total	%		
1815–20	50,359	40.8	70,438	57.0			2,731	2.2	123,528	100.0
1820–30	99,801	40.3	139,369	56.3	6,417	2.6	1,805	0.7	247,392	100.0
1831–40	308,247	43.8	322,485	45.9	67,882	9.7	4,536	0.6	703,150	100.0
1841–50	1,094,556	65.0	429,044	25.5	127,124	7.5	34,168	2.0	1,684,892	100.0
1851–60	1,495,243	65.4	235,285	10.3	506,802	22.2	49,875	2.2	2,287,205	100.0
TOTAL:	3,048,206	60.4	1,196,621	23.7	708,225	14.0	93,115	1.9	5,046,167	

Source: Bureau of Census, *Population of the United States in 1860; Compiled from the Original Returns of the Eighth Census under the Direction of the Secretary of the Interior* (Washington, 1860), 'Introduction', table: 'Emigration from Great Britain and Ireland', p. xxv.

regularly crossing back and forth for work. As the century progressed, road improvements, but particularly the development of the Erie Canal (1825), were critical. The canal dominated many of these towns, each of which was underpinned by strong links to the other impressive new water, road and rail transport systems. The latter system connected these Ontarian, New York and New England communities to the ports of Boston, New York itself and others. We see in this earlier period the origins of the idea that the 'United States–Canada border was a "permeable membrane" in the second-half of the nineteenth century'.[53]

These great advances in transport in the 1820s to 1840s enabled westward movement from New England into northern New York State and Upper Canada, or the United Province of Canada. Still diversity was essential to avoid competition: one town could not simply replicate another. Thus, Little Falls and Utica were textile towns. The latter attracted a diversity of Britons.[54] The Welshman William Davies, writing from Utica when it was a town of 500 dwellings in 1821, and with the canal still a few years from completion, anticipated the positive effects that would be enjoyed there when Lake Erie and the Hudson were connected.[55] Meanwhile, Schenectady – seventy-five miles from Utica and sixty from Little Falls – was a centre of heavy industry. It grew on the strength of transport access and the movement of resources. From the 1830s, the town became a 'pioneer in the world in railroad traffic'.[56]

One of the factors in this American and Canadian growth was a heavy influx of surplus British capital from investors looking for good returns on sound investments. This was true, for example, in the fur trade in Canada, where the merger of the Hudson's Bay and Northwest companies provided an early nineteenth-century boost to investment (though most of those involved were Scots). As Smith has argued, in pre-Confederation Canada many political stakeholders wanted to remain part of the British Empire not only for reasons of loyalty and shared roots, but more instrumentally because they 'were personally involved in projects that were dependent on the continued inflow if British capital'.[57] Early railroad growth provides us with further examples. In the United States, from 1828, when the Baltimore and Ohio line opened, it was not only English capital that played a critical role, as iron rails manufactured in England enabled freight pulled by English engines to extend the city's economic possibilities.[58] At the same time, local merchants were developing their own cotton industry, which attracted workers from England whose background was not only in cotton production but also in factory work. The Baltimore Steamworks Factory, the Washington Cotton Manufacturing Company and the Powhattan Cotton Mills all expanded in the 1830s.[59]

Encounters with Irish migrants sometimes had explosive results. The Irish in Philadelphia, for example, faced hostility that sometimes became exceptionally violent – notably in the 1820s and 1830s, when increasing immigration and rising Protestant anti-Catholicism turned the 'city of brotherly love' into the 'city of brotherly hate', as contemporaries unflatteringly renamed it.[60] 'Philadelphians with English roots or English ties', Gary Nash averred, 'looked down on them as "wild Irishmen"', though the necessity for cheap labour ensured that the Irish continued to flow in and, ultimately, as elsewhere, were welcomed.[61] Social superiority to the Irish did not always guarantee an easy transition into United States society. Englishmen and Germans – especially those militant 'refugees from Chartism and revolution' – enjoyed an easy association with 'American radicals'.[62]

Lest we should think all English arrivals were prosperous, skilled or independent, we need to note the presence of much less fortunate immigrants. Certainly, the role of emigration schemes played some part in creating an illusion of the widespread undesirability of the poor English. Such feelings should not surprise us when emptying poor houses and orphanages to meet labour demands in the colonies occupied the minds of colonial administrators, agents and commentators. However, as Baines points out, these schemes made a statistically unimportant contribution to the overall flow – some 1,400 per year between 1835 and 1846. More important, perhaps, is the coincidence of English emigration in the first half of the nineteenth century with years of depression and poor harvest yields.[63]

Among the Irish, Laurie argues, there was a basic gratitude at having a job, and preserving an ethnic culture was placed ahead of 'pursuing economic justice'.[64] An English observer noted that in New York in 1827, long before the famine inrush, 'the lowest stations of the hard working-classes' are 'generally filled by Irishmen, who are as much vilified here … as in England or Scotland'.[65] Such factors encouraged the anti-Irish views that were increasingly part of American culture and certainly strengthened after the famine as waves of poor immigrants entered the country's cities and large towns and as Fenians began plotting the downfall of British rule from bases on American soil.[66] Thus the conflicts that had characterized host–immigrant relations in urban Britain from the early nineteenth century also came to mark out the American city. The principal difference, however, was that now the Irish outnumbered the English and the character of tension became more complicated.

If it is virtually impossible to unpick the English immigrant from the wider British population, it is also difficult to deduce the effect of immigrants who were English over those who were Scottish, Welsh or from Ulster. This is particularly true in the spheres of mining, engineering, shipbuilding and steelmaking, but less so in textiles – the latter providing many of our most interesting examples of a retained English culture. Migration is an enormously complex series of processes. Where specific planned migrations took place, with Scottish colliers hired to establish new mines in Illinois or Welsh miners transplanted directly to hard-rock mining areas for their deep-mining expertise, or when the Cornish established the tin plate industry in Pittsburgh, such differentiations are relatively easy. The English had this type of measurable effect, for example, within the first industrial ventures in Baltimore, the Baltimore Cotton Factory (1829).[67] Steam-powered factories making flooring, as well as technologies for other types of mechanized carpentry, soon followed.

Migration and urbanization from the mid-nineteenth century

Some time before May 1861, two Worcestershire miners named Burton and Skidmore had emigrated for work in Scranton, Pennsylvania, in the heart of the main American anthracite district. The region had attracted many miners from Cornwall, the English Midlands and especially Wales. In that month, the two miners' families arrived in Philadelphia. Sarah Burton and her sister, Phebe Skidmore, were those miners' wives. They travelled to the United States with Sarah and Phebe's four young children, and their nineteen-year-old brother, the coal-miner William Whale, accompanied them. We know about this extended family because, immediately upon arrival, its members fell on the mercy of the Philadelphia Sons of St George, one of the oldest patrician English societies in America. The Sons of St George, along with the Albion Society and six individual subscribers, helped the newly arrived in their moment of terrible misfortune: Sarah's husband had been killed in an accident at work that also badly injured Phebe's husband. Their wives had crossed the ocean and were sick, 'having suffered much in the voyage and [being] in great distress of mind + destitution' because of rough seas and the tragedy that had befallen them. Their patrons in Philadelphia donated $16.50 to convey them all 'to Scranton where they have friends and will find work'.[68] There is no evidence of a major pit disaster in the region in 1861, but perhaps a smaller event befell the men, and neither woman appears to have been in Scranton in the 1870 census. However, in 1880, Phebe, her coal-miner husband, Richard, and their seven children aged from one to twenty were living in Superior, Kansas.[69] Phebe had long since left behind the melancholy fortunes that elicited critical charitable aid from the Sons of St George twenty years earlier.

The English associational networks that supported the Burton and Skidmore families developed in accordance with the rhythms of migration. From the mid-nineteenth century, this meant that ethnic societies proliferated and spread far wider as migration streams grew and further territories were developed. Exploring the nature of these migrations and assessing where the English settlements were located in the period from the 'Hungry Forties' to the First World War provides important context for our examination of English associations in the following chapters.

The middle years of the century saw migration from England, the rest of Britain and Ireland entering a vastly more expansive phase (see Figure 1.1). While the famine flight from Ireland contributed more significantly to this development than any other single event, the 1840s were hard times in Britain too. With rising migration and increasing numbers of poor emigrants, ethnic associational cultural also expanded. In particular, English associations spread beyond the old colonial vanguards of Charleston, Philadelphia and New York as ever larger numbers of English were attracted to towns in the growing industrial regions of New England, the Atlantic states, Pennsylvania and the Mid-West. Within increasing immigrations, both the United States and Canada witnessed the planting of English, Scottish and Irish societies alongside a flowering of similar organizations for European immigrants. The balance, however, strongly favoured the United States, which also drew an increasing share of all immigrants bound for the North American continent.

Emigrations from Britain and Ireland also became more focused on American destinations as the United States share grew to 65 per cent of all persons leaving Great Britain. Equally, those heading for Canada declined to 25.5 per cent in the 1840s and then 10.3 per cent in the 1850s. Australasia took up most of the remainder. In the 1840s, of course, the majority of emigrants by far were from Ireland or were Irish people outward bound from British ports – a trend also clearly reflected in census figures documenting the number of those of Irish birth resident in Toronto, for example, which rose in mid-century from 1,695 in 1848 to 12,441 in 1861.[70]

Despite Irish dominance, the outflows of the English- and Scots-born still were significant (Tables 1.3 and 1.4). In the 1820s, those born in England had represented nearly 71 per cent of all British and Irish emigrants. In the next decade, as Irish migration climbed, the English share dropped to 35.9 per cent. In the 1840s this figure had fallen once more to around one-quarter the 1840s. In the 1850s, as the Irish famine exodus began to fall back, English emigration rose again to account for nearly 40 per cent of all those leaving the British and Irish Isles. The hard figures for that period are striking: between 1820 and 1860 some 302,665 English-born and 47,890 Scots-born entered the United States, compared with nearly one million Irish-born.[71] This core English population was strong enough to create (and to require) the firm bedrock of an immigrant ethnic culture. For, while the English often are characterized as skilled workers and farmers, the overall group was large enough to include significant numbers of the poor and unskilled too, thus ensuring that there was both the manpower to run English charities and also the demand for help.[72]

Figure 1.1 'Leaving old England for America' (*Harper's Weekly*, 22 January 1870, image courtesy of Library of Congress, LC-USZ62-118128)

British and Irish emigrant traffic was focused on the great centre of New York, though other places were significant or developing too. In 1860, New York received 131,565 immigrants. Numbers were much smaller elsewhere, but also significant. In the same year, Boston landed

Table 1.4 *Countries of birth of passengers arriving in the United States from foreign countries, 1820–60*

	1820–30	*1831–40*	*1841–50*	*1851–60*	*ALL*
England	15,837	7,611	32,092	247,125	302,665
Scotland	3,180	2,667	3,712	38,331	47,890
Wales	170	185	1,261	6,319	7,935
Great Britain	19,187	10,463	37,065	291,775	358,490
Ireland	27,106	29,188	162,332	748,740	967,366
GB % Ire.[a]	**70.79**	**35.85**	**22.83**	**38.97**	**37.06**

Note: [a]GB % Ire. = the flow from Britain as a percentage of the flow from Ireland.
Source: Bureau of Census, *Eighth Census, 1860*, 'Introduction', tables, p. xxxii.

12,825 immigrants, New Orleans 13,080 and San Francisco (5,817), so entering the top-listed ports. But the old colonial ports of Baltimore (with 6,932) and Philadelphia (with 3,898) were falling behind. Many of these immigrants were from Britain, or else were Europeans trans-shipped through Britain. Between 1855 and 1860, British ports sent 1,531, or over half, of all ships landed in the United States ports, which amounted to 1,149 ships from Liverpool, 296 from London and 86 from Glasgow.[73] While the Irish and Germans accounted for the largest proportions of these vastly increased numbers, in all, in the years from 1814 to 1860, some 'three and a quarter millions of the natives of Great Britain and Ireland, "a population for a kingdom" … emigrated to this country', wrote Joseph C.G. Kennedy, Superintendent of the Census.[74]

Urban centres and industrial work attracted most of the English as they journeyed on from their ports of embarkation. Van Vugt's close reading of statistical data on British immigration in 1851 shows that 70 per cent of British immigrants (most of them English) working in industrial trades prior to arrival in the United States settled in the most industrial places in America: New England (19.8 per cent) and New York and Pennsylvania (50.6 per cent).[75] Specific industries also attracted precise inter-regional connections. Thus, the tens of thousands of English making new lives in New England and New York State included signifi-cant numbers of Lancastrians who headed for United States mill towns because of their experience in the manufacture of cottons. While mill operatives were plentiful in Manchester, Massachusetts or Oneida, New York State, the English were foremost an aristocracy of English labour, such as the English engineers and mechanics who helped commission the factories. They were then hired and overseen by fellow countrymen who were managers and foremen. If the English were pioneers in all facets of the American industrialization process, they also brought their propensity for complaint, demonstration and trade unionism.[76]

Industrial towns and key ports attracted the English, and one marker of their presence was the growth of English ethnic associational activity. Places such as Fall River, Boston and Providence in New England were major settlements. Albany, Buffalo, Rochester, Utica, Oneida and many others in New York State, were important, aligning closely with the Canada-based neighbours only a few miles north. Philadelphia, Pittsburgh and the mining districts around Scranton in Pennsylvania drew in thousands of English. Fanning further west, Cincinnati and Cleveland in Ohio and St Louis in Missouri ranked highly. Since colonial times Baltimore had been a major centre of English settlers, and this continued in the 1840s and 1850s. These were centres either with long-established St George's societies or else ones that developed between the 1840s and 1860s (see Tables 1.5–1.10).[77] They were also the places that, as seen in the next chapter, united with their Canadian cousins to form the NAStGU, a transnational confederation of similar societies across the continent.

While the English came to the United States in large numbers, they were outstripped by other major emigrant nations. In mid-nineteenth-century New York City, for example, they were in third place behind the Irish and Germans. Ernst characterizes the English there as a primarily Protestant group whose similarities to Americans enabled them to blend in. They formed no distinct ethnic neighbourhood in the early part of the century. By the 1840s, this had changed with the emergence of an English cluster in the Fourth Ward. As further such communities appeared, it was apparent that the English, Scots and Welsh tended to live quite close to each other, separated from the Irish. Around 23,000 of them, a large majority of the whole group, apparently lived in Manhattan. A further indicator of the superior buying power of the English and Scots was their disproportionate presence in Greenwich Village, which neither the poorer Germans nor the Irish achieved.[78] The English and Scots were more strongly represented, as a percentage of their respective populations, in the building trades than the Irish or Germans. Indeed, in 1855, if we add the Welsh and Canadians to the group, no other nationalities provided any serious share of the city's 13,583 foreign-born building workers. Ernst opens up a fascinating world in which the English-speaking workers (not merely the English-born ones) were able to enjoy advancement in America in a trade that was highly familiar to them from their homelands. With work being seasonal, moreover, Ernst tells us, workers moved south to warmer climes to continue their trades, or else went to types of work, such as shipbuilding, that were not so much restricted by the weather.[79] The English laid great store in carrying letters of recommendation to vouchsafe both their skill

Table 1.5 *British-born and Irish-born in the major United States centres of English associational activity: overview, 1860–1900*

	English-born		Scots-born		Welsh-born		British-born		Irish-born		TOTAL	No. of cities
	Total	%	Total	%	Total	%	Total	%	Total	%	TOTAL	
1860	109,711	12.3	27,911				137,622	15.5	615,564	69.1	890,808	25
1870	137,033	15.5	35,145	4.0	10,591	1.2	182,769	20.6	704,033	79.4	886,802	28
1880	169,967	18.2	40,671	4.4	11,527	1.2	222,165	23.8	711,443	76.2	933,608	26
1890	242,111	22.6	70,556	6.6	13,083	1.2	325,750	30.4	744,767	69.6	1,070,517	32
1900	264,192	24.6	71,270	6.6	16,948	1.6	352,410	32.9	719,704	77.1	1,072,114	34

Sources: Bureau of Census, *Eighth Census, 1860*, introduction, 'Principal Cities and Towns; Native and Foreign Population', pp. xxxi–xxxii;1870: Bureau of Census, *Ninth Census*, vol. 1: *The Statistics of the Population of the United States, Embracing the Tables of Race, Nationality, Sex, Selected Ages, and Occupations … From the Original Returns of the Ninth Census (June 1, 1870), under the Direction of the Secretary of the Interior* (Washington, DC, 1872), 'Nativities of the Population of Principal Cities', table VIII: 'Fifty Cities', pp. 388–89; 1880: Bureau of Census, *Statistics of the Population of the United States at the Tenth Census(June 1, 1880), Embracing Extended Tables of Population of States, Counties, and Minor Civil Division, with Distinction of Race, Sec Age, Nativity, and Occupation; together with Summary Tables …* (Washington, DC, 1880), table XVI: 'Foreign-Born Population of Fifty Principal Cities', p. 540; 1890: Bureau of Census, *Report of the Population of the United States at the Eleventh Census*, part 1 (Washington, DC, 1894), table 34, 'Foreign-Born Population Distributed According to Country of Birth for Cities Having 20,000 Inhabitants or More', pp. 670–71, 674–75; 1900: Bureau of Census, *Census Reports*, vol. 1: *Twelfth Census of the United States*, part 1 (Washington, DC, 1901), table 35: 'Foreign Born Population Distributed According to Country of Birth for Cities Having 25,000 Inhabitants or More', pp. 796–803.

Table 1.6 *English-, Irish- and Scots-born populations of major United States urban centres with English associations, 1860*

	English-born	Irish-born	Scots-born	Total of all foreign-born	Total
New York, NY	27,082	203,740	9,208	383,717	818,699
Philadelphia, PA	19,278	95,548	3,290	169,430	565,529
Brooklyn, NY	15,162	56,710	2,785	104,589	266,661
Baltimore, MD	2,154	15,536	524	52,497	212,418
Boston, MA	4,073	45,991	1,321	63,791	177,840
New Orleans, LA	3,045	24,398	736	64,621	168,675
Cincinnati, OH	3,730	19,375	921	73,614	161,675
St Louis, MO	5,513	29,926	1,101	96,086	160,773
Chicago, IL	4,354	19,889	1,641	54,624	109,260
Buffalo, NY	2,965	9,279	799	37,684	81,129
Newark, NJ	2,833	11,167	509	26,625	71,941
Albany, NY	1,490	14,780	527	21,619	62,367
Washington, DC	893	6,282	234	10,765	61,122
San Francisco, CA	2,412	9,363	659	28,454	56,802
Providence, RI	1,387	9,534	455	12,570	50,666
Pittsburgh, PA	1,346	9,297	262	18,063	49,221
Rochester, NY	2,342	6,786	374	18,897	48,204
Detroit, MI	2,353	5,994	1,168	21,349	45,619
Milwaukee, WI	1,265	3,100	375	22,848	45,246
Cleveland, OH	2,822	5,479	452	19,437	43,417
Charleston, SC	368	3,263	209	6,309	40,522
Syracuse, NY	1,047	4,030	76	10,052	28,119
Utica, NY	1,449	2,952	173	8,327	22,529
Savannah, GA	348	3,145	112	28,454	22,232
TOTAL	109,711	615,564	27,911	1,354,422	3,370,666

Total of all British-born: <u>137,622</u>

Total of all Irish-born: <u>615,564</u>

Note: No Welsh census data for 1860.
Source: Bureau of Census, *Eighth Census, 1860*, Introduction, 'Principal Cities and Towns; Native and Foreign Population', pp. xxxi–xxxii.

Table 1.7 *English-, Irish-, Scots- and Welsh-born populations of major United States urban centres with English associations, 1870*

	English-born	Irish-born	Scots-born	Welsh-born	Total population
New York, NY	24,442	201,999	7,562	584	942,292
Philadephia, PA	22,034	96,698	4,175	501	674,022
Brooklyn, NY	18,843	73,985	4,098	539	298,977
St Louis, MO	10,027	39,988	4,197	147	310,864
Chicago, IL	5,367	32,239	1,202	565	396,099
Baltimore, MD	2,142	15,223	525	84	267,354
Boston, MA	5,977	56,900	1,795	113	250,526
Cincinnati, OH	3,526	18,624	787	507	216,239
New Orleans, LA	2,020	14,693	568	70	191,418
San Francisco, CA	5,172	25,864	1,687	247	149,473
Buffalo, NY	3,563	11,264	996	94	117,714
Washington, DC	1,235	6,948	298	23	109,199
Newark, NJ	4,041	12,481	870	64	105,059
Cleveland, OH	4,533	9,964	668	285	92,829
Pittsburgh, PA	2,838	13,119	584	1,036	86,076
Detroit, MI	3,284	6,970	1,637	46	79,577
Milwaukee, WI	1,395	3,874	423	242	71,440
Albany, NY	1,572	13,276	427	29	69,422
Providence, RI	2,427	12,085	575	26	68,904
Rochester, NY	2,530	6,078	428	31	62,386
Charleston, SC	236	2,180	114	8	48,956
Indianapolis, IND	698	3,321	253	41	48,244
Syracuse, NY	1,345	5,172	138	108	43,051
Scranton, PA	1,445	6,491	366	4,177	35,092
Toledo, OH	694	3,332	119	7	31,584
Utica, NY	1,352	3,496	198	992	28,804
Savannah, GA	252	2,197	72	9	28,235
Fall River, MA	4,043	5,572	383	16	26,766
TOTAL	137,033	704,033	35,145	10,591	4,850,602

Total of all British-born: <u>182,769</u>

Total of all Irish-born: <u>704,033</u>

Source: Bureau of Census, *Eighth Census, 1860*, Introduction, 'Principal Cities and Towns; Native and Foreign Population', pp. xxxi–xxxii.

Table 1.8 *English-, Irish-, Scots- and Welsh-born populations of major United States urban centres with English associations, 1880*

	English-born	Irish-born	Scots-born	Welsh-born	Foreign-born	Total
New York, NY	29,664	198,595	8,683	929	478,670	1,206,299
Philadelphia, PA	26,315	101,808	5,696	680	204,335	847,170
Brooklyn, NY	20,324	78,814	4,682	425	177,694	566,663
Chicago, IL	13,045	44,411	4,152	722	204,859	503,185
Boston, MA	8,998	64,793	2,662	221	114,796	372,839
St Louis, MO	6,212	28,536	591	241	105,013	350,518
Baltimore, MD	2,286	14,238	591	86	56,136	332,312
Cincinnati, OH	3,086	15,077	650	379	71,659	255,189
San Francisco, CA	7,462	30,721	2,243	333	104,244	233,959
New Orleans, LA	1,786	1,786	426	47	41,157	216,090
Cleveland, OH	7,527	11,708	426	1,061	59,409	160,146
Pittsburgh, PA	5,111	17,110	1,058	2,012	44,605	156,389
Buffalo, NY	4,319	10,310	1,169	95	51,268	155,134
Washington, DC	1,408	6,448	436	47	14,242	147,293
Newark, NJ	4,478	13,451	1,090	56	40,330	136,508
Detroit, MI	4,200	6,775	1,783	71	45,645	116,340
Milwaukee, WI	1,630	3,659	479	242	46,073	115,587
Providence, RI	5,013	16,939	1,198	63	28,075	104,857
Albany, NY	1,866	12,575	572	27	23,765	90,758
Rochester, NY	2,703	6,136	470	34	26,622	89,866
Indianapolis, IN	957	3,660	317	37	12,610	75,056
Syracuse, NY	1,363	4,451	137	28	13,018	51,792
Toledo, OH	899	2,941	180	18	14,340	50,137
Charleston, SC	236	1,611	109	7	3,950	49,984
Fall River, MA	7,521	8,118	570	50	23,575	48,961
Scranton, PA	1,558	6,772	301	3,616	15,857	45,850
TOTAL	169,967	711,443	40,671	11,527	2,021,947	6,478,882

Total of all British-born: <u>222,165</u>

Total of all Irish-born: <u>711,443</u>

Source: Bureau of, Census *Tenth Census, 1880*, table XVI, 'Foreign-Born Population of Fifty Principal Cities', pp. 538, 540.

Table 1.9 *English-, Irish-, Scots- and Welsh-born populations of major United States urban centres with English associations, 1890*

	English-born	Irish-born	Scots-born	Welsh-born	Foreign-born	Total
New York, NY	35,907	190,418	11,242	965	639,943	1,515,301
Chicago, IL	28,337	70,028	9,217	1,613	450,668	1,099,850
Philadelphia, PA	38,926	110,935	8,772	935	269,480	1,046,964
Brooklyn, NY	26,493	84,738	7,417	510	61,700	806,343
St Louis, MO	6,507	24,270	1,370	262	114,876	575,283
Boston, MA	13,454	71,971	4,490	305	158,172	448,477
Baltimore, MD	3,098	13,389	666	88	69,063	434,439
San Francisco, CA	9,828	30,718	3,181	357	126,811	298,997
Cincinnati, OH	2,950	12,323	621	328	71,408	296,908
Cleveland, OH	10,950	13,512	2,060	357	97,095	261,353
Buffalo, NY	7,098	11,664	1,625	99	89,485	255,664
New Orleans, LA	1,599	7,923	270	24	34,369	242,039
Washington, DC	2,126	7,224	578	71	18,770	230,392
Detroit, MI	7,168	7,447	2,459	84	81,709	205,876
Milwaukee, WI	2,409	3,436	686	342	79,576	204,468
Newark, NJ	5,625	13,234	1,570	46	55,571	181,830
Rochester, NY	5,002	6,484	718	57	9,775	133,896
Providence, RI	8,143	19,040	1,749	57	40,364	132,146
Indianapolis, IN	982	3,547	348	29	14,487	105,436
Albany, NY	1,698	9,812	495	40	22,293	94,923
Syracuse, NY	2,560	6,314	300	49	22,342	88,143
Toledo, OH	1,487	2,878	213	57	22,189	81,434
Scranton, PA	3,065	8,343	576	4,890	25,573	75,215
Fall River, MA	11,062	9,130	930	106	37,734	74,898
Charleston, SC	224	994	67	4	3,133	54,955
Bridgeport, CT	1,916	5,985	374	25	14,189	48,866
Utica, NY	1,451	3,010	214	1,314	11,769	44,007
Savannah, GA	353	1.269	87	9	3,408	43,189
Augusta, GA	76	556	29	31	1,208	33,300
Bay City, MI	559	566	226	3	10,945	27,839
Auburn, NY	1,058	2,644	239	26	5,659	25,858
TOTAL	242,111	744,767	70,556	13,083	2,663,764	9,168,289

Total of all British-born: <u>325,750</u>

Total of all Irish-born: <u>744,767</u>

Source: Bureau of Census, *Eleventh Census, 1890*, part 1, table 34, 'Foreign-Born Population Distributed According to Country of Birth for Cities Having 20,000 Inhabitants or More, 1890', pp. 670–71, 674–75.

Table 1.10 *English-, Irish-, Scots- and Welsh-born populations of major United States urban centres with English associations, 1900*

	English-born	Irish-born	Scots-born	Welsh-born	Total foreign-born	Total
New York, NY	68,836	275,102	19,836	1,686	1,270,080	3,437,202
Chicago, IL	29,308	73,912	10,347	1,818	587,112	1,698,575
Philadelphia, PA	36,752	98,427	8,479	1,033	295,340	1,293,697
St Louis, Oo	5,800	19,421	1,264	238	111,356	575,238
Boston, MA	18,174	70,147	4,473	308	197,129	560,892
Baltimore, MD	2,841	9,690	594	92	68,600	508,957
Cleveland, OH	10,621	13,120	2,179	1,490	124,631	381,768
Buffalo, NY	6,908	11,292	1,868	158	104,252	352,387
San Francisco, CA	8,956	15,963	3,000	386	116,885	342,782
Cincinnati, Oh	2,201	9,114	461	240	57,961	325,902
Pittsburgh, PA	8,902	18,620	2,264	2,539	84,878	321,616
New Orleans, LA	1,262	5,298	218	35	30,325	287,104
Detroit, MI	6,412	6,412	2,496	101	96,503	285,704
Milwaukee, Wi	2,134	2,653	667	307	88,991	285,315
Washington, DC	2,299	6,220	574	82	20,119	278,718
Newark, NJ	5,874	12,792	5,511	91	71,368	246,070
Providence, RI	9,639	18,683	1,914	82	55,855	175,597
Indianapolis, IN	1,154	3,765	429	41	17,122	169,164
Rochester, NY	8,999	5,599	663	69	40,748	162,604
Toledo, OH	1,636	2,684	256	73	27,822	131,822
Syracuse, NY	2,383	5,717	307	65	23,757	108,374
Fall River, MA	12,268	7,317	1,045	102	50,402	104,863
Scranton, PA	3,692	7,198	576	4,621	28,973	102,026
Albany, NY	1,361	6,612	395	39	17,718	94,151
Bridgeport, CT	2,755	5,974	471	32	22,281	70,996
Utica, NY	1,474	2,548	213	1,165	13,470	56,383
Savannah, GA	316	865	78	5	3,434	54,244
Charleston, SC	144	621	64	1	2,592	53,807
Augusta, GA	56	362	22	1	995	39,441
Schenectady, NY	632	1,103	242	20	7,169	31,682

(Continued)

Table 1.10 (*Continued*)

	English-born	Irish-born	Scots-born	Welsh-born	Total foreign-born	TOTAL
Auburn, NY	1.023	2,084	198	23	5,436	30,345
Bay City, MI	402	389	166	5	8,485	27,628
TOTAL	264,192	719,704	71,270	16,948	3,651,789	12,595,054

Total of all British-born: British: <u>352,410</u>

Total of all Irish-born: Irish: <u>719,704</u>

Source: Bureau of Census, *Twelfth Census, 1900*, table 35, 'Foreign Born Population Distributed According to Country of Birth for Cities Having 25,000 Inhabitants or More', pp. 796–80.

and their reliability; they also utilized regional, local and personal bonds to secure work. In 1847, in New York, a Coventry ribbon weaver named Benjamin Tilt finally secured work after he 'by "accident found M.M. Roy [also] a Coventry man and he promised us employment"'.[80]

Utica in New York was a growing textile town that continued to attract English migrants on a sizeable scale long after its factories started up. Typically of many United States towns, however, the industrial structures, planted by British settlers and managed with English experts, soon attracted diverse other workers. By the 1850s, Yankee and English mill girls in Lowell, Massachusetts, were being threatened by waves of Irish immigrants, who rapidly came to dominate the New England textile labour force.[81] Germans, Irish and, later on, Poles, Italians and Jews flocked to Utica, and one result was notable residential segregation by ethnicity and class. The city's story was not, however, spectacular. After that, unskilled Europeans provided the primary staff so that the town quickly was compared unfavourably with Buffalo and Syracuse – the former because of its location on Lake Erie, and the latter because it embraced new industries, such as chemicals.[82] High levels of Welsh settlement in Utica pointed to strong connections to the coal-mining districts of north-east Pennsylvania, where their countrymen were many times more numerous than in all but the largest cities. This was due to the fact that Utica's position on the Mohawk River and Erie Canal made it an ideal place for the trans-shipment of coal. Utica, then, was the site of some of the most notable small-town English ethnic associationalism and was connected, too, with the places of the fiercest interethnic rivalries imported from Britain, notably Scranton and environs, where the Irish Ribbonmen, known as the Molly Maguires, burst into ignominious life.

Immigrants from northern England were strongly attracted to New England because of its dominance in the American textile industry. By mid-century, that region contained half the largest mills and three-quarters of the country's spindles. Massachusetts, New Hampshire and Rhode Island were the regional centres. New England mill-owners were quick to exploit English technologies and know-how, and labour drawn from the surrounding areas and from England. By 1836, eight firms in Lowell employed 6,000 hands, and the industrial revolution was well under way.[83] Here, the English, mostly from Lancashire, brought both technical skills and trade union organization. They also introduced English societies, churches, culinary culture and features of pastime culture. Yorkshire immigrants had a similar influence in Lawrence, Massachusetts, where they were responsible for establishing the worsted woollen industry.[84]

Cotton was not the only textile trade in which English know-how and labour were vital. In the post-bellum period, 'practically the entire English silk industry was transferred by skilled British immigrants from Macclesfield and Coventry to Paterson, New Jersey'.[85] Here, in New Jersey, however, immigrants were less organized than in New England and so less able to impose trade unions and effectively to bargain with capitalism.[86]

Textiles also had purchase in Philadelphia. However, this city's organizational structures and principles were different. Here, 'proprietary capitalism' prevailed, whereby 'a factory system based on small firms initially owned individually or by partnerships that primarily employed British immigrant skilled workmen, produced specialty goods'. The economic principles were to specialize outside the cheap, mass market; paternalism, high pay, strong unions and 'industrial peace and sustained prosperity' dominated the ethos of the labour process. Consequently, 'by 1880, 250,000 workers of English, Irish, German and native-born backgrounds crowded' Philadelphia, 'this most diversified industrial centre in the United States'.[87]

Generally, the English group was over-represented with immigrants who were well prepared for industrial work, from mining to textiles, engineering to shipbuilding. The copper mining and smelting industries are particular cases in point. In northern Michigan, where mining for copper began in 1844, Englishmen from Cornwall were something of an industrial vanguard. Experienced in the art of mining and metal manufacture, they 'carried on their work successfully and in many cases made large fortunes'.[88]

While skilled workers were an important component of the English labour flows to the United States, scholars have disagreed as to how much. Erickson and Van Vugt subjected the profile of British immigrants to intense scrutiny in high-quality quantitative research, with Cohn challenging their weighting of skilled and unskilled elements.[89] While Cohn disagrees with Erickson and Van Vugt about the quantity of skilled workers in the emigrant cohort, his interpretation spins on a different, less critical reading of available data, with Cohn not challenging the many instances where those logging data simply repeated categories of work. Regardless of the disagreements, none can demur from the fact that skilled industrialists were heavily represented among the English. Additionally, the data also reveal that farmers were not poor or small tenants, but wealthier men of capital, often those accompanied by large families and possessions. At the same time, beyond skilled men and farmers, the largest group (and one that Cohn would have us revise up) was the poor unskilled workers.

We certainly find many of these less well-resourced individuals – men and women heavily represented in the huge immigration figures for the 1840s and 1850s – appearing in lists of immigrants given alms by the St George's societies. Moreover, not all of the skilled who came to the United States were independent and well resourced. In 1861, striking numbers of textile workers, for example, found themselves in receipt of support from the stewards of the Sons of St George, Philadelphia. Of 335 individuals receiving relief, 120 were identifiably involved in textiles, with weavers and spinners the largest groups.[90] In 1879, the same society relieved 928 persons in a year, the two largest groups being labourers (178; 19.2 per cent) and clerks (67; 7.2 per cent).[91] The picture painted by such instances of alms-giving is one in which local and national conditions (war in one case, economic depression in another) bit hardest at the unskilled but could buffet lower-grade white-collar workers too. We are also left with a sense that sometimes the spur to migration was the redundancy of old trades, speciality occupations and handicrafts, which impelled people to embark on the hopeless task of retaining their occupational status in a new land whose economy was less likely to accommodate them in their trade than was the old country.

Overall, the work of these scholars of English emigration data chimes with our presentation here of, on the one hand, poor immigrants needing help, which their wealthier fellow countrymen happily provided, and, on the other, industrial workers at the cutting edge of American industrialism who, in their own struggles to control the labour process, formed ethnic societies which at once threw the protective veil of the friendly society around co-ethnic workers and excluded others, especially Catholics.

The skilled men, women and their families – those able mostly to avoid the charity of English societies – were undoubtedly a great boon to American cities and industries. They had specific skills, however: not handloom weaving or shoemaking so much as the likes of hard-rock mining and engineering. New York State's industries featured prominently the craft skills of English workers and the technical know-how of foremen, overseers and the like, who had significant experience of factory work back home. Until the Civil War, the state had attracted more immigrant agriculturalists. Upon the cessation of hostilities, however, the balance was tipped to industrial and urban opportunities and so to different types of immigrants – those who lacked capital but often were equipped with skills; and certainly those commanding significant experience of urban life and work. In mid-century New York City, immigrant workers, including the English, were breaking into the printing industry. English and Scottish workers also prospered in metallurgical trades. Though vastly outnumbered by both groups, the English and Scots proportions in those trades (7.5 and 9 per cent respectively) were double the German rate and treble the Irish.[92]

These migratory pathways explain why we focus upon these well-established centres and the westward outgrowths from them that followed. In the broadest terms, this was the Atlantic seaboard area from Maine to the Carolinas, usually no more than 250 miles inland from the ocean.[93] While we see relatively little English associational activity further inland from the southern extent of this original colonial settlement area, the westward push from Boston, New York, Philadelphia and Baltimore, from New England, New York and Pennsylvania towards the Great Lakes, to the south of there into Ohio, Indiana and Michigan, and to the west of the Lakes, in Illinois and Wisconsin, is where most of the activity we will describe took place. True, there was activity in the south, in the far west and in most states where the English settled. But the preponderance was in the most populous, industrial, northern and Mid-Western places. At the same time we must recognize the diffusion of the English. Even as early as 1860, there were some interesting developments in terms of this spread across the United States. English-born immigrants accounted for at least 1.4 per cent population of sixteen states, among which California ranked highest, with 4 per cent English-born. While most of the states that featured these higher rates of English settlement were in the north and east, states such as Iowa, Illinois, Tennessee, Wisconsin and Minnesota also were included (see Table 1.11 below). Concentration was, therefore, one theme; but dispersal was another.

Mass immigration, urbanization and territorial expansion

Until the mid-nineteenth century, most English immigrants settled in the industrial north-east before a broader-based diffusion ensued. Indeed, the middle Atlantic states accounted for half of all British immigrants in the mid-nineteenth century. Thereafter, there was an increasingly wide distribution of such immigrants – a development in line with the growth and spread of English associations. Farming was a persistent dream for the English and British, as it was for so many other groups, but it was the expansion of the frontiers or urbanization that really accounted for the diversification of English settlement. By 1890, California, the south, mining towns in the west and many other places beyond the usual eastern axis welcomed English-speaking arrivals. Figures from the United States illustrate this shift. While, also in 1890, Gilpin County, Colorado, was 25 per cent English-born, Nevada County, California, was 10 per cent English, and Silver Bow County, Montana, was at 12 per cent.[94] Pressing west led to the development of later-arriving hubs based on agricultural and mineral exploitation. Alongside the established tidewater cities in the United States, where the English and their associations dated to the eighteenth century, Mid-Western settlements, such as St Louis, mushroomed. That acme of urbanization, Chicago, became one the western world's great boom cities, rising from a mere 4,470 in 1840 to 2.7 million in 1920.

Canadian urbanization, in this phase of development, was, as Tables 1.12–1.16 show, small by United States standards. In 1851, no Canadian conurbation totalled even 50,000; by 1900, Toronto, with 208,000 souls, was still 50 per cent smaller than Baltimore; Ottawa and Hamilton, the next-placed of our Canadian cities, were roughly the same size as the demographically stagnant Charleston. These then were regional hubs as well as major American centres, pieces in a global economic network and sites of significant English settlement. Along with smaller Ontarian cities, such as Kingston, London and Guelph, and the Quebec city of Montreal, Toronto was the major place of English associational activity (Tables 1.11–1.16).

Toronto was the largest city in Ontario, and the nation's second-placed centre behind Montreal. Additionally, Toronto was country's largest English-speaking city and a major industrial centre. It was initially very English-speaking, though Irish and Scots outnumbered the English-born. To Ephraim Hathaway, in 1870, it was 'the most comfortable English-looking place he had struck yet'.[95] From the 1880s, however, it was attracting large numbers of eastern Europeans, Jews, Catholics and others quite outside the British and Irish norms on which it had been established. It remained mostly Protestant, but became less so as the population diversified; and it maintained a reputation for fierce sectarian, Anglo-Saxonist and racist aggression, perpetrated by Irish Protestant Orangemen and English and Scottish workers against Irish Catholics, the French, eastern and southern European Catholics and the Chinese.[96] That said, the Irish Catholic population was, by the 1880s, rising quickly up the social scale.[97]

Table 1.11 *English- and Irish-born populations in key states of English settlement in in the United States, 1860*

	English-born		Irish-born	
	Total	*%*	*Total*	*%*
California	12,227	4.00	33,147	10.85
Connecticut	8,875	1.93	55,445	12.05
Delaware	1,581	1.41	5,832	5.41
Illinois	41,745	2.44	87,573	5.12
Iowa	11,533	1.71	28,072	4.16
Massachusetts	23,848	1.94	185,434	15.07
Michigan	25,743	3.44	30,049	4.01
Minnesota	3,462	1.99	12,831	7.37
Missouri	10,009	0.85	43,464	3.68
New Jersey	15,853	2.36	62,006	9.23
New York	106,011	2.73	498,072	12.84
Pennsylvania	46,546	1.6	201,939	6.95
Rhode Island	6,356	3.64	25,285	14.48
Tennessee	2,001	0.18	12,498	1.12
Virginia	4,104	0.26	16,501	1.03
Wisconsin	30,543	3.94	49,961	6.44
	350,437	**2.15**	**1,348,109**	**7.49**

Ratio Irish to English = **3.5:1**

Note: Table includes only states with 2,000+ English and states where 1.4+% of the population was English.
Source: Bureau of Census, *Eighth Census 1860*, 'Introduction', Tables, pp. xxix, xxxi.

Table 1.12 *British-born and Irish-born in the major Canadian centres of English associational activity: overview, 1871–1901*

	English & Welsh		Scots	British		Irish		TOTAL	No of cities
	Total	*%*	*Total*	*Total*	*%*	*Total*	*%*		
1871	30,647	45.3	12,322	42,969	63.5	24,741	36.5	67,710	10
1881	35,636	42.9	13,731	49,367	59.4	33,716	40.6	83,083	10
1891	45,117	49.2	14,724	59,841	65.2	31,945	34.8	91,786	10
1901	50,547	56.7	13,156	63,703	71.4	25,481	28.6	89,184	6

Sources: See Tables 1.13–1.16.

54 The English diaspora in North America

Table 1.13 *British-born and Irish-born in the major Canadian centres of English associational activity, 1871*

	England and Wales		Ireland		Scotland			
	Total	%	Total	%	Total	%	Total	%
Montreal	5,022	4.7	1,059	1.0	3,111	2.9	107,225	100
Toronto	11,089	19.5	10,366	18.1	3,263	5.7	56992	100
Hamilton	4,781	17.3	3,543	12.8	2,315	8.4	27646	100
Ottawa	1,488	7.0	2,548	11.8	549	2.5	21,545	100
London	3,192	20.2	1,917	12.1	1,091	6.9	15,826	100
Kingston	1,107	9.0	2,658	21.4	394	3.2	12,407	100
Brantford	1,388	17.1	919	11.3	452	5.6	8,107	100
St Catharines	726	9.2	1,053	13.4	293	3.7	7,864	100
Belleville	651	9.0	1,031	14.1	239	3.3	7,305	100
Guelph	1,203	23.6	695	13.6	615	12.1	5,102	100
TOTAL	**30,647**		**25,789**		**12,322**		**270,019**	

Source: Census of Canada, 1870–71, vol. 1 (Ottawa, 1871), table III, 'Birth Place of the People', pp. 335ff.

Table 1.14 *British-born and Irish-born in the major Canadian centres of English associational activity, 1881*

	English-born		Irish-born		Scots-born			
	Total	%	Total	%	Total	%	Total	%
Montreal	5,406	3.8	9,789	7	3,289	2.3	140,747	100
Toronto	14,667	17.0	10,781	12.5	4,431	5.1	86,415	100
Hamilton	5,502	15.3	3,343	9.2	2,397	6.7	35,961	100
Ottawa	1,458	5.3	2,388	8.7	540	2.0	27,412	100
London	3,280	16.6	1,885	9.5	1,065	5.4	19,746	100
Kingston	1,040	7.4	2,266	16.1	415	3.0	14,091	100
Brantford	1,329	13.9	724	7.5	413	4.3	9,616	100
St Catharines	873	9.0	1,015	10.5	267	2.8	9,661	100
Belleville	823	8.7	827	8.7	228	2.4	9,516	100
Guelph	1,258	12.7	698	7.1	686	6.9	9,890	100
TOTAL	**35,636**		**33,716**		**13,731**		**363,055**	

Source: Census of Canada, 1880–81, vol. 1 (Ottawa, 1871), table IV, 'Birth Place of the People', pp. 303ff.

Table 1.15 *British-born and Irish-born in the major Canadian centres of English associational activity, 1891*

	English-born		Irish-born		Scots-born			
	Total	%	Total	%	Total	%	Total	%
Montreal	9,117	5.0	9,460	5.2	3,776	2.1	182,695	100
Toronto	22,801	15.9	13,253	9.2	6,347	4.4	144,023	100
Hamilton	6,536	13.8	3,389	5.4	2,571	7.2	47,245	100
Ottawa	1,947	5.2	2,336	6.3	614	1.6	37,269	100
London	3,156	14.1	1,611	7.2	894	4.0	22,281	100
Kingston	1,560	6.4	1,896	7.8	522	2.2	24,269	100
TOTAL	**45,117**		**31,945**		**14,724**		**457,782**	

Source: *Census of Canada, 1890–91* (Ottawa, 1891), table XVIII, 'Birthplace of the People by District'.

Table 1.16 *British-born and Irish-born in the major Canadian centres of English associational activity, 1901*

	English-born		Irish-born		Scots-born			
	Total	%	Total	%	Total	%	Total	%
Montreal	14,042	5.2	6,796	2.5	2,564	1.00	267,730	100
Toronto	24,901	12	11,804	5.7	6,464	3.10	208,040	100
Hamilton	5,626	10.7	2,524	4.8	2,120	4.00	52,634	100
Ottawa	2,436	4.1	2,021	3.4	727	1.20	59,928	100
London	2,489	6.6	1,141	3	942	2.50	37,981	100
Kingston	1,053	5.9	1,195	6.7	339	1.90	17,961	100
TOTAL	**50,547**		**25,481**		**13,156**		**644,274**	**100**

Source: *Fourth Census of Canada, 1901* (Ottawa, 1902), vol. 1: *Population*, table XIV, 'Birthplace of the People by District', pp. 418ff.

Toronto and other eastern centres in the Province of Canada continued their urban sprawl at this time, finally catching up with other large North American population centres. This growth was still financed primarily from Britain.[98] Not all investment opportunities were, however, successful. While British capital continued to flow, some of the most promising schemes – on paper anyway – such as the Grand Trunk Railway, did not perform well: 'shares were not popular with investors', and the scheme ended in financial disaster for many investors.[99] More positive were the opportunities that arose – for new intending migrants as well as investors – after Confederation in 1867.

At this point, the new Dominion Government first mooted settlement proper of the Canadian prairies, the eventual goal being to establish Canada as a state from the Atlantic to the Pacific coast. Early migration to the west was channelled through the gateway of Winnipeg, particularly after the completion of the transcontinental railway in the mid-1880s, which played a critical role in peopling Canada's western shores.[100] Other early centres in the west were, certainly in the late nineteenth century, little more than tent campsites or, at best, assemblages of wooden log houses as in the case of late nineteenth-century Saskatoon. But overall growth continued and was fast. Edmonton, Alberta, for example, had a population of 200 in 1878, but this had grown to 55,000 by about 1910.[101]

The migrants building European Canada at his time often were highly mobile. A case recounted by Dirk Hoerder offers a useful example. This is the story of an English mason who, in 1872, travelled to Liverpool with the expectation of going to the United States. Instead, he immediately fell in with a crowd heading for Canada, and so he went with them for Toronto via Maine. Once there, he took lodgings with an English family, and worked for a while as a quarryman west of the city. The money was poor, but since the city's houses were made of wood, there was much less demand for those skilled in stone-cutting than was true of England. The man then heard how the 'Great Fire' had created a building boom in Chicago, and he joined the flood of workers who headed south from Toronto. He then became embroiled in labour disputes that saw the stonemasons turned out, so he headed to Buffalo. After that, he made the short return journey to Toronto before, in 1873, heading home to England because of the economic downturn. This one life captures the kinds of journey that many of his compatriots made. It captures the hope, enterprise, disappointment and environmental exigencies affecting the lives and decisions of ordinary men and women heading back and forth across the Atlantic, and between towns, cities and nations. Such peripatetic experiences were especially common for young, unattached, childless immigrant male workers as they quested after decent livings.[102]

This mason's transnational wanderings were part of a larger movement between Canada and the United States, which saw migrants born in British North America, as well as more recent migrants, crossing borders with remarkable regularity, and in large numbers. Table 1.17 shows just how many of these British North Americans, later simply 'Canadians', made the journey. It also shows how the largest such populations were to be found in the American cities. There are certain clear patterns. While the major cities of Boston, New York, Chicago, Philadelphia, San Francisco, and later Los Angeles, all feature prominently, the lion's share of these cross-border settlers went to the closest industrial cities (e.g. Buffalo and

Table 1.17 *The largest British North America-/Canadian-born immigrant populations in United States cities, 1860-1900*

1860: cities of 1,000+		1880: cities of 2000+		1900: cities of 2000+			
City	BNA total	City	BNA total	City	Canada (Fr.)	Canada (Eng.)	Canada total
Boston, MA	6,813	Boston, MA	23,156	Boston, MA	2,908	47,374	50,282
New York, NY	3,899	Chicago, IL	13,914	Chicago, IL	5,307	29,472	34,779
Detroit, MN	3,088	Detroit, MI	10,754	Detroit, MI	3,541	25,403	28,944
Buffalo, NY	2,464	Lowell, MA	8,768	Fall River, MA	20,172	2,329	22,501
Chicago, IL	1,867	Fall River, MA	7,028	Lowell, MA	14,674	4,485	19,159
Brooklyn, NY	1,673	New York, NY	7,004	Buffalo, NY	733	16,509	17,242
Rochester, NY	1,619	Buffalo, NY	6,021	Cambridge, MA	1,483	9,613	11,096
St Louis, MO	1,332	Brooklyn, NY	4,363	Lawrence, MA	6,999	1,683	8,682
Lowell, MA	1,082	Cleveland, OH	4,331	Cleveland, OH	772	7,839	8,611
Troy, NY	1,041	Cambridge, MA	3,981	Holyoke, MA	6,991	865	7,856
		Rochester, NY	3,884	Duluth, MN	1,285	5,099	6,384
		San Francisco, CA	3,860	Gloucester, MA	800	4,388	5,188
		Lawrence, MA	3,499	Haverhill, MA	2,403	1,651	4,054
		Worcester, MA	3,220	Bay City, MI	1,075	2,413	3,488
		Minneapolis, MN	3,009	Grand Rapids, MI	169	3,318	3,487
		Providence, RI	2,508	Los Angeles, CA	214	2,683	2,897
		Lynn, MA	2,423	Denver, CO	245	2,623	2,868
		Philadelphia, PA	2,354	Brockton, MA	532	2,199	2,731
		St Louis, MO	2,091	Hartford, CT	781	1,809	2,590
				Butte, MO	556	1,518	2,074
TOTAL	24,878		116,168		71,640	173,273	244,913

Source: Bureau of Census, *Eighth Census 1860,* pp. xxxi–xxxii; *Tenth Census, 1880,* table xvi, p. 538; 1900, table 35, p. 796 (see Tables 1.3–1.8 for full citations).

Detroit), the mill towns of both New York State and Massachusetts. Data from the census of 1900 show that 40 per cent of immigrants from British North America were French Canadians, many of them arriving to work in the mills, like their fellow Anglo-Canadian countrymen. We cannot be sure how many of the English-speaking part of this migration stream comprised the offspring of more recent immigrants (of any nationality), but even so, the numbers are significant enough to suggest that they would have buttressed the British-born immigrants in their Protestant, anti-Catholic outlook and in their suspicion of Irish Catholics. Those who were of French origins, moreover, would have added grist to those Protestants who were vigilant about the creeping effect of 'Romanism'. Taken together with the larger immigrant profile of American cities, these migrations, in all their various possible hues and textures, added an important dimension to the world which created an ethnically conscious, association-forming English immigrant character.

By the fourth quarter of the nineteenth century, emigration was on a vastly larger scale than at any time since the Irish famine. It had become a cheaper, faster option. Steamships by then crossed the Atlantic in days, not weeks; fares were within the compass of ordinary workers; and, for those who wished to consider it, returning to Europe, permanently or temporarily, became a possibility.[103] In this same period, English immigrants continued to flow into the United States in large numbers. They were at this time the least unskilled of all America's new arrivals, with only 30 per cent being labourers and the like. It was partly a function of their skill levels that the English also had the highest return rates of all European immigrants, except the Italians, who were sojourners par excellence, despite their much lower skill levels. Skilled industrial workers, such as miners, have long been recognized as sojourning strategists, for whom a season in the shipyards of Baltimore or the anthracite mines of Pennsylvania could be interspersed with periods of work or idleness at home – a clearly preferably alternative to short-time, unemployment or reduced wages in the pits and yards of Britain. Such returning also became possible for personal reasons, such as holidaying, seeking brides and attending funerals, as well as for reasons of business.[104]

The numbers of arrivals designated as 'British' in the decades between the agricultural depression, beginning in the early 1870s, and the outbreak of the First World War, ran at between 300,000 and 810,000. Van Vugt aligns these figures with upturns in the American business cycle, rather than with agricultural downturns in Britain, because so many of these arrivals were travelling from city to city. Miners, labourers and skilled industrial workers, female domestic servants and textile workers of both sexes were noteworthy. The pastoral idyll lured many, with one-third of English and Welsh settlers counted in the 1890 census as farmers.[105] But these people did not organize the kinds of associations that we explore here.

A more variegated English immigrant group

There also were some remarkably strong, long-term immigrant connections between regions of the old country and regions and industries in the new. A good example is what Blewett calls 'the transnational culture of Lancashire'.[106] The textile industries of New York, Massachusetts and Pennsylvania relied heavily on English immigrants. Over the longer term, these connections provided more than just a particular character. They also, for example, provided the framework for the development, in the 1870s, in a town such as Fall River, Massachusetts, of female activism involving female weavers, single and married women and female leadership and public participation – in other words, a challenge to capital and to men. Such occurrences were in advance of the degrees of female union and political participation in British textile towns.[107] While the 1875 strike was broken by lock-outs and expanded into a broader range of protests, including bread-riots, Blewett describes the employers' resistance to Lancashire mores and tactics, while Americans recognized 'extraordinary English cool-headed control'.[108]

Demonstrations of calm organization were, however, shaped by what the immigrants found in the United States. Laurie, writing of industrial conflict in the 1870s and 1880s, explains the culture-shock effect of American conditions for English workers, and other Europeans, thus: 'English, French and German workers were citizens of nations with strong governments and deeper traditions of the exercise state power.'[109] Stott reckons that 'English workers ... were often distressed by American unpredictability.' Whether more uncertain than English life, 'higher New World standards meant further to fall, and ... serious economic unpredictability called into question the decision to emigrate'.[110] News of the hardship reached England as surely as did recommendations for emigration. The *Cotton Factory Times*, in 1885, ran news from the United States, including wage comparisons between Fall River, Massachusetts, that epicentre of English settlement, and English mill towns. 'It noted the lack of "whole association as in England," and discussed "the development of American cooperatives."' Tellingly, 'the paper ended its maiden issue with advice to Lancashire workers: "No families should think of leaving England for America unless they have engaged places ... and have sufficient means to tide them over."'[111]

English workers were not alone in their concerns with the, at times, savage thrust of industrial relations in the United States. Englishmen, both elites and workers, could display serious unease with America capitalism. The role of Englishmen in the establishment of trade unions and unionism is one well-known example of their expression of discontent at the world they found in the United States. English capitalists were no less unsure about the direction and intensity of 'Gilded Age' capitalism – not so much a form of capitalism of that age as an emerging American standard. Members of the new country's various St George's societies, for example, pressed government for legislation and codes that would formalize fairer relations between capital and labour in the form of arbitration. Certainly, from the 1870s, as the next chapter shows, placing pressure upon governments and employers to follow more paternalistic English modes of industrial relations became a keystone of the NAStGU.

How do we assess the position of the English in United States and Canadian society? In one sense, they were, of course, dominant. Their sharing of language and certain customs clearly helped integration. The numbers of capitalists and businessmen among them also positioned them above other immigrant groups and next to the Americans themselves. For skilled workingmen, or immigrants in well-paid work, there were also continuities and strengths which social commentary and state investigation revealed. English and Welsh miners, for instance, appeared to keep all immigrant groups but the Swedes to very low proportions of miners; moreover, they continued to occupy the positions of authority – as foremen, overseers and managers – more than any other groups.[112] Even at the turn of the century in less long-established centres, the English stood out. In Tennessee the English had by far the highest proportion (91 per cent) who were 'working for wages' before they came to the United States. While the English included a sizeable 12.5 per cent of agricultural labourers, 62 per cent had already worked in copper. Only the Norwegians (21.7 per cent) and the Swedes (47.6 per cent) had high levels of experience of copper mining before arrival. Among southern Europeans, such as the Slovenes 72 per cent) and Croatians (40 per cent), these proportions were lower. Among the Croatians, 28 per cent of such workers had previously been 'working for profit', presumably as small traders. Almost none had worked with copper or in mining before.[113] For them, the transition to mining and the factory was much more of a leap. Consequently, the English held the best-paid work – only they had anyone earning over $20 a week and over 68 per cent of them earned $15 or more, regardless of the period of time in the United States. No other nationality could match that, though the Finns were close on key indicators.[114]

There was, however, another side to this. Not all Englishmen or women were well established in strong or skilled trades. In Canada, in 1881, there was a change to the Dominion Lands Act that enabled indigent immigrants to be set up on homesteads with debts of up to $500 per head.[115] These debts had to be cleared before land titles would be issued. Of course, many failed to establish themselves on new land in a tough climate. It was argued by some commentators that 'non-success' rates among such English emigrants was caused by the role of state and philanthropic organizations in helping the poorest, least-prepared groups to emigrate. 'In Scotland, where the proportion of emigrants to the population is more than double what it is in England, there are no such philanthropic societies and no such charitable organizations engaged in emigration work, and you can not but have observed how few cases of non-success there are among Scottish emigrants.'[116] Moreover, English and Welsh rates of deportation were higher in the early 1900s in Canada than those of any other groups.[117] And writing in 1908, P.H. Bryce, chief medical officer of the Canadian Department of Immigration, stated:

> Not only does the large number of people from English cities come to our large cities, but it is especially true of that class of 'ne'er-do-wells,' social and moral derelicts, and ineffective in general. They are not only physically unequal to the task of farm life, but they are further usually incapable of enduring the quiet of rural life. Hence if sent to the country they too frequently drift back to town, and when winter comes and work fails they seek aid in those institutions set apart for the city poor and helpless.[118]

Evidence given to the Ontario Bureau of Industries made similar points. Farmers and employers wanted 'good servant girls', for example, not 'these English street Arabs' or 'this pauper class of English lads', both of which were considered 'a curse on the country'. Preference was instead given for 'good, honest, steady German or Scotch farm hands'.[119] Two years later, the same message was being received: '[we] don't think we require [in Howick, Huron] any importation of farm labourers – especially not gutter children from the cities of England. They are an unmitigated curse.'[120] Less than a year later, notice had been taken, and the same bureau was able to report a recent 'great improvement' in the quality of English farmhands.[121] While the majority of English workers were not paupers shipped to agricultural work for which they were unsuited, there nevertheless were other issues that challenged notions of easy transfer from one Anglo-world culture to another.

Rates of return migration represent one of the most relevant challenges to ideas of English integration in Canada and the United States. Wyman's pioneering work on European return migrations indicates that the Jews and Irish were the least likely to return. The English, on the other hand, were more likely than any other groups from the British Isles to return home to England, or to leave for Canada and other parts of the Empire, and these factors could have diminished English ethnic solidity in the United States even more.[122] Erickson, in a detailed examination of over 200 English and Scottish immigrant letters, highlighted that English arrivals were perhaps not very different from other migrants in America in that they held the same hopes and aspirations and also could experience the same disappointments. Wilbur Shepperson's study of English repatriates shows how they, as much as other groups, could struggle in the United States and come to reject it – this notwithstanding the cultural, religious and linguistic advantages they had over, for example, Irish Catholics or southern European migrants.[123] Our research certainly chimes with the works of Shepperson and Stephen Fender,

which describe the English as an immigrant people whose ethnic formations dealt with the limitations of the Arcadian American dream.[124]
Complaining letters to families, trade union formation and participation
in acts of industrial militancy each point to an English working-class
response to the realization that capitalism, give or take levels of paternalism, was a similar beast on either side of the ocean. A combination
of such factors resulted in the Dillingham Commission's findings that,
between 1899 and 1910, only the Italians outmatched the 103,828 English
who were counted as re-returners to the United States, having been there
at least once before (see Tables 1.18 and 1.19).[125]

Re-return suggests something slightly different from permanent
re-emigration home. In one sense, it was a positive thing that, as
Thistlethwaite found many years ago, the Atlantic was a highway for
diverse workers, from English miners to Italian waiters, and a multiplicity
of tradesmen and merchants. Such people used America temporarily as
they saw fit.[126] At the same time, it is impossible to discount that for a considerable body of emigrants and re-emigrants – often regular sojourners –
the United States, Canada and other New World destinations simply
did not offer enough of what they idealized or desired to make the move
permanent. The key point to stress is that the flow of people across the
Atlantic was two-directional for many.

Table 1.18 *Emigrants previously in the United States, 1899–1910: top ten
percentages*

			In USA previously	
Rank	Origin	Total number	Number	%
1	Chinese	22,590	13,791	61.0
2	Cuban	44,211	25,937	58.7
3	Spanish American	10,669	3,942	36.9
4	West Indian (except Cuban)	11,569	3,941	34.1
5	French	115,783	33,859	29.2
6	Spanish	51,051	14,797	29.0
7	ENGLISH	408,614	103,828	25.4
8	Mexican	41,914	8,902	21.2
9	Welsh	20,752	4,232	20.4
10	Scotch	136,842	27,684	20.2
	All	9,555,673	1,189,283	12.4

*Source: Reports to the Immigration Commission, 42 vols, Statistical Review of Immigration,
1820-1910, document 756, presented by Mr W.P. Dillingham (Washington, DC, 1911),
vol. 3, table 37, p. 359.*

Table 1.19 Emigrants previously in the United States, 1899–1910: top ten totals

Rank	Origin	Total number	In USA previously Number	%
1	Italian (north and south)	2,284,601	319,246	14.0
2	ENGLISH	408,614	103,828	25.0
3	Scandinavian	586,306	86,700	14.8
4	Irish	439,724	80,636	18.3
5	German	754,375	80,458	11.5
6	Slovak	377,527	71,889	19.0
7	Croatian-Slovenian	355,543	43,037	12.8
8	Magyar	338,151	39,861	11.8
9	French	115,783	33,859	29.2
10	Scotch	136,842	27,684	20.2
	All	9,555,673	1,189,283	12.4

Source: Reports to the Immigration Commission, 42 vols, Statistical Review of Immigration, 1820–1910, document 756, presented by Mr W.P. Dillingham (Washington, DC, 1911), vol. 3, table 37, p. 359.

Conclusion

From the colonial period to the end of the First World War, emigration from Britain to North America was never less than impressive. Although it occurred in heavy numbers in all years and decades, the main movements to the United States came in three waves, which Baines ascribes to the power of the American business cycle, rather than to downturns in Britain. The first, in the 1840s and 1850s, carried farmers, builders and skilled workers across the Atlantic; the second occurred after the American Civil War and lasted to the early 1870s; and the final large wave of the century occurred between the 1880s and the economic crash of 1893. English emigration to Canada was less significant in the early nineteenth century, but a large number arrived between 1900 and 1930 – a result of westward expansion in Canada, as well as post-First World War initiatives like the British Empire Settlement Act (1922). By that point figures and proportions in the United States had fallen significantly: it was now the Empire that received most British migrants. Moreover, after the Wall Street Crash of 1929 and the onset of the Depression in the 1930s, more Britons returned home than ever before. The spectre of dislocation, dissatisfaction and rejection loomed in the lives of English immigrants too.

What we have described here is the emergence of three types of English immigrants to the United States and Canada. The first, and the most familiar to scholars of ethnicity in the United States, is the well-to-do group. The second group is the better class of workers. Skilled, sought-after and well paid, these were the men who were as likely to join a St George's society as to seek aid from one. Even more than that, they were likeliest to sign up to an English mutual aid association. The third group were the poor, sick, old and unfortunate. Often the wives and children of dead, injured, sick or disappeared workers, or else workingmen who had fallen on hard times, these were the beneficiaries of ethnic societies; indeed, they were the very *sine qua non* upon which the principles of immigrant charity were built. The extent to which these various layers of English immigrants constituted a conscious ethnic community can be measured in various ways. One such test-bed is ethnic association. Although societies varied, and sometimes had different class impera-tives and social compositions, they were united by their commitment to expressing a common culture and shared roots. The next two chapters explore the emergence of the elite St George's societies and the more working-class English friendly societies, which lay at the heart of English ethnic associationalism in North America.

Notes

1 Michael MacCarthy-Morrogh, *The Munster Plantation: English Migration to Southern Ireland, 1583–1641* (Oxford, 1986).

2 M. Percival Maxwell, *The Scottish Migration to Ulster in the Reign of James I* (Belfast, 1990).

3 Historical Manuscripts Commission, *Calendar of the Manuscripts of the Most Honourable the Marquess of Salisbury ...*, vol. 10: 1609–1612 (London, 1970), p. 121, quoted by Jane H. Ohlmeyer, 'Colonization within Britain and Ireland', in Nicholas Canny (ed.), *The Oxford History of the British Empire*, vol. 1: *The Origins of Empire* (Oxford, 1998, reprinted 2001, p. 126.

4 Nicholas Canny, *Making Ireland British, 1580–1650* (Oxford, 2003), explores that process in Ireland, via the influence of Edmund Spenser's thinking, from the Munster plantations to the Cromwellian invasion. Processes of assimila-tion and integration are explored through several hundred individuals and families in Jane Ohlmeyer, *Making Ireland English: The Irish Aristocracy in the Seventeenth Century* (New Haven, CT, 2012).

5 Thomas Bartlett, '"This famous island set in a Virginian sea": Ireland in the British Empire, 1690–1801', in Peter Marshall (ed.), *Oxford History of the British Empire*, vol. 2 (Oxford, 1998), pp. 273–74. On the Arthurian dimen-sions, see Glyn Parry, 'Mythologies of Empire and the First English Diaspora', in Tanja Bueltmann, David T. Gleeson and Donald M. MacRaild (eds), *Locating the English Diaspora, 1500–2010* (Liverpool, 2012), pp. 15–33.

6 MacCarthy-Morrogh, *Munster Plantation*; R.J. Hunter and J.S. Morrill, *Ulster Transformed: Essays on Plantation and Print Culture, c.1590–1641* (Belfast, 2012).

7 Cited by Audrey Horning, *Ireland in the Virginian Sea: Colonialism in the British Atlantic* (Chapel Hill, NC, 2013), p. 1.

8 Malcolm Gaskill, *Between Two Worlds: How the English Became Americans* (Oxford, 2014), pp. 3–21.

9 Abigail L. Swingen, *Competing Visions of Empire: Labor, Slavery, and the Origins of the British Atlantic Empire* (New Haven, Conn., 2015), explains how declining or insufficient free labour migration contributed materially to the rise of slavery.

10 Samuel Purchas, *Hakuylut Posthumus or Purchus his Pilgrimes*, 20 vols (Glasgow, 1905), vol. 1, pp. xxxvii–xxxviii, quoted in Canny (ed.), *The Oxford History of the British Empire*, vol. l, p. 2.

11 B. Bailyn, *The Peopling of British North America: An Introduction* (New York, 1986), pp. 4–5.

12 David Hackett Fischer, *Albion's Seed: Four English Folkways in America* (New York, 1989), p. 16.

13 Unlike in previous ages, however, the frightened or the disgruntled, the abused or the victimzed had alternatives. Although these outlets primarily lay in emigration to North America and the Caribbean, some 20,000 went to Ireland in the same period, 20,000 to the West Indies and Old Providence Island, and similar numbers to Holland and the Rhineland. Hackett Fischer, *Albion's Seed*, p. 16. Some of those who went to Holland returned to join the 1620s migrations to New England. See Virginia DeJohn Anderson, 'New England in the Seventeenth Century', in Canny (ed.), *The Oxford History of the British Empire*, vol. 1, pp. 193–217. For further numbers on this early migration, see also Russell R. Menard, 'British Migration to the Chesapeake Colonies in the Seventeenth Century', in Lois Green Carr, Philip D. Morgan and Jean B. Russo (eds), *Colonial Chesapeake Society* (Chapel Hill, NC, 2000), pp. 100ff.

14 When Scots and Irish became involved, it was, Canny tells us, as 'a plural rather than a singular endeavour'; and even that applied only in places where colonization was not viewed as 'an exclusively English enterprise'. Canny (ed.), *The Oxford History of the British Empire*, vol. 1, pp. 2–3.

15 2009 American Community Survey, 5able 52: 'Population by Selected Ancestry Group and Region', http://www.census.gov/compendia/statab/2012/tables/12s0052.pdf (last accessed 18 June 2015).

16 This figure is based on single and multiple ethnic origin responses; the number of people identifying English as their single ethnic origin was 1,367,125, still giving it first place when compared with other groups from the British and Irish Isles. Statistics Canada, 2006 Census of Population, catalogue no. 97-562-XCB2006006 (Canada, Code01), http://www12.statcan.gc.ca/census-recensement/2006/dp-pd/index-eng.cfm (last accessed 26 June 2014).

17 It does not, however, seek to replicate key studies of the early period, e.g. Alison Games, *Migration and the Origins of the English Atlantic* (Cambridge, MA, 1999), ch. 7 and passim.

18 For an example see early movements of English fishermen, see Peter E. Pope, *Fish into Wine: The Newfoundland Plantation in the Seventeenth Century* (Chapel Hill, NC, 2004).

19 A.E. Smith, *Colonists in Bondage:* White Servitude and Convict Labor in America, 1607–1776 (Chapel Hill, NC, 1947), p. 3. The view has subsequently been proved to be fallacious: Mildred Campbell, 'Social Origins of Some Early *Americans*', in James Morton Smith (ed.), *Seventeenth-Century America: Essays in Colonial History* (Chapel Hill, NC, 1959); David Galenson, '"Middling People" or "Common Sort"? The Social Origins of Some Early Americans Re-Examined', *William and Mary Quarterly*, 3rd series, 35 (1978), pp. 499–524.

20 R.J. Dickson, *Ulster Emigration to Colonial America, 1718–1775* (London, 1966); Donald M. MacRaild and Malcolm Smith, 'Migration and Emigration, 1600–1945', in Liam Kennedy and Philip Ollerenshaw (eds), *Ulster since 1600: Politics, Economy, and Society* (Oxford, 2013), pp. 140–59.

21 The Germans, for example, are better called German-speaking because they came from so many diverse territories. Importantly, in the vast expanse of the Delaware valley, it was these continental migrants who both predated and outnumbered the Ulster emigrants whom British and Irish scholars usually look to as the pioneers of the great eighteenth-century exodus. Overall, from 1700 to the 1770s, the Delaware region received about 110,000 Germans and a little over 50,000 Scots and English planters from Ulster. Marianne S. Wokeck, *Trade in Strangers: The Beginnings of Mass Migration to North America* (Philadelphia, 1999).

22 A. Roger Ekrich, *Bound for America: The Transportation of British Convicts to the Colonies, 1718–1775* (Oxford, 1987); Gwenda Morgan and Peter Rushton, *Eighteenth-Century Criminal Transportation: The Formation of the Criminal Atlantic* (Basingstoke, 2004).

23 In the 1760s, there were five such years, and these spurred emigration. Between 1770 and 1775, some 7,000 English went to the American colonies, a figure outmatched only by the Scots and Scotch-Irish and ahead of the Germans (5,200) and Irish Catholics (3,900). Jon Butler, *Becoming America: The Revolution before 1776* (Cambridge, MA, 2001), p. 35.

24 Richard Price, cited by Mildred Campbell, 'English Emigration on the Eve of the American Revolution', *American Historical Review*, 61:1 (October 1955), p. 3.

25 Between 1773 and 1776 customs officials were required to count the numbers of people leaving the country. Excluding those who were not immigrating to the colonies ('Irish workmen returning home', 'soldiers on their way to Bengal' and others), some 6,000 left in this period, 5 per cent of them convicts. Their number included 258 different types of crafts and trades. Moreover, 23 per cent of the women emigrants registered a trade. For further details, see Campbell, 'English Emigration', pp. 5–7.

26 R.C. Harris, G.J. Matthews and R. Louis Gentilcore, *Historical Atlas of Canada: The Land Transformed, 1800–1891* (Toronto, 1987), pp. 21ff.

27 Campbell, 'English Emigration', pp. 3–4, 5–6, 7–8; Butler, *Becoming America*, pp. 35–36, 187; J. Potter, 'The Growth of Population in America, 1700–1860',

in *Population History: Essays in Historical Demography* (London, 1965); B. Bailyn, *Voyagers West: A Passage in the Peopling of America on the Eve of Revolution* (New York, 1966).

28 William E. Van Vugt, 'English', in Peter Eisenstadt and Laura-Eve Moss (eds), *The Encyclopaedia of New York State* (Syracuse, NY, 2005), p. 507.

29 Robert A. McCaughey, *Stand, Columbia: A History of Columbia University* (Columbia, NY, 2013).

30 Noah Webster, *Sketch of American Policy …* (Hartford, CT, 1785), p. 29.

31 Peskin suggests that a new breed of writer espousing 'pro-manufacturing rhetoric' articulated the value of indigenous industry. L.A. Peskin, *Manufacturing Revolution: The Intellectual Origins of Early American Industry* (Baltimore, 2003), pp. 10–11 (quotation at p. 10).

32 T.H. Breen, '"The baubles of Britain": The American and Consumer Revolutions of the Eighteenth Century', *Past and Present*, 119 (1988), pp. 74–109.

33 Data here drawn from Carl Briderbaugh, *Cities in the Wilderness: The First Century of Urban Life in America, 1625–1742* (New York, 1938), pp. 6, 143, 303, and Carl Briderbaugh, *Cities in Revolt: Urban Life in America, 1743–1776* (1955), p. 5; Thomas L. Purvis, *Colonial America to 1763* (New York, 1999), p. 220. In 1750, Sheffield, Leeds and Manchester each contained fewer than 20,000 people; and only Liverpool, Birmingham, Bristol and London contained more.

34 Gilbert A. Stelter, 'The Political Economy of Early Canadian Urban Development', in Gilbert A. Stelter and Alan F.J. Artibise (eds), *The Canadian City: Essays in Urban and Social History* (Ottawa, 1984), p. 13.

35 Ibid., p. 15.

36 Even in 1841, Toronto still had a population of fewer than 15,000. Census, cited in Brian P. Clarke, *Piety and Nationalism: Lay Voluntary Associations and the Creation of an Irish-Catholic Community in Toronto, 1850–1895* (Kingston and Montreal, 1993), p. 16, table 1.

37 Richard Pomfret, *The Economic Development of Canada* (Abingdon, 2006), p. 12.

38 Notable cohorts of waged workers, expressing what labour historians consider to be a language inflected with class, were beginning to stress a shared identity. On the United States side, this was especially true of Philadelphia, where workers commenced running their own candidates for public office. Greg Nobles, 'Class', in *A Companion to Colonial America* (Oxford, 2003), pp. 277–81.

39 James T. Lemon, 'Colonial America in the 18th Century', in Thomas F. McIlwraith and Edward K. Muller (eds) *North America: The Historical Geography of a Changing Continent* (Lanham, MD, 2000), ch. 6; Ian Barnes and Charles Royster, *The Historical Atlas of the American Revolution* (New York, 2000), pp. 36–37.

40 Van Vugt, 'English', p. 507, col. 3.

41 Lemon, 'Colonial America', p. 120.

42 Peskin, *Manufacturing Revolution*, p. 62.

43 Ibid., pp. 62–63.

44 James M. Bergquist, *Daily Life in Immigrant America, 1820–1870* (Westport, CT, 2008), pp. 87–89.
45 Although Philadelphia neighboured the town of Northern Liberties, which it would merge with in 1854.
46 Dean E. Esslinger, 'Immigration through the Port of Baltimore', in M. Mark Stolarik (ed.), *Forgotten Doors: The Other Ports of Entry to the United States* (Philadelphia, 1988), pp. 61ff.
47 Seth Rockman, *Scraping By: Wage Labor, Slavery, and Survival in Early Baltimore* (Baltimore, 2010), p. 29.
48 Bruce Laurie, *Artisans into Workers: Labor in Nineteenth-Century America* (Champaign, IL, 1997), p. 43.
49 Charles G. Steffen, *The Mechanics of Baltimore: Workers and Politics in the Age of Revolution, 1763–1812* (Champaign, IL, 1984), p. 6. On Ulster, see David Hempton and Myrtle Hill, *Evangelical Protestantism and Ulster Society, 1740–1890* (London, 1992); also David Hempton and Myrtle Hill, 'Did Ulster Presbyterians have a Devotional Revolution?', in James Murphy (ed.), *Evangelicals and Catholics in Nineteenth-Century Ireland* (Dublin, 2005), pp. 38–54.
50 Germans dominated the Maryland and Pennsylvania hinterlands, where they grew vast amounts of wheat. James M. Berguist, *Daily Life in Immigrant America, 1820–1870* (Westport, CT, 2008), p. 88; Steffen, *Mechanics of Baltimore*, p. 7.
51 Barbara J. Messamore, 'Canada and Migration: Kinship with the World', in Barbara J. Messamore (ed.), *Canadian Migration Patterns: From Britain and North America* (Ottawa, 2004), p. 2.
52 See also Bruce S. Elliott, 'Regional Patterns of English Immigration and Settlement in Upper Canada', in Barbara J. Messamore, *Canadian Migration Patterns: From Britain and North America* (Ottawa, 2004), pp. 51–89.
53 William Jenkins, *Between Raid and Rebellion: The Irish in Buffalo and Toronto, 1867–1916* (Kingston, Ont., 2013), p. 12. See a lso, more generally, John J. Bukowyzck et al (eds), *Permeable Border: The Great Lakes Basin as a Transnational Region, c.1650–1990* (Pittsburgh, PA, 2005).
54 E. P. Kraly and P. Vogelaar, '"Starting with Spoons": Refugee Migration and Resettlement Programs in Utica, New York', in J.W. Frazier, E.L. Tetley-Fio and N.F. Henry (eds), *Race, Ethnicity, and Place in a Changing America* (Herndon, VA, 2011), p. 393.
55 Davies to Revd Ellis Evans, Denbighshire, 24 September 1821, in Alan Conway, *The Welsh in America: Letters from the Immigrants* (St Paul, MN, 1961), pp. 64–65, and see passim for the Welsh in Utica. Such developments clearly helped give Utica a strong British character, with particularly the Welsh heavily represented in its population of 8,000 or so in the 1830s. Not that the ethnic history of the place recognizes the English in this way. James S. Pula, 'Ethnic Utica', in *Oneida County Historical Society* (Oneida, 2005), contains no essay on the English.
56 Austin A. Yates, *Schenectady County, New York, Its History to the Close of the Nineteenth Century* (New York, 1902), pp. 163–64. Later on, it emerged as

the centre of the electrical trade and home to the General Electric Company. During the First World War, the city became a site of significant labour militancy and industrial action led by left-wing union men with British ancestry, e.g. the 'sharp-tongued Scottish immigrant' John Bellingham. See Joseph A. McCartin, *Labor's Great War: The Struggle for Industrial Democracy and the Origins of Modern American Labor Relations, 1912–1921* (Raleigh, NC, 1997), pp. 60–61.

57 Andrew Smith, *British Businessmen and Canadian Confederation: Constitution-Making in an Era of Anglo-Globalization* (Montreal and Kingston, 2008), p. 18.

58 *Annual Report of the President and Directors of the Baltimore and Susquehanna Railroad* (Baltimore, MD, 1828), vol. 1, pp. 35, 36, 75; William R. Sutton, *Journeymen for Jesus: Evangelical Artisans Confront Capitalism in Jacksonian Baltimore* (Philadelphia, 1998), p. 139.

59 Esslinger, 'Port of Baltimore', p. 64.

60 Patrick Steward and Bryan P. McGovern, *The Fenians: Irish Rebellions in the North American World, 1858–1876* (Knoxville, TN, 2013), p. 12.

61 Gary B, Nash, *First City: Philadelphia and the Forging of Historical Memory* (Philadelphia, 2002), p. 129.

62 Among such men, both Americans and advanced immigrant workers, there was a reverence for English radicals, including Tom Paine. Laurie, *Artisans into Workers*, pp. 66, 68, 212.

63 Dudley Baines, *Migration in a Mature Economy: Emigration and Internal Migration in England and Wales 1861–1900* (1985; Cambridge, 2002), p. 71.

64 Laurie, *Artisans into Workers*, p. 212.

65 Mark Beaufoy, *Tour Through Parts of the United States and Canada* (London, 1862), pp. 147–48.

66 Niall Whelehan, *The Dynamiter: Irish Nationalism and Political Violence in the Wider World, 1867–1900* (Cambridge, 2012); David Sim, *A Union Forever: The Irish Question and US Foreign Relations in the Victorian Age* (Ithaca, NY, 2013).

67 Sutton, *Journeymen for Jesus*, p. 140.

68 Philadelphia, Historical Society of Pennsylvania [HSP], (PHi) 1733, Sons of St George Archive, Stewards' Books, vol. 1, 1860s–1870s, entry 81 of W.M. Attwood and H.H. Peacock, Monday 20 May 1861.

69 Bureau of Census, *Statistics of the Population of the United States at the Tenth Census (June 1, 1880), Embracing Extended Tables of Population of States, Counties, and Minor Civil Division, with Distinction of Race, Sec Age, Nativity, and Occupation; together with Summary Tables* ... (Washington, DC, 1880), district 37, 2, Schedule 1, Inhabitants in Superior Township, Osago, Kansas, B, p. 6.

70 Census, cited in Clarke, *Piety and Nationalism*, p. 16, table 1.

71 We cannot know what proportion of these British-born were the children of onward-travelling Irish migrants.

72 Over a period of a century, the English immigrants, who had comprised the largest arriving group in the American colonies in the seventeenth century, happened also to constitute 80 per cent of the 2,760,360 people

(of specified national origins) who left Britain for the United States between 1820 and 1910. Meanwhile, the Scots accounted for 488,789 (17.7 per cent) and the Welsh for 59,540 (2.2 per cent). A further 793,801 did not specify origins. 61st Congress, 3d Session, Doc. 756, *Reports of the Emigration Commissioners: Statistical Review of Immigration, 1820–1910*, vol. 3: *Distribution of Immigrants, 1850–1900* (Washington, DC, 1911) [chair: William P. Dillingham], tables 8, 13; Erickson, *Invisible Immigrants.*

73 Bureau of Census, *Eighth Census, 1860*, 'Introduction', p. xxiii. Bremen, Le Havre, Hamburg and Antwerp together sent 1,397.

74 Ibid., p. xxii. At that point, the Germans numbered 1.47 million.

75 William E. Van Vugt, *Britain to America: Mid-Nineteenth Century Immigrants to the United States* (Urbana and Chicago, 1999), table B5, p. 168.

76 Mary H. Blewett, 'USA: Shifting Landscapes of Class, Culture, Gender, Race and Protest in the American Northeast and South', in Lex Heerma van Voss, Els Hiemstra-Kuperus and Elise van Nederveen Meerkerk (eds), *The Ashgate Companion to the History of Textile Workers, 1650–2000* (London, 2010), pp. 535–36.

77 Van Vugt, *Britain to America*, table B4, p. 167.

78 Robert Ernst, *Immigrant Life in New York, 1825–63* (1949; Syracuse, NY, 1994), pp. 43–44.

79 Ibid., table 1, pp. 74–75.

80 Quoted by Richard B. Stott, *Workers in the Metropolis: Class, Ethnicity and Youth in Antebellum New York* (Ithaca, 1990), p. 91.

81 B.C. Mitchell, *The Paddy Camps: The Irish of Lowell, 1821–61* (1988; Champaign, IL, 2006).

82 Alexander R. Thomas, *In Gotham's Shadow: Globalization and Community Change in Central New York* (New York, 2003), pp. 22, 25–26.

83 Blewett, 'USA: Shifting Landscapes', pp. 531–58 (data on Lowell at p. 534).

84 Ibid., p. 535.

85 William E. Van Vugt, 'British (English, Scottish, Scots Irish, and Welsh) and British Americans, 1870–1940', in Elliott R. Barkan (ed.), *Immigrants in American History: Arrival, Adaptation, and Integration*, 4 vols (Santa Barbara, 2013), vol. 1:2, p. 237.

86 In the late 1840s and early 1850s, during what was early strike activity and general protest, English mule spinners and native-born workers formed an alliance that sought to embrace all workers in the face of severe employer hostility. They also made donations to strikers in their native Lancashire in the mid-1850s. Mary H. Blewett, *Constant Turmoil: The Politics of Industrial Life in Nineteenth-Century New England* (Amherst, 2000), pp. 94ff.

87 Blewett, 'USA: Shifting Landscapes', p. 536.

88 *Reports of the Immigration Commission: Immigrants in Industries*, part 17: *Copper Mining and Smelting*. [chaired by William P. Dillingham], 1911, p. 81.

89 Many sources by Charlotte Erickson, among which 'Emigration from the British Isles to the USA in 1841, Part I: Emigration from the British Isles', *Population Studies*, 43 (1989), pp. 347–67, and 'Emigration from the

British Isles to the USA in 1841, Part II: Who were the English Emigrants?',
Population Studies, 44 (1990), pp. 21–40; William E. Van Vugt, 'Prosperity
and Industrial Emigration from Britain during the Early 1850s', *Journal of
Social History*, 5 (Winter 1988), pp. 390–405, and William E. Van Vugt,
'Running from Ruin? The Emigration of British Farmers to the USA in
the Wake of the Repeal of the Corn Laws', *Economic History Review*, 41
(August 1988), pp. 411–28; Raymond L. Cohn, 'The Occupation of English
Immigrants to the United States, 1836-1853', *Journal of Economic History*,
52:2 (1992), pp. 377–87.

90 HSP, (PHi) 1733, Sons of St George Archive, Stewards' Books, vol. 1, sample
of 1861.

91 Ibid., sample of 1879.

92 Ernst, *Immigrant Life*, p. 82.

93 Bureau of Census, *Tenth Census, 1880*, 'Introduction. General Discussion of
the Movements of Population – 1790 to 1880', Francis A. Walker and Henry
Gannett, p. xii.

94 Van Vugt, 'British and British Americans, 1870-1940', p. 238.

95 Dick Hoerder, *Creating Societies: Immigrant Lives in Canada* (Kingston,
1999), p. 105.

96 The key global study is Marlyn Lake and Henry Reynolds, *Drawing the Global
Colour Line* (Cambridge, 2008). Also see, for instance, see Arlene Chan,
The Chinese in Toronto from 1878 (Toronto, 2011); Zofi Shahrodi, 'The
Experience of Polish Catholics in the Archdiocese of Toronto, 1905-1935',
in Mark McGowan and Brian P. Clarke (eds), *Catholics at the 'Gathering
Place': Historical Essays on the Archdiocese of Toronto, 1841-1991* (Toronto,
1993), pp. 141–54.

97 By 1921, McGowan argues, 'the most distinctive cleavage in working-class
Toronto did not run along a Catholic--Protestant axis but along lines of
occupation and neighbourhood'. The coming together of groups formerly
separated by sectional, geographical and national divisions undoubtedly was
enhanced not only by the pioneering work of the Friendly Sons of St Patrick
Benevolent Society, which helped to ground the life-chances of the poorest
community members, but also by the emergence of a stronger, broader Irish
middle class with commitments to such organizations as the Catholic Mutual
Benefit Association. Mark McGowan, *The Waning of the Green: Catholics,
the Irish, and Identity in Toronto, 1887–1922* (Kingston and Montreal, 1999),
pp. 43–44, table 4.1, pp. 53, 167.

98 Indeed, Pentland estimates that, in the 1850s alone, the Provinces of Canada
imported $100 million 'in mostly British capital'. Referred to in Smith,
British Businessmen and Canadian Confederation, p. 30.

99 Ibid., pp. 39ff. See also P.J. Cain and A.G. Hopkins, *British Imperialism,
1688-2000* (Abingdon, 1993), p. 238 for later figures of British capital investments in Canada.

100 Hoerder, *Creating Societies*, p. 121.

101 Ibid., p. 138.

102 Ibid., pp. 108–09.

103 Frank Thistlethwaite, 'Migration from Europe Overseas in the Nineteenth

and Twentieth Centuries' and 'Postscript', in R.J. Vecoli and S.M. Sinke
(eds), *A Century of European Migrations 1830–1930* (Champaign, IL, 1991).

104 Van Vugt, 'British and British Americans, 1870–1940', pp. 235–36.

105 Ibid., pp. 235–37.

106 Blewett, 'USA: Shifting Landscapes', p. 542.

107 Lydia Murdoch, *Daily Life of Victorian Women* (Santa Barbara, 2014), p. 34
notes campaigns for female suffrage among northern female textile workers.
Alan Fowler, *Lancashire Cotton Operatives and Work, 1900–1950: A Social
History of Lancashire Cotton Operatives in the Twentieth Century* (London,
2003) reveals continuing gendered male attitudes to women, skill and
unionism.

108 Blewett, 'USA: Shifting Landscapes', pp. 542–44 (quotation at p. 544).

109 Laurie, *Artisans into Workers*, p. 208.

110 Stott, *Workers in the Metropolis*, p. 188.

111 Horace Huntley, 'Ethnicity and the American Working Class, 1850–1900:
Fall River, 1850–1900', in Robert Asher and Charles Stephenson (eds), *Labor
Divided: Race and Ethnicity in United States Labor Struggles, 1835–1960*
(New York, 1990), pp. 161–62.

112 *Reports of the Immigration Commission: Immigrants in Industries*, part 17:
Copper Mining and Smelting, table 74, pp. 87–88.

113 Ibid., tables 12, 13, pp. 21–22.

114 Ibid., table 21, p. 29.

115 N. Kelley and M.J. Trebilcock, *Making the Mosaic: A History of Canadian
Immigration Policy* (Toronto, 2010), p. 72.

116 J. Bruce Walker, Interior Department of the Government of Canada, 'Aims
and Methods of Charitable Organizations Promoting Emigration from
Canada to the British Isles', reproduced in full in Immigration Commission,
Reports of the Immigration Commission, 42 vols (Washington, DC, 1910),
vol. 40: *The Immigration Situation in Other Countries: The Immigration
Situation in Canada* (1 April 1910), 61st Congress, 2d session, document no.
409 [William P. Dillingham Commission] (Washington, DC, 1910), appendix F, p. 160.

117 Immigration Commission, *Immigration Situation in Canada*, p. 52.

118 Ibid., p. 53.

119 'Remarks of Correspondents', in *Annual Reports of the Bureau of Industries
for the Province of Ontario, 1895*, parts I, II and II: *Agricultural Statistics*
(Toronto, 1896), p. 120.

120 *Annual Reports of the Bureau of Industries for the Province of Ontario, 1898*,
parts I, II and II: *Agricultural Statistics*, part IV: *Chattel Mortgages* (Toronto,
1899), p. 98.

121 *Annual Reports of the Bureau of Industries for the Province of Ontario, 1906*,
parts I: *Agricultural Statistics*, part II: *Chattel Mortgages* (Toronto, 1906),
p. 19.

122 Walter Nugent, *Crossings: The Great Transatlantic Migrations, 1870–1914*
(Bloomington, 1992), p. 44. See also Randy W. Widdis, *With Scarcely
a Ripple: Anglo-Canadian Migration in the United States and Western
Canada, 1880–1920* (Montreal, 1998), esp. ch. 5, pp. 294–304; Marjory

Harper (ed.), *Emigrant Homecomings: The Return Movement of Emigrants, 1600–2000* (Manchester, 2005), especially the essay by Mark Wyman, 'Emigrant Returning: The Evolution of a Tradition', pp. 16–31.

123 Wilbur S. Shepperson, *Emigration and Disenchantment: Portraits of Englishmen Repatriated from the United States* (Norman, OK, 1965).

124 Ibid., and also Wilbur S. Shepperson, *British Emigration to North America* (Norman, OK, 1965); Stephen Fender, *Sea Changes: British Emigration and American Literature* (Cambridge, 1992).

125 61st Congress, 3d Session, Doc. 756, vol. 3: *Distribution of Immigrants, 1850–1900*, table 8, table 37, p. 359.

126 Thistlethwaite, 'Migration from Europe Overseas', passim.

2

Elite associations:
from local to transnational

May the Society long continue its useful course and may it ever be worthy
of the great country – England – of which we are all so justly proud. (John L.
Sanford, *History of the St George's Society of Baltimore*, 1929, p. 16)

While arguing for the ethnicity of English associations we also recognize
wider and more practical aspects of their work. For instance, the earliest type of these associations, the St George's societies, served a range
of functions: civic, financial, social, cultural and emotional. They were
places to meet and dine, sources of help and pillars of immigrant communities. Their core philosophy was, however, the belief that wealthy
and fortunate individuals, who had enjoyed the benefits of settlement
in the New World, should use their good fortune to bless those of
their countrymen less fortunate than them. The St George's Society
of Kingston, Ontario, rallied members with a quotation from Admiral
Nelson: "'England expects every man to do his duty".[1] These societies
were part of a much larger and wider spirit of middle-class charity and
social care.[2]

In the second half of the nineteenth century, however, a new brand of
English ethnic organization was founded that mixed sectarian exclusivity with friendly-society collective self-help in a direct challenge to the
benign, elitist, hierarchical beneficence of the gentlemen of the St George's
societies. These new associations, the Sons of St George and the Sons of
England, became much larger than the St George's societies, were more
working-class in composition, and though sharing the same essential
social and cultural desires, added dimensions of exclusivity that extended
beyond those of the St George's societies. The Sons of England was widespread in Canada and South Africa, but never took root in the United
States; for English workers in America, the Sons of St George became the
standard vehicle of ethnic associational culture, but it never crossed north
to Canada. Reflecting sectarian conflict between working-class groups

and the inherent anti-Catholicism of British culture, these working-class communities normally admitted only English, and sometimes Welsh, Protestants.[3] It is thus not possible to write of a single, uniform organized ethnic tradition created by English communities in North America.

It has been said that such societies and associations 'were less prevalent among the English than among other nationalities'.[4] Indeed, the English certainly directed much collectivist energy towards the Oddfellows and Foresters, and towards other forms of non-ethnic, non-sectarian mutualism that had their roots in England and which they introduced to the New World. American scholars consider the inherent Englishness of the host country as the principal bar to ethnic behaviour. Esslinger argued:

> Because the majority of Baltimore's residents were either English-born or descended from English ancestors, immigrants of that nationality tended to be quickly absorbed into the social and economic structures of the city. Rather than forming separate organizations, English newcomers joined the native-born majority in local political parties and social organizations.[5]

While Esslinger's point reveals a core truth, he also acknowledged that Englishness was recognizable in the city and so demanded action: 'there was a constant complaint in the press about the influx of English paupers ... [and] the trustees of the city almshouse in 1832 tried to per- suade the government to put a limit on the number of indigent English who seemed to be "dumped" on Baltimore'.[6]

It was this precise kind of problem that caused wealthier English and Anglo-American citizens to act. Indeed, when it came to specifically ethnic, largely secular, charities set up for the aid of immigrants – which is what all early English associations were – then they looked hardly less numerous than their Irish equivalent (either the St Patrick's Society or the Hibernian Society). In terms of community presence, they also matched the associational life of the Scots with their St Andrew's Society or Caledonian Society. As a consequence of their similarity to other groups, English associations existed and were part of a wider world of ethnic, immigrant organizations of, or involving, British citizens, such as the British-American Society, the Canadian Club and several others, to name but a few.[7] Chicago, in the 1890s, was not untypical in having three different English groups: the Sons of St George, the St George Benevolent Society and the British-American Society, while, the Order of St George from neighbouring Joliet joined them for celebrations.[8] Meanwhile, in the east, St George's societies were supplemented by smaller organi- zations, such as the Albion Society, which continued to hold annual dinners in the 1880s and 1890s.[9] In pre-war New York, a large society gathering could attract similar numbers of organizations, as well as associations of Scots, Welsh and guests from other European immigrant clubs. Such was the case when 700 people turned out, in 1909, for a huge dinner in honour of the Royal Navy's Admiral of the Fleet, Sir Edward Hobart Seymour.[10] These ambitious and large-scale events and organizations were, by the Edwardian period, far removed in size and scale from the first shoots that appeared in the early eighteenth century.

Following the rhythms of emigration and settlement, the English first organized themselves in the American colonies, then in Canada and later in Australasia and Asia. At the earliest points these developments took root in the tidewater communities of the eastern American colonies, following the patterns of English settlement there that we have traced in the previous chapter. The associations that they formed were localized instances of Enlightenment cosmopolitanism, underpinned by sociability and charity; their remit extended overseas only insofar as it was the ocean that bore the beneficiaries of their charity – poor immigrants – towards them. Otherwise, they had no continuing connection to England itself.

In the nineteenth century, however, things changed, as this 'unimagined community' became something akin to Anderson's 'imagined community'.[11] Since most of the people who joined English societies knew about, but never met, their peers in far-flung lands, we find Anderson's model, with its emphasis on the importance of modern media communication, appealing to explain this transnational identity of English ethnic societies, which formed and maintained impressive transoceanic systems of ethnic celebration.[12] What is clear in all this is that, in an age of mass migration and epic continental expansion, these types of societies simply spread, through identified necessity, in line with European growth in the United States and British colonies.

The first aim of this chapter, then, is to chart the development of the different types of English societies within American and Canadian settings. We begin in the eighteenth century when organized Englishness first developed, before moving on to assess associational developments in the age of mass migration. Critically, by the 1870s, these developments took a transnational turn from their local United States and Canadian developments, when the Canadian and American societies began to exert their collective interests through sharing intelligence, expressing common principles and meeting at least annually. As Englishmen in Toronto or Philadelphia, and numerous other places, tended to the needs of the indigent, aged or infirm, as they embraced orphans and widows, the leaders of these associations recognized that knowledge of experiences and labour markets in other places of English settlement could be vital. The result was, in 1873, the formation of the NAStGU. Though no manuscript records survive,[13] the Union is a useful and important gauge of the reach of such pro-immigrant societies, particularly the extent of their transnational communication.

What makes the shift from local to transnational particularly important is that it was still local developments and local leaders who were at the helm. It was as a result of their local activities, concerns and experiences that they sought transnational connection through the NAStGU: the associational remit gave them a structured means to connect the local to the regional and beyond, while also enabling the development of a new set of goals through the NAStGU as a common organizational framework. Consequently, English transnational activity was not simply a 'type of consciousness',[14] but an active engagement through fraternal networks and associations. Critically, the process worked both ways,[15] as the leaders driving these transnational developments through the NAStGU returned to their local groups, where they disseminated news, but also actively pushed for change in line with discussions at NAStGU annual meetings.

Colonial roots

English ethnic societies planted roots in the eighteenth century, forming part of the networks of clubs and societies, so brilliantly described by Peter Clark, which honeycombed the Atlantic world.[16] Recognized as an intrinsic part of a developing civil society, and a signature of an emerging polite discourse in the New World, associations promoted both private enjoyment and public values.[17] Freemasonry represented one of the earliest and most consistent of these fraternal organizations that provided charity.[18]

In the earlier colonial age, the English actually were quick to organize immigrant aid charities. They were faster than the Irish by far (owing partly of course to the early timing of their first arrival), though generally slower than the Scots (despite arriving *en masse* before them). The Scots' Charitable Society of Boston was founded in the mid-seventeenth century, long before either the English or the Irish fashioned similar organizations.[19] In 1729, we first read of a Welsh Society of Philadelphia, whose members gathered on 1 March, St David's Day, and 'walk'd in regular order with Leeks in their Hats, to the Church, where was preach'd in the old British language [i.e. Welsh], an excellent sermon'. The Society also enjoyed a fine dinner, and had stewards to uphold this 'Yearly Custom' – though there was no talk of charity at this point.[20]

In 1733, some four years after the Philadelphian Welsh made a mark, the English of Charleston formed the American colonies' first St George's Society. It was decades after that, in 1762, that St George's Day was first mentioned as an event. On that occasion Sir Jeffrey Amherst hosted a ball for ninety-six persons at Crawley's New Assembly Rooms, New York. In 1770, the city's newspapers contained an account of how 'Gentlemen of the English Nation, residing in this City, and those descended from English Families, gave an elegant entertainment at Bolton's [Hotel].'[21] New York's Society of St George appeared in that same year, 1770, though formal appurtenances – constitution, written rules and recorded minutes – date to 1786, according to the Society's own history.[22] In 1771, the St George's Day celebration was the most striking yet, with around 120 English folk and descendants of England, gathered once more at Bolton's Hotel for a fine dinner and a list of twenty-three toasts, from the king and queen down to 'the Sons of St George in every quarter of the Globe, etc.', the latter implying that they knew of other similar gatherings.[23]

Philadelphia had a 'British Club', as the Society of the Sons of England was labelled, that dated to 1759. This was some thirteen years before the benevolent society of the same name was founded at Byrne's Tavern on St George's Day 1772.[24] Even after its formation, the Philadelphia Sons of St George existed alongside other societies, such as the Ancient Britons.[25] Like the St David's Society for the Welsh, or the Sons of Hermann for the Germans, the St George's Society was established as a wide-ranging benevolent society whose primary aim was to give support to new immigrants. The early years of the Philadelphia Society were fraught because of the outbreak of the revolutionary war, and the Society went into abeyance until March 1776 and then was suspended until St George's Day 1787, when Governor Penn was re-elected as president. In 1798 a healthy gathering of the Society ate dinner and raised sixteen toasts of the usual degree of Anglo-American loyalty; in 1804 the routine was almost identical; but in 1805 the toasts had climbed to twenty-one in number.[26]

The suspension of activities in Philadelphia during the American War of Independence documents how, at times of geopolitical crisis, English identity could be difficult to negotiate and highly risky to express. The American Revolution, as John Adams noted, caused a three-way split in the Philadelphia Sons of St George. Members were sitting in session in April 1775 when Robert Morris, the Society's first vice-president, broke news of the Battle of Lexington. Thereafter members were divided between loyalty to Britain and patriotism to the infant United States.[27] So it was that 'staunch Americans' met in one tavern, ' staunch Britons' in another, and 'half-way men' in yet another.[28] Such separations were, however, mild compared with the public humiliation of the Sons of St George member and physician John Kearsley, whose 'zealous attachment to the Royal cause' and his 'impetuous temper', not to mention his Tory speeches against the Whigs, saw him carted through the street, threatened with tarring and feathering and finally thrown in prison, where he died, with all his property and possessions confiscated. 'It thus was seen', the Society's historian glibly noted, 'that when he [Kearsley] was expelled from the Society in March 1776, he was already under public notoriety obnoxious to many of the members of the Society'.[29]

The colonial-age societies, especially the larger ones in New York and Philadelphia, set the tone for subsequent developments. They also locked into a wider set of cultural trends of that age. Voluntary benevolent societies, including those named for the United Kingdom's national saints, were commonplace in the eighteenth century. Crucially, however, they had by then thrown off sectarian entry requirements of seventeenth-century variants and so embraced all of their kinsmen by nation and not by religion.[30] Such societies were part of a large-scale trend which encompassed associations for every form of enjoyment, behaviour, viewpoint and tradition, from Freemasonry and politicking, hunting and reading, to drinking and eating. And while shorn of divisive religious bars, they were, as Bradburn correctly deduces, 'never completely apolitical, since they fortified and reinforced notions of the social and fraternal function of the leading figures of colonial and imperial society – men in positions of public power'.[31] Although the American Revolution disturbed the activities of Britons declaring their loyalty to an enemy country and king, these Britons soon returned to their normal business (what Clark calls 'philanthropy combined with high socializing') after hostilities had ceased.[32]

On its establishment in 1772 the Society of George set the standard in eating, drinking, toasting and helping out their fellow poor countrymen. The essential ritual, structure and approach in the major port cities remained the essence for what came later. Their toasts were not much changed in later years. Something much larger would develop from this small set of English associations welcoming English folk (and sometimes Welshmen) into their ranks. But the emphasis on camaraderie and sociability, and, above all else, the collective duty of offering benevolence towards their poor countrymen, was immediately set in stone. Importantly, sociability and charity were often linked, with big social events such as dinners and balls often serving the purpose of collecting additional funds for subscription lists for relief projects or contingency funds. The history of Philadelphia's Sons of St George put it rather more poetically and expansively. We are told that the first gathering:

> [C]ame thither from the pure dictates of Christian benevolence – to unite themselves into an association, whose ministrations were to be carried into the humblest abodes; to succor the distressed, to assuage the anguish of the sick, to assist the unfortunate, to give counsel to the stranger, to aid the industrious, and to carry out into effective exercise the principles of Him 'who went about doing good.'[33]

Typically, the founding statutes of the Philadelphia's Society of the Sons of St George affirmed that 'doing good' by declaring it existed 'for the ADVICE and ASSISTANCE of ENGLISHMEN in DISTRESS'.[34]

Some of the later-developing English associations in other places also had colonial predecessors, even if they did not initially last. While the St George's Society of Baltimore dated only to 1869, the notable tea merchant Thomas Twining recorded in his 1795 travelogue how, on arriving in Baltimore, he was invited to celebrate St George's Day with an unnamed English society there. His remarks convey a real sense of an active network welcoming visiting Englishmen and looking after less fortunate ones. Here he met Robert Field, an English miniature painter – one of the finest working in eighteenth-century America – with whom he had breakfasted the next day. He also ate dinner with the Society's president on another occasion.[35]

Initially at least, these societies were formed by Englishmen, for English members, with the object of aiding Englishmen and Englishwomen in the United States and Canada. The definition of 'English' caused some discussion, and, as in other ethnic organizations, precise definitions could prove challenging when membership numbers slumped, or as long-serving members retired, died or drifted away. From inception, the St George's Society of Kingston, Ontario, declared itself to 'consist of native born Englishmen and Welshmen, and the sons and grandsons of such Englishmen and Welshmen'.[36] Beyond those normal limits the constitution also declared that 'all subjects of Her Majesty, born in the British Colonial possessions, and naturalized subjects of Her Majesty, shall be eligible as Honorary Members of the Society'.[37] Baltimore St George's Society initially declared itself constitutionally to be a narrower, English society. At the same time the word 'descendants' was crucially added to those nationalities so that, for instance, the American son of a Canadian could join.[38] This was no longer the case after 8 February 1869, when the words 'English and Wales' were replaced in the constitution with 'United Kingdom' in the second article 'so that Scotch and Irish and their descendants could become members'.[39] Aside from the specifics of nationality, Kingston's St George's Society reflected the sectarian nature of Canadian society, a feature that lay at the heart of article 5: 'No person shall be a member who does not profess to believe in the Holy Scriptures.'[40] In short, no Catholics need apply. The same sectarian injunction also was true of the later nineteenth-century working-class benevolent societies that we discuss in the next chapter.

Members' subscriptions rates for these associations varied considerably, though the English charities usually set the bar higher than did other groups of their type. In the early 1800s, the Sons of St George, Philadelphia, were charging, at $10, ten times the amount asked of the Hibernians, five times the rate for the Scots Thistle Society and $2 more than the Welsh Society.[41] Immediately, we can imagine class-based relativities. Montreal's St George's Society, in 1834, embraced 'those who are natives of England, or descendants of natives of England'. By-laws from the 1860s make further membership specifications that resonate with those elsewhere: 'Any person who is a native of England or Wales, born in the British Possessions, may become a member of this Society, after being proposed and elected by open voting ... and paying a subscription fee of no less than three dollars.'[42] Welshmen were also 'eligible as members' in Baltimore (though 'natives of Scotland and Ireland' were excluded), while the St George's Society of British Columbia had the sole concern of 'bringing together Englishmen for their mutual benefit'.[43] Regardless of whether they were English or Welsh, the process of electing members was common for most associations, including that of Philadelphia (Figure 2.1).

More than a century later, the New York St George's Society stressed similar principles with the added espousal of sociability. The Society 'arose from the congenial feelings of some native English settled here, who felt, that though this was to be their permanent residence, they could not restrain the gratifying recollections of their native land, or be

Figure 2.1 Membership certificate from 1826, Philadelphia Society of the Sons of St George (image courtesy of Historical Society of Pennsylvania, Society of the Sons of St George, Collection no. 1733)

unmindful of the condition of any who might resort to their vicinity in a state of indigence or distress'.[44] Through such efforts, the English became successful in accumulating 'endowments and annually dispensed several thousand dollars among hundreds of persons'.[45] Charity remained a constant throughout, but it was with mass migration in the nineteenth century that the necessity of such support became a more persistent issue, with English associations in North American moving from charity to strategy, offering financial support but also labour-market advice.[46]

Expansion, migration and English associations

In the 1820s, a half-century after their original St George's Society was formed in the empire city, a New York St George's Cricket Club was founded and St George's Day was established as a holiday for the English there.[47] Traditional celebrations were also noted in Charles A. Murray's 1830s American travel diary, in which he recorded a fine dinner hosted by the New York St George's Society to mark its saint's day. Murray recollected some 150 well-off New Yorkers, both English and American, sharing a good dinner. For the event, 'the toasts were all thoroughly English, and given with English feeling'. In fact, he doubted if 'King William's health was ever drunk at the Thatched House of London Tavern with such unbounded, uproarious, and long-continued cheers, as at this transatlantic meeting'.[48]

Canadian English societies came later and reflected the pace of development within the northern colonies. Toronto's first English association was established in 1834, as was that of Montreal; Quebec was next in 1835 and Ottawa in 1844. Hamilton followed suit in the later 1840s.[49] In all cases urban growth – and by extension the growth of civil society – facilitated and required the formalization of English ethnic associations, as migrant communities expanded and civil society progressed. The first English associations in Canada mirrored their American counterparts, focusing chiefly on the provision of charity.[50] But it was, of course, a charity mixed with patriotism – and this, as the Revd Norman noted lyrically in a sermon delivered to the Montreal St George's Society on St George's Day later in the century, was 'the river-bed, the channel through which the stream of sympathetic kindness wends its healing way'.[51]

Despite the re-awakening of public, associative Englishness in the United States, the 1830s were still a tense time. The year 1832, in Charleston, captures this well. At that point, the St George's Society of Charleston evoked the essence of England with a toast to 'The British Constitution – The greater of charter of rational liberty – destined to flourish, in undiminished strength, amidst the wreck of tyrants and the overflow of demagogues.'[52] The toast was, though, deliberate and

defensive, since members were publicly resisting Henry Clay's questioning of British Americans' 'eulogy of the British Constitution', something
that the Society felt had no relevance to local or national politics in the
Carolinas or the United States.[53] Time and again, geopolitical disagreements would impact on how the English were seen and how they acted.

Englishmen also founded less well-known societies in the nineteenth century, most of them with no remaining manuscript records.
Philadelphia had an Albion Society, formed in December 1855, which
was active for many years but left no record. We really know of it only
through the press, and because it was occasionally referenced in the Sons
of St George minutes.[54] Its members were noticed, for example, when
they contributed funds to relieve the poor English, often in concert with
St George's societies. Such societies also enjoyed some commonalities
in membership and among officers. John Thomson, English-born librar-
ian of the free library in Philadelphia, served on many committees and in
many organizations, including the Sons and the Albion Society, both of
which enjoyed his services as officer.[55]

In light of these establishment patterns in both the United States and
Canada, a continental picture began to emerge that transcended locality,
region and country: English associations proliferated quickly in response
to the poverty of a certain noticeable minority of immigrants; societies
and clubs were founded in communities large and small, urban and
rural; they offered conviviality for members as well as help for hard-up
countrymen and women; and each of these developments occurred
in a broadly westward direction – southerly too in the American case.
Burgeoning settlement in Ohio resulted in the emergence, in 1837, of the
St George's Society in Cincinnati.[56] Even older, eastern colonies, which
experienced new waves of urban growth and immigration, founded such
societies where they had not previously been part of the colonial wave of
developments. Thus, in 1841, the English of Providence, Rhode Island,
followed their Mid-Western counterparts in planting a society.[57]

Equivalent societies appeared in towns at the heart of north-eastern
transport developments between the Great Lakes and the sea. Such was
the case in Utica (1858) and in other places nearby, such as Oswego,
Cohoes and Onondanga. Canadian developments also clustered near the
Lakes. Kingston, Ontario (1859), is a notable example, though a dozen
other Ontario towns followed suit between the 1850s and early 1870s.
At the same time, the earlier organizations became much stronger.
Toronto's St George's Society was, for instance, incorporated in 1858,
with the relevant bill 'pass[ing] both Houses without opposition'.[58]
Further north, in Quebec, the bishop of the city praised the continuous good work of the St George's Society there, noting how it spoke to
'the Christian grace of self-denial' by 'furnish[ing] an opportunity for
the cultivation of ... systematic, high-toned, benevolence' through its

operations.[59] Indeed, an increasing public profile meant that some of these societies' events were spectacular. On 11 January 1859, New York's St George's Society held a 'an elaborate Grand Festival' at the Academy, which, though well attended and acutely planned, fell victim to prima donna behaviour by the two leading singers, who squabbled publicly on stage over the singing, in English, of 'God Save the Queen'.[60]

Most of these elite English associations were primarily Protestant, their utilizing of Episcopal churches for their services being one measure of that. Members' names suggested English ethnicity. In the first two days of 1901, the Baltimore St George's Society's 'members and dues' book listed fifteen names, twelve of which – Alcock, Bennett, Bowes, Clough, Courtney, Hodge, Metcalfe, Oldham, Purcell, Robson, Rowland, Russell – bore strong association not only with England, but particularly with the north.[61] The ritual and celebration they enjoyed also reflected their clear English identifications: St George's Day celebrations with roast beef dinners; Gilbert and Sullivan sing-songs; and courses on menus accompanied by quotes from Shakespeare.

However, membership also was complicated by ethnicity over birth-place. As well as Americans of many generations' settlement, English associations also attracted those who did not fit a narrow English, Protestant, elite characterization. A notable individual such as Frank Dawson, head of Charleston's principal newspaper and proponent of modernization in the post-bellum period, offers a vignette of this com-plication. Dawson was a London-born Catholic, a proud American Confederate during the Civil War and an avid supporter of industrial modernization for the South. But as well supporting the St George's Society with his membership, he also joined the Hibernian Society and a number of other committees and bodies.[62] Dawson's profile as one of life's joiners suggested civic responsibility and activity as well as, possibly, recognition of both English and Irish roots.

As the Mid-West was opened up, the communities of the American western Great Lakes also welcomed thousands of English settlers. In 1856, for instance, Madison, Wisconsin, reported the existence of its St George's Society. Two years later the tradition had made its way east to Milwaukee, as the number of English settlers proliferated.[63] The prominence of English societies, as evinced by the press, suggests that the established pattern of middle-class leadership remained key. Thus, in 1858, with their society newly formed, the Milwaukee English held their first major St George's Day dinner.[64] In Chicago, the St George's Society was founded in 1860, and in 1864, members made an impressive splash with their sustained celebrations of the tercentenary of the birth of the bard, William Shakespeare.[65] One large American centre that did not fit within this general pattern was the Baltimore's St George's Society. Founded in 1866 at the behest of the local British consul, Andrew Darrell, it was a comparatively late development – but one that continued the tradition of earlier St George's societies resolutely as poor relief, tickets for onward travel, hospital beds, burial plots, general fund-raising and sociability were its stock-in-trade too.[66]

Within this wider context, imperial and monarchical occasions provide historians with a useful stock-taking opportunity. Thus, among the throngs of people and groups who welcomed Prince Albert when he visited Newfoundland in 1860 as part of his tour of the Empire and colonies were members of the St George's Society, who paraded along with the masons, the Benevolent Irish Society, the St Andrew's Society and several others.[67] Similar waves of support were planned for Upper and Lower Canada when the prince made his way there. Indeed, we learn a little about the organizational mechanisms behind such public expressions of support by associations rather than individuals from the minutes of the Ottawa St George's Society. In preparation for his visit to their city, the men of the St George's Society called a special meeting of officers and members utilizing adverts in the press to ensure a full turnout. The meeting's purpose was to agree an address to be forwarded to the Governor-General in good time, so that he could ensure the prince saw it via the hand of his personal private secretary. One of the members, Mr Lee, wished the address to ask the prince to be the Society's patron, 'just as his father was of the German Society of Montreal'.[68]

Spreading across the east, south and Mid-West, Englishmen gathered under the banner of St George in Little Rock, Racine and Knoxville.[69] In the following decades, associations continued to move further west, finding their way to Anaconda and Butte, Montana, and to southern California at both Los Angeles and Pasadena, to name only a few.[70] These patterns of geographic diversification were fully in tune with the migratory pathways of the English: their ethnic associations were not the response of marginalized groups, but were established in the centres of English settlement throughout North America.

As the societies were first being planted out west, the signs were of established associations becoming yet more powerful and wealthy back in the east. Philadelphia's Sons of St George, who, for over a century, had met in rented rooms, marked a significant development in 1875 when they acquired a marble building on 13th and Arch Streets, which they adorned with 'an elegant equestrian group in bronze, representing St George killing the dragon'. The newly created St George's Hall became, and remains, an imposing public building.[71] The power implied by this development should not be taken to be the ultimate measure of elitism. While Erickson has dismissed English ethnic societies as middle class and therefore above and out of touch with the common English immigrant, the reality in most places was more complex; in Philadelphia, it was simply quite different. Here, as Olton explained, political challenges from

below in the city, in the revolutionary era, came not from Jacobin radicalism but from a 'burgeoning community of manufacturing entrepreneurs
with continuing and accelerating upward social, economic, and political
aspirations to reorient existing structures and patterns of behaviour'.[72]
This was a protean middle class asserting its civic role through ethnic
expression.

The building of St George's Hall was not the result of individual beneficence but of collective effort. Moreover, as Olton goes on, artisans, independent masters and better sorts of workingmen were not excluded from
the social and political fabric of the city and so were not 'so estranged
as to contemplate radical reconstruction of the ... social milieu'.[73] In
this period, social institutions such as the Sons of St George included
artisans as well as merchants, thus embracing common cause rather than
social isolation or conflict.

The geographic spread and numeric proliferation of English associations throughout the United States and Canada highlight the wide
permeation of English ethnic organizations as they became an intrinsic
part of English immigrant community life (Map 2.1). The St George's
societies who celebrated their saint's day in 1883, 'throughout the eastern
provinces', exchanged telegrams of good wishes between themselves and
some American societies.[74] They knew of each other's existence, their
locations and their secretary's addresses. They were able to communicate
mutual sympathy and goodwill, and they did. What aided these associations' durability across temporal space and through time was an umbrella
organization, the NAStGU, which brought the various elements together
transnationally to create or maintain some sort of standard among them,
in terms of both charitable work and cultural activities.

Consolidating the continent: the North America St George's Union

An active diaspora is denoted both by the geographical range of its
adherents and by transnational communication between them. The
English, with their growing North American associational culture, demonstrated both of these facets of diaspora. Furthermore, their vitality and
range soon led to the formation of an overarching, continental structure.
There was nothing new in this, for many such friendly societies, the
Orange Order, Catholic confraternities and societies and groups of every
conceivable kind maintained national, continental and global structures
in what was one of the surest measures of the ability of cultures to survive
mass emigration.[75] The Orange Order in Ireland, for instance, formed the
Triennial Council in 1865 in order to maintain standardized structures
and to ensure that a scriptural Protestant message endured.[76]

Though the St George's societies and Sons of England societies across

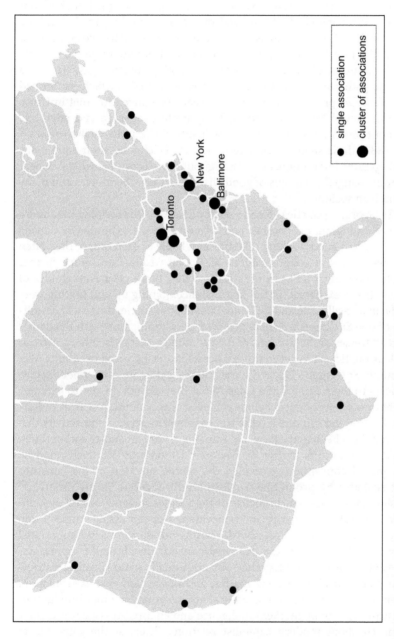

Map 2.1 Locations of the principal St George's societies in North America

North America at times appeared like localized, individual, almost
masonic organizations, they also had limited knowledge of kindred
societies elsewhere. They exchanged messages and good wishes, but
little more concrete had emerged by 1870. According to the address
of President George Francis Dawson at the Washington convention of
1882, the idea for the NAStGU first sprouted in Onondaga, New York,
in the autumn of 1872. The original planning meeting gave rise to a
further gathering, also at Onondaga, in February 1873, which established
the NAStGU proper.[77] The following year, the convention met in Utica,
also in New York State, and declared itself 'expressive and advisory',
without any attempt to 'govern' or 'control' the individual societies.[78]
By 1883, these same St George's societies celebrated their saint's day
with greater interconnection 'throughout the eastern provinces', where
they exchanged telegrams of good wishes between themselves and many
American societies.[79]

St George's societies close to each other – in Philadelphia, Baltimore
and Washington, or Toronto and Ottawa across the border in Canada
– clearly had good working relations and knew of each other. They often
received notes of congratulations and good wishes from much further
afield, especially on St George's Day, so they had a clear enough idea of
each other's existence. In the first instance, joining up and uniting were
done in a small-scale and individual way. For example, the relief committee of one St George's Society provided poor immigrants with the names
and addresses of the wardens of their kindred societies in other towns, as
well as rail tickets to get to those places. On the big social occasions – for
example St George's Day – the societies would invite each other's senior
officers to their dinners and galas. What they did not do was to federate;
what they never sought, let alone achieved, was a common central authority. Yet they did evince a level of transnational awareness and activity that
moved them beyond the local and trans-local attachments of earlier times.

The initial aim of the St George's Union was relatively modest.
Its annual conventions extended the ethnic function of the constituent societies by promoting Englishness throughout North America.[80]
Discussions about new branches of the various societies across the continent; developing charity and benevolent aid; expressing Anglo-Saxon
unity; and developing cross-border amity – these were among its stated
objectives.[81] However, the principal concern that brought representatives of these societies together was not initially nationalism or patriotism, but instead a practical matter, and one which exercised many of
their annual meetings: the need to share information about immigrants,
focusing on labour-market intelligence and charity. At issue was a grave
concern about modern capitalist relations. Thus, at the gathering at
Hamilton, Ontario, in 1876, attempts were made to promote arbitration
over confrontation to prevent labour unrest.[82] As the 1889 convention,

also held at Hamilton, was told, the Society had two ideals: to maintain the organizations' collective benevolent character and to disburse charity to those less fortunate than them.[83] The St George's Union was 'modelled on the plan of our American general conventions' and appeared to be strongly endorsed from inception by local and regional units such as the St George's Benevolent Association of Chicago, whose members were addressed directly by Mr G.G. Jones, secretary of the federating Society.[84] No rewriting of constitutions or common rituals was suggested. The NAStGU was not a replacement organization. In organizational terms, though there was some talk of making Philadelphia the base for all NAStGU meetings, the Union adopted the principle of holding its annual convention on a roving basis.[85] For three decades or more, conventions were held in a different city each year.

Although the union was focused on charity and Englishness, there also was a political element in the form of an emerging desire for the regulation of workplace disputes by way of 'a system of arbitration into the mixed struggles of capital and labor'.[86] Meetings of the NAStGU heard much about this desire to be important English models of social harmony, thus suggesting that capitalists as well as workers perceived differences between their culture and that of America. Talk concerned the desirability of English-style labour relations, laced with an inference of English superiority. Interestingly these societies, which mixed the wealthy with the more modestly monied, were promulgating concerns similar to those of English workers. If labourers from England reviled the lack of workers' rights in the United States, the employers and professionals who ran the St George's Union were greatly agitated by the underlying conflict and sometimes open hostility of labour relation at the dawn of the 'Gilded Age'. Certainly, by the 1890s, there was a more general interest among American Progressives in the fact that the Canadians had passed a 'conciliation and arbitration law similar to the English act of 1896'.[87]

The NAStGU appeared when it did with the express intention of bringing together diverse American and Canadian English organizations. A main aim was to help societies that 'are for the most part officially unknown to each other' to avoid repetitive fraud and to support worthy migrants who would benefit from tramping between towns and societies, seeking support in each. The convention in 1875 was in Buffalo, New York State. Here travelling cards of membership were proposed and ordered. In 1877, the issue was, however, raised again, suggesting imperfections in the system.[88] Moreover, a committee was appointed to 'show the legislature of New York the propriety of restoring the capitation tax on immigrants at the ports of New York from $1.50 to $2.50 per capita to prevent the crippling of the New York Commissioners of Emigration'.[89] Another issue raised at the NAStGU was the perpetual problem of 'vagrant tramps who prey upon National Societies'.[90] The same convention also expressed a wish to develop links with Englishmen in South and Central America, but there is little evidence that this subsequently came to pass. Disraeli's performance at the 1878 Congress of Berlin was the major talking point, in 1879, at the seventh convention, which was held at Bridgeport, Connecticut.[91] After the sending of congratulations to the queen and government on the triumph of British diplomacy, friendship between 'the elder and younger Englands' was marked in the formation in London, on St George's Day 1879, of the St George's Society of London.[92]

The eighth convention, held in Ottawa in August 1880 and hosted by the city's St. George's society (see Figure 2.2), returned to practical themes associated with helping unfortunate English people in North America: child emigration, and the necessity of both British and North American governments ensuring that emigrants had good information

Figure 2.2 Emblem of the St George's Society of Ottawa, c.1875 (John Henry Walker for the Ottawa St George's Society, gift from David Ross McCord, image courtesy of McCord Museum, M930.50.7.499)

before travelling. The societies on the American side of the Atlantic found themselves having to pick up the pieces for pauper emigrants, the likes of handloom weavers with no prospects in their own trades or those who arrived at times of economic hardship. Applying pressure to governments and ensuring good labour-market intelligence were prime aims.[93] In this respect, they were merely building on the ethos of individual St George's societies, which, in straitened times, took to writing to English newspapers to discourage emigration.[94] In April 1884, the meeting of the St George's Society in Montreal demonstrated the continued local concerns about 'reckless emigration' by people induced with 'false representations'. Such migrations had necessitated the relief, repatriation or onward migration westwards of over 500 'unfortunate victims'. All this was of course code for pauper emigration. Newspapers, including American ones, ran with the Montreal theme:

> The President and Secretary have been authorized to prepare a draft of a communication to the leading English newspapers, denouncing the system of indiscriminate emigration [currently] in vogue, and explaining the disastrous effect to all concerned of people coming to this country who are not suited to its requirements.[95]

The St George's societies were not the only ones worried about immigrants lured across the Atlantic with false prospectuses for the good life. On 20 May 1884, the St George's Society of Montreal passed a resolution to 'put itself in communication with other national societies with the object of devising means for enlightening public opinion in England as to the class of immigrants needed in this country, and impressing upon the Dominion Government the necessity of providing shelter for needy immigrants'.[96] In 1885 John Armstrong, who was leader of the Tories in the Toronto Trades and Labour Council, 'proposed that the council send a representative to England to combat the Macdonald government's misleading propaganda aimed at recruiting British workers to Canada'.[97] Thus we can see that transnational activity such as that manifested by the NAStGU just picked up on things, such as 'reckless emigration', partly because the issues exercised local associations. But in offering opinions harmonious with those of Tory politicians in Canada, the societies were demonstrating connection to wider political viewpoints.

If transnational activity such as this, as well as the many informal connections between individual associations across national boundaries, was noticed for the Scots or Irish, it would be accepted unquestioningly as evidence of strong ethnic identity and actual or emerging power. It follows that similar acknowledgment thus needs to be given to the English. At its meeting in 1876, the St George's Union discussed and supported a large-scale celebration of Queen Victoria's fifty-eighth birthday that the British Association of Virginia was organizing. By seeking audiences with consuls and ambassadors and writing to St George's and Albion societies, the organizers ensured high interest and many promises of attendance, including that gleaned at the NAStGU from members in Kingston, Toronto, Bridgeport, Baltimore, Philadelphia and several others, all of whom pledged support.[98] In the following year, 1877, some members of the British Association of Virginia attended the fifth annual convention, held in Philadelphia, though the local press expressed a little disappointment that not more would be heading north for the 'very attractive programme' advertised.[99] In addition to the delegates counted here, there also were the *ex officio* officers of the Union, and sundry men of Western Ontario who were neither delegates nor officers. But attendances could be patchy.

The geographical origins of NAStGU delegates and their resulting attendance reflected the vastness of the United States and Canada. The Kingston men, who were relative stalwarts in the context of the smaller cities and towns, were, for example, not represented at Philadelphia in 1877.[100] There was no one from further south than Philadelphia, and no one from further west than Chicago – even though societies thrived well beyond the middle Atlantic, New England and Ontario. Baltimore and Charleston had societies, but sent no one. New York also was absent, and seemingly remained so throughout the period, but not for reasons of geography. Eight years after the convention with the representation noted above, New York still was not there; moreover, delegates 'voted down' a proposal to ask New York 'to come into the union' because 'neither the union nor their own societies had received courteous treatment from the New York societies'.[101] Clearly, the New Yorkers were, for whatever reason, aloof from their peers. Yet still the NAStGU had grown again by 1888, to 4,000 members organized into twenty-six 'affiliating societies'.[102] Investments totalled $130,000, an increase of $15,000.[103] New York, in 1883, counted permanent funds at $42,000.[104] These figures can be contextualized by reference to the financial position of one of the oldest of their societies, the Philadelphia Sons of St George: in 1887–88, it alone had an income of $3,030, with $76,000 invested.[105]

While distances imposed limits on attendance, delegates to the 1878 convention wished to stress the true extent of the branches of the NAStGU. At that point, Canada had twenty-five such societies; the state of New York alone had over twenty; and 'Pennsylvania and each of the Eastern States [had] a proportionate number' (see also Map 2.2; for a detailed list of societies, see Appendix 1). The Kingston representatives, R.J. Barker and E.J.B. Pense, produced a handbill for the event, reporting with flourishes of information and colour. They ascribed the geographical range of their societies to the fact 'an Englishman's heart beats more warmly for the Old Home as his travels bear him from her and lessen

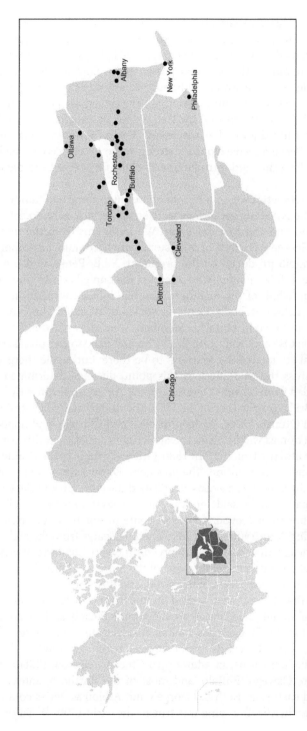

Map 2.2 Branches of the North America St George's Union in the eastern border region

the number of his associated brethren'. This was why they heard also of branches in 'far distant California, Omaha, Nebraska and Georgia'. The delegates seemed moved that even far-removed places such as 'Hannibal, Missouri had 'during the past year presented an English celebration on a grand scale, one that would do honour to any city in the Empire, the centre of British loyalty and affection'. These English-born Canadian representatives were surprised by 'the fervour of affection for England and her most loved jewel, her sovereign' shown by American speakers. Barker and Pense also developed a strong sense of what concerned the Union: 'the fostering and introduction of clubs for literary and personal benefit'.[106]

Although societies were numerous and though some had hundreds of members, the NAStGU gatherings were small because each society sent only between one and four delegates. We know this from the minutes of the St George's Society of Kingston, which contain an important printed handbill produced by the president, E.J.B. Pense, and the first vice-president, R.W. Barker, who attended the annual convention of the NAStGU on behalf of the members. The handbill shows that, in 1878, forty-seven delegates of St George's societies attended the NAStGU convention in Guelph, Ontario. Members were drawn from Toronto, Philadelphia, Oswego, Kingston, Waterloo and many other places; some of the members made long journeys to be there, but, while there were societies across the Mid-West by this point, distance determined that none attended from beyond Ontario and the American north-east.[107]

At the Bridgeport gathering in 1879, the 'influential delegates' were drawn from Ottawa, Utica, Bridgeport itself and Chicago, and hoped 'to take such action as will bring all the St George's societies in this country and Canada into the Union'.[108] In 1880, Ottawa, 'capital of the Dominion', hosted the eighth convention. The president, Dr Sweetman, spoke of the purpose of the Union. His words re-affirmed the core spirit of the Union. They were gathered, he said, 'not for political, communistic, or religious principles, but to endeavour to devise some means to secure relief for their suffering countrymen'. He welcomed delegates from far and wide: from America in the south to this city 'on the very outskirts of civilization'. The men from Philadelphia, one of the more southerly delegations, were drawn from both the Albion Society and the Sons of St George.[109]

Indeed, the delegate list settled in the later 1870s and remained constant – although the Charleston St George's Society archive contains a handbill for the St George's Union, no delegate from there is ever listed. New York retained its aloof distance. Toronto, Ottawa and many smaller Canadian towns, in addition to Chicago, Boston, Philadelphia, Washington, Oswego, Buffalo 'and most of the northern states', were represented each year. Both St George's and Albion societies continued to stand together.[110] The same was true in the early 1890s.[111] Baltimore, in spite of its continuous activity, seems to have shown no interest, and its archives contain no reference to the NAStGU. By contrast, many of the smaller towns in the state of New York were well represented at all times, including years when they hosted the events.[112]

The St George's societies' vision and its limits

Meetings filled with mutual appreciation and visions of unity were underpinned by more mundane explains of their shared culture in action. The Ottawa gathering, for example, heard reports of many events organized by the St George's Union. These included meetings, picnics and larger regional gatherings, and were reported as far afield as San Francisco and Petersburg, Virginia.[113] The ground-level work was revealed in the local minutes of, for example, the St George's Society of Kingston, whose stalwart activist Bro. E.J.B. Pense was elected to the executive committee.[114] In July of the same year, 1880, at a meeting of the St George's Society of Baltimore 'it was moved + seconded that the president be authorized to subscribe for the Soc[iet]y to the North American St George's Union, if upon investigation he thought it advisable to do so'.[115] The result was not the attendance of Baltimore men at the convention; nor were they listed in any other year. Connections with other, similar societies were not much in evidence in the records of the Baltimore St George's Society, though in 1883 it did invite Revd Dr Parker Morgan of the New York Society to preach to the members at their St George's Day church service.[116] Another minute, also in 1883, noted that a telegram was being sent to the sister organization in Toronto apologizing that business engagements prevented more of the members from attending a convention in the Ontarian city.[117]

Remarking on the connections between England's constitution and those of both the United States and Canada, a Mr Benjamin, drew warm applause when he noted the amity 'not only existing between Canada and the United States but also between the United States and Great Britain.' The second vice-president, Edward C. Barber, felt as though he was 'speaking to men who were born and lived within the sound of Bow Bells'. Barber described the Union as honourable and selfless since no political gain was to be had from travelling hundreds of miles to attend a convention with 'no prizes to offer'. Mr Lawson of Philadelphia then praised the development of civilization in Ottawa, the 'enterprise displayed by Canadians' and 'the success of Englishmen in every sphere of life'. These meetings were indeed about formulating common policies for dealing with the indigent migrant English, and they were also about forging a group identity; as a result of both, they involved long encomia to the spirit, ideal and commonality of them all. Such was true when

G.W. Longstaff of Bridgeport, Connecticut, commented positively on the nature of the English, before expressing a wish for expansive growth: 'Scatter the Englishmen where you may, he will still retain his national character, his love of country. He hoped the gatherings would long continue, and the St George's Union extend from Canada to Mexico, and from the Atlantic and the Pacific.'[118] For all that, Longstaff, a naturalized American, living in his adopted home of Connecticut, in 1884, doubtless retained his English passions but also showed how the immigrant also had to negotiate new identities.[119]

The members of the Philadelphia Sons of St George heard 'accounts of the operations of sister societies at San Francisco and Winnipeg', which suggests that the westward roll was on.[120] Grand visions of a continent-straddling organization continued into the 1880s. In 1881, the press reported a strong showing among the Englishmen of Washington, DC, whose St George's Society was growing strongly, doubling since it was inaugurated on St George's Day 1879. A well-attended six-course dinner on the saint's day two years later announced that the Society would host the NAStGU in the national capital.[121] Only a couple of months later, and over a year from the event itself, the Philadelphia Sons of St George elected its delegates for Washington.[122] The delegates had been expecting to travel to the Convention in the autumn of that year, but the murder of the president caused the St George's Union to postpone it: Washington, of all places, was heavily shadowed by the events, which 'saddened every Anglo-Saxon heart on the globe'.[123] Thus, in May 1882 the Canadian press noted the intention of numerous branches to be represented. Moreover, since 'each of the Toronto, London, and Winnipeg societies have passed resolutions inviting the members to hold the next convention [1883] in its city, a lively struggle is anticipated'.[124] In the same year, the Union lost three stalwart officers: a former president, Lewis Thompson of Philadelphia, Captain J.A.H. Andrews, 'a leading member of the English colony in Virginia', and William Tomlin, a past secretary, of Bridgeport, Connecticut.[125]

Washington, then, hosted the ninth convention, in 1882, at the Willard Hall. Attendees came from all of the major centres of St George's society activity. The president, Mr Dawson, described how the number and strength of their individual societies were greater than ever before, with some of the societies having 600 members. Although the attendance was small, he said, compared with other conventions, 'we really represent very many thousands of English Canadians and English Americans banded together in societies, for purposes benevolence and philanthropic and patriotic to both the motherland and the Lands in which we live and which we love so dearly.' The president also made some clear recommendations to ensure stronger governance: the president and secretary both from the same towns, national as well as transnational unions, a push for union with all similar societies and not just most St George's ones, the appointment of a roving lecturer to visit all such societies, a charge of ten cents per capita on all members to provide funds and the selection of a particular newspaper to be the Union's organ for communicating good information. One of the recommendations contained an interesting and lofty ambition: that the word 'international' replace 'North America' to reflect an expectation of expansion beyond North America. Dawson also sought the official laudation of both the Canadian parliament and the American Congress, and a policy of lobbying both polities for protection for new immigrants. In a pre-echo of later global developments, he also expressed a deep desire that 'St George's Day should be celebrated in all lands people by the Anglo-Saxon race as our common race-day'.[126]

In line with so many traditionally male associations, the NAStGU in the later nineteenth century witnessed profound social change. A principal matter of interest at the 1891 Oswego convention was preponderance of women, all adorned in 'the badge of the St George's Society'. Ladies numbered over half of all attendees. Mr Neal, president of the Oswego St George's Society, Canada, tried to appease the emerging new order by introducing a traditional message with a word for the ladies:

> Your coming to us revives vivid memories of motherhood, and rekindles the flame of love for the dear old home, towards which ... we turn with pride and affection at all times, and more especially on occasions like the present when we meet as representatives of the United States and the Dominion of Canada, to promote and advance the good and welfare of the North American St George's Union, an organization which, international in its scope and most beneficent in its operation, commends itself to the support of Englishmen everywhere.[127]

Neal spoke of the meeting as held 'under the intertwined flags of England and America to take counsel in the interests of the North America St George's Union'. The mayor of Oswego then spoke words of welcome and was followed by Mr T.B. White, who stated that 'there was not a drop of English blood in his veins although he might have the outward appearance of and Englishman'. In fact, 'he was to the manor born a Yankee'. This did not prevent an affinity with the St George's Union or Englishmen in general, since 'he felt his country was the offspring of Britain'.[128] Overall, the tenor of the speeches was to emphasize English and American linkages and to stress Anglo-Saxon connections. Mr Smythe, a long-serving member of the delegation from Kingston, Ontario, used a variant of Churchill's pet phrase of many years later – 'English-speaking nation' – in a short and approving speech.[129]

By the early 1900s, the principles that held the St George's Union in place were still strong; but the transcontinental union was had almost run its course. The year 1902 was not, as Bianchi says, its final session.[130] An impressively well-attended meeting did, however, occur that year in Philadelphia, with co-operation between Britain and the United States reportedly a topic of discourse and discussion.[131] The St George's Union continued for several more years, but the rise of the Sons of England in Canada and of the Order of St George in the United States, the failure of the St George's Society of New York ever to become involved and the barrier of distance, which blocked participation by southern and western associations, signalled the demise of the practice, if not the spirit, of transnational co-operation. In 1904, members formed up for the thirty-second convention and went through the usual election of officers for the upcoming year: president, James Stark, Boston; first vice-president, F.W. Gates, Hamilton, Ontario; second vice-president, Frank Thrappleton, Philadelphia; and secretary-treasurer, Thomas G. Yeates, Washington, with committeemen and chaplain drawn from Philadelphia and Toronto.[132]

A decade later, however, local societies were talking in past tense about the once-impressive cross-border co-operation. The absence of such common cause bothered Englishmen in Canada, not least J.C. Anderton, whose efforts were written about in a lengthy article in *The English Race*, the journal of the London-based RSStG, an organization founded in 1894 to create a global network of pro-English activists. With strong metro-politan, middle- and upper-class credentials, and with royal patronage by the early 1900s, the RSStG clearly was something to which Anderton and many of this countrymen clearly wished Canadian groups to affiliate. The article, however, revealed as much about weaknesses as strengths, as much about accident as planning. Anderton asserted that English people, 'the backbone of the Dominion, are at last becoming aware that their position is being systematically assailed and undermined by the more active, self-assertive, but united minor nationalities'. The problem was the rising power of the Irish, and to some extent the Scots. Noting the same superiority of the (Celtic) 'fringe' nations at home, the imperialist, assertive RSStG feared that this imbalance between the English and their British and Irish neighbours, 'if unchecked, must eventuate in the disin-tegration of the Empire, which has been created and developed almost entirely by the genius and energy of the English people'.[133]

'This awakening of the slow, phlegmatic, far-too-patient concern arose after a meeting' of sixteen societies from St John, New Brunswick, Ottawa, Quebec, Hamilton, London and Montreal. The awakening was not, however, universal. Canada's oldest English association, the St George's Society of Toronto, reported correspondence from its Anderton's St George's Society in St John, New Brunswick, in support of affiliation of societies across Canada and proposing two delegates from each branch being sent to a joint meeting, with each grouping 'paying a portion of, at best, the travelling costs'. Toronto decided to 'write for further suggestions'.[134] The meeting went ahead without them. The gathering elected J.C. Anderton as temporary president and resolved to bring together all known English organizations in Canada.[135]

The meeting held in Montreal in October 1910 revealed 'how "wide apart" these Societies are' since 'the existence of several others only became known at this meeting'. The result was recognition that the organized English in British North America comprised about 9,000 paying members.[136] Anderton, their president, painted a vision of greater success than that, with his words aimed expressly at 'truant Societies' who had not joined the federating meeting:

> The advisability of Englishmen acting as a united body, enlarging their membership, and increasing their influence at the present time was felt by all to be a necessity. As far as known, there are 9,000 members of St George's Societies in Canada. There is no reason, if loyal and energetic effort is made, why this should not be increased to 50,000 in a reasonably short time.[137]

With immigration running at higher levels in the early 1900s than at any time since the first half of the nineteenth century, Anderton stressed the need to work on recruitment in the west of the country. More generally, he also emphasized the importance of trying to 'influence our newly arrived countrymen to become members, thus maintaining the spirit of English connection, customs, and historic tradition of which we as Englishmen are so justly proud'. Anderton still spoke as a man beginning a mission rather than one who could draw upon the long traditions of forerunners of his own efforts – namely, the NAStGU, which had met in 1904, in Toronto, for its final convention. Both Anderton and *The English Race* picked up on the connection between what these English folk in Canada were doing in 1911 and what their predecessors had done in the early 1870s, which was very much the same thing. Like them, Anderton believed the English could be an ethnic force disseminating 'the principles we hold – patriotism, unswerving loyalty to the Flag and Country [and] social intercourse among members'. For now, he bemoaned the 'decadent state' of the societies. While he found

> no want of patriotism or racial sentiment amongst the members ... there is an utter lack of co-ordinate action; each Society is a law unto itself, and like raw levies, which give way and fail to maintain a position in the face of disciplined forces, they succumb to the up-to-date methods employed by more attractive organizations.[138]

Anderton also speculated on why the societies were individual and distinct, and, he felt, less favourable to collaboration than they should be: 'We must bear in mind that most of these Societies were established before the days of railways and steamboats, when inter-communication was extremely difficult and its need not so apparent.' He had no notion of why the NAStGU had failed but thought perhaps national boundaries were the cause: 'Perhaps a distinct organization for the two countries would meet with better success?'[139] In any case, when minutes of the meeting were received by the St George's Society of Toronto, the president expressed the intention to respond to each item. He asked members for their views (none of which was minuted). The Toronto minute books referred to the new organization as the (proposed) Federation of St George's Society in Canada, but no enthusiasm or participation was logged.[140] By early 1911, the Toronto Society clearly had tired of the issue of federation. A further three communications – presumably letters of encouragement or persuasion – were recorded from Hamilton, Guelph and London societies, and the Toronto group decided 'no further action would be taken in the matter'.[141]

Overall this was a strong appeal for intra-Canadian fellowship between the St George's Society, the Sons of St George Benefit Society and the Sons of England. Yet such a plan for official, organized fellowship was not realized – not even by St George's societies that had once before been affiliated together and now had the chance to unify under a London standard, but chose not do to so. Affiliation was, instead, haphazard.

Conclusion

Like their Scottish or German counterparts, English migrants established ethnic associations soon after their first footfall in the New World. From the 1730s to the mid-twentieth century, most North American cities and towns of any size had examples of English ethnic organizations – whether charities or friendly societies. As for other groups, English folk were aware of the basic functions such societies served: they were safety nets, network facilitators and providers of sociability. The foundations of English associational culture were elite in nature, and dated to the eighteenth century; these early examples, in the major seaboard ports, were inherently driven by middle-class migrants and shaped, in the first instance, by the provision of charity.

From these foundations the tradition of St George's societies proliferated quickly, spreading first throughout the American colonies, and then Canada in the 1830s, before moving west with newly arrived migrants in the course of the nineteenth century. As societies founded by immigrants for immigrants, they naturally looked outwards to England and their peers elsewhere. The NAStGU was formed in the early 1870s with the express intention of bringing together diverse American and Canadian

English organizations. Within a few years, local English societies hosted roving conventions for this organization, each in a different city. Many of the St George's societies were durable. In the big cities in both Canada and the United States, they still exist. However, even at the time, there were divisions and separations, some triggered, in part, by the socially limited nature of St George's societies due to their middle-class focus. This has led scholars to view these charities as narrow elite organizations rather than as ethnic ones.[142] It was precisely this narrowness and exclusivity – and the resulting conditional, humiliating charity – that led working-class English immigrants to establish their own associational culture based on mutual aid through the Order of the Sons of St George in the United States, and the Sons of England in Canada. Together, these two organizations eventually provided millions of dollars to support their members, and, as such, cannot be excluded from consideration if a fuller appreciation of the civic–ethnic dichotomy is to be developed. These associations, therefore, their ideals and activities, are the focus of the next chapter.

Notes

1 Kingston, Ontario, Anglican Diocese of Ontario Archives [ADOA], XM-72A, St George's Society [StGS], Kingston, Constitution, 6 April 1858, Article no. 1, p. 4.
2 The St Vincent De Paul Society, founded in 1849 to look after poor famine victims, was perhaps the period's largest example of a charity based on this type of ethos. B. Aspinwall, 'The Welfare State within the State: The Saint Vincent de Paul Society in Glasgow, 1848–1920', in W.J. Sheils and D. Wood (eds), *Voluntary Religion* (Oxford, 1986), pp. 445–59; Donald M. MacRaild, *The Irish Diaspora in Britain, 1750-1939* (2nd edn, Basingstoke, 2010), pp. 62, 81, 231.
3 The Welsh were permitted entry where they were too few to have their own society. The much older connection between England and Wales perhaps smoothed this connection, though it was not expressly referred to in these terms.
4 Gary B. Magee and Andrew S. Thompson, *Empire and Globalisation: Networks of People, Goods and Capital in the British World, c.1850–1914* (Cambridge, 2010), p. 88, n. 102.
5 Dean E. Esslinger, 'Immigration through the Port of Baltimore', in M. Mark Stolarik (ed.), *Forgotten Doors: The Other Ports of Entry to the United States* (Philadelphia, 1988), p. 65.
6 Ibid.
7 *By-Laws of the Canadian Club, with a list of officers and members* (New York, 1885). This was a social club for Canadians and former Canadian residents, the express design being to meet and aid Canadians in New York.
8 *Daily Inter Ocean*, 22 April 1895.

9 Its twentieth anniversary was remarked upon in 1875: *North American and United States Gazette* (Philadelphia), 15 December 1875.

10 *New York Times*, 6 October 1909.

11 S. Condor, 'Unimagined Community? Some Psychological Issues Concerning English National Identity', in G.M. Breakwell and E. Lyons (eds), *Changing European Identities: Social Psychological Analysis of Social Change* (Oxford, 1996); Benedict Anderson, *Imagined Communities: Reflections on the Origins and Spread of Nationalism* (London, 1983).

12 Newspapers, and later radio and television, maintained the webs. Simon Potter, *News and the British World* (Oxford, 2003); Wendy Webster, *Englishness and Empire, 1939–1965* (Oxford, 2007).

13 There is no discrete archival source base. However, several printed reports are contained in the records of various St George's societies, and handwritten references to the NAStGU are also traceable in society minute books.

14 Steven Vertovec, 'Conceiving and Researching Transnationalism', *Ethnic and Racial Studies*, 22:3 (1999), p. 447.

15 See also Alejandro Portes, 'Conclusion: Towards a New World: The Origins and Effects of Transnational Activities', *Ethnic and Racial Studies*, 22:2 (1999), p. 473.

16 Peter Clark, *British Clubs and Societies 1580–1800: The Origins of an Associational World* (Oxford, 2000), pp. 3, 388–429.

17 J. Habermas, *The Transformation of the Public Sphere* (Cambridge, MA, 1989).

18 Freemasonry in the colonies dates to 1733, when Bostonians opened the first lodge. David T. Beito, *From Mutual Aid to the Welfare State: Fraternal Society and Social Services, 1890–1967* (Chapel Hill, NC, 2000), p. 5. See Steven C. Bullock, *Revolutionary Brotherhood: Freemasonry and the Transformation of the American Social Order, 1730–1840* (Chapel Hill, NC, 1996) for the wider context.

19 The society was founded in 1657 (Rowland Berthoff, *British Immigrants in Industrial America, 1790–1850* (Cambridge, MA, 1953), p. 165), though the early history is patchy, with activities more clearly traceable from the later seventeenth century; see also John M'Culloch, *A Concise History of the United States, from the Discovery of America till 1795 ...* (Philadelphia, 1795), p. 195; Scots' Charitable Society of Boston, *The Constitution and By-Laws of the Scots' Charitable Society of Boston (Instituted 1657) with a List of Members and Officers, and many Interesting Extracts from the Original Records of the Society* (Boston, 1878). The society is still in operation today, and is the oldest charitable society in North America. See also Scots' Charitable Society, Boston, http://scots-charitable.org (last accessed 18 March 2016).

20 HSP, Welsh Society of Philadelphia, Wj 502, vol. 1 [1980]; *Pennsylvania Gazette*, quoted in George Edward Hartmann, *The Welsh Society of Philadelphia: History, Charter and By-Laws*, pamphlet produced for the 250th anniversary (Philadelphia, 1979), p. 3.

21 *New York Gazette and Weekly Post Boy*, 29 April 1762; *New York Gazette and Weekly Mercury*, 30 April 1770; St George's Society of New York, *History of St George's Society of New York, from 1770–1913* (New York, 1913), pp. 25–26.

22 St George's Society of New York, *History of St George's Society of New York*, p. 21.
23 *New York Journal*, 25 April 1771.
24 Robert N. Rosen, *A Short History of Charleston* (Columbia, 1997), p. 40. The *Charleston Mercury*, 24 April 1858, announced the 125th anniversary of the society in that city, thus corresponding to an establishment year of 1733. For the Philadelphia Society of the Sons of St George, see minute book vol. 1; this includes the minutes of the founding meeting, held on St George's Day 1772. HSP, (Phi) 1733, Sons of St George Archive. For a global perspective on English associationalism, see Tanja Bueltmann and Donald M. MacRaild, 'Globalizing St George': English Associations in the Anglo-World to the 1930s', *Journal of Global History*, 7:1 (2012), pp. 79–105 and, more extensively, Chapter 7 below.
25 Peter Thompson, '"The friendly glass": Drink and Gentility in Colonial Philadelphia', *The Pennsylvania Magazine of History and Biography*, 113:4 (October 1989), pp. 556–77.
26 *Philadelphia Inquirer*, 27 April 1798; *Poulson's American Advertiser*, 27 April 1804; *Daily News*, 25 April 1805.
27 J. Thomas Scharf and Thompson Westcott, *History of Philadelphia, 1609–1884*, 3 vols (Philadelphia, 1884), vol. 3, p. 1467.
28 Thompson, '"The friendly glass"', pp. 564–65.
29 T.C. Knauff, *A History of the Society of the Sons of St George* (Philadelphia, 1923), pp. 28–29.
30 Douglas Bradburn, *The Citizenship Revolution: Politics and the Creation of the American Union* (Charlottesville, VA, 2009), p. 212.
31 Ibid., p. 213.
32 Clark, *British Clubs and Societies*, p. 305.
33 Knauff, *A History of the Society of the Sons of St George*, p. 13.
34 Society of the Sons of St George, *Rules and Constitution of the Society of the Sons of St George* (Philadelphia, 1772), p. 6. See also the minutes of the founding meeting, held on St George's Day 1772, HSP, (PHi) 1733, Sons of St George Archive.
35 Thomas Twining, *Travels in America 100 Years Ago* (1894; Bedford, MA, 2007), pp. 88, 93, 113.
36 ADOA, XM-72A, StGS Kingston, Minutes, 'Constitution and Bye-Laws', dated 6 April 1858, p. 4.
37 ADOA, XM-72A, StGS Kingston, Article no. 3, p. 4.
38 Baltimore, Maryland Historical Society [MdHS], MS 1881, StGS Baltimore, Minutes, 19 February 1867. Quotation from Sanford, *History*, p. 6.
39 St George's Society of Baltimore, *Book of the St George's Society of Baltimore* (Baltimore, 1954), p. 5, pamphlet in MdHS, MS 1881 files.
40 ADOA, XM-72A, StGS Kingston, Article no. 5, p. 5.
41 A. Kristen Forster, *Moral Visions and Material Ambitions: Philadelphia Struggles to Define the Republic, 1776–1836* (Oxford, 2005), p. 55.
42 *The act of incorporation and bye-laws of the St George's Society of Montreal, founded by Englishmen in the year 1834, for the purpose of relieving their brethren in distress* (Montreal, 1867), pp. 3 and 8.

43 MdHS, MS 1881, StGS Baltimore, Minutes, 6 December 1866; *Constitution, by-laws and standing rules and orders of the British Columbia St George's Society* (Victoria, 1886), p. 2.

44 Robert Waller, *A Sketch of the Origin, Progress and Work of the St George's Society, A.D. 1786–1886* (New York, 1887), p. 3.

45 Berthoff, *British Immigrants*, p. 165.

46 The role of these societies was recognized by the British government, e.g. 1872 [C. 617] *Reports on the present state of Her Majesty's colonial possessions. Transmitted with the blue books for the year 1870. Part III. North American colonies; African settlements and St. Helena; Australian colonies and New Zealand; and the Mediterranean possessions, &c.*, p. 50; 1892 [C. 6795-XI] *Royal Commission on Labour. Foreign reports. Volume II. The colonies and the Indian Empire. With an appendix on the migration of labour*, p. 89; 1906 [Cd. 2979] *Departmental Committee on Agricultural Settlements in British Colonies. Minutes of evidence taken before the Departmental Committee appointed to consider Mr. Rider Haggard's report on agricultural settlements in British colonies, with appendices, analysis, and index.* II, 208, 5490.

47 St George's Society of New York, *History of St George's Society of New York*, p. 32.

48 Charles A. Murray, *Travels in North America during the years 1834, 1835, & 1836, etc.*, 2 vols (London, 1839), vol. 2, p. 293.

49 According to a history read at the annual convention of the NAStGU, 1889. *Toronto Daily Mail*, 23 August 1889, p. 5. Also in the *Ottawa Citizen*, 15 January 1946, which notes the 102nd anniversary of the city's St George's Society.

50 See for instance St George's Society of Montreal, *The Constitution and By-Laws of the St George's Society* (Montreal, 1855); also St George's Society of Quebec, *Officers and Members with the Reports* (Quebec, 1847).

51 Revd R.W. Norman, *'Our Duties and Opportunities': Annual Sermon by Rev. R. W. Norman* (Montreal, 1877), p. 4.

52 *Political Register*, 6 (1832), p. 229.

53 The refutation was delivered at their annual St George's Day dinner by My Battersby: *Political Register*, 6 (1832), p. 229.

54 HSP, (Phi) 1733, Sons of St George Archive, Stewards' Books, vol. 1, 3 May and 10 June 1861; Albion Society, *Constitution and By-Laws* (Philadelphia, 1856, 1858); Albion Society, *Constitution and By-laws of the Albion Society of Philadelphia: Together with a List of the Officers and Members in the Year 1888, and a Complete List of Members Since the Foundation of the Society* (Philadelphia, 1888).

55 'Biographical Sketch of John Thomson, A.M.', in Ellis Paxson Oberholtzer (ed.), Philadelphia: A History of the City and its People. A Record of 225 Years, 4 vols (Philadelphia, 1912), vol. 3, p. 38.

56 William E. Van Vugt, *British Buckeyes: The English, Scots, and Welsh in Ohio* (Kent, OH, 2006), p. 34.

57 *Albion*, 15 May 1841, quoted by Hanael P. Bianchi, 'St George's Day: A Cultural History', unpublished PhD thesis, Catholic University of America, 2011, p. 185.

58 Quotation from committee's report, in St George's Society of Toronto, *Charter and By-Laws, with the Report of the Committee for 1858* (Toronto, 1859), p. 15.

59 J.W. Williams, *A Sermon Preached before the St George's Society* (Quebec, 1868), p. 2.

60 Vera B. Lawrence, *Strong on Music: The New York Music Scene in the Days of George Templeton Strong* (Chicago, 1999), vol. 3: *Repercussions, 1857–1862*, pp. 224–25.

61 MdHS, MS 1881, StGS Baltimore, Members and Dues Book 1, 1901, p. 1.

62 Joan Marie Johnson, *South Carolina Women* (Athens, GA, 2009), vol. 1: *Their Lives and Times*, pp. 74–75.

63 *Wisconsin Patriot* (Madison), 23 August 1856; *Milwaukee Daily Sentinel*, 12 March, 3 April 1858.

64 *Milwaukee Daily Sentinel*, 26 April 1858.

65 *Chicago Tribune*, 2 May 1861, 26 April 1864. The fourth annual general meeting was reported in the same newspaper on 5 and 12 April 1864. Also see *Chicago Tribune*, 16, 22, 27, 28 and 31 March 1864.

66 MdHS, MS 1881, StGS Baltimore, Minute Books, 7 vols; also Bianchi, 'St George's Day', p. 185, citing Daniel E. Wager, *Our County and its People: Oneida County* (Boston, 1896), pp. 146–48.

67 *Royal Gazette*, 28 August 1860.

68 Ottawa, Library and Archives Canada [LAC], MG28-V3, StGS Ottawa, Special Meeting, 16 July 1860, p. 35.

69 *Daily Cleveland Herald*, 8 January 1864; *Milwaukee Daily Journal*, 21 April 1890; *Little Rock Daily Arkansas Gazetteer*, 27 December 1874; *Knoxville Journal*, 8 February 1918.

70 *Salt Lake City Intermountain and Colorado Catholic*, 24 March 1900; *Los Angeles Times*, 24 April 1885, 6 April 1887, 1 January 1891, 25 April 1895, 25 April 1904. See also David Emmons, *The Butte Irish: Class and Ethnicity in an American Mining Town 1875–1925* (Urbana, 1989).

71 Scharf and Westcott, *History of Philadelphia*, vol. 3, p. 1467.

72 Charles S. Olton, *Artisans for Independence: Philadelphia Mechanics and the American Revolution* (Syracuse, NY, 1975), pp. 33–34.

73 Ibid., p. 34.

74 *Manitoba Free Press*, 24 April 1882.

75 For Freemasonry, see Jessica L. Harland-Jacobs, *Builders of Empire: Freemasonry and British Imperialism, 1717–1927* (Chapel Hill, NC, 2007). On the Atlantic reach of Orangeism, see Jessica L. Harland-Jacobs, '"Maintaining the Connexion": Orangeism in the British North Atlantic World,' *Atlantic Studies*, 5 (April 2008), pp. 27–49, Donald. M. MacRaild, 'Orangeism in the Atlantic World', in David T. Gleeson (ed.), *The Irish in the Atlantic World* (Columbia, SC, 2010), pp. 307–26; Kevin Kenny, *The American Irish: A History* (New York, 2000), pp. 195–96.

76 Donald M. MacRaild, *Faith, Fraternity and Fighting: The Orange Order and Irish Migrants in Northern England, c.1850–1906* (Liverpool, 2005), ch. 8.

77 *Washington Post*, 20 May 1882; *Evening Critic* (Washington), 20 May 1882.

78 *Ottawa Daily Citizen*, 26 August 1880.

79 *Manitoba Free Press*, 24 April 1882.
80 Bianchi, 'St George's Day', pp. 185–87, offers a brief outline of the NAStGU.
81 Royal Society of St George, *Annual Report and Year Book 1904* (London, 1904), p. 64.
82 North America St George's Union, *Report of the Fifth Annual Convention, held at St George's Hall, Philadelphia, PA, September 12th, 13th and 14th, 1877* (Bridgeport, CT, 1877), pp. 12–16.
83 *Toronto Daily Mail*, 21 August 1889.
84 *Chicago Daily Times*, 9 March 1873.
85 See letters from the NAStGU to the Society of the Sons of St George, Philadelphia, HSP, (Phi) 1733, Sons of St George Archive, Minute Books, vol. 6, 1888.
86 Handbill: a report by members of the delegation at the 'St George's Convention, 1878 to St George's Society, Kingston', ADOA, XM-72B, StGS Kingston, dated 3 September 1878.
87 *Bulletin of the Bureau of Labor Statistics of New York*, vol. 2 (Albany, 1901), p. 270.
88 North America St George's Union, *Report of the Fifth Annual Convention*, p. 7.
89 *Philadelphia Inquirer*, 12 September 1877; *New York Times*, 13 September 1877.
90 *British Daily Whig*, 4 April 1877.
91 *New York Evening Express*, 11 September 1879; history of the conventions, *Evening Critic* (Washington), 20 May 1882.
92 *New York Times*, 11 September 1879.
93 *Evening Critic* (Washington), 20 May 1880.
94 For example the Philadelphia Sons of St George's Society wrote to the *Manchester Guardian* in 1874 to discourage migration. Reported in the *Freeman's Journal*, 18 August 1874. Also see 1878–79 [C. 2372] *Eighth annual report of the Local Government Board*, British Parliamentary Papers, p. 152, letter from the St George's Society, Toronto, complaining at rates of pauper migration to Canada.
95 *Newark Daily Advocate*, 4 April 1884.
96 *Brooklyn Eagle*, 20 May 1884.
97 Gregory S. Kealey, *Toronto Workers Respond to Capitalism, 1867–1892* (Toronto, 1980), p. 233.
98 *Petersburg Index and Appeal*, 16 December 1876.
99 *Petersburg Index and Appeal*, 8 September 1877; *New York Herald*, 14 September 1877; *New York Evening Times*, 14 September 1877.
100 *British Daily Whig*, 3 April 1878.
101 *New York Times*, 27 August 1886.
102 *Washington Critic*, 29 August 1888; *Washington Post*, 30 August 1888.
103 *Philadelphia Inquirer*, 30 August 1880.
104 *New York Times*, 24 April 1883.
105 *Philadelphia Inquirer*, 30 August 1888.
106 Handbill, ADOA, XM-72B, StGS Kingston. The description of the extent of the St George's society movement is the fullest we have before the setting up of the London-based society in the mid-1890s.

107 Ibid.
108 *New York Times*, 11 September 1879.
109 *North American* (Philadelphia), 21 August 1880; *New York Times*, 25 August 1880.
110 *Washington Post*, 29 August 1888.
111 *Chicago Daily Tribune*, 28 August 1891.
112 For example at Oswego in 1891. *Oswego Palladium*, 28 August 1891.
113 Letters from the NAStGU to the Society of the Sons of St George, Philadelphia, HSP, (PHi) 1733, Sons of St George Archive, Minute Books, vol. 6, 1888; *North American* (Philadelphia), 21 August 1880; *Chicago Daily Times*, 20 August 1884; *Daily Evening Bulletin* (San Francisco), 18 April 1877; *North American* Philadelphia), 21 August 1880.
114 ADOA, XM-72B, StGS Kingston, Minutes, Annual Meeting, 5 April 1881.
115 MdHS, MS 1881, StGS Baltimore, Minutes, 19 July 1879, p. 26.
116 Ibid., 23 April 1883.
117 Ibid., 29 August 1883.
118 This, and the previous quotations, from *Ottawa Daily Citizen*, 25 August 1880.
119 National Archives and Records Administration, Washington, DC; *Index to New England Naturalization Petitions, 1791–1906 (M1299)*, microfilm serial M1299, microfilm roll 22, L523, vol. 2, p. 235, 16 October 1884.
120 *Washington Post*, 25 July 1881.
121 Ibid., 24 April 1881.
122 *Philadelphia Inquirer*, 25 July 1881.
123 *Evening Critic* (Washington), 20 May 1882.
124 *Toronto Daily Mail*, 17 May 1882.
125 *Critic-Record* (Washington), 24 May 1882.
126 This, and the previous quotation, from *Evening Critic* (Washington), 20 May 1882.
127 *Oswego Daily Times*, 26 August 1891; *Daily Inter Ocean* (Chicago), 28 August 1891.
128 *Oswego Daily Times*, 26 August 1891.
129 Smythe appeared in the records of the Kingston St George's Society at least to the mid-1870s: report of annual meeting, *British Daily Whig*, 5 April 1876.
130 Bianchi, 'St George's Day', p. 186. Bianchi cites Knauff for this fact, but Knauff, in fact, refers to how the NAStGU 'finally held' a meeting in Philadelphia, having twice before planned to do so without it happening. Knauff, *History of the Society of the Sons of St George*, p. 74.
131 *Philadelphia Inquirer*, 11 September 1902.
132 *Saint Paul Globe*, 3 September 1904.
133 *The English Race*, 2:9 (January 1911), p. 22.
134 Toronto, City of Toronto Archives [CTA], Series 1093, StGS Toronto Records, File 26, Monthly Meetings Minutes, 1908–20, 4 March 1910, p. 41.
135 *The English Race*, January 1911, p. 22.
136 Ibid.
137 Ibid.

138 Ibid.
139 Ibid.
140 CTA, Series 1093, StGS Toronto, File 26, Monthly Meetings Minutes, 1908–20, 2 December 1910, p. 53.
141 Ibid., 6 January 1910, p. 57.
142 Charlotte Erickson, 'English', in Stephan Thernstrom, Ann Orlov and Oscar Handlin (eds), *Harvard Encyclopaedia of American Ethnic Groups* (2nd edn, Cambridge, MA, 1980), p. 333.

3

Independent and sectarian:
working-class English associational culture

In the early 1870s, English associational culture took a significant new turn with the formation of two parallel, though nearly identical, associations in the United States and Canada. The OSStG was established in 1870 in the coalfield communities of Pennsylvania; and four years later, in 1874, the Sons of England Benefit Society held its inaugural meeting in Toronto. Within ten years, these would become the largest English associations in the world – far outmatching the St George's societies. Members of both the OSStG and the Sons of England wore 'elaborate badges of the order with the famous words: "Honi Soit Qui Mal Y Pense"' ('shamed be he that thinks evil of it').[1] The motto also could be seen, from early 1904, on the masthead of the *Sons of England Record*, the Sons' official journal. These words, first associated with the medieval Order of the Garter, were neither idly acquired nor accidentally adopted. Heraldic and knightly orders, like latter-day confraternities, were noted for ritualized secrecy and oath-bound loyalty. What connected the medieval and the modern manifestations was this aspect 'of an ethical integrity that can turn into secrecy',[2] for this underpinned forged bonds of fraternity and, later, sorority.

The emergence of the OSStG and the Sons of England marked a shift in English associational culture in North America. The elite charities named for St George remained a strong and persistent force, but these were middle-class and civic-elite instances of 'hierarchical' aid, where moral as well as financial judgements often were passed upon passive recipients who requested help. Now, in the 1870s, the elite charities were outmatched by these new English ethnic friendly societies that offered 'reciprocal' – that is, collective – self-help in the form of members-only mutual aid.[3] Societies such as the OSStG and Sons of England were part of a large and growing body of North American confraternal membership organizations with initiation rituals, highly sculpted ceremonies, rigorous rules and customs and masonic-style paraphernalia. They expressed independence of spirit and guarded against the vagaries of the workplace, unemployment, injury and sickness by their mutual funds. These monies aided only those who paid in, and their families, when members were sick or had died. In essence, they offered the obverse of the charity of the St George's societies.

Such enterprises were not new. Workingmen in Europe had for centuries nurtured guilds and societies that provided a collective shield against the caprices of life. These were, like the organizations that followed them, a 'risk-sharing' enterprise.[4] In nineteenth-century Britain, such ventures became increasingly popular as expanding numbers of workers were pressed together in larger units of production, with paid work, and reliance upon wages, reducing the independence of the ordinary man and woman. Collective self-help occurred most notably through the independent orders, such as the Oddfellows and Foresters, but also in many other lesser societies.[5] Indeed, 'the idea of fraternity, and how to organize it, was one of nineteenth-century Europe's most visible exports to the New World'.[6] One strategy was for existing friendly societies that gathered funds from members (and for the benefit of members) to be transported overseas, as indeed many were.[7] Another tactic was to form new organizations, so that, by later in the century, a plethora of local, regional and national organizations such as these existed in Canada and especially the United States. Newspapers in the United States reported the activities of dozens of local branches of national orders dubbed 'secret societies' on account of their closed initiation ceremonies and regular rituals and rites.[8] Organized by trade, ethnicity or religion, they sought fastness, trust and durability through strong memberships and sound finances. They also offered social connections, activities, sports and leisure pursuits. In sum, they became lynchpins of the modern, urban 'subscriber democracy'.[9]

Given their remarkable similarities, it is possible that there was some umbilical link between the OSStG and Sons of England. It could be that English immigrants who had spent time in the United States and migrated (or re-migrated) north to Canada had experience of the OSStG and so introduced a nearly identical organization there. The American–Canadian border was a permeable one, with Canadians forming a significant component of the immigrant populations of major United States towns and cities, especially in the Great Lakes region.[10] It is difficult to imagine that two groups with such similar rules, rituals, restrictions and ambitions could have developed in parallel, just four years apart, without any mutual knowledge. However, this research has uncovered no such organic connections. Later in the century, the two groups came into regular contact and considered merging. This was prevented by one insurmountable point of difference: the OSStG's perfectly realistic admittance of United States citizens as well as British subjects. For the

Sons of England, members could only be British. What emerges, then, is a parallel development that began on a relatively small and localized scale in both countries, but which soon grew into simultaneous nationwide organizations. The Sons of England even extended overseas to South Africa and, to a lesser extent, Australia.

As these two societies evolved, they adopted many of the same outward strategies and roles as the St George's societies. Dinners, events, excursions and the hosting of prominent visitors all became part of their social calendars. Such blurring continued with the investment, by both the OSStG and the Sons of England, in hospitals, orphanages, burial plots and gifts to the poor of England, especially during wartime. Charity-versus-self-help, however, continued to divide the two communities of interest in North American English associational culture.[11] While the St George's societies reminded the world of their members' ethnicity through their high-profile acts of civic celebration, and although they catered for the wider English immigrant community with important charity, ultimately they were a preserve of elites. Contact with the ordinary worker was primarily restricted to dispensing hand-outs when times were hard.

English ethnic mutual associations evinced a strong class ethos. Indeed, the development of this type of friendly society suggested the English were capable of matching groups by coalescing along ethnic lines. Such fraternity also shows that, unlike Gutman's 'new industrial workers', many English immigrants *were* 'associated with industrial necessities and the industrial ethos'.[12] Certainly, classes of workers such as textile operators – among whom the English were pioneers – were at the forefront of collectivized mutual aid. Little wonder then that the OSStG would branch out quickly to New England and New York State, where such workers were found in profusion. Even less surprisingly, the OSStG and Sons of England developed broader bases of support than the elite associations we have previously explored, something we ascribe directly to the socio-economic profile of their memberships. Poorer members were much less likely to remain involved in charitable societies because their own finances often were only marginally less parlous than those of the people they helped. Once they were in an ethnic friendly society, however, the benefits of membership came into play precisely when members were pinched by unemployment or sickness. The effect, therefore, was the opposite of that which pressured charities such as the St George's societies: instead of difficult circumstances weakening bonds (as occurred with trade unions), they strengthened them.

Although the OSStG and Sons of England differed from the St George's societies over the issue of charity, more prosperous men could be members of both. Abel Robinson, who died on St George's Day 1915, was a long-standing member of the St George's Society of Toronto and also was said to be 'present at the formation of the Order [of the Sons of England] in 1874'.[13] There certainly was overlapping membership, and this was matched at the organizational level, when St George's societies and OSStG or Sons of England lodges shared pews for church services, or when, in 1890, the Sons of England and the St George's Society in Manitoba attended the same charitable smoking concert in the hall of another membership association, the Knights of Phythias.[14] Both the Sons of England and the OSStG thus served as a locus of collective memory and sociability, aiding their members in keeping alive a connection with England, its culture and heritage, providing a principal cornerstone that made a diaspora.[15]

The following discussion charts the rise and development of the Sons of England and OSStG. Critically, their expansion is illustrative of the realities of English immigrant experiences. The extensive range and durable character of these societies make notions of the invisibility of the English seem a yet more distant and untenable conceptualization of the immigrants' lives. Overall, the two Sons' organizations in the United States and Canada not only grew much larger than the St George's societies, but also, in the early 1900s, drew support away from the charitable form of ethnic consciousness. While both the Sons of England and OSStG illustrated ethnic responses to class imperatives, sectarian tension (and open aggression) between the English and Irish was an important factor shaping the OSStG in its early years. In the context of turbulent labour relations in the anthracite mining regions of Pennsylvania an emotional and practical blend of Old World customs, traditional ethnic community cleavages and variant responses to labour organization, both open and clandestine, caused enduring hostilities. Such divisions promoted battles between workers on ethnic and class lines, as well as more sharply defined hierarchical conflicts with employers. For over a decade straddling the 1860s and 1870s, America's formative labour conflict unfolded with the customary disconnections of English/British-versus-Irish animosity exuding a powerful influence on the course of events.[16]

The emergence of the Benevolent Order of the Sons of St George

The OSStG was, then, born out of a heightening ethnic consciousness. Conflict had been a feature of urban life for the English and Irish, both Protestants and Catholics, back home and where Irish immigrants met a hostile host in the industrial community of England, Wales and Scotland. Such divisions were carried with emigrants to the United States, and were reformulated in new communities such as those of the coalfields.

Table 3.1 *British-born and Irish-born in the major United States centres of English associational activity: overview, 1860–1900*

	English-born	% Eng	Scots-born	% Scots	Welsh-born	% Welsh	British-born	% Brit	Irish-born	% Irish	TOTAL	No. of cities
1860	109,711	12.3	27,911	3.1			137,622	15.5	615,564	69.1	890,808	25
1870	137,033	15.5	35,145	4.0	10,591	1.2	182,769	20.6	704,033	79.4	886,802	28
1890	169,033	18.2	40,671	4.4	11,527	1.2	222,165	23.8	711,443	76.2	933,608	26
1890	242,111	22.6	70,556	6.6	13,083	1.2	325,750	30.4	744,767	69.6	1,070,517	32

Sources: Bureau of Census data, 1860–1900, cited in Table 1.6–1.11. The cities chosen (25–34 in number) qualify by having English associations and being big enough to warrant individual recording in each relevant census.

Ethnicity thus separated workers who otherwise shared sectional and class interests. The result quite was probably a benefited American capitalism through fractured unionism.

If ethnic tensions were enduringly strong in Britain in the period after the Irish famine, what erupted in the Pennsylvanian anthracite coal-mining districts, in the 1860s and 1870s, was far more serious. The focal point was the town of Scranton, Pennsylvania, where Irish-born and British-born communities were closer in size than in most other urban centres. The norm was that the Irish, driven to migrate in huge numbers by famine and hardship, would be three to four times more numerous than the British-born, as Table 3.1 shows. At Scranton, as the balance was more even, resulting in much deeper-seated and durable tension than might be expected if one community far outmatched the other (see Table 3.2).

Scranton was home to overlapping and connected traditions within systems of labour organization. The town and its mining environs gained national notoriety for harbouring a movement of violent proto-trade unionists, mostly Irishmen, who imported some of the techniques and tactics of particularly Ulster Ribbonism to industrial and communal relations in the new community.[17] These were the Molly Maguires. As with the strategies adopted by later Fenian operatives, the Mollys used legitimate fronts to hide their activities.[18] The core of activists proffered vigorous, sometimes violent collectivism in which the mystique of the oath- and ritual-bound secret society was blurred with primitive trade unionism. It was in places such as Scranton that miners who had known each other in England or Ireland – Irishmen, Welshmen and Cornishmen – once more found themselves mixing in close proximity and characteristically uneasy relations.[19]

Table 3.2 *British- and Irish-born populations of Scranton, Pennsylvania, 1860-90*

	Born in England	Born in Wales	Born in Scotland	Born in Britain	Born in Ireland	Irish:British ratio[a]
1870	1,445	4,177	366	5,988	6,491	1.08:1
1880	1,558	3,616	301	5,475	6,772	1.23:1
1890	3,065	4,890	575	8,530	8,340	0.97:1
1900	3,692	4,621	576	8,889	7,198	0.81:1

[a]This column represents the ratio of Irish-born to British-born.

Sources: Bureau of Census: 1870: *Ninth Census,* vol. 1: *The Statistics of the Population of the United States ...*, 'Nativities of the Population of Principal Cities', table VIII: fifty cities, pp. 388-89; 1880: *Statistics of the Population of the United States at the Tenth Census,* table XVI, 'Foreign-born population of fifty principal cities', p. 540; 1890: *Report of the Population of the United States at the Eleventh Census,* table 34, 'Foreign-born Population Distributed According to Country of Birth for Cities Having 20,000 Inhabitants or More', pp. 670-71, 674-75; 1900: *Census Reports,* vol. I, *Twelfth Census of the United States,* table 35, 'Foreign born population distributed according to country of birth for Cities having 25,000 inhabitants or more', pp. 796-803.

Scranton also gave rise to a strong, but at this point protean, labour movement that outwardly derived more from orthodox class-based precedents. Indeed, it is reasonable to assert that the Molly Maguires were as much an Irish element of the miners' trade union, the Workers' Benevolent Association, as they were an instance of Irish Ribbonism adopted in and adapted to American mining capitalism.[20] Equally, English workers had their own clandestine societies from which protean, new unions were born, but these deepened sectarian cleavages by tending not to include or attract Irishmen.[21] Their Irish associations derived from their responsibility for a dozen or more deaths; in other facets they were like primitive trade unions elsewhere in America, Britain and Ireland. The Mollys represented worker interests against local authorities, mining chiefs and their agents and managers; they meted out numerous lesser acts of violence and intimidation. The Irish elements sought reprisals for discrimination and poor working conditions against Welsh and English foremen, policemen and workers. What Kenny describes as a more specific story of the emergence of a protean trade union movement, others – both contemporaries and historians working prior to him – viewed as an essentially Irish Catholic, pro-nationalist conspiracy of secrecy and violence.[22] In this regard, they looked like Ribbonmen on the Irish canals or the union of English saw-grinders in Sheffield, who tyrannized labour with techniques known as 'carding' and 'rattening' whereby men were warned, threatened and beaten to maintain union discipline and control of the labour supply and wages.[23] Ultimately, the work of the Mollys mixed clandestine Irish rural tactics – attacking the agents of tyrants, rather than the tyrants themselves, striking out at authority figures, engaging in petty crime that turned violent. Certainly, the Mollys suggest that class and ethnic considerations cannot easily be unpicked from each other.

Scranton also witnessed apparent class-oriented developments that immediately became mired in ethnic issues. The town was the site of a famous attempt to develop a grand union of all workers, the Knights of Labor. The Knights' pedigree made them an unlikely attraction to English workers. Their leader, Terence V. Powderly, the son of Irish immigrant parents, was closely involved in the Land League and Clan-na-Gael. He battled against claims that his politics and industrial relations work were merely extensions of the code of the Molly Maguires.[24] Powderly's position as rising star of the Knights of Labor helped him in 1878 to win the mayoralty of Scranton on a Greenback-Labour ticket.[25] From its base in the Pennsylvania anthracite fields the Knights spread to other mining districts, most spectacularly throughout the hard-rock fields of the American west.[26] The OSStG spread through the same mining regions, and was principally associated, in its initial forays, with 'Cousin Jacks', Cornish miners – men who, like the Welsh, were common in Pennsylvania, but also in Upper Peninsula, Michigan, and the western mining belt.[27]

Resistance to the Mollys was broad-based and went beyond Welsh and Cornish miners and included the hierarchy of the Catholic Church, which generally proscribed such clandestine and violent association. At a service on 21 December 1875, at the Catholic church in Mahoney Plain, Pennsylvania, the Revd Daniel O'Connell 'read a letter from the archbishop of Philadelphia, which was a formal excommunication of the society known as the Molly Maguires, otherwise the Ancient Order of Hibernians'.[28] More specifically, Bishop O'Hara of Scranton, who had given favour to the Order for several years, excommunicated its members, who he said had 'deceived him as to the real character of the organization': that is, as a front for the Mollys.[29] At the community and neighbourhood level, however, there was a different perspective. It caused some bitterness among the English and Welsh that Irishmen and women with no apparent connection to the Mollys kept quiet about the identities of men they knew were involved, while 'two of the known murderers and their families were quietly spirited away from the processes of the law'.[30] Such rumours merely enforced the general climate of conflict that saw Cornish and Welsh miners demonstrate little pan-Celtic brotherhood towards the Irish on account of religious differences, occupational competition and Old World grievances reintroduced to the mining belts of Pennsylvania, upper Michigan and the west.[31] Irish miners in Cork worked for English, Welsh and Cornish owners, or in pits often financed by British capital; and Cornish elite miners were found in the Cork mines in the first half of the nineteenth century, receiving more than three times the monthly pay of their Irish peers. Resulting enmities travelled with the migrants, as O'Neill's work demonstrates.[32]

The murderous behaviour of Pennsylvanian Irish workers, some of whom were still British subjects, drew the attentions of the British Consul-General in Philadelphia, R.C. Clipperton, who described 'the well-remembered "Molly Maguires"' as 'an organization of assassins said to be a wing of the Ancient Order of Hibernians'.[33] At the very least, the Mollys diverted energy from the Order, albeit temporarily.[34] The consul was probably the first external agent to describe the English response to the Mollys, though recent scholarship suggests he generally had relied on paid informers, raising some questions about his evidence.[35] He noted that British and some American workers of English descent got together to form the OSStG as a counter to the Mollys, after 'three Englishmen were brutally murdered in the coal regions' of Pennsylvania.[36]

The story is not so straightforward. Some disagreement exists as to whether the Mollys were the catalyst, or merely a later focus for attention. Moreover, even if sectarianism lit the touch-paper for the OSStG, it is also the case that more prosaic, class-based considerations underpinned the durability of what, ultimately, became a friendly society for Englishmen. For immigrant workers in a tough, alien environment, with few friends or networks, both camaraderie and financial good sense added to the appeal of the mutual aid society.[37] Social events, such as banquets, were common, (Figure 3.1). Moreover, the sectarian explanation of the OSStG is countered by a different version of events, which dates the OSStG very precisely to unfortunate events on the evening of 4 June 1870 when, after a boozy pub crawl, a Cornishman called Benjamin Jaco accidentally locked out his roommate, Williams. Williams, quite possibly a Welshmen, apparently swore to get even with Jaco, and some weeks later the two men argued in a pub 'frequented by Englishmen' and Williams shot Jaco dead.[38] It was said that the English then gathered under the leadership of Thomas R. Lyddon to ensure that the dead man, who had no friends or family in the United States, was given a decent burial. Other sources credit Joseph Davenport and William Maylin with the society's foundation.[39] A civic history of Scranton noted the presence of these two men, and another ten, as the founders who received the first charter.[40] Still other narratives claimed Williams had many influential friends in Scranton whom were likely to protect him.[41] Corruption certainly seems to have been a common beef on the coalfields in these times, with Welsh and English magistrates, cops and managers roundly condemned. Certainly, regardless of origins, the Irish, Welsh and English lined up in ethnic formation using whatever influence they had among office-holders or the general population to protect their interests. Usually these expressions of collective self-interest fell along ethnic fault-lines.

The OSStG gained a reputation for vigilance against the Irish. Despite later moderation, it never entirely lost this feature. The OSStG announced itself as exclusively English (though it was not, since Americans could join). It also averred a Protestant exclusivity, through which both the Sons of St George and the Sons of England expressed their national identity and occasionally their prejudices. Their lodge names generally spoke only of English places, heroes and ideals. Many Sons of England lodges adopted names of towns and counties, such as three of the four original lodges, which called themselves Kent, Middlesex and Essex. Both organizations chose iconic English heroes or royalty, such as Cromwell, Queen Victoria, Nelson, Charles Dickens and the Duke of Cornwall. Still other lodges chose timeless classics, such as Albion, Anglo-Saxon, Old England, Commonwealth, Hearts of Oak, St George, Britannia and British Lion.[42]

In many ways, and deliberately so, the English association was the inverse of the Irish and Catholic Molly Maguires. While it is no surprise to find that the Irish fell back on a century-long tradition of clandestine resistance to the perceived exercise of arbitrary power by Scranton's local administrators and officials, this was more of a novelty for the English. English class fault-lines had resulted in sometimes highly organized, clandestine behaviour among English trade unionists, radicals and rural redressers; but organizing in this way along ethnic lines was new. What the English (that is, mostly Cornish) and their Welsh neighbours faced in these anthracite coalfields was an imported Irish tradition of clandestine resistance to authority, and they came up with a collective response formalized in an association that matched this tradition.

Canada's Sons of England Benefit Society

The Canadian context for the Sons of England was nowhere near as tense as that which spawned the OSStG. However, the founders of the Sons of England did perceive a climate of anti-Englishness as well as a degree of ethnic competition in which the English were bearing up poorly against others from the British and Irish Isles and beyond. Indeed, various extant constitutions note the existence of these societies for the Scots, Irish, Germans and others. The founders were George F. Carrette, a bricklayer from Middlesex, and G.B. Brooks, a book-keeper from Nottinghamshire.[43] These men established Court Albion no. 1 of the Sons of England with seven Middlesex men, all but two of whom were unemployed. Elliott correctly sees the Sons as emerging from an English tradition of mutual self-help where confraternity was favoured over charity, with charity viewed as undesirable and weak.[44]

The Sons of England, unlike their St George's society peers, were not an elite: their most elevated members were foremen or from the lower middle class of traders and small businessmen, rather than the true men of influence. Indeed, the organization's strengths included the fact that butchers, agents, higher-ranking blue-collar workers and clerks joined lodges side by side with labourers. Indeed, the sheer size of the Sons of England suggests a continued and growing appeal to ordinary workers, even though some of the leading lights became quite wealthy. The Sons of England was not as large or influential as the Orange Order, Elliott tells us, but its membership ran into tens of thousands and spread nation-wide, from British Columbia to the Maritimes.[45] Friendly-society aspects offered protection that independently minded individuals desired. Once in a lodge, the natural inclination was to continue paying to maintain access to funds. The several hundred members of the seven lodges of Ottawa City and the Ottawa Valley included some middle-class pro-fessions.[46] The same also was true (though less so) of the five lodges in Ottawa and one in Hull, Ontario, in 1899. Here, among 299 members, we find an array of trades mixed with white-collar workers, some profession-als and many unskilled. Thus, 21 out of 299 (7 per cent) of members were listed as carpenters, 4 per cent were butchers, and only a few less were skilled machinists (see Table 3.3). However, the remainder cut in various directions and included the unskilled and the better off. The largest single group, for example, were labourers (9.7 per cent), while civil servants and clerks together were equal second with 8.7 per cent. Shopkeepers, traders, merchants and manufactures accompanied clerks, journalists, physicians, editors and funeral directors; these in turn met in lodges with plumbers, firemen, cab-drivers and clergymen. What strikes the observer is not the members' particular classes, but the sheer range of crafts and occupations present, from the presumably comfortably off estate agent to the more modestly remunerated caretaker.

Ethnicity was an impermeable membership barrier for both the OSStG and the Sons of England. From inception, both excluded even other Britons and certainly the Irish. Only Englishmen, their sons and their grandsons were admitted. Even the otherwise usually fellow-travelling Irish Protestants could not be admitted. For the Sons of England, it was just the same: membership was restricted to 'Englishmen and their descendants',[47] and this was closely adhered to. The St George's societies could be more open in this respect, customarily accepting, certainly in the early years of their development, Welsh members.[48]

Both the Sons of England and the OSStG upheld religious quali-fications. Intrinsically entwined with loyalty to the crown, the Sons of England, for example, firmly expressed that it 'owes allegiance to God and the Protestant religion'.[49] In this, the Sons' societies were both like the Orange Order. Equally, English independent orders had

Figure 3.1 Banquet given by the Order of the Sons of St George, St George's Day, 23 April 1904, Auditorium, Chicago (image courtesy of Library of Congress, PAN SUBJECT – Groups no. 289 (E size) [P&P])

elaborate and mysterious initiation ceremonies, paraphernalia and rituals. The early historian, himself a member, captures the essence of a secret, ritual-bound society well: '[at the second meeting] certain secret work was adopted, consisting of a pass-word, raps for admission, a grip, a sign of recognition and a salutation sign. No badge or regalia was decided upon, save the adoption of a broad blue sash.'[50] Inner and Outer Guards were appointed to make sure meetings could take place without intruders, with the latter responsible for 'prevent[ing] the intrusion of all improper or disorderly characters, and under no pretense [sic] whatever, be on duty without wearing regalia'.[51] While this changed as time went by, many lodges certainly continued to be wary of too much public knowledge of their activities. In Calgary, for example, Bro. Beaufort moved in early November 1890 'that no communication be given to the newspapers without permission of the Lodge'.[52] In any case there was an immediate reason for a degree of secrecy: it was meant 'to enable us to protect each other and prevent imposition'.[53]

The Sons of England relaxed the English-only requirements as time went by. In the 1892 version of their constitution, for example, they were expressly admitting 'Welshmen and those from the Isle of Man, Anglesey and the Channel Islands'.[54] Moreover, in the United States, the OSStG (like American St George's societies) allowed naturalized American citizens of English birth to join. To the Sons in Canada, however, British citizenship was a critical requirement. In a country that was still part of

Table 3.3 *Occupations of the Sons of England, Canada, 1899: Ottawa and Hull*

	Ottawa					Hull		
	Derby Lodge No. 30	Bowood Lodge No. 44	Stanley Lodge No. 55	Russell Lodge No. 56	Queen's Own Lodge No. 233	Tennyson Lodge No. 165	Total	%
Labourer	7		3	2	2	15	29	9.7
Carpenter, wood, etc.	10	2		2	7		21	7.0
Clerk	1	1	1	4	7	1	15	5.0
Butcher	8	2	2				12	4.0
Machinist	4	2	4		1		11	3.7
Civil servant	2	9					11	3.7
Driver	3		3		1	1	8	2.3
Baker	4		2	1			7	2.3
Painter	3				3	1	7	2.3
Physician/surgeon	1	2	2		2		7	2.3
Papermaker						7	7	2.3
Messenger	2	1	2		1		6	2.0
Gardener	4			1			5	1.7
Coachman	3			1		1	5	1.7
Printer	3	1	1				5	1.7
Merchant	3	2					5	1.7

Bookbinder	1	4				5	1.7
Tailor	3	1				4	1.3
Fitter	2	2				4	1.3
Grocer	1	1		1	1	4	1.3
Clergy	1	1		1	1	4	1.3
Moulder	2		1			3	1.0
Stonecutter/mason	2				1	3	1.0
Agent	2	1				3	1.0
Manufacture	1	1		1		3	1.0
Blacksmith	1		2			3	1.0
Engineer	1	1		1		3	1.0
Waiter	1	1	1			3	1.0
Bricklayer	1			1	1	3	1.0
Caretaker		1	1	1		3	1.0
Confectioner	2					2	0.7
Firemen	2					2	0.7
Watchman	1			1		2	0.7
Gunsmith	1	1				2	0.7
Salesman	1			1		2	0.7
Gilder	1				1	2	0.7

(Continued)

Table 3.3 (Continued)

| | Ottawa | | | | Hull | | | |
	Derby Lodge No. 30	Bowood Lodge No. 44	Stanley Lodge No. 55	Russell Lodge No. 56	Queen's Own Lodge No. 233	Tennyson Lodge No. 165	Total	%
Storeman	1		1				2	0.7
Funeral director	1	1					2	0.7
Shipper	1	1					2	0.7
Manager	1	1					2	0.7
Plumber	1				1		2	0.7
Press		1	1				2	0.7
Book-keeper		1			1		2	0.7
Real estate agent		2					2	0.7
Saddler		1	1				2	0.7
Porter				1	1		2	0.7
Other							58	19.4
TOTAL							299	99.9

Source: Sons of England, Business Directory of the Sons of England for the Cities of Ottawa and Hull (Ottawa, 1898), pp. 7–29.

the British Empire, and whose head of state was the British monarch, there simply was no question of naturalizing.

With their lodge systems, initiation, rituals and ceremonial form these two organizations also upheld the mysteries associated with the masons, Orange Order and other apparently similar secret, oath-bound or friendly societies.[55] They were not secret societies so much as slightly mysterious. After all the Sons of England happily announced meetings in local papers and reports on their activities circulated widely.[56] Their version of secrecy sought to excite inquisitiveness and to pique interest so that new people would join. That said, societies with initiation ceremonies also risked criticism or ridicule. This undoubtedly occurred in 1896 at Waltham, Massachusetts, when a bizarre story emerged claiming two men were 'seriously assaulted and branded upon the body with red hot irons while being initiated into Victoria lodge, [of the] Sons of St George'. The judge heard their claims in secret session. 'The evidence', it was reported, 'is alleged to be very damaging to the officers of the lodge'.[57] As much as outsiders liked to imagine that these mysterious rites were like this, few actually were. Nothing more was reported of this case.

St George's societies had been collaborating closely through the NAStGU since the early 1870s.[58] In 1894 the London-based RSStG emerged, and it eventually functioned as a global umbrella for many.[59] Despite this, the St George's societies were neither governed as uniformly nor as closely connected through organizational structures as the Sons of England. They comprised the Supreme Grand Lodge, Grand Lodge and subordinate lodges; presidents were at the helm of the day-to-day business, each being supported by vice-presidents, a secretary, a treasurer and a committee. Subordinate lodges, who governed many of their own affairs directly, normally met twice a month. In Moose Jaw, Saskatchewan, the local lodge decided to meet every second and fourth Saturday of the month, renting the local masonic hall,[60] while further west the meetings of Pride of the Island Lodge in Victoria, British Columbia, took place at St George's Hall on the first and third Wednesday of the month, starting at 7.45 p.m.[61] Apart from these localized activities there were also district meetings in areas with a larger number of lodges, as well as annual (and from 1900, bi-annual) meetings of the Supreme Grand Lodge. Composed of delegates from all lodges, the Supreme Grand Lodge conventions were sizeable gatherings, organized and hosted by a different lodge in a different location on each occasion, as at Calgary, 1983. (see Figure 3.2).

The spread and growth of organized English ethnicity

In the first few months, the OSStG was small and regionally limited, primarily spreading within Pennsylvania, to such places as Hazleton,

Figure 3.2 Officers of Calgary Lodge No. 240, Sons of England Benefit Society, Calgary, Alberta, 1903 (image courtesy of Glenbow Archives, PB-165–1)

Pittston, Carbondale and Mahonoy City. Developments thereafter were rapid. As early as January 1872, a regional Grand Lodge was organized on the coalfield, with a 'full board of officers'. Later in the same year, the organization spread to New York and New England, and in August a Supreme Lodge was founded at Providence, Rhode Island.[62] Sources also point to developments much further afield, with a flourishing culture in Salt Lake City, Ogden and elsewhere in Utah (Map 3.1).[63]

From inception, the Order emphasized benevolence and collective self-help. While the initial context had been one of sectarian conflict, the Order also shifted to the cultural dimensions of ethnicity: 'the families of the various lodges meet together socially on stated occasions, thereby keeping live the English love of the country and the festivities of her fête days'.[64] In addition, the social class of the Order was extended in the early 1880s. This was reflected, for example, in the decision by the New York St George's Society to make an annual donation of $150 for a labour bureau – an act that suggested strong relations between the two different types of English organizations. The bureau was organized by the Order, which counted among its members 'a great many employers of labour' who were behind the idea of harmonizing labour supply and demand.[65]

In Canada, westward expansion carried the Sons of England to the prairie states at Calgary, Alberta, and Winnipeg, Manitoba. In Calgary,

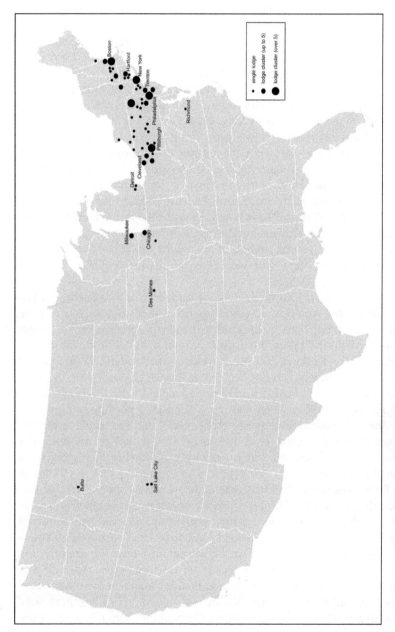

Map 3.1 Locations of the main lodges, Order of the Sons of St George

the local press welcomed the establishment of Sons of England in the area, noting that 'we shall be greatly surprised if the Calgary lodge does not prove to be one of the largest and most prosperous in Canada'. Two years later in Winnipeg, the Sons were advertised specifically as a benevolent society, organized into lodges and holding regular meetings and annual events.[66] The Sons of England also spread east from their base in Toronto across Ontario to Quebec, and, by the early 1890s, to the Maritimes and then to Newfoundland (Map 3.2; see also Appendix 3). They also thrived in the prairie states: Winnipeg, Manitoba, announced a branch being organized in May 1882. Describing it as 'essentially a mutual benevolent society', the press felt it would do very well.[67] And indeed it did. One reason for the success of the Sons of England was that Grand Lodge members worked hard to spread their orders. When a branch was opened in Winnipeg for the first time in July 1882, the development was prefaced by a visit from Richard Caddick, the Grand Lodge President from Toronto.[68] Two weeks later the lodge was launched, with Caddick present at the inaugural event.[69] A few years later, in Calgary, United Roses Lodge was 'organized at 8pm, by Bro Harry Symons, delegate from Grand Lodge, with twenty charter members'; all were 'initiated into the Red Rose Degree'.[70]

To the south, the story also was of spreading and developing. Alas, we have for the American organization none of the rich society records that exist for the Sons of England. Instead, the press is our principal guide. Early in the 1880s, the organization of the OSStG spread to New York and New England. In 1882, it was reckoned to have 7,000 to 8,000 members nationwide.[71] It was decided, in August the same year, to found a Supreme Lodge at Providence, Rhode Island.[72] By the 1880s, the Order was firmly established as far west as Wisconsin, according to reports in the *Sons of England* journal (see Appendix 2) and the *Anglo-American Times*. Between August 1883 and June 1884, it had grown from 125 lodges to 159 in just nine months, with membership increasing from 11,643 to 'about 17,000'. One report claimed proudly that the Order 'is swelling at the rate of 5,000 to 6,000 members yearly – a wonderful growth when the restricted field from which membership can be taken is considered'. In that same year, lodges had received $85,895 and had disbursed $28,730 'for sick and funeral benefits and donations'. Nearly $20,000 was invested, mostly in United States government loans. Importantly, the Order, by the mid-1880s, was located in thirteen states. According to one press report in the United States, Pennsylvania had the most lodges (50), followed by New York (20) and New Jersey (9); the others were in Massachusetts, New Hampshire, Connecticut, Ohio, Illinois, Iowa, Michigan, Wisconsin, Kentucky and Virginia.[73] The figures produced for the same year, 1884, in the *Sons of England* journal differ slightly but nevertheless show a similar range and spread (see Appendix 2). By the end

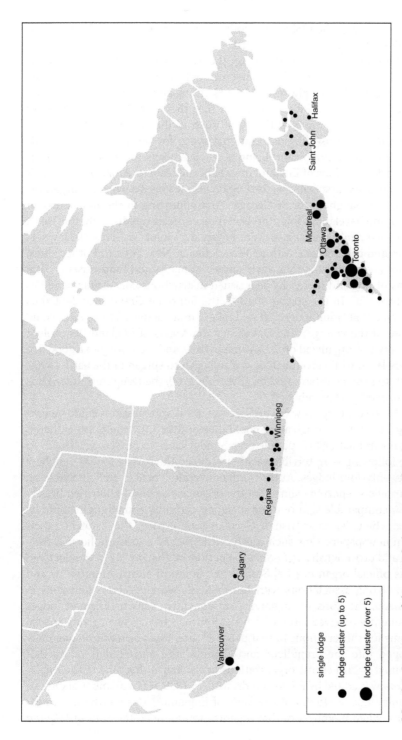

Map 3.2 Locations of the main lodges, Sons of England

of the century, the OSStG had lodges and members from Montana and Utah back to the eastern seaboard.

Another feature sponsored by the key organizers was to cater for women and juveniles, the former through a distinct association in its own right – the Daughters and Maids of England – the latter through an associated juvenile lodge system. In this, they were like so many other fraternal organizations of this time, such as the Orange Order and the Maccabees.[74] Providing associational space for the young was considered especially important, being a crucial means for forming the next generation of Sons of England members and leaders. Alongside its men's branches and associations, the OSStG also fostered a women's organization, the Daughters of St George. First appearing in the newspaper in 1885, in Cleveland, Ohio, the Daughters spread rapidly.[75] By the 1890s these women's lodges also were engaged in joint St George's Day services and celebrations with male societies in New York and other cities, as well as organizing their own soirees, concerts and fund-raisers.[76] The Sons of England hierarchy also issued instructions concerning juveniles and women. In the spring of 1897, the Supreme Grand President thus stressed that 'adult lodges' should take 'a more active and live interest in' those of the young.[77] The Daughters and Maids of England Benevolent Society was organized on 7 November 1890, and incorporated a good five years later, while juvenile lodges also began to spread in the early 1890s, with four being established by 1896.[78] In 1900, the Daughters and Maids recorded 1,162 members.[79]

As the century drew towards a close, local organizations could be very large. In 1895, Chicago alone could muster over 1,000 members gathered for the annual OSStG parade on a Sunday close to St George's Day.[80] In the following year, terrible weather reduced the parade to 600 members of twenty-four lodges. At the ninth convention, held in 1897 in Syracuse, journalists reported claims that the organization had 40,000 members.[81]

A comparable sign of these societies' certainty and strength could be seen when, like their Irish or German counterparts, they launched their own newspapers. One such was the reactionary, anti-Catholic, pro-British and pro-English *Anglo-Saxon*, a periodical that, in 1877, 'was declared "the official organ of [the] St George's union of North America"',[82] and had strong associations with the OSStG's working-class equivalent in Canada, the Sons of England. Consequently, Sons of England lodges frequently received letters from the journal's head office, 'giving special terms for subscriptions to that paper'.[83] The *Anglo-Saxon* fundamentally tapped into the prejudicial anti-Catholic and anti-French values that typified British ethnic organizations in Canada at this time.[84] The *Anglo-Saxon* was edited by E.J. Reynolds, who, in 1899, was a member of Ottawa Stanley Lodge No. 55 of the Sons of England.[85] Despite these connections, when members of that organization founded the *Sons of England*

Record, things seem to have gone a little sour. As an early editorial note in the *Record* documents, the editors 'have been shocked and grieved at the un-fraternal spirit in which our Ottawa contemporary' – and with this we must assume the *Anglo-Saxon* was meant – 'has taken notice of our existence, and it has been distressing to observe the envy, hatred, malice and all un-charitableness which has marked its every reference to ourselves'.[86] The *Sons of England Record* was by far the more comprehensive of these journals, growing in popularity in particular after it had been endorsed as the Sons' official organ from June 1897. In the United States, the OSStG developed its own periodical, the *St George's Journal*, which it published in Philadelphia between 1876 and 1891. The association also launched a short-lived title, the *English-American*, published in New York, which ran for just one year, from 1884 to 1885. The importance of communication, and by extension the need to have a clear published outlet for it, was recognized too by the RSStG: its foundation was accompanied by the launch of *The English Race*, a monthly periodical distributed to branches of the Society and also to kindred groups that were unaffiliated. Among the latter was the St George's Society of Toronto, which received copies and also requests for copies from other societies.[87]

The early twentieth century

By the Edwardian period both the OSStG and the Sons of England were strongly established across North America, from Newfoundland in the north-east to California and British Columbia in the west; however, both organizations were strongest still in that broad, Great Lakes transnational zone of industrial enterprise that connected Ontario and Quebec with New England, New York, Pennsylvania and the Mid-West (see Appendices 2 and 3).[88] For the Sons of England in 1900, then, 74 per cent of members were to be found in Ontario and 8.5 per cent in Quebec. In contrast, 5 per cent resided in Manitoba, 3.3 per cent in British Columbia and a little over 10 per cent spread across the Maritimes, Newfoundland and the other prairie states. The membership of 13,793 in 1900 was more than double that of a decade earlier.[89] By 1910, it had almost doubled again to 26,218,[90] reflecting a trend that attests powerfully to the Sons of England's growing appeal. This expansion – both numeric and geographic – is also clearly traceable in overall subordinate lodge numbers: while there were, for instance, two subordinate lodges in Assiniboia (Saskatchewan) in 1901, by 1906 there were ten.[91] A similar picture emerges, in 1901, for the OSStG. In that year, eleven states – Pennsylvania, New Jersey, Massachusetts, Rhode Island, Connecticut, New York, Ohio, Illinois, Michigan, Montana and California – were represented at the Philadelphia convention.[92] The presence in the foothills of the Rockies and out west notwithstanding the focus clearly was in the north, east and Mid-West.

The early 1900s were marked by changes that strengthened both groups. The move to diversify locations for meetings of the Grand Lodge is reflective of the general spread of the Sons of England throughout Canada – a spread that broadly followed the late nineteenth- and early twentieth-century migratory streams of the English, moving into the prairie states and further west into British Columbia.[93] As English migrants were answering the call of the 'best great west',[94] the Sons of England increasingly took hold, 'establishing itself', as a Quebec newspaper noted, 'with increasing energy'.[95]

Local organizations and regional conventions also gave insights into new initiatives. In 1907, seven years after the women's English association was recorded, there was news from Trenton, New Jersey, which welcomed OSStG delegates from all over the country. Included in their business was the intention to create a state funeral fund and a move to biennial conventions.[96] Boston hosted the convention of 1913, when a local man, William F. Barlow, was elected Supreme President. Barlow, it was said, had worked hard to make 'Massachusetts ... the banner jurisdiction', which he seemed to have achieved. The article reported how membership there had climbed to 5,318, an increase of 273 in the year of 1913, whereas Pennsylvania, the initial heartland, had seen a 126 decline to 5,300. That said, both states were 'in a very prosperous condition, both financially and numerically'.[97]

For the Sons of England, the 1902 national meeting marked a watershed. Held in Winnipeg, it was the first convention to take place outside Ontario and its more immediate environs – a move designed to abolish the regional bias towards the eastern provinces, which, for many new lodges in the west in particular, was a principal concern.[98]

Yet while desirable, a meeting in a prairie state brought complications due to increased travel costs for a large number of delegates as most hailed from the east. To facilitate attendance, therefore, the Sons of England negotiated reduced rail fares on the Grand Trunk Railway and Canadian Pacific Railway, as well as the Inter-Colonial Railway.[99] The desired effect was achieved, with delegates beginning to arrive in Winnipeg around 10 August 1902, including 'some thirty ... by the lake route', and 'a number arrived by way of Chicago', taking temporary residence in several of the city's hotels.[100] The proceedings of the national meeting commenced with a welcome of delegates to Winnipeg by the city's mayor, with a plethora of sessions being held over the ensuing days. As had long since been common at Supreme Grand Lodge meetings, the programme of events also included social pursuits, for instance 'a trolley ride over the lines of the Winnipeg Electric Street railway'[101] and a banquet in the Oddfellows' hall, 'for which nearly 300 members of the society sat down' and many a toast was cheered.[102] There was also an excursion in the form of a cruise on the Red River. More than 'two hundred delegates and friends crowded the boat comfortably', and a visit was paid to St Paul's Indian Industrial School.[103] The Winnipeg convention was important not only because it generally was a success, but because it presented 'a casting off of the last shreds of localism and provincialism' that the prior concentration of meetings in Ontario and Quebec had established.[104]

By 1904, the Sons of England had over 300 lodges with membership estimated at between 20,000 and 25,000.[105] The territory-wide reach of its membership was shown in 1905 when the Sons nominated sixty-five members from its various district lodges just for work on its General Purpose Committee. While the bulk of these individuals came from Ontarian towns and cities, with Toronto most numerously represented, they also originated in Vancouver, Halifax, Winnipeg, Ottawa, Montreal and certainly Newfoundland.[106]

The huge successes of the Sons of England in garnering new lodges and attracting large increases in membership, in the decade up to the First World War, had the effect of causing corresponding reductions in interest in the St George's societies, which waned somewhat. In terms of the number of lodges, the Sons of England and the OSStG were far larger than the St George's societies, collectively, ever became. The NAStGU counted a little over fifty affiliated St George's societies in Canada and the American east and Mid-West (see Appendix 1in relation to Chapter 2). Even if we add those lodges that we know existed out west and in the south, the individual St George's society branches were far fewer than either the Sons of England, for which we have good data, or the OSStG, for which only press reports and one tabular digest of the lodge's pervasiveness, in 1885, survive (see Appendix 3). Also in this period, the Sons of England and the Sons of St George were drawing life from their fellow English societies, with their combination of large-scale public parades, church services, socials, dances, lectures and, crucially, collective self-help. A further source of pressure for North American St George's societies developed in 1894 with the foundation of the RSStG. For this was an attempt to take the organization of English associations beyond even the geographical range manifest in the North American St George's societies. Each layer of English ethnic associationalism, and each separate organization formed, did not suggest only competition, and certainly did not seem to imply overt competition or hostility. More simply, the list of St George's societies, Albion societies, the Sons of England and the OSStG, and doubtless some other lost local examples, simply reflected the absence of any desire to collapse all manifestations of organized Englishness under one central authority. There were specific attempts to develop an overarching St George's culture, such as the NAStGU; but their friendly-society-forming fellow countrymen in the two largest

English societies, the Sons of England and the OSStG, could not agree a merger, even though they were virtually identical. At the annual convention of the Sons of St George at Scranton, Pennsylvania, in 1904, such a union was proposed between that society and the Canadian Sons of England, 'since the former order was organized for the same purpose'. The discussion went on: 'The Sons of England is the younger order, and first made overtures to bring an amalgamation about. After the amalgamation both orders will probably be known as the Sons of St George.'[107] Perhaps it was the prospect of losing their name that dampened the appeal to the Sons of England; and in any case, both organizations were strong and the merger did not proceed, despite the Pennsylvania delegations apparently voting for it.

If merger did not work for these associations, the fact did not prevent them from maintaining strong central authority within their respective groups. The Sons of England Supreme Grand Lodge, for example, worked hard to ensure strong relations. One initiative was to support networking between lodges through visits from the head lodge, with Supreme Presidents and Past Supreme Grand Presidents, as well as other lodge officials, frequently travelling throughout Canada to visit subordinate lodges. Moose Jaw thus saw the visit of Past Supreme President Bro. John Aldridge during his 1904 tour of western Canada, arranging several activities for him throughout his stay.[108] As the *Moose Jaw Signal* reported, Aldridge 'complimented the lodge upon the way it discharged its duties and upon its great numerical strength for such a young lodge'.[109] After his visit in Moose Jaw, Aldrige continued to travel further west to visit other lodges, including Lodge Calgary, where an 'enthusiastic celebration' was held.[110] On a smaller-scale level there is also clear evidence of visiting members in attendance from other lodges.[111] In 1908, 100 lodges were represented at the Grand Lodge meeting in August 1908 at Hamilton, Ontario; in 1911, 124 delegates made the meeting, held in Windsor, also in Ontario.[112] This was not, however, the peak of their powers. In 1923 an impressive 373 delegates were entered on the roll for the 1923 Grand Lodge meeting.[113]

After the First World War, there was a notable shift in the emphasis of the OSStG – a shift that can be discerned in the emergence of still another new periodical. In 1919, Ernest H. Bennett, of the OSStG's Anglo-Saxon lodge, edited another short-lived monthly called *The English-Speaking World*, which covered a dizzying array of Anglo-American organizations, initiatives and activities, including news of the OSStG itself.[114] The latter journal pointed to a turn in the OSStG's mission from a patriotic friendly society to a collection of politically Anglo-Saxonist agitators. This tendency was strengthened by the increasing profile of the London-based RSStG, which increasingly made its presence felt as a global force that wished to unify the various societies in celebration of the historical and global contribution of English culture.[115]

By the 1920s, the OSStG had nearly doubled in size from the 1880s, though claims of 60,000 to 70,000 members seem too high in relation to other estimates reported in this chapter.[116] For many membership societies, the inter-war period marked a high peak of activity.[117] It was at this point that the OSStG had broadened its appeal still further to persons of a higher socio-economic class. Now, civic leaders and small and medium businessmen – and not just miners, textile hands and other blue-collar men – were part of the scene. It is possible that this development was part of a bleeding of members from the St George's societies to the OSStG; certainly, there was a feeling, on the part of the much smaller, elite-focused St George's societies, that these alternative societies must 'absorb the young' because 'benevolence alone is not sufficient'; and they recognized that 'benefits must also accrue'.[118]

Other changes were discernible in this period, not least a further strengthening of a more comfortably off leadership class. The major lights in the Upper Peninsula of Michigan give us an insight that may be used to generalize. Evidence here shows a network of substantial men who were active in three or more societies, with certain key ones – the OSStG itself plus the Freemasons, the Elks and the Knights of Pythias – recurring in most cases. James H. Dale, English-born florist, of Houghton, Michigan, was typical. A self-made man who worked his way up in the horticultural industry, he became owner of his own company. Dale was a classic nineteenth-century joiner: the masons, Elks, Knights of Pythias and Society of American Florists, as well as the Sons of St George and others, at times called on his exertions as a solid member. Dale had numerous aspects in common with his fellow Sons of St George members. Frank Elsworth Keese, superintendent at the Oliver Iron Mining Company in upper Michigan and the grandson of an Englishman, also was in the Sons of St George, as well as being a Freemason and Knight of Pythias. This also was true of William Trebilcock, son of a Cornishman, stationary engineman and later greenhouse manufacturer. In addition to the Sons and Knights, Trebilcock joined the Oddfellows, Maccabees and Modern Woodmen of America. William J. Billing, motor sales company owner, was the son of a Cornish miner, and joined the Sons of St George. Judge John G. Stone, of Houghton, Michigan, also was in the Sons of the St George, the Freemasons, the Elks and, additionally, the Knights Templar. James H. Thomas, also descended from English immigrants, is interesting: he was a funeral director in Calumet and a member of the OSStG and several other confraternities, while his wife joined the Rebekahs, Eastern Star and Phythian Sisters, and was active in charitable circles.[119] These were men of substance: not politicians, mayors or ambassadors and consuls, but commercialists, traders and sturdy, largely self-made men. They were the classic, successful, second-generation scions of immigrant families. In the United States, Cornish miners could produce offspring who progressed up the socio-economic scale to be funeral directors, wholesale florists and owners of medium-sized businesses: men who, despite their new comfort and privilege, retained connection to the friendly societies and clubs that their fathers had founded and nurtured.

The Sons of England also reflected support from influential stalwarts like these OSStG men. One such was George Clift King, who was the first president of the United Rose Lodge, which was Calgary's first. Born in Chelmsford, Essex, in 1848, King had immigrated into Canada in 1874 and joined the North-West Mounted Police that year, making his way to the prairies. After being discharged, King settled in Calgary and was appointed postmaster, also serving as the city's mayor in the later 1880s and as a councillor thereafter. Appointed, in 1934, to the Order of the British Empire, King is a suitable representative of the type of middle-class Englishmen who loyally acclaimed the old home through associative behaviour.[120]

Ethnicity identity and anti-Irishness

The Toronto St George's Society monthly meeting of November 1909 heard a resolution from its sister society in Ottawa on the issue of 'Chinese Coolie Labour on the Grand Trunk Pacific Railway'. However, 'the [members of the] meeting were of the opinion that the subject was not a suitable one for this society to deal with'.[121] The same could not be said for ethnic prejudice towards the Irish, sectarianism and anti-Catholicism, all of which connected these societies. Such prejudices united all British Protestants, English or not. Indeed, with strong Calvinist and chapel traditions, Scots and Welsh were capable of even more fiercely anti-Catholic and anti-Irish rhetoric than their English counterparts. This was observable in the sectarian tensions that occurred in Britain;[122] and it was a fundamental feature of the urban American fabric. The Welshman John H. Evans, in a letter to John Richards, vicar of Llanowddin, Montgomeryshire, in 1842, wrote of both the good and the bad things for immigrants about the state of New York. Among the good, he recalled: 'I do not think that they punish thieves with death as often as they do in England.' Among the bad, he reported in matter-of-fact tones, 'it is generally said there is no great punishment for killing an Irishman'.[123]

To the earliest Sons of England, declarations of sectarian loyalty were as much political as cultural – a marked challenge to the rise of both French and Irish Catholic power in Canada. The Sons' early history views things this way: 'as a political institution it [the Sons of England] was to know no party, but to inculcate the preservation and perpetuity of the British Empire, loyalty to Crown and country under Protestant rule'.[124]

These exclusivist views led the Order of the Sons of St George, along with other imperialist and Tory organizations, such as the League of the Rose and the Daughters and Maids of the Revolution, to be wooed by the reactionary *Anglo-Saxon* periodical.

Anti-Catholicism and anti-Irishness were unifying cultural discourses across the British World. The mass emigrations of the 1840s, during the Great Irish Famine, amplified all negative relations between the English and Irish. In 1846, the *Liverpool Times* divided the Irish into 'the emigrants of hope', who went to the United States or Canada, and 'the emigrants of despair', who languished in Britain.[125] In the industrial and commercial cities of Liverpool, Manchester and Glasgow, and many dozens of smaller urban centres, Irish Catholics were met with hostility from the English and Welsh, Scots and Irish Protestants. Sectarian tensions marked out communal life, stratified employment opportunities and segmented community life along ethno-religious lines. Irish Catholics overwhelmingly were unskilled and occupied the least secure, ill-paid work.[126] In the United States, such hope as the *Liverpool Times* imagined was filtered through initial hardship but then was distilled into stronger and clearer opportunities for advancement than Britain offered. While America's English immigrant workers 'trained in Britain's industries formed the Aristocracy of the American labour force' and 'received favoured treatment', the Irish were 'left to fend for themselves'.[127]

Politics, however, offered the Irish a release. While the Irish faced intense prejudice and often clashed with working-class Britons and Yankees, their numbers made them formidable. These post-famine arrivals did not shrink or stand still. They pursued naturalization, citizenship and attendant voting rights with alacrity and then, deploying their sheer weight of numbers effectively, they exerted political power that the English and British failed to match. Irish-Americans in the typical United States city supported a variety of Irish political nationalist organizations, including the Fenians. Large numbers provided financial aid, and a smaller hard-core participated in the dynamite bombing campaigns in Britain.[128] Irish hostility complicated the lives of the English and sometimes brought them under severe duress, but did not make the Englishman's lot in the United States worse than that of the average Irish immigrant.[129] Not even three generations of post-famine settlement could put the Irish precisely on a par with the English. Moreover, all immigrant groups from Britain and Ireland arrived in North America with extensive experience of communal discord and long histories of religious and ethnic division.[130] Many of these gut feelings of enmity simply were replayed in the new communities, but with some differences. In Canada, the English were never so severely outnumbered as in the United States, and the Irish there were generally more cautious because numbers did not favour them and because they still lived, effectively, under British and pro-British rule. In 1871, the Irish-born in ten major Canadian towns totalled two-thirds of the English-born and a little over one-half of the British-born; by 1901, the proportions had fallen to one-half and two-fifths respectively (see Table 1.12). Further layers of tension were created by the addition of Francophone Catholic populations, which in places were much more numerous than the Irish. In this context, then, sectarianism was a shared cultural disposition for the Canadian Sons of England and the American OSStG. As the latter struggled against the viciousness of the Molly Maguires, the former made claims of being 'oppressed' by other ethnic groups. As the *Anglo-Saxon* somewhat apocalyptically put it: 'The bondage these Anglo-Israelites are laboring under – the whips and scorns they are enduring from their Franco-Egyptian and Hiberno-Egyptian taskmasters.'[131]

Also added to the mix were Irish Protestants, though they tend to be overlooked when assessing the creation of the type of anti-Catholic culture that affected Irish immigrants in Britain and the United States. In the 1880s, it was the said Irish Protestants who became exaggerated nativists in organizations such as the American Protective Association to distinguish themselves from their Irish Catholic countrymen. As a consequence, wrote an Irish Catholic editor, 'Wherever there is a street-preaching riot, or an attack on Catholic Church or convent, be sure that certain faithful *Irish* Calvinists are foremost among the enlightened Protestants upon the ground.'[132] Finally, middle-class Irish Protestants, who were part of one of Canada's largest ethnic blocs, would regularly find common cause with like-minded English folk of the type found in the Protestant exclusive OSStG.

It is hardly surprising, then, that the Irish were suggestible to the propaganda of Irish-American nationalists. Revenge against Britons, not merely in the United Kingdom but also in the United States, acquired a currency with increasingly assertive Irish Catholic communities. Anger and hostility resulting from Anglo-Irish relations and personal experiences of poverty and hunger, especially during the Great Irish Famine, coloured ethnic relations in the American city, often to the detriment of the English. Moreover, American ethnic politics provided voice for such feelings. According to Ernst, the list of undimmed grievances harboured by the Irish included 'all things English, including the hapless English immigrant in America'.[133]

Baltimore's English witnessed a brief light thrown on to the issue of Irish revenge and how it might work in practice. In 1874, the treasurer of the St George's Society used his annual address partly to report the imprisonment of several Englishmen who, not being able to afford lodgings, had taken temporary refuge in the old station house. However, the local Irish police had arrested them. To the secretary of the St George's Society of Baltimore this was a stain on United States liberties. Wider anxieties about the pressures of American life were at the heart of his words: 'Few Englishmen would credit the oppression and tyranny which their countrymen have to undergo in this boasted land of freedom.' He continued:

> The boast 'Britons never shall be slaves' will be a mockery when any Fenian policeman or Magistrate can incarcerate an Englishman as a felon to 'feed fat his ancient grudge' imported from the Emerald Isle, where prejudice and bigotry and religious animosity warp men's minds and bend their reason ... The St George's Society is essentially ... a Benevolent Society and one important duty is to guard the friendless immigrant from oppression by petty tyrants.[134]

A sense of the differences between Irish and English, or Protestant and Catholic, was also emphasized from cultural and political positions adopted by Irish Catholics. By controlling forms of labour where they predominated for their own people, they merely mirrored the exclusionary practices that they themselves fell victim to. When they introduced their networks of Ribbon and Hibernian societies to the new communities of settlement, which they did in Britain as well as the United States,[135] they far exceeded their fellow immigrants but were, in their minds, natural resisters to the pressures they faced from capitalists and bosses, who, in America, were surrogates for landlords in Ireland. There was, then, an absolutely clear sense in which the Irish were shaped by ethnic as well as class considerations. They did not simply graduate from ethnic consciousness to class consciousness, as would suit most Marxist interpretations. For Emmons, the Irish were so involved in feelings of nationalism and anti-Britishness that ethnicity often undermined their class concerns. For him, prejudices based on historic injustices at home explained the Irish worker's ultimately limited interest in pan-ethnic class solidarities. Emmons states persuasively:

> There were enormous differences between the [mutualist] Sons of Italy, say, or the Sons of St George, and the [ethno-political] Clan-na-Gael, and the conclusion is inescapable that the history of American labor – as surely as that of the English – would have been different had the Anglophobic Irish not been so early and dominant a component of the working classes of both nations.[136]

To Emmons, the Irish were caught in a suspicious half-light, viewing no one – not the English, Germans or others – as allies in matters of class. Consequently, 'the Irish worker was an unlikely candidate for working-class radicalism'.[137]

While working-class organizations, whose daily associations brought them closest to the Irish, were most likely to evince anti-Celtic bile, even the elite St George's societies sometimes let their veil of politeness slip. At the usual St George's Day dinner in 1883, the presence of guests from the Hibernian Society did not prevent the Baltimore St George's Society discussing Anglo-Irish political matters.[138] In particular, they were interested in Phoenix Park, where on 6 May 1882 – some eleven months previously – Lord Frederick Cavendish and his under-secretary, T.H. Burke, had been murdered.[139] President Spencer of the Baltimore St George's Society made mention in a light-hearted way. During a toast to 'Old England', and drawing up the Irish-American bombing campaigns in Britain,[140] he commented:

> Unfortunately John Bull had a crown in which there is an emerald, and he has just found out it contained dynamite [Laughter.] Irishmen are not alone responsible for this. There are influences at work to foster these fearful conspiracies in every country, and it behoves Americans to go hand in hand to suppress them. What would our railroads and canals be had it not been for John Bull's pocket? Where do you go today for money to build your railroads? If it were not for John Bull the world might as well shut up shop – [Laughter and applause.][141]

Irish nationalist violence placed Revd Dr Campbell Fair, an Irish Anglican clergyman associated with the St George's Society of Baltimore, in an invidious position requiring considerable diplomatic skills. On the one hand, Fair was a British loyalist, but on the other he was a proud, reasoning Irishman. Even in difficult times, he was not going to evince one identity at the expense of another. So, among the St George's Society of Baltimore, it fell to Fair to address Irish issues. He spoke in measured tones about Ireland as a country of 'unresolved issues' while pointing out that 'there were people there as loyal to the crown as any Englishmen'.[142] He also picked up the theme of English, Irish and American relations in his speech of the following year.[143] At around the same time, further implacable hostility to the Irish extremists among them was announced when Syracuse Sons of St George adopted the name 'Lord Frederick Cavendish lodge'.[144]

On the same night, in April 1883, as their countrymen in Baltimore made mention of the Phoenix Park murders, members of the New York's St George's Society also listened to talk of dynamite. This time a clear attempt was made to soothe potential tensions, albeit in a different way. Their president, Mr Hill, pointed out that the government of the city of New York dated to a charter of the late seventeenth century: 'its author was an Irishman, pure and simple, and he made it before dynamite was invented'. It was a worthy, reasoned and sensible comment in such an Irish city, and one guaranteed not to embarrass Judge Jack Shea, of the Friendly Sons of St Patrick, who was one of several responding to a toast to 'Our Sister Societies'. 'There are occasions when silence is the safest eloquence,' he said, 'and this was one.' Perhaps this too was a reference to the dynamite bombing campaigns. He could see no reason why his society should not celebrate St George's Day, and 'remarked with pride of the great weight Ireland had in the formation and evangelization of the British nation'.[145] Ancient history was the safest site for common ground.

Despite the focus on mutualism, the provision of sick benefit and social activities the Sons of England also were, at times, tainted by political militancy and secretive practice.[146] At their inception, the exclusivist Protestant, English Sons of England were strongly shaped by anti-Irish feeling. One particular episode – opposition to a lecturing tour through North America by the Irish Nationalist MP and president of the Irish Land League William O'Brien– brought the Sons wider attention in the press in the late 1880s.[147] Protesting against the Irish nationalist movement, the Sons were cast as an aggressive, conservative political bloc, being lumped together with the Orange Order and the local militia.[148] Even the suggestion that O'Brien should be protected by 'the whole military force if necessary' seemed pointless, a newspaper report suggested, as 'this is composed of every three out of five men who belong to the Orange [O]rder or to the Sons of England'.[149] The Sons described here were overtly anti-Catholic, unionist and belligerent. Yet the Sons themselves were always adamant that they were not political – a belief they later framed by casting the organization as an 'independent entity':[150] an entity independent not only of particular political views, but also of other associations and their activities. Still it is clear that the level of independence was limited given the Sons' loyalty to 'the Protestant religion, to our Queen and country'.[151] While there may not have been an overt political agenda, this framing of the organization reflected a particular mind-set that was not 'independent'.

The OSStG's initially sectarian context cleared in the mid-1870s and it began to focus on cultural dimensions of ethnicity, with 'the families of the various lodges meet[ing] together socially on stated occasions, thereby keeping live the English love of the country and the festivities of her fête days'.[152] The charming depiction of a proud, patriotic people enjoying their Englishness together in largely serene ways does not, however, tell all of the story. Regardless of what changes may have occurred, they never welcomed Catholic members; and they retained sectarian teeth. Emmons, in his major study of ethnicity and class in Butte, the heavily Irish copper-mining colony in Montana, noted a different aspect to English ethnic associationalism. As late as 1892, goading and challenging still went on along ethnic lines. In that year, the 'Sons of St George asked the RELA [Robert Emmet Literary Association] if the Irish organization would hang a picture of Queen Victoria in Hibernia Hall. The Emmets "threw the request away".'[153] A willingness and desire to mark out differences with the Irish actually grew stronger, not weaker, as the nineteenth century faded. The progress of Irish nationalism, both at home and in the diaspora, ensured an English response that showed that ethnic cleavages remained pronounced.

The anti-Irish sentiments that had fired up the OSStG in the first place and which had coloured St George's societies too during the 1870s and 1880s re-emerged with even greater force as Irish Home Rule came closer to realization and when bloodshed and war stood between the Irish and their freedom. What shape that might take was not clear in 1919, when the OSStG founded the *English-Speaking World* newspaper to express not only its unionist philosophies, but also those of, for example, the Ulster League of North America, whose connections to the Unionist leader, Edward Carson, were regularly reported. By this time, the OSStG had 500 or more lodges and tens of thousands of members, had disbursed nearly a million dollars and eclipsed the St George's societies. However, it had not abandoned that initial sectarian, anti-Irish anti-Catholic ethos. Its rules still excluded non-Protestants. More importantly, it came to appear more like the Orange Order: sectarian, potentially paramilitary in its marches and parades and sharply opinionated with respect to the Irish Question. Thus, in the post-war period, Mr Brown, 'supreme organizer' of the OSStG, reported a recruitment drive in 1920 and an upsurge in members. What caused this growth spurt in the wake of the First World War? According to Brown,

> there seems to be an awakening in the minds of the Englishmen and they realize what a great factor for good they can be, in the shop, store, factory or among their friends who are not of British origins, in offsetting the harmful and insidious work of the Sinn Feiners, pro-German or anti-British.[154]

In keeping with the mood of the moment, the benevolent society remained an instrument of giving and helping; but its edges also had been sharpened. In what were turbulent times of ethnic and racial conflict, immigration controls and fear at the easing spectres of Communism and Fascism, the OSStG's Anglo-Saxonism, which had initially fired it up against Irish Ribbonmen, was once more coming more fully to the fore.

While anti-Irish fervour united the English in the United States and Canada, the latter, being a British colony still, had different dimensions of imperial and religious conflict. Indeed, the Sons of England existed only in Canada and South Africa and could not have prospered in the United States, because of the fervour of their loyalty to the crown and Empire. Such vehemence would have been impossible to assert in a republican context. An important sub-plot was the issue of United States–Canadian relations, border conflicts and the way the Sons of England viewed the relationship between the two countries. One member of the Sons was particularly vocal on the subject, writing regularly in the *Record* about matters relating to the British Empire: John Castell Hopkins. Born in Dyersville, Iowa, Hopkins came to Canada as a child when his parents relocated to Bowmanville in Ontario. He worked as a bank clerk but was known chiefly as an author and imperialist, having been involved in the establishment of the Ontario branch of the Imperial Federation League.[155] Hopkins's fundamental assumption was this: that 'British connection' had had '[t]he greatest influence ... in the development of Canadian institutions and the moulding of Canadian patriotism'.[156] In his writings, therefore, he can frequently be found to criticize the present state in which, to his mind, Canada was becoming more removed from the motherland. This was all the more problematic given the 'Americanization' of the world. 'In the popular mind', Hopkins asserted, '"America" obscures "Canada"':

> Under the former name is included the latter geographically, and as the people of the United States have arrogated to themselves the national use of the word 'America,' everything Canadian is naturally mixed up in the ideas of the masses with the concerns of the United States. Besides this fact, and contributing to enhance it, is the sending of cable news regarding Canada via New York, and it must be confessed that a further puzzling complication is given by Canadians themselves in the use of Provincial abbreviations, such as 'Ont.,'instead of writing in their business and others communications of Canada as a whole. The use of provincial hieroglyphics does it serious harm in the present somewhat dazed state of geographical knowledge.[157]

To be able to progress within the Empire and to allow it to stand strong against the United States, Canada would have to assert its position more vocally, and in distinct separation from that of the United States. Only this could ensure that Canada would grow as an integral partner in an imperial federation with Britain, rather than being overshadowed by its republican neighbour.

It was this thinking, Hopkins's 'unqualified support' for any 'imperial crusade',[158] that pitted his views – and by extension the views of the Sons of England – against those of the famous businessman and philanthropist Andrew Carnegie, who became a frequent victim of attack in the *Record*. While the Sons, writing in the context of McKinley's presidential election, believed that '"our hatred of England," has lost much of its old time power with the majority of the voters of the United States',[159] Carnegie antagonized them greatly as he still represented that hatred in his criticism of the British Empire. Hence even when Carnegie offered support to two Canadian cities through philanthropic contributions, there were voices of unease. A Sons of England member, William

Robbins of Walkerville, Ontario, for instance, wrote a pamphlet stating that such gifts should not be accepted because of Carnegie's views. Robbins included extracts from Carnegie's writings in his pamphlet to trace where the problems lay – and they lay especially in Carnegie's dismissal of the queen.[160] Unsurprisingly, this did not go down well with the Sons of England: to them it represented a 'series of fabrications and insults',[161] and to the person they held most dear. Sentiments heightened in the context of the question of an inter-imperial tariff. Carnegie did not support it and sent warning messages in the direction of Canada. For the Sons such interference was unacceptable:

> We beg Mr. Carnegie's pardon. He is not an American. He is a natural-ized British subject ... not all his lavish expenditure for colleges, hospi-tals and libraries in any part of the British Empire can hide the fact that Mr. Carnegie's real love is for the land where his dollars were made ... The fear which inspires his cry of warning is not that Canada may be tripped by the United States as she marches into an imperial preferential tariff, but that Canada may tread heavily on the corns of the Republic.[162]

The impact of economic considerations in the relationship between Canada and the United States was certainly not lost on the Sons, and Carnegie was not the only person to rouse their sentiments. In a piece published in the *Record* entitled 'Keep the Flag Afloat' the Sons cautioned, for instance, that the supremacy of the Empire was under threat 'not by the fleets and armies of avowedly hostile nations, but by the financial machinations of the plutocracy of an alleged friendly power', the United States. It was 'Yankee capitalists' who had helped establish 'for the United States that shipping supremacy of the Atlantic which was first obtained by England', and therefore, 'American money has dealt our Motherland a heavier blow than she ever received from foreign foe.' How could it come to that? In part, the problem was republicanism, which the Sons saw as facilitating the development of a 'despotic form of govern-ment': in a 'land where money is king and where that King both makes and administers the law' this happens quickly. The Sons thus cast having a monarch as head of state as a means to liberty. But more practical solu-tions were required, and it was the Imperial Order of the Daughters of Empire who 'have shown the way', pledging 'to purchase and to induce others to purchase Canadian and other British goods in preference to those of foreign manufacture'.[163]

There was, then, a more practical side to Canadian—United States relations and the views of the Sons of England – and one that was of all the more immediate relevance in the context of the status of Yukon and Alaska. At a meeting of the Supreme Grand Executive held in early April 1898, it 'proscribed for residence by members of the Order all that portion of North America lying north of the 60th parallel of north lati-tude, which embraces a portion of Alaska and the Yukon and adjacent territories. Notice is therefore hereby given that the Society will not be responsible for any benefits claimed on account of sickness or death hap-pening on or by reason of residence within the district above named.'[164] The Alaska boundary dispute was rearing its head.[165] Yet despite these issues that complicated the view that the Sons of England held regarding the United States, there were associational interactions that transcended them, speaking strongly to the strength of English diaspora connections across the globe.[166] Personal links played an important part in this, for instance through Sons of England members who had relocated to the United States but maintained contact.[167]

The complexities inherent in United States–Canadian relations seem small, however, when compared with Canada's internal dynamics in the relationship between English- and French-speaking Canadians. From the 1870s, as Canada was increasingly seeking its way as a nation in its own right after Confederation in 1867, French Canadians had to find their place in the new constitutional set-up.[168] For many contemporary observers this brought with it a series of problems. Goldwin Smith, for instance, saw the monarchism of French Canadians as a fundamental problem, noting that 'French Canada is a relic of the historical past pre-served in isolation, as Siberian mammoths are preserved in ice.'[169] There were also growing concerns that French-speaking Canadians harboured, at best, divided loyalties to both the new Dominion and the British Empire. Contributions in the *Sons of England Record* document that the Sons certainly viewed the latter possibility as problematic.

In general terms, many of the contributors to debates concerning French Canadians emphasized that subjects of French origins should not be automatically prejudiced against: concerns were levied towards indi-viduals for whom there was clear evidence of activity that, in the mind of the Sons, did not show an adequate level of loyalty. One such individual was Joseph Israel Tarte. Born in Lanoraie, Lower Canada, in January 1848, Tarte commenced his political career in the Conservative Party, and was elected to the Quebec Legislative Assembly in 1877. Given the party's indifferent stance towards questions concerning French Canada, Tarte, who had since been elected to the Canadian House of Commons, eventually joined the Liberals and became Minister of Public Works in the Laurier government in the summer of 1896.[170] While Tarte's views on French Canada were by no means unknown, it was in 1899 that his pro-French statements caused the Sons to attack him openly. At the time, Tarte was, as Canada's chief commissioner at the universal exposi-tion, based in Paris, there choosing, as a report in the *Record* observed, to 'openly avow in effect that he is a Frenchman first and a British subject afterwards'.[171] Therefore, and while 'not animated by party feeling in one direction or the other', the Sons sought to 'join forces ... and insist upon the retirement from British official life of such variegated patriots as Monsieur Tarte'.[172] It was not acceptable to the Sons that a minister of the Canadian government, and thus by extension of Her Majesty's government, should express loyalty to another country as a result of his personal sentiments. Almost a year later, with Tarte again in Paris, the Sons' attack resurfaced. While the Sons expressed clearly that they 'never had any sympathy with the cry of disloyalty hurled against the French-Canadian', believing 'them to be true British subjects with a natural feeling of affection for the land of their ancestors', Tarte's story remained different, since he still 'look[ed] to France'. What made his new statements more problematic was that he actively 'urged Frenchmen to emigrate to Canada'. The Sons wondered what Tarte, as a minister of the British crown, meant when saying '"*We* look to France." "Englishmen can make their homes among *us*."' For the Sons the situation was clear: with loyalty to the crown a central pillar, 'We know of no British colony that looks to a foreign power.'[173]

As in the examples relating to the relationship with the United States, the question of loyalty lay at the core of these concerns, but, in the case of French Canadians it was overtly tied up with the issue of religion. For the Sons the situation was clear: given that the monarch made reference in the oath only to the Protestant faith, the Sons had to follow that line. The Roman Catholic Church was 'an organization seeking to exercise political power to the advancement of its own interests and the detriment of those of other creeds'.[174] Whether through French-speaking patriots like Tarte, or Irish nationalists like O'Brien, the prevention of such 'detriment' was fundamental to the Sons' mind-set.[175]

Within both themes explored – United States – Canadian relations and the complexities of French Canada – one development amplified the situation: the Second Anglo-Boer War (1899–1902). It was a time when some commentators began to wish 'for the humiliation of the Anglo-Saxon race and the downfall of the British Empire',[176] while pro-Boer sentiments, for instance as expressed by many a United States journalist, could keep alive 'the insensate hatred of England ... among a large class'.[177] The Sons did, of course, agree that any war is best prevented, but with respect to the Second Anglo-Boer War it was their firm belief that 'it is not only the lesser of two evils, but it will be productive of much that will make for peace for years to come over a far wider area than South Africa'.[178] Importantly, there was also clear recognition of the wider relevance in terms of the English diaspora – and its active recognition: the war was 'a lesson in the solidarity ... which England's covert enemies will not very soon forget',[179] a solidarity shown in how quickly the English in Canada, and the Sons of England specifically, answered the Empire's call.

Conclusion

While the range and extent of the Sons of England and OSStG was impressive, the full potential strength of the different types of English societies was never fully realized. While various attempts were made to combine efforts and unify in order to maximize strength, clarity and common purpose, these efforts got no further than loose federation. The NAStGU represented a degree of federalism between the 1870s and the early 1900s and clearly demonstrated strong and persistent transnational communication between primarily elite Englishmen and Americans of English descent. However, the two largest, popular English friendly societies – the OSStG in the United States and the Sons of England in Canada – never managed to agree on terms for merging although they considered doing so several times. Moreover, after the First World War, the organizations still appeared quite separate, the difference being that now, in addition to the established North American St George's societies, the late Victorian, London-based RSStG had become a prominent third force. We explore the latter, and its global reach, in Chapter 6.

Regardless of their failure to unite or federalize their operations, the English associations we have explored here remained broadly in union. Neither faction fighting nor warring has been uncovered; neither has any difference of principle or expression, other than the difference between charity (St George's) and collective self-help (OSStG and Sons of England). Patriotism to England remained a constant for both. Suspicion and fear surrounding the rise of Irish-American power clearly also connected them. So did the plethora of activities that St George's and other societies pursued to celebrate English culture and express loyalty to the crown – themes we now turn to in our exploration of the structures and activities of English associations.

Notes

1 *Syracuse Daily Herald*, 14 July 1897.
2 L.O. Aranya Fradenburg, 'Pro Patria Mori', in Kathy Lavezzo (ed.), *Imagining a Medieval English Nation* (Minneapolis, 2004), p. 23.
3 David T. Beito, *From Mutual Aid to the Welfare State: Fraternal Society and Social Services, 1890–1967* (Chapel Hill, NC, 2000), pp. 18–19.
4 Daniel Weinbren, 'Beneath the All-Seeing Eye: Fraternal Orders and Friendly Societies' Banners in Nineteenth- and Twentieth-Century Britain', *Cultural and Social History*, 2 (2006), p. 167.
5 P.H.J.H. Gosden, *The Friendly Societies in England, 1815–1875* (Manchester, 1961); Simon Cordery, *British Friendly Societies, 1750–1914* (Basingstoke, 2003).

6 David Fitzpatrick, 'Exporting Brotherhood: Orangeism in South Australia', in *Immigrants and Minorities*, 23:2–3 (2005), p. 277.

7 Marcel van der Linden (ed.), *Social Security Mutualism: The Comparative History of Mutual Benefit Societies* (Bern, 1996).

8 This term, however, carried none of the quasi-revolutionary freight that the term acquired in Britain, where legislation at various points in the 1820s and 1830s sought to eliminate illegal, treasonable secret oaths among Irish rural redressers, trade unionists and political radicals. Much government pressure in Britain was levelled against Irish illegal oaths, on which see: Petri Mirala, 'Lawful and Unlawful Oaths in Ireland, 1760–1835', in Allan Blackstock and Eoin Magennis (eds), *Politics and Political Culture in Britain and Ireland, 1750–1850: Essays in Tribute to Peter Jupp* (Belfast, 2006), pp. 209–22.

9 R.J. Morris, 'Voluntary Societies and British Urban Elites, 1780–1850: An Analysis', *Historical Journal*, 26:1 (1983), pp. 95–118.

10 John J. Bukowyzck et al. (eds), *Permeable Border: The Great Lakes Basin as a Transnational Region, c.1650–1990* (Pittsburgh, PA, 2005); Randy W. Widdis, *With Scarcely a Ripple: Anglo-Canadian Migration into the United States and Western Canada, 1880–1920* (Montreal, 1998).

11 See for example *Manitoba Free Press*, 14 August 1893, for a donation by the Sons of England to the Winnipeg General Hospital; *Manitoba Daily Free Press*, 2 March 1892, and the same paper, 30 October 1894, for examples of Sons of England concerts.

12 Herbert G. Gutman, 'Work, Culture and Society in Industrializing America, 1815-1919', *American Historical Review*, 83:3 (1973), pp. 540–41.

13 CTA, Series 1093, StGS Toronto, File 26, Monthly Meetings Minutes, 1908-20, 4 February 1916, p. 176; John S. King, *The Early History of the Sons of England Benevolent Society* (Toronto, 1891), p. 9, list of founding members.

14 *Manitoba Daily Free Press*, 9 January 1891.

15 See Tanja Bueltmann, Andrew Hinson and Graeme Morton, *The Scottish Diaspora* (Edinburgh, 2013), ch. 2.

16 Mark Bulik, *The Sons of Molly Maguire: The Irish Roots of America's First Labor War* (New York, 2015).

17 See Kyle Hughes and Donald M. MacRaild, *Ribbonism in Ireland and Britain* (Liverpool, forthcoming), which explores the Irish roots and trans-national spread of this form of clandestine ethno-sectarian trade unionism.

18 David Sim, *A Union Forever: The Irish Question and US Foreign Relations in the Victorian Age* (Ithaca, NY, 2013) and Niall Whelehan, *The Dynamiters: Irish Nationalism and Political Violence in the Wider World, 1867–1900* (Cambridge, 2012).

19 Timothy N. O'Neill, 'Miners in Migration: The Case of Nineteenth-Century Irish and Irish-American Copper Miners', in Kevin Kenny (ed.), *New Directions in Irish-American History* (Madison, WI, 2003), pp. 61–77.

20 For the most thorough treatment, see Kevin Kenny, *Making Sense of the Molly Maguires* (New York, 1998), esp. pp. 14–34, for their origins. Bulik's *Sons of Molly Maguire* is a fine account of the long-run origins, activities and

legacies of Mollyism, incorporating (as Kenny does) antecedents in Ireland. Classic early works, which differ in emphasis from Kenny, are: J. Walter Coleman, *The Molly Maguire Riots: Industrial Conflict in the Pennsylvania Coal Region* (1936; paperback, New York, 1969); Wayne J. Broehl, *The Molly Maguires* (Cambridge, MA, 1964).

21 This was true of the Association of Miners and Laborers of Schuykill County, according to an English miner writing home. Cited by Bulik, *Sons of Molly Maguire*, pp. 135–36.

22 Kenny, *Making Sense* and Bulik, *Sons of Molly Maguire* offer the fullest, exposition on the Irish dimensions.

23 Virginia Crossman, *Politics, Law and Order in Nineteenth-Century Ireland* (Belfast, 1996), p. 22; M.R. Beames, 'Ribbon Societies: Lower-Class Nationalism in Pre-Famine Ireland', in C.E.H. Philpin (ed.), *Nationalism and Popular Protest in Ireland* (Oxford, 2002), p. 246; Sidney Pollard, 'The Ethics of the Sheffield Outrages', *Transactions of the Hunter Archaeological Society*, 8:3 (1953–54), pp. 118–39.

24 Kenny, *Making Sense*, p. 187; Eric Foner, 'The Land League and Irish America', in Eric Foner (ed.), *Politics and Ideology in the Age of the Civil War* (New York, 1980), pp. 170–74.

25 Joseph Gerteis, *Class and the Color Line: Interracial Class Coalition in the Knights of Labor* (Durham, NC, 2007), p. 31; Mathew Hild, *Greenbackers, Knights of Labor, and Populists: Farmer-Labor Insurgency in the Late-Nineteenth-Century South* (Athens, GA, 2010), p. 47; Robert E. Weir, *Beyond Labor's Veil: The Culture of the Knights of Labor* (University Park, PA, 2010), p. 10.

26 Mark Wyman, *Hard Rock Epic: Western Miners and the Industrial Revolution, 1860–1910* (Berkeley, 1979), pp. 161–66.

27 'Cousin Jacks' were so called on account of the Cornish exhortation to save a job for cousin Jack – itself a function of chain migration and communication between homeland and new home. Ronald C. Brown, *Hard-Rock Miners: The Intermountain West, 1860–1920* (College Station, TX, 1979), p. 8; see also pp. 108–09, 114–15. See specifically O'Neill, 'Miners in Migration', pp. 61–77.

28 *Daily News* (Newport, RI), 22 December 1875, p. 2.

29 Reported in England in the *Grantham Journal*, 3 March 1877.

30 R.C. Clipperton, HM's Consul, USA, 1886 (C.4783) *Commercial*, No. 20 (1886), *Reports by Her Majesty's Representatives abroad, on the System of Co-operation in Foreign Countries*, p. 138.

31 See Brown, *Hard-Rock Miners*, pp. 40, 155, 157, who actually shows violence was general, not merely sectarian. Wyman, *Hard Rock Epic*, pp. 42, 45, 158, 167, gives ample evidence of Cornish-Irish grievances, as does John B. Martin, *Call it North Country: The Story of Upper Michigan* (1944; Detroit, MI, 1986), pp. 87–90, 194–95.

32 O'Neill, 'Miners in Migration', pp. 61–77.

33 Clipperton, *Reports by Her Majesty's Representatives*, p. 138.

34 A.C. Hepburn, 'The Ancient Order of Hibernians in Irish Politics, 1905–1914', *Cithara*, 10 (1971), pp. 5–18.

35 Whelehan, *Dynamiters*, p. 86.

36 *Canadian-American*, 10 June 1887; Rowland Berthoff, *British Immigrants in Industrial America, 1790–1850* (Cambridge, MA, 1953), p. 188.

37 Brown, *Hard-Rock Miners*, p. 48.

38 *Syracuse Sunday Herald*, 1 October 1897.

39 *Kane Daily Republican*, 9 August 1912, p. 4.

40 The full roll was Thomas O. Jones, S.S. Bice, Richard Tyack, Joseph Davenport, William Maylin, George Allen, George Cooper, Edward C. Fletcher, Albert Roskelly, William Jarvis, H.S. Wyatt and Thomas Atkins. *History of Luzerne, Lackawanna, and Wyoming Counties, Pa; with Illustrations and Biographical Sketches ...* (New York, 1880), p. 425; David Crafts, *History of Scranton, Pennsylvania ...* (Dayton, OH, 1891), p. 544.

41 *Syracuse Sunday Herald*, 1 October 1897.

42 King, *Early History*, pp. 40–43; Ottawa, Archives of Ontario, F 1155 – MU 2864, Sons of England Benefit Society Records, Minute Books, Grand Lodge Meeting, Windsor, Ontario, 11 August 1911, pp. 287–90 includes a hand-written list of over 100 lodges and names; Grand Lodge Meeting, minutes, 13 August 1912, pp. 227–30, lists 138 lodges; see *New York Times*, 24 April 1882, 31 July 1883, for the activities of several OSStG lodges.

43 King, *Early History*, p. 9.

44 Bruce S. Elliott, 'English', in Paul T. Magocsi (ed.), *Encyclopaedia of Canada's Peoples* (Toronto, 1999), pp. 462–88 (quotation at p. 483).

45 Ibid., pp. 483–84.

46 *The Directory of the Members of the Sons of England for the City of Ottawa and the Ottawa Valley* (n.p., 1899), unpaginated.

47 Sons of England, *The Business Directory of the Sons of England for the Cities of Ottawa and Hull* (Ottawa, 1898), p. 8.

48 See for instance MdHS, MS 1881, StGS Baltimore, Minutes, 6 December 1866.

49 *Sons of England Record* [hereafter *Record*], 15 October 1896, p. 4; the later constitutions, however otherwise modified, confirmed the religious exclusions: 'the founders of this society excluded Roman Catholics from membership because all members were required to be Protestants.' Sons of England, *Constitution of the Sons of England* (Toronto, 1890), p. 5.

50 King, *Early History*, p. 17.

51 Sons of England, Constitution of the Sons of England Benevolent Society, under the Supreme Jurisdiction of the Grand Lodge of Canada (Belleville, 1889), p. 39.

52 Calgary, Alberta, Glenbow Museum Archive[GMA], M-1659, Sons of England, United Roses Lodge No. 117 Records, Minute Book, 6 November 1890.

53 *Record*, 15 July 1896, p. 8.

54 Sons of England, *Constitution of the Sons of England Benevolent Society ... 1892* (Belleville, 1892), p. 8.

55 *Manitoba Free Press*, 7 August 1894.

56 A search of Peel's Prairie Provinces newspaper archive, hosted by University of Alberta Libraries and covering over 100 newspapers from throughout the

Canadian prairies, is indicative of the wide coverage of Sons of England activities. A search of the exact phrase 'sons of England benefit society' alone yields well over 700 results in the period from the Sons' establishment to the Second World War. While such a simple search does not fully capture the complexities of the Sons of England's activities, nor of mass-scale digital newspaper searching, it nonetheless is suggestive of the wider trends. For the archive visit http://peel.library.ualberta.ca/newspapers/ (last accessed 18 March 2016).

57 *Bangor Whig and Courier* (ME), 11 August 1896, p. 2.
58 Tanja Bueltmann and Donald M. MacRaild, 'Globalizing St George: English Associations in the Anglo-World to the 1930s', *Journal of Global History*, 7:1 (2012), p. 95.
59 For a detailed studied of the role of the RSStG, see Lesley C. Robinson, 'Englishness in England and the "Near Diaspora": Organisation, Influence and Expression, 1880s–1970s', unpublished PhD thesis, University of Ulster, 2014; also Hanael P. Bianchi, 'St George's Day: A Cultural History', unpublished PhD thesis, Catholic University of America, 2011.
60 Moose Jaw Public Library, Archives Department, MJ-6.001, Moose Jaw Sons of England Benefit Society Fonds, Minute Book, 1904–07, 28 May 1904. The decision to meet at the local masonic hall was made at a later date: see 11 June 1904. The hall was rented for $60.00 per year, with the rent 'to include light, use of furniture and a locker'.
61 Sons of England, *By-Laws of Pride of the Island Lodge, No. 131, Sons of England Benevolent Society: instituted January 15th, 1891, established A.D. 1874, under the supreme jurisdiction of the Grand Lodge of Canada* (Victoria, BC, 1891), p. 4.
62 *Syracuse Sunday Herald*, 10 January 1897.
63 C.W. Heckethorn, *The Secret Societies of All Ages and Countries*, 2 vols (London, 1897), vol. 2, p. 275.
64 Clipperton, *Reports by Her Majesty's Representatives*, p. 138.
65 St George's Society of New York, *Annual Report of the St George's Society of New York for the Year 1884* (New York, 1884), p. 8.
66 *Manitoba Free Press*, 2 March and 7 April 1892.
67 Ibid., 18 July 1882.
68 Ibid., 3 July 1882.
69 Ibid., 18 July 1882.
70 GMA, M-1659, Sons of England, United Roses Lodge, Minute Book, 1 August 1890.
71 *New York Times*, 24 April 1882.
72 Noted in a retrospective piece many years later: *Syracuse Sunday Herald*, 1 October 1897.
73 This and previous quotations from *Anglo-American Times*, 27 June 1884.
74 Donald M. MacRaild and D.A.J. MacPherson, 'Sisters of the Brotherhood: Female Orangeism on Tyneside in the Late 19th and Early 20th Centuries', *Irish Historical Studies*, 34:137 (May 2006), pp. 40–60; Beito, *Mutual Aid*, pp. 31–37; Keith L. Yates, *An Enduring Heritage: The First One Hundred Years of the North American Benefit Association (formerly Women's Benefit Association)* (Port Huron, MI, 1992).

75 Bianchi, 'St George's Day', p. 188.
76 *New Castle News*, 6 July 1892; *Boston Daily Globe*, 29 August 1893, 12 May 1896; *New York Times*, 24 April 1899.
77 *Record*, 15 April 1897, p. 1.
78 Ibid., 15 December 1896, p. 13.
79 *Report of the Inspector of Insurance and Registrar of Friendly Societies of Ontario 1900* (Toronto, 1900), p. C 82.
80 *Chicago Daily Tribune*, 22 April 1895.
81 *Syracuse Daily Herald*, 14 July 1897.
82 Paula Hastings, '"Our glorious Anglo-Saxon Race shall ever fill earth's highest place": The *Anglo-Saxon* and the Construction of Identity in Late-Nineteenth-Century Canada', in R. Douglas Francis (ed.), *Canada and the British World: Culture, Migration and Identity* (Vancouver, 2006), pp. 104–05.
83 GMA, Sons of England, United Roses Lodge, no reference number, 5 November 1896.
84 Hastings, '"Our glorious Anglo-Saxon Race"', pp. 92–93.
85 Sons of England, *Business Directory of the Sons of England of Ottawa and Hull Lodges* (Ottawa, 1899), p. 19. This directory was published by the Anglo-Saxon.
86 *Record*, 15 September 1896, p. 8.
87 In 1916, the Society received a request for copies from Mr C.W. Rowley of Winnipeg, and agreed to send some. CTA, Series 1093, StGS Toronto, File 26, Monthly Meetings Minutes, 1908–20, 3 March 1916, pp. 184–85.
88 See Bukowyzck, et al. (eds), *Permeable Border*, passim, and Chapter 2 above.
89 Figures for 1900 are confirmed in *Report of the Inspector of Insurance and Registrar of Friendly Societies of Ontario 1900*, p. C 43.
90 *Report of the Inspector of Insurance and Registrar of Friendly Societies of Ontario 1911* (Toronto, 1911), p. C 26.
91 Based on statistics extracted from the Society's journal, the *Record*.
92 *News* (Frederick, MD), 2 October 1901, p. 1.
93 For further details see for example Donald Kerr and Deryck W. Holdsworth (eds), *Historical Atlas of Canada: Addressing the Twentieth Century, 1891–1961* (Toronto, 1990), especially ch. 17; also Barbara J, Messamore (ed.), *Canadian Migration Patterns: From Britain and North America* (Ottawa, 2004).
94 See for instance R. Douglas Francis and Chris Kitzan (eds), *The Prairie West as Promised Land* (Calgary, 2007); W. Peter Ward, 'Population Growth in Western Canada, 1901–71', in John E. Foster (ed.), *Developing the West* (Edmonton, 1983), pp. 157–78.
95 *Quebec Saturday Budget*, 28 April 1906.
96 *Trenton Evening Standard*, 30 August 1907.
97 *Lowell Sun*, 7 October 1913, p. 32.
98 *Record*, March 1902, p. 1.
99 Ibid., p. 1.
100 *Manitoba Free Press*, 11 August 1902.

101 Ibid., 12 August 1902.
102 Ibid., 14 August 1902.
103 Ibid., 15 August 1902. Photographs of the visit can be found in *Record*, September 1902, pp. 4–5.
104 *Record*, September 1902, p. 1.
105 Royal Society of St. George, *Annual Report and Year Book 1904*, pp. 66–67; Bianchi, 'St George's Day', p. 189.
106 Ottawa, Archives of Ontario, F 1155 – MU 2864, Sons of England, Minute Books, Grand Lodge Meeting, Hamilton, Ontario, 14 August 1905, pp. 157–58.
107 *Philadelphia Inquirer*, 4 August 1904.
108 Moose Jaw Public Library, Archives Department, MJ-6.001,Moose Jaw Sons of England Benefit Society, Minute Book, 1904–07, 8 October 1904.
109 *Moose Jaw Signal*, 10 October 1904, reprinted in *Record*, November 1904, p. 2.
110 *Calgary Daily Herald*, 19 October 1904.
111 Ibid., 8 July 1905.
112 Ottawa, Archives of Ontario, F 1155 – MU 2864, Sons of England, Minute Books, Grand Lodge meeting, Hamilton, Ontario, 11 August, 1908; Windsor, Ontario, 11 August 1911; Minute Books, pp. 116–18, 280–81.
113 Ibid., Minute Books, Grand Lodge meeting, Toronto, Ontario, 11 August 1911; Minute Books, pp. 433–38.
114 *English-Speaking World*, 4:11 (January 1919), p. 23.
115 Lesley Robinson, 'English Associational Culture in Lancashire and Yorkshire, 1890s–c.1930s', *Northern History*, 51:1 (March 2014), pp. 131–52; Bianchi, 'St George's Day', pp. 213–14, 224–28.
116 *English-Speaking World*, 3:1 (January 1919), p. 16.
117 Though it is worth noting that this was not a uniform development: many smaller ethnic associations ended activities at this time as members decided not to renew subscriptions for lack of funds – an immediate effect of the war. Yet many mutual societies expanded significantly: they were clearly especially attractive for 'the smaller man' at this time of ongoing crisis.
118 Royal Society of St George, *Annual Report and Year Book 1904*, cited by Bianchi, 'St George's Day', p. 187.
119 George N. Fuller, *A History of the Upper Peninsula of Michigan*, 3 vols (Dayton, OH, 1926), vol. 3, pp. 144, 195, 198, 202, 222, 230.
120 See interview with his son Edward King in 1959, GMA, M 4030 D920.K52, George Clift King fonds; *Calgary Weekly Herald*, 6 August 1890.
121 CTA, Series 1093, StGS Toronto, File 26, Monthly Meetings Minutes, 1908–20, 5 November 1909, pp. 28–29.
122 Hughes and MacRaild, 'Anti-Catholicism and Orangeism'; Paul O'Leary, 'When was Anti-Catholicism? The Case of Nineteenth- and Twentieth-Century Wales', *Journal of Ecclesiastical History*, 56:2 (April 2005), pp. 308–25.
123 Alan Conway, *The Welsh in America: Letters from the Immigrants* (St Paul, MN, 1961), pp. 62–63.
124 King, *Early History*, p. 17.

125 Reported in the *Nation*, 14 November 1846, cited by Graham Davis, 'The Irish in Britain, 1815-1939', in Andy Bielenberg (ed.), *The Irish Diaspora* (Harlow, 2000), p. 19.

126 Donald M. MacRaild, *The Irish Diaspora in Britain, 1750-1939*, 2nd edn (Basingstoke, 2010), ch. 2.

127 Charlotte Erickson, *American Industry and the European Immigrant, 1860-1885* (New York, 1958), p. 5.

128 Though a percipient new account, Sim, *Union Forever* demonstrates that the political pressure applied to the American administration was generally not successful. For the broadest trajectories of Irish-American power, see the excellent Whelehan, *Dynamiters*.

129 Even as late as the early twentieth century, the Dillingham Commission reported the superior social status of the English, for example, as foremen and works managers. *Reports of the Immigration Commission. Immigrants in Industries*, part 17: *Copper Mining and Smelting* [chaired by William P. Dillingham], 1911, table 74, p. 87; p. 88.

130 MacRaild, *Irish Diaspora*, ch. 5; S. Fielding, *Class and Ethnicity: Irish Catholics in England, 1880-1939* (Buckingham, 1992), esp. introduction and ch. 1.

131 *Anglo-Saxon*, quoted by Hastings, '"Our glorious Anglo-Saxon Race"', p. 96.

132 Quoted in Ernst, *Immigrant Life*, p. 168.

133 Ibid., pp. 54, 105.

134 MdHS, MS 1881, StGS Baltimore, Minute Books, vol. 1, Treasurer's Report, 19 January 1874.

135 J. Belchem, '"Freedom and friendship to Ireland": Ribbonism in Early Nineteenth-Century Liverpool', *International Review of Social History*, 39:1 (1994), pp. 33-56; Hughes and MacRaild, *Ribbonism*, chs 2-4.

136 David Emmons, *The Butte Irish: Class and Ethnicity in an American Mining Town 1875-1925* (Urbana, 1989), p. 293.

137 Ibid., p. 209.

138 MdHS, MS 1881, StGS Baltimore, Minutes, 23 April 1883. See *Baltimore American*, 24 April 1883, for report of the church service.

139 T.H. Corfe, *Phoenix Murders: Conflict, Compromise and Tragedy in Ireland, 1879-1882* (London, 1968).

140 K.R.M. Short, *Dynamite Wars: Irish American Bombers in Britain* (Dublin, 1979); Whelehan, *Dynamiters*.

141 *Baltimore Sun*, 24 April 1883.

142 Ibid.

143 Ibid.

144 *Syracuse Herald*, 12 July 1908, p. 16.

145 *New York Times*, 24 April 1883, p. 2.

146 *Freeman's Journal*, 15 July 1878; *Leeds Mercury*, 20 July 1878; *Lloyd's Weekly Register*, 21 July 1878.

147 See also Mark McGowan, *The Waning of the Green: Catholics, the Irish, and Identity in Toronto, 1887-1922* (Kingston and Montreal, 1999), p. 3; Gerald J. Stortz, 'An Irish Radical in a Tory Town: William O'Brien in Toronto, 1887', *Eire-Ireland 19* (1984), pp. 35-58.

148 See for instance *Aberdeen Weekly Journal*, 18 May 1887.
149 *Elyria Daily Telephone*, 15 May 1887; but the same account circulated more widely and was printed in several other papers either verbatim or in digested form.
150 *Record*, 15 October 1896, p. 4.
151 Ibid.
152 Clipperton, *Reports by Her Majesty's Representatives, p. 138.*
153 Emmons, *Butte Irish*, p. 218.
154 *English-Speaking World*, 3:7 (July 1920), p. 18.
155 For details see Jeffrey A. Keshen, 'Hopkins, John Castell', in *Dictionary of Canadian Biography*, vol. 15, University of Toronto, http://www.biographi. ca/en/bio/hopkins_john_castell_15E.html (last accessed 13 March 2014).
156 *Record*, 13 December 1899, p. 2.
157 Reprinted in *Record*, 15 August 1896, p. 2.
158 Keshen, 'Hopkins'.
159 *Record*, 15 November 1900, p. 6.
160 Andrew Carnegie, *Triumphant Democracy Or: Fifty Years' March of the Republic* (London, 1886), p. 351. The stance is clear from the outset, as Carnegie added an acknowledgement 'to the beloved Republic under whose equal laws I am made the peer of any man, although denied political equality by my native land, I dedicate this book with an intensity of gratitude and admiration which the native-born citizen can neither feel nor understand'.
161 *Record*, May 1901, p. 2.
162 Ibid., September 1903, p. 4.
163 This and the previous quotes from *Record*, May 1902, p. 1.
164 Ibid., 15 April 1898, p. 135.
165 See for instance Iestyn Adams, *Brothers across the Ocean: British Foreign Policy and the Origins of the 'Special Relationship' 1900-1905* (London, 2005), esp. the section on America and Canada; F.M. Carroll, 'Robert Lansing and the Alaskan Boundary Settlement', *International History Review*, 9:2 (1987), pp. 271-90; and Edward P. Kohn, *This Kindred People: Canadian-American Relations and the Anglo-Saxon Idea, 1895-1903* (Kingston and Montreal, 2004).
166 Particularly with respect to initiatives concerning the Order of the Sons of St George based in the United States, see *Record*, November 1903, pp. 4-5.
167 For example ibid., 15 March 1900, p. 3; Widdis, *With Scarcely a Ripple.*
168 Phillip Buckner, 'Introduction: Canada and the British Empire', in Phillip Buckner (ed.), *Canada and the British Empire* (Oxford, 2008), p. 7.
169 Cited in Donal Lowry, 'The Crown, Empire Loyalism and the Assimilation of Non-British White Subjects in the British World: An Argument against "Ethnic Determinism"', in Carl Bridge and Kent Fedorowich (eds), *The British World: Diaspora, Culture and Identity* (London, 2003), p. 106.
170 Michèle Brassard and Jean Hamelin, 'Tarte, Joseph Israel', in *Dictionary of Canadian Biography*, vol. 13, University of Toronto, http://www.biographi. ca/en/bio.php?id_nbr=7097 (last accessed: 20 March 2014).
171 *Record*, 16 October 1899, p. 4.

172 Ibid., p. 5.
173 This and the previous quotations from ibid., 15 June 1900, p. 5.
174 Ibid., May 1901, p. 1.
175 See also 'England's Greatness': Anniversary Sermon Delivered to the Members of St George's Society of Ottawa and the Sons of England by Rev. Dr. Herridge (Ottawa, 1899).
176 This quotation comes from *La Semaine Religieuse*, a Quebec-based journal that was very vocal in its anti-Englishness; see *Record*, 15 February 1900, p. 5.
177 Ibid., 15 October 1900, pp. 5-6.
178 Ibid., 16 October 1899, p. 4.
179 Ibid.

4

Ethnic activities and leisure cultures

It is proposed to hold the Anniversary dinner as usual on St George's Day ... to promote one of the primary objects of the original Founders, that of 'cherishing social intercourse among themselves'. (*Annual Report of the St George's Society of New York* (New York, 1870), p. 5)

Let us then as Englishmen, and as Englishmen loving our country and countrymen, have a Society from which we can when in sickness or distress claim aid as our right and not as charity. (John S. King, *Early History of the Sons of England Benevolent Society* (Toronto, 1891), p. 30)

The St George's Society is, therefore, essentially an American patriotic society. (St George's Society of Baltimore, Minutes, 20 January 1869, MdHS, MS 1881)

Despite their different social composition and emphases, the elite and middle-class St George's societies shared a number of characteristics with the broader-based Albion societies, Canada's Sons of England and the American OSStG. Whether they were charities run by the better off or mutual societies offering collective self-help, all of these societies publicly venerated England, Britain, its monarch, the global Empire; each evoked a shared Anglo-Saxon inheritance. Adopting the posture of their age and their nation, the speech-makers and event organizers – whether wealthy lawyers or working-class journeymen – focused on the expression of a sometimes pugnaciously superior identity within which St George was the identikit icon, invested with whichever powers or qualities they wished to ascribe to their nationality: military valour, imperial reach, beneficent charity, moral leadership or spiritual supremacy. St George's Day saw all associations feasting, toasting and praying for England, the hub of the world and centrepiece of a pronounced Anglo-world hegemony. Ethnic togetherness enjoined appreciation of national glories that appeared chauvinistic. Moreover, English celebrations also denoted a conscious collective across borders – society members were visiting each other or sending telegrams of camaraderie – expressing transnational diasporic consciousness.

The basic rules and procedures of the various St George's societies remained quite similar. Their membership rules and rituals were relatively standardized in terms of joining and fee-paying; their practices conformed to established principles; and they undertook to organize an array of social and cultural events, and to engage with their countrymen, English visitors and the homeland with a shared zeal. While the St George's societies did not utilize Orange-style regalia, the Sons of England and the Sons of St George drew upon them heavily. Still, the assiduous maintenance of minutes and records, their upholding the principles of electing officers and their dispensation of charitable 'good cheer', their promotion of grand St George's Day dinners and their celebration of monarch, Empire and notable dates in English history all pointed to a clear and shared identity among these different associations. Though ethno-symbolism was not normally associated with western nationalism, Anthony D. Smith observes it in English behaviour, whether in their private gatherings, in public celebrations or through the deployment of powerful ethno-cultural symbols, such as St George slaying the dragon.[1] Indeed, English associations often utilized rituals similar to those of other ethnic societies established by migrants from the British Isles – societies often framed by a broadly pro-imperialist world-view.

Yet the English associations' habit of gathering in public places to toast the queen, Empire and England sometimes yielded sharp rebuke from Americans. Indeed, Anglo-American politics – at times very fraught in the nineteenth century – determined a significant frostiness to the idea of England and her Empire. This presented problems to those of American nativity who were proud of their English stock and who wished to demonstrate it by joining the likes of these ethnic societies. This is why, as one of the quotations that open this chapter suggests, love of England had to be matched by a duty to the United States. In 1832, the St George's Society, Charleston, was in defensive mode in resisting Henry Clay's questioning of British Americans' 'eulogy of the British Constitution', something denounced as irrelevant to local or national politics in the Carolinas or the United States.[2] Given that so many St George's society members were Americans, this warning was taken seriously; indeed, its essential character caused some division between English- and American-born members. Even the Order of the Sons of St George, which had been forged in the fires of sectarian anti-Irishness, sought citizenship (and thus political power), not ethnic ghettoization, for its members.

This chapter investigates English associational culture in terms of social life, cultural expression and national identity and affinity. Having explored the rise of English associations in the preceding chapters, we now focus, first, on the inner workings of the societies. This involves exploring the quarterly and annual rituals of being an Englishman or Englishwoman in an ethnic society in the nineteenth and early twentieth centuries and, secondly, the social aspect of dinners, smokers, church services, sporting events, annual picnics and outings and attendance at city functions. For these were critical components for all associations examined in this study.[3] To the small, tightly focused core group which ran such societies, social occasions cemented the principles of shared working, service and trust; where societies were larger, often with hundreds of members, social occasions were vital to maintaining shared identity, thereby serving as important sites of memory. The final feature we explore concerns the ideas, views and expressions that underpinned English associational culture. Notions of Anglo-Saxon unity and racial supremacy shaped the imperial nationalism of the English in the half-century or so to the advent of the First World War, and activities organized by associations provided a ready platform for them.

What is apparent is that, while men with close associations had founded these societies, they could very quickly become socially more strung out – a fact we have already documented in the phenomenal rise in membership, as well as the geographic spread. Keeping a handle on members was important, for the proliferation of these membership societies was a key part of the emergence of an empowered, confident middle class within a growing and increasingly complex urban, civic society.[4] Equally, the same phenomena could, as Chapter 3 has documented, also boost the social capital of the working class. What emerges overall is the story of a focused and wide-ranging range of expressions and activities of Englishness, both social and practical.

Principles and structures

The nineteenth-century St George's societies were founded in many towns and cities because ethnic community leaders accepted responsibility for the paupers and poor workers lurching down the gangways of the emigrant ships in their harbours. Americans, recently naturalized, and English stock of many generations' residence in the New World shared this responsibility. For these men, Englishness primarily was expressed through such work on behalf of immigrants and represented civic as well as ethnic behaviour. Those efforts benefited the United States in a deliberate way. The secretary of the Baltimore St George's Society, speaking at the inception of his organization in 1869, captured it well: '[t]his is generally seen as a Society to support English interests [but] it is really a society that advances American interests'[5] – a society which, as the secretary went on to record, served America, patriotically, more than England, by dealing with the problem of English immigrant poverty without drawing upon American purses.

Importantly, the social side contributed to the charitable side, since a popular organization, with a reputation for good dinners, dances and other events, was likely to increase and maintain membership, as well as generate additional funds for charitable pursuits. Hence, associations also sought to raise income from individual donations, dinners, musical concerts and other fund-raisers. The New York St George's Society organized a full social calendar, from the usual St George's Day dinner to musical concerts around Christmas time and an annual ball for Valentine's Eve.[6] Chicago St George's Society held its twenty-third annual 'sociable' in 1881, between Christmas and New Year. Members and wives, daughters and sons, associates and friends, were entertained with singing, music, dancing and good food at the city's Palmer House.[7] In 1887, the Albion Society of Denver hosted a large New Year ball.[8] As with so many such masculine organizations, 'smokers' or 'smoking concerts' were means of socializing and raising money.[9] One such was proposed and agreed for the king's birthday in 1908.[10] Another suggestion was for a 'carnival gathering' at the St George's house.[11]

Each society created a set of meetings, committees, annually elected officers and entrance fees, periodic dues and so on. Meetings occurred quarterly, with sub-committees meeting more frequently as necessary. Toronto's Committee of Management, for example, which was chaired by the president and involved most of the senior officers, met weekly to oversee the work of the Society, its sub-committees and special committees, and so on.[12] Each St George's Society had a president, vice-president, treasurer, secretary, several chaplains and also quite often general medical practitioners. Members were proposed and seconded before existing members voted on whether or not to admit them. The quarterly meetings were open to all members and were chaired by the president, with reports from the treasurer and secretary providing the mainstay of proceedings. An annual general meeting was held in the early part of the year to elect the year's officers, their nominations having normally been garnered in October or November of the previous year. At its foundation, the St George's Society of Kingston precluded the president and vice-president from being elected for consecutive years; however, in 1869 the members adjusted article no. 4 of their constitution to allow further re-election.[13] Immediately upon their election, the Society, headed by its new committee, ordinarily received annual statements of finances and other business. Officers' appointments were usually announced at St George's Day dinners, held on or close to 23 April each year. A specially appointed sub-committee organized these social occasions, with members charged with booking a hall or hotel dining room, pricing and distributing tickets and urging members to bring families and friends along, since the dinner was both a social occasion and a fund-raiser.[14] The enormous society dinners held by the New York Society were society occasions, but even the more modest Baltimore and Ottawa St George's Societies each headed for one of their own city's better eating places.

Principal officers were the organizational heart of the St George's societies, but because the *sine qua non* of these organizations was the body of poor and hard-up to whom they dispensed charity, the relief or stewards' committee was crucial. The stewards always included a couple of doctors who were able to give medical assessments of claimants for relief. They worked closely with five or six of the most reliable, long-serving and dedicated members. Relief committees assiduously maintained very detailed ledgers of every cent given to each person, how many times, for what reason and with what effect. The Kingston Society was set upon on a similar basis to the other societies: a president, two vice-presidents, secretary and treasurer were supported by 'one or more Chaplains, and one or more Physicians, and Six Stewards',[15] thus implying the full range of charitable and medical services for hard-up or vulnerable English immigrants.

All such societies struggled to maintain members and to acquire full dues from everyone. With a hard economic winter approaching in 1873, the beginning of a severe depression, James Belden, secretary of the Society in Baltimore, issued a handbill, which was reproduced in local papers, calling for members to pay their subscriptions and for 'those who are able, to send in an extra donation' to relieve the rising numbers of English poor, with nearly $60 raised this way.[16] The year was one of depression, and so it 'made large demands upon its resources'. With sixty paying members, the Society had an income of $300 per annum.[17] While lamenting the fiscal state of affairs, the secretary also perceived a lack of interest among the English in the welfare of their fellow countrymen in the United States:

> The year 1876 has been remarkable for the productiveness of centenni-als [of the American Revolution] and hard times. Perhaps there never occurred in the history of this country such a juxtaposition of luxury and poverty, and as a consequence of this latter, the resources of our Society have, in common with others, been taxed to the utmost ... It is to be regret-ted that so many Englishmen and persons of English descent living in our midst should stand aloof and withhold the aid so much needed to extend our usefulness. Many perhaps, it is true, are only awaiting our invitation to join our ranks, while others may be deterred from lack of funds. To the former we would say 'Do not stand upon the order of your coming, but come at once,' and to the latter, 'Give us at least your sympathy and countenance.'[18]

Belden, one of the most active members and the former and founding secretary, had a solution to another sort of apathy, and moved
that members two years in arrears be written to saying 'unless prompt
payment is made they will be considered to have resigned their membership as provided in Art. 5 of Bye laws'.[19]

The secretary's report of January 1877 continued to paint a bleak picture
of the economy of Baltimore: 'perhaps there never occurred in the history
of this country such a juxtaposition of luxury & poverty, & as a consequent
result of this latter the resources of our Society have ... been taxed to the
utmost'. This meant that 'private resources' had to be called upon. The
secretary, the Islington-born architect E.G. Lind, ended this passage with
an appeal for further donations and criticism that so many 'Englishmen &
persons of English descent ... should stand aloof and withhold their aid'.
At this point, they were down to thirty-six paying members.[20]

Individuals were pursued for tardiness and non-payment. One
Mr Crouch was written to in July 1883 to obtain funds, as the bill for his
St George's Day tickets was still unpaid.[21] A month later – presumably
after no response or a refusal to come before them – the members moved
that he be excluded. Telling punctuation accompanied the secretary's
recording of the result: 'unanimously carried!' Precisely the same formulation and emphasis were recorded when the members voted to notify
Mr Vaughan and others who had not paid for three years that they were
at risk of being struck from the record.[22]

During the 1890s the secretary's annual reports sometimes include
snipes at those who showed 'considerable apathy' and complaints against
those critics of the Society 'who did not take an active interest' in
it.[23] Moreover, in 1894 the quality of the Baltimore Society's minutes
declined; less business was apparent in what they reported, and, in
October that year, in a recruitment drive, the entrance fee ($5) was
waived until 1896 and a committee was formed to plan entertainments to
be held 'from time to time ... particularly at the meetings of the society'.[24]
In 1896 and 1897, only a couple of pages of terse minutes were penned at
the hand of the secretary, Stewart Darrell, one of the founding members
of thirty years' standing. No officers are listed for either year.[25] In mid-
1897, things came to a head. With no new members being recorded, and
small attendances, the sense of decline was made more acute in July 1897
when the almoner, Mr Rowland, expressed concern that while 'the call
upon him [for funds] was more numerous than usual ... there are practically no funds now to hand available to meet the urgent and deserving
applications being daily made'.[26]

The outlook had become less insular with the formation of the
NAStGU, and this effect was multiplied many times over with the formation of the RSStG in 1894. The RSStG was not, however, directly related
to the existing body of St George's societies – even today the New York,

Philadelphia and Baltimore societies are merely affiliates. The impor-
tance of the RSStG for these groups, it may be argued, was that it enabled
Englishmen at home to connect with their fellow nations in the wider
Anglo-world and also to influence them. Robinson has, however, questioned the extent of this connection, and certainly finds little evidence
of a direct influence of the American system upon that emerging in late
Victorian England, though she accepts the likelihood of some link.[27]
Besides, the RSStG appears to have prompted the development of a host
of competing branches bearing the 'royal' prefix. This was particularly
true in the British Empire and former colonies, but not in the United
States. Here the American St George's societies certainly communicated
with the London RSStG but did not become subordinate to it. The scanty
archives of the Charleston St George's Society, for example, include a
beautiful programme for the RSStG festival dinner of 1905 in London,
raising the possibility that a member may have attended. If not, then at
least transnational communication extended to sending invitations out
across the Atlantic.[28]

Membership dues tell us much about the class of an organization.
For most working-class organizations in the nineteenth century, when
English ethnic associations were taking off, they tended to be quite low,
little more than a sixpence per monthly or four-weekly meeting. The
strongly elitist constituency of the St George's Society of New York, in
the colonial and early republican periods, charged members the large
membership fee of thirty shillings per annum and fined them ten shillings
if they missed the annual dinner, 'unless prevented by sickness'.[29] Small
traders, let alone workingmen, could barely afford such charges. By contrast, at its founding meeting many years later, in 1859, the St George's
Society of Ottawa set the entrance fee at five shillings and the annual
subscription at five shillings, 'payable in advance'.[30] This was equivalent
to roughly one American dollar at that time, with an exchange rate of
£1 to $4 or $5. The Baltimore St George's Society, which was founded in
the mid-1860s, charged the similar sum of $5 per annum in dues, with
an entrance fee of another $5. In 1939, this same figure was still being
charged.[31] Since dues were often hard to extract, it is clear that not all
members followed the Baltimore treasurer's entreaty, in 1871, that they
should 'as a labor of love, pay them speedily and cheerfully' or 'send in his
resignation in writing to the Secretary'.[32]

An important newspaper clipping – regrettably without an indication
of the year of publication – survives in the minute books of the Kingston
St George's Society. The report, dated 25 January, almost certainly was
from 1860. While reaffirming the Society's commitment to supporting
down-at-heel fellow countrymen and helping immigrant settlement, the
report detailed a special meeting of the Society, where some important
changes were introduced. The meeting proposed to extend its purview

from the city to the wider electoral division, to reduce the membership dues to $1 per annum, and to declare a donation of $20 to result in life membership, a reduction of the quorum from nine to five and the establishment of the 'St George's Society Reserve Fund'.[33] Coming at a time when Canada had recently adopted the dollar at United States rates, the value of that membership cost was approximately four shillings – very significantly lower than that which New York members paid. In 1877 there was a change, with fees doubled to $2 per annum with an entrance charge of one dollar. Life membership was then set at $10 (or four quarterly payments of $3, making $12 in total).[34]

Variations in the wealth of societies were marked by the nature of their accommodation. The Sons of England in Calgary (United Roses Lodge) met in the local masonic hall, while others, for instance in Toronto, had their own lodge rooms.[35] Among the St George's societies too there were significant variations. Whereas some, like the Philadelphia Sons of St George, had their own buildings, others were less well positioned. In New York the St George's and St Andrew's societies shared offices for some time in the 1870s, primarily to facilitate the more co-ordinated dispensation of charity, while several decades later, in the 1920s, the St George's Society moved offices in quick succession after a series of robberies, including one in which its almoner was shot in the groin, though 'luckily without fatal results'.[36]

The seemingly endless debates within the Baltimore St George's Society about where to hold its meetings, and whether or not to invest in a building, are signs of the less confident society with either less wealthy members or fewer adherents overall. Almost six years after its founding, in October 1872, the 'feasibility and advantage of having a St George's Hall in an eligible situation' was discussed, with 'funds to be raised by shares of stock'.[37] The same issue was mooted in January 1877, with Mr Spiller promising to donate $500 or $100 per annum for five years.[38] Three months later, the members were discussing the more modest proposition of a suitable room.[39] And at the beginning of the following year, the president was lamenting Spiller's death.[40] But it was to take more than another twenty years until the Society finally secured a 'permanent home', forming a committee in April 1900 to consider a proposal that $500 be drawn from the Society's savings account as long as it was matched in an issue of stock in order to furnish a place at 10 West 20th Street, which the Society had leased.[41] Not all members liked the use of funds in this way: the one-time president W.H. Perot wrote to the Society 'in earnest terms' against it, though the secretary's reply no longer exists.[42] Perhaps Perot foresaw the long-term financial impact this would have – an impact that meant that, by early 1911, it was stated that a more central and cheaper home was preferable, and that, by April 1911, the Society had returned to Rennart's Hotel, a place it had used many years previously.[43]

Principles and supporters

No matter what they were and when they existed, and regardless of the class or ethnicity of their members, these membership societies had several recurring things in common. First, they corresponded to what Morris called a 'subscriber democracy'. Money was collected from members. The funds were distributed and activities organized by a committee and officers elected by the subscribers at the annual general meeting.[44] Secondly, as a result of the structure described so well by Morris, these societies relied inordinately on the good work of small numbers of committed men or women. Moreover, the initial impetus to form these organizations usually came from someone with clout or office, a respected civic figure, someone with a prior history in the tradition being developed, maintained or expanded. In Philadelphia, James Allen, a long-serving member and officer of the city's Sons of St George, provided this type of leadership. When he died in 1875, the press covered his funeral in a fulsome piece. After arriving from England sixty years previously, Allen had become a successful businessman. He served as president (for sixteen years), vice-president, secretary and treasurer, and was highly involved the relief committee. Allen was instrumental in the purchase of St George's Hall, on the corner of 13th and Arch Streets, and, wrote the press, 'it is somewhat remarkable that the last time he used his pen was to sign a check for his subscription to his hall'.[45] Not long before Allen died, the St George's Society of Toronto was, in 1871, electing James Cooper to life membership. Serving as steward, as first, second and third vice-presidents and as president, he was an early-generation arrival in Toronto, who developed strong business interests as a merchant and was a thorough stalwart of the Society. In the same minute, several members' deaths in 1915 were recorded. They were all men of substance and service: Walter Beardmore, who ran his own company; Mr H. Blackburn, 'prominent insurance man'; Henry Buckland, 'prominent real estate and insurance agent'; William Clow, businessman; and, among others, Charles Parsons, 'one of the oldest businessmen in the city'.[46] These were committed members who conformed to Morris's categorization: they stood repeatedly for usually uncontested elections; and where there was a contest, it was managed, with both men eventually serving whichever office they ran for. These were local power elites: they probably were not quite the oligarchs Morris considers to have been common in subscriber societies such as these, but they certainly wielded influence over charity, business, civic life and politics.[47]

Kingston's St George's Society could not have had a better pedigree in this respect. A meeting intended formerly to organize the branch occurred on Saturday 30 April 1859 at the city's Macrow's Hotel.[48] In the chair was Colonel William Foster Coffin, Bath-born soldier, civil servant and author. Coffin had fine credentials to chair such a meeting. His father, John, was a Boston-born loyalist who moved to Quebec in the mid-1770s, as one of the United Empire Loyalists who migrated *en masse* to Canada and elsewhere in the Empire. Here, Coffin's father played 'a distinguished part in its defence against the Americans in 1775–76'. Coffin's family came to Quebec in 1813, where he rose, in the 1830s, to be assistant civil secretary for Lower Canada, where his job was to organize a police force. In the meantime he had married a woman with, like him, Boston loyalist credentials. By the 1850s, when he had acquired wealth and influence, he also organized militia units after the British greatly reduced Canadian garrisons because of the Crimean War. This was the man of acumen, power and wealth who sat to chair the emerging English society.[49] The Toronto St George's Society could boast men such as Captain Mason, past president, who died in 1915. Members at the annual general meeting heard of his commitment, his honorary life membership and his military experiences in the Royal Grenadiers, including 'repelling what is known as the Fenian Raid 1866 and received the medal for that event'.[50] Then there was Captain Frederick Caston, born in the Norfolk village whose name he bore. Caston rose to captain in the Royal Grenadiers, and was involved in the suppression of the Riel Rebellion in 1885, especially at the Battle of Baroche.[51]

Consular officials were regular attenders at these dinners, though Consul George Matthew refused to attend Philadelphia's 1855 celebrations because, in a heated political climate between the two countries, its committee 'omitted the toast to the queen'.[52] In Baltimore a decade later, relations with English authority and prestige were much less varied. With a very rich set of records from the first minute books and membership lists, we are able to see how important the consular office was. Thus on 6 December 1866 it was announced that the British Consul, Stewart Darrell, was to 'organize and commence a St George's Society for the relief of distressed English subjects at once so long as fifteen persons will assent to become members at an annual subscription of ten dollars each'. Darrell, a substantial merchant with interests in Baltimore and later Bermuda,[53] was joined by his Vice Consul, the Royal Insurance Co. representative for the American South, J.J. Jackson, also a founder member, as was Darrell's brother, Charles – the latter serving in several offices, including that of president, a post he had to relinquish in 1909 'on account of his want of eyesight'.[54] Twice the required number of founding members stepped forward, and many others joined in the early months.[55] The Society was thus organized officially on 21 January 1867 and was incorporated under Maryland law in the following month.[56]

Darrell and his brother remained involved until the early 1900s, by which time they were old men. The desire to maintain such a connection with British officialdom can be noticed throughout the Darrells' tenures. Denis Donohoe, also British Consul-General at Baltimore, was proposed for membership 20 October 1873 and was duly elected on 19 January 1874. Darrell and Donohoe involved the Society in numerous high-profile society events, such as the visit south of Edward Thornton, British ambassador to Washington, and the Earl Dufferin, Governor-General of Canada, which was being organized in 1876 for May 1877, the queen's birthday, by the British Association of Virginia. The Association's representatives called on Donohoe's 'immediate patronage and personal attendance'; Darrell, then president of the St George's Society of Baltimore, 'said he would do all he could to interest his Society in the movement' for a large British celebration.[57] Forty years after Darrell first called these Englishmen to arms, and decades after Donohoe became involved, there was still hope of consular support. In February 1909 members formed a committee to approach Mr Frazer, the British consul, to ask him 'to become associated with the Society'.[58] The Darrell connection crossed the generations, with the founder Stewart Darrell's son, the lawyer H. Cavendish Darrell, chairing the relief committee. [59]

Besides the Darrells and various British consuls, there also were other strong continuities. In July 1875, the secretary of the Baltimore St George's Society, John Belden, stepped down from this office and from the relief committee and was replaced by E.G. Lind.[60] Lind served as secretary from 1876 to 1882, resigning in March that year to move to Atlanta, where he stayed for ten years or so.[61] George H. Williams, who was serving as president and treasurer, also temporarily took up the duties of secretary in what was confirmation of a familiar theme to historians of associations: that good health relied on the energies of a few.[62] His work was recognized when, in July 1883, he was made a life member, 'without entrance fee or subscription'.[63] Similarly, in April 1890, the then president and founding member W.H. Perot, who had given over two decades' service, resigned because of poor health.[64] W.H. Perot's presidency was regularly challenged by the candidacy of his vice-president, George H. Williams.[65] Nevertheless they both served the Society for many years, as did Williams's son. In 1918, the Society announced the death of Williams Jnr, 'one of its [the Society's] most faithful and esteemed members, and, for many years, its treasurer', capturing the Society's sense of lineage in a resolution which noted his

> gracious courtesy and ever-ready response to all calls of charity ... endeared him to his fellow-members, who ever found him a straight-forward, honourable, honest gentleman who faithfully carried on the interest in the Society evinced by his distinguished father, the late George Hawkins Williams, one of the founders and first Presidents of the St George's Society of Baltimore.[66]

St George's Day

Dinners, feasting, toasts and merrymaking – all embroidered with ritual form and etiquette – were fundamental outward expressions of civic, ethnic and group identity by English societies. In this regard, they were no different from a plethora of other membership associations: in the club world of New York as much as small-town Kingston, Ontario, dinners were key milestones in the annual calendars of societies, serving to bring together members and guests for a common activity. Only the gravest circumstances caused the annual celebrations of St George to be cancelled: New York abandoned its dinner in the teeth of the Irish famine in 1847, and most American societies did not meet during the years of the American Civil War.[67] On a smaller, local scale, 'the Ottawa St George's Society felt the benefits of this mutual alliance in 1900 when, in the wake of "the disastrous fire", which destroyed much of Hull, Quebec and large parts of Ottawa, the parent society in London sent their heartiest sympathies along with a donation of 10s 6d to help those affected'.[68] Baltimore's St George's Society cancelled its dinner of April 1912 on hearing of the sinking of the *Titanic* and instead donated ticket funds to the disaster relief fund.[69] Otherwise, attendance at the meetings was a fundamental requirement of membership, with sometimes severe penalties for not turning up. Minutes often contain irritated or exasperated comments about the failure of members to do this annual service. John Belden, secretary of the Baltimore Society, was a hard-line character, and in April 1874 he proposed that Englishmen who were not members of the Society should not be able to attend the St George's Day dinner. His colleagues did not, however, agree: his motion was not carried.[70]

St George's Day dinners were usually the most elaborate annual gatherings, offering an important show of unity – and one not only between members seated at the dinner table, but also with other societies, both nationally and transnationally. Messages were received from the same brethren they had been sent to. Typical were those from 'one hundred jolly Englishmen' in Guelph and the '300 strong' Oswego St George's Society, both of which groups sent 'fraternal greetings' and hopes for 'good health' to their 'brethren in Kingston'.[71] But gatherings in the English saint's name were not all about expressing identity. Dinners were often attended by civic dignitaries from beyond a society's own ranks and offered an opportunity to raise additional funds for charitable good works. Events were also arranged around the visits of dignitaries and officials. In 1851, Sir Henry Lytton Bulwer, a man exiled to Washington but who fell in love with the country and sought to improve Anglo-American relations during his three years there, gave a long and characteristically witty after-dinner speech at the sixty-fifth anniversary dinner of New York St George's Society.[72] Meanwhile, in 1859 the St George's Society of

Chicago announced that the former MP and corn law reformer Richard Cobden was to be present at its annual saint's day dinner.[73]

St George's Day dinners were usually attended by members of the clergy, who consistently opened proceedings with sermons. These clerics were drawn usually from Episcopalian churches, and if not then from the Protestant sects. This research has uncovered no instance of a Catholic clergyman leading the prayers; nor did any of the societies record ever attending a Catholic service. In the 1840s, the English of New York opened the Anglo-American Free Church of St George the Martyr, the emphasis altogether suggesting the English roots of the church. This initiative was led by the Revd Marcus Moses, chaplain of the St George's Society, whose aim was to prevent English from drifting away from Anglicanism. The fact that free seats were offered for British immigrants in an era of pew charges indicated how directly the measure was aimed at the poor classes of workingmen and their families.[74] These societies also liked to be seen at the better religious venues. Thus, in 1909 and 1910, Toronto St George's Society noted the decision to reserve seats at St James' Cathedral for England's saint's day service.[75]

The societies each had several chaplains, and one of these provided a church for a service on the Sunday closest to St George's Day and also blessed the dinners. During the 1880s, the Baltimore St George's Society regularly attended a special service at the Ascension Church, where its own Revd Dr Campbell Fair was rector.[76] Thirty years later, a resolution of congratulations was sent to Fair's contemporary Revd David Prescott Allison MA, who had offered services all this time at St Michael and All Angels. The resolution offered 'love and gratitude of this Society for the time and service he has never failed to give willingly in burying our Dead, honouring the friendless emigrant with the same reverent and solemn rite he would celebrate the notable and distinguished citizen'.[77]

From an early point the St George's Society of Kingston took great care to have a religious service at the time of St George's Day. The year 1878 was typical enough: the dinner was held on Tuesday 23 April, but a religious service at St George's Cathedral was conducted two days earlier by two of the Society's chaplains, Revd Mr Bousfield and Revd Mr Rogers.[78] The St George's dinner on Tuesday 23 April 1878 was a well-attended affair at the British American Hotel. The gathering of some ninety members heard that their president and secretary had been invited to annual banquets in London and Oswego. The Society sent a message to London, Toronto, Oswego, Hamilton and Ottawa:

> St George's brethren greet you with their best wishes for your welfare, and that God may prosper you throughout the year, save to the old land, her honour and renown, and, brethren, may all unite in making Canada the land of our adoption, the brightest jewel in the diadem of the Queen.[79]

In Toronto the St George's Society received invitations each year from the city's Sons of England to attend 'divine service', but not always around St George's Day. In 1908, the date was set for 8 November.[80] This was the Sunday nearest to the anniversary of the Gunpowder Plot. In 1915, the tradition remained strong, and the Toronto St George's annual general meeting early in the next year entered a minute of 'apprecia- tion of the interest and appreciation taken, as heretofore, by the Sons of England, on their large attendance and joining with our Society in the process to the church'.[81]

Baltimore also made clearly sectarian charitable decisions, reaching out to local charity organizers in the process. Miss Margaret Purviance was thanked for admitting 'sick Englishmen at a mere nominal fee into the Union Protestant Infirmary'.[82] Established in 1854 on account of all existing hospitals being 'under Catholic control', the board of managers had as its first president the Miss Purviance to whom thanks were now being given.[83] Following that, the Society agreed to write to the infirmary to praise its work in looking after the members' ill fellow nationals.[84] Similarly, Kingston St George's Society made what we might dub sectar- ian donations, for example in 1869 when it awarded $10 to the Carleton Protestant Hospital.[85]

Dinner halls and restaurants, as Bianchi has noted, were adorned with flags, emblems of St George, paintings of Queen Victoria (of which several were commissioned) and various other symbols and icons of national identity. Flags also marked contemporary events or the pres- ence of other national groups.[86] Press reports noted how, in New York in 1841, 'the union jack of Old England and the stars and stripes of Young America were mingled together in harmonious concord'.[87] Flags were certainly a critical element in decorations. Hence the Grand Lodge of the Sons of England, in 1896, decided that its flag should be the White Ensign. As was explained:

> The 'Jack' with its three crosses of St. Patrick, St. Andrew and St. George, is a sign of 'British Empire,' thus added to the red cross of St. George, the emblem of 'England,' combines to make a flag eminently suited to a national society such as ours, whose dominant idea is that of 'British Connection'.[88]

Elsewhere, at Ottawa, in 1860 the St George's Society discussed the size and design of rosettes to be worn at the upcoming ball, and planned to add streamers and other materials to decorate the room.[89] Decorations served as commemorative symbols and, together with speeches and food, were intrinsic elements of what were fairly standardized and ritu- alized gatherings. Given their often symbolic nature, decorations helped to condense and make accessible to attendees particular meaning and messages.[90] Especially widely used for decorations were flags. Details of the 1868 gathering in Baltimore provided a little detail of the flags adorning the walls. Behind the president of the Society the 'Union Jack' was 'supported either side by the French and American flags', owing to the presence of the French; to the rear of the vice-president, 'the English and American flags intertwined' – a fitting symbol of a society such as this. Eleven toasts were raised to the usual individuals, countries and feelings, with the addition of 'our allies' – a further nod to the French presence.[91] In 1870, the flags of Germany and France were both added to the ensemble in Baltimore.[92] Three months later, the two nations would be at war. In 1872, Baltimore St George's Society saw the British and French flags intertwined with the cross of St George; at the other end of the table, the Scots saltire was added to the Stars and Stripes and the Union flag.[93] A little teasing of other nations seemed not to cause offence.

One of the common toasts made was to our 'sister societies'. This meant Irish, Scottish and Welsh societies in the main, but also French, German and other ethnic associations where they existed. Indeed, togetherness and a general lack of rancour between them was a sign of the fundamentally polite and middle-class nature of these societies, and perhaps a recognition of their shared purpose in alleviating immigrant hardship. 'Several other national benevolent Societies' were present, in April 1814, at the dinner of the Sons of St George of Philadelphia.[94] In addition to the four societies from the (then) United Kingdom and the Germans, New York, in 1841, also entertained the New England Society.[95] A few years later, the city's St George's Day Society, for its annual dinner at the City Hotel, had also invited the St Nicholas Society, the British vice-consul, Lieutenant Walker of the United States Navy and the Swedish consul, as well as sundry editors and civic dignitaries.[96]

Overall, toasts changed little over time. Key office-holders were lauded first. In the colonial period, the monarch and colonial officials, along with military men, headed the roll of honour to which glasses were raised. Once the United States was an independent nation, the president was added. Baltimore was typical. The first toast was usually for St George, 'the day we celebrate'. On most (though not all) occasions the next toast, to Queen Victoria – which 'elicited the enthusiasm which an Englishman's love of country carries with him' – was followed by glasses raised to the Prince and Princess of Wales, the president of the United States, 'Her Majesty's Ministers and Representatives', 'Old England', 'Englishmen', 'Our Sister Societies throughout the world' and 'the press, the great enlightener of mankind'.[97] Monarch, Empire, the global reach of Englishmen and the cherished liberties of their race were each captured in different ways.[98] Toasts could reflect particular moments. At Madison,

Wisconsin, in 1865, the dinner was postponed because of President Lincoln's assassination.[99] This act was also reflected in the toasts:

1. The day we celebrate.
2. The Queen and old England.
3. The memory of our late President ABRAHAM LINCOLN.
4. The president of the United States.
5. The Army and Navy of the United States.
6. Our Sister Societies.
7. The press.
8. The ladies.

In 1870, the St George's Society of Baltimore toasted 'The Press. May it ever be the incorruptible guardian of what is known around the world as English Liberty.'[100] Englishmen in Washington sat down to a sumptuous dinner on their saint's day in 1881, amid a 'handsomely decorated' hall. President George F. Dawson chaired an event which saw toasts to the United States president, the queen, 'the Day We Celebrate', 'Our sister societies', 'the Land We Live in', 'the Army and Navy', 'the Press' and 'Our guests'. Messages of goodwill were received from Ottawa, from Philadelphia and from Hyde Clark, 'chairman of the Societies of St George and corresponding secretary of the North American Union of Societies of St George' in England.[101] At Baltimore, Andrew Darrell, the British vice-consul and a member since the 1867, said in an 1896 address to the annual dinner of the St George's Society of Baltimore what the anniversary meant to him: 'the 23rd April, St George's Day, meant the beginning of England, and more than that, the beginning of the Anglo-Saxon race'.[102]

In Canada, the speeches required no compromise between English, British and host identities and institutions. Indeed, the journal of the Sons of England carried a tone of strident patriotism that evoked race, Empire and martial culture as indistinguishable features of their shared identity. In 1897 members in Toronto were twice given the chance to hear a former soldier, Charles E. Swait, draw upon his military experience in a paper entitled 'India beyond the Indus', in which he described the 'raw-boned and long faces' and 'Jewish caste of features' that he found among the 'good fighters' of the Afridi people of the North-West Frontier. Swait finished a talk of rippling chauvinism with bellicose declarations about the 'power, world-wide and all-pervading of the British people', expressing pride at how few nations and peoples had not felt British military might.[103]

By comparison other outpourings were mild, even if still patriotic. Many years later, in 1930, 100 persons gathered in Lethbridge, Alberta, to celebrate their saint's day with toasts for the 'King', 'the Empire', 'St George and his Day' and 'the Ladies'.[104] By about the same time, the English Americans were no longer so averse to toasting the Empire as once they might have been. At their dinner on 23 April 1929, the members of Baltimore's St George's Society raised their glasses to 'Old England and the Dominions'.[105] Speeches (which we consider later), recitals and singing were part of the general merrymaking. Shakespeare was read; menus often saw each course accompanied by a line from the Bard. In 1872, the members, families and friends of the Baltimore Society thought the highlight of the after-dinner entertainment was William Miniside reciting a 'witty and humorous poem entitled "the History of the St George's Society"'.[106] National anthems featured every year, as in 1894, when, after feasting on beef and beer, the 'Englishmen in Gotham' sang 'God Save the Queen' and 'The Star-Spangled Banner'.[107]

The St George's Society of Baltimore gradually built up its membership base from thirty or forty attendees at annual dinners to over 100. In 1878 it was forty; the figure shot up to sixty-seven within a year. The year 1878 saw a number of interesting developments. The French consul was among distinguished guests including a healthy sprinkling of Johns Hopkins University professors, who had lately joined the Society. The gathering heard a rousing speech by Revd Kirkus, who spoke fondly of the American reception of Englishmen. To him, St George's Day 'spoke of the freedoms allowed to Englishmen in this country on political and social subjects, although he did not think they ever showed as much candor on the subject as Americans'. He went on to say that despite the warmth Americans showed to Englishmen, 'they still continue to look upon the old country as their home'.[108] The toasts included the usual ones plus the Johns Hopkins University and the founding members. Songs included 'Rule Britannia' and 'The Englishman' from Gilbert and Sullivan's *H.M.S. Pinafore*.[109] In 1880, the Society met at Barnum's Hotel for a fine gathering. Shakespeare was added to the toasts, and 'The Englishman' from *H.M.S. Pinafore* was sung once more.[110] In 1883, the attendance had climbed to eighty persons, and the gathering commenced the toasts with 'Old England – Her bulwarks are the hearts and strong arms of her children. Her Standards protect all nations.' The queen, the president and the United States all received suitable deference and cheer.[111] In the same year, on the same night, as the Baltimore men sat down to dinner, so too did the 'the Sons of "Merrie England"' in Winnipeg, with over 100 sitting down to a banquet – at which all the royals were nobly toasted – organized by the St George's Society there.[112] Simultaneously, 'Englishmen Makes Merry' was the *New York Times* headline as members of the Society there chanced the 'dismal, drizzling rain and snow' to join their president and Her Britannic Majesty's new Consul-General, William Lane Booker. Around 150 took up the opportunity, including representatives of the Scots, the St Nicholas Society and the New England Society. Among them was Revd Benjamin F. De Costa, a stalwart of the wider Anglo-Saxon traditions of later nineteenth-century America. A light-hearted feature was a sugar table piece 'of the transit of Venus, including the famous "black drop". Uncle Sam was viewing the transit through a straw, John Bull through a reversed spy-glass, a Frenchman through a champagne bottle, and a Dutchman through a pretzel. A Russian was also seen making measurements to determine the sun's distance.'[113]

But of course the dinners also were that, with menus rich in masses of solid English food. At Albany in 1860 the enormous menu, served to over 100 persons, included English giblet soup, rib of beef, South Down mutton, smoked tongue, lamb chops, veal, plum pudding and many other dishes on what must have been a groaning table.[114] St George's Day dinner usually included the national sirloin of beef and plum pudding and brandy sauce. In the 1880s, sirloin of beef and Yorkshire pudding were served with chicken cutlets. St Andrew's and other societies, however, ate similar fare.[115] In 1886, this now familiar British – if not only English – meal was washed down with Bass Ale shipped from England.[116] There was, it is clear, an important connection between migration and food-ways, with particular dishes provided for want of invoking Englishness.[117]

Queen and the limits of country

Effusive monarchical resolutions and toasts were commonplace features of English celebrations overseas, and royal occasions were moments for concentrated associational activity. Equally, fund-raising was prompted by Britain's wars and disasters, from the Crimean War to the sinking of the *Titanic*. Both monarchy and war thus provided distinct hooks for members of associations to come together for a common goal. Hence, in 1841, the birth of the Prince of Wales, the future Edward VII, led the New York St George's Society to organize a ball, which was a tremendous success, realizing a surplus of $700.[118] In 1852, the same Society offered a typically gushing note to the queen:

> In venturing, therefore, to intrude upon your Majesty with this expression of their gratitude, the committee beg to assure your Majesty that the members of their [St George's] Society, though far from the land of their fathers and their love, can never cease to think of it with tenderness, and that the prayers which they offer to God from their home in this friendly republic, for the long continuance of your Majesty's health and prosperity, *flow from hearts as loyal*, and are uttered by lips as true, as can be found in any part of your Majesty's almost boundless dominions.[119]

In the United States toasts such as this sometimes elicited stern rebuke. The recorder of this particular message argued strongly that some of those who signed the address – for example the local British Consul – of course had every right to 'reiterate their loyalty and subjection to her most excellent Majesty, even to the kissing of her most excellent Majesty's little toe-nail'. Others, however, did not. English immigrants who had become American citizens, for example, had 'solemnly abjured and renounced' Victoria and sworn allegiance to 'plain Uncle Sam'. Expressions by them of loyalty to a foreign head of state – especially a monarch – were deemed highly unacceptable. For uttering such disloyal words, the naturalized English Americans were no different from other immigrants whom nativists considered suspicious because no ritual of citizenship could really 'swear a man out of his [old] home attachments'.[120] The situation was much less complex in Canada.

The queen's birthday celebration dinner, set for 24 May 1860, was a major event for the Ottawa St George's Society. Mr S. Morrell of Warren Street, New York, proprietor of the Victoria Hotel, wrote a letter to the St George's Society there allowing it the use of his premises for the queen's birthday ball.[121] The Society asked the Royal Insurance Company to insure its next event at the Victoria Hotel, and it also received several other quotes.[122] This followed a 'late heavy charge for Insurance' by the hotel. [123] The cost of the insurance, which the Society eventually took out with the British American Insurance Company, amounted to $28 and completely wiped out the profits of what was supposed to be a charitable ball. The stewards then contacted the insurers asking for a portion of the premium back, and recorded that the British American 'most generously returned the whole of the amount received by them'.[124]

In 1882 another of the queen's birthdays – this one her sixty-third – was celebrated with 'British shipping in the [New York] harbour gaily bedecked with flags', and 'the English ensign was displayed from the masthead of the American and other vessels in the port'. Meanwhile, the Albion Society and the British Football Club held dinners at the Arion Hall and Delmonico's – a favourite posh haunt of the English – respectively.[125] At Washington, seat of political power, members of the St George's Society were strongly in attendance at a sumptuous dinner organized by the British envoy Mr Sackville West. With floral tributes, British flags and a powerful guest list including the President of the Senate, the speaker of the House and envoys from many countries, this was a fine example of the powerful position enjoyed and sought by the English middle classes in the nation's capital. The president of the St George's Society and also of the NAStGU, George F. Dawson, recited 'an original poem "Freedom's Oak"' amid toasts to the queen, royals, 'The Day We Celebrate' and various American individuals, institutions and office-holders.[126]

Monarchical events stretched beyond the dining rooms of America's and Canada's finest hotels and restaurants, particularly for the queen's diamond jubilee – a global tour de force of English associationalism – which we examine in detail in the final chapter. Just as celebrations of queenly longevity provided moments of bonding and warmth, graver news of the old queen's death, in January 1901, prompted sombre reflection, but also a startling fight among the English- and American-born of the Baltimore St George's Society.

Initially there was no controversy. Several English associations in Baltimore were called together specially 'in order to afford you an opportunity of prompting on record an expression of the heartfelt grief of the St George's Society of Baltimore upon the death of our beloved Queen'.[127] President Robson then linked events to the Society's 'Contingent Fund', a pot of cash being built up to buy a large plot for burying the English poor and for a permanent bed at the local charitable hospital. He continued:

> When the wide world is today united with the Royal Family in doing honour to the dead, what greater tribute can the St George's Society lay at the feet of the dead Queen than that of perpetuating her noble name by means of this living Charity[?] ... I propose that this Fund shall hereafter be known as the 'Victoria Memorial Fund'.[128]

Members agreed that it would be appropriate to 'show to the world the reverence in which we hold the Queen, by taking care of the sick and burying the dead out of this fund', and the motion was passed unanimously. Members then also agreed to form a committee to make appropriate resolutions of sympathy that would be passed, via the consul in Baltimore, to the British Embassy in Washington.[129] After a short recess, the committee reported back with this proposed resolution:

> Whereas it has pleased Almighty God in his inscrutable wisdom, to take to himself our most beloved Queen Victoria, bringing grief and sadness to all her subjects, and whereas while humbly submitting to the will of God, we desire to testify to the deep sense of personal loss we all feel in the death of Her, whose pure, upright, and noble life as Queen, wife and mother, has endeared her to every son of the flag in every part of the world.[130]

Englishmen were then invited by the rector of St Paul's Church to attend a memorial service that was planned for precisely the moment when 'the Funeral Services for the late beloved Queen Victoria are held in England'. The rector asked that the members also invite Scots and Irish to join the service. Dr W.P. Ryan, president of the Hibernian Society, communicated in response to say that, while official sanction was impossible (presumably because of time constraints) many members would accept the invitation.[131] In an interesting insight into the types of organizations the St George's Society had links to, the chairman and president also then stated that several related organizations had accepted invitations. Other than the obvious St Andrew's Society, two lodges, one probably masonic, the other Orange – Lord Baltimore's Lodge No.433 and the Pride of Baltimore Lodge No. 136 – reported acceptance alongside the Sons of St George and the Daughters of St George.[132]

At this point, tensions emerged at a meeting of 9 February 1901. A lengthy discussion ensued about the rectitude of forwarding minutes of condolence to the royal family via the British consul and ambassador in Washington. 'Formidable doubts had emerged', the chair stated, about this course of action, since 'a large majority of its members were American citizens'. Given this fact, he added, 'it looked as if the society had been unintentionally guilty of a breach of etiquette.' Instead, Mr H.W. Rowland, a relief committee member, argued 'that the proper channel for the resolutions to follow was through the Secretary of State in Washington'. Rowland explained that he was also a member of the Sons of St George, 'who had sent their resolutions direct to the British Government', but he reckoned that they would have taken a different route had they been aware of the formalities being discussed that night. At this point, Rowland stepped down, and Austin Hirst and Thomas Gwilliam proposed and seconded a motion, unanimously carried, that because the members were primarily American citizens, the action taken was a 'breach of etiquette, and therefore [should] be reconsidered'. It was then resolved to send resolutions, as alternatively proposed, to the United States Secretary of State.[133]

The queen's death raised once more the issue of Anglo-American identity, and the matter was to cause serious debate. The death caused meetings to be called more frequently than the normal monthly schedule, minutes ran for page after page, and debate was clearly heated as members discussed whether etiquette demand they send condolences to Buckingham Palace via the British or United States authorities. When it was agreed to send a resolution of condolence through the United States Secretary of State, some members sponsored a debate about whether the Society was English or American. A mood emerged in favour of a resolution that the Society was, in fact, American: it alleviated burdens on the American state and charity, so the arguments went, and was incorporated under Maryland law. The former president Perot, however, fiercely resisted the resolution. During a lengthy meeting in April 1901, Perot argued:

The Society always has been an English Society and had merely secured a charter of incorporation from the State of Maryland for the purpose of holding property. It was absurd to say that Society was American on that ground. It was established by Englishmen for Englishmen and nothing had occurred to change its complexion.

Instead, Perot proposed another resolution for adoption: 'that the action of the Society in determining to send its resolutions to Secretary [of State] John Hay was out of order and that the original resolutions to send them through the British Consul be adhered to'.[134] Charles Darrell, brother of the British consul in Baltimore, Andrew Darrell, seconded the motion. However, a counter-motion was then tabled to set aside this discussion and return to the original point, which was that the Society was American. This resolution was defeated by thirteen votes to twelve. The president, Arthur Robson, bitterly regretted the decision, and the minutes contained his words: 'it was impossible for him as an American citizen to remain President of a Society which had just been declared to be an English organization'. Thereafter he tendered his resignation and the secretary, Michael Wild, followed suit. Stewart Darrell, consul and vice-chair, and one of the principal protagonists in favour of asserting the Society's Englishness, then took up the chair.[135]

Some members moved that the resignations not be accepted, but neither senior officer was prepared to continue. The debate was resurrected once more. Mr Guthrie 'proceeded to expound the law and to instruct the Society generally as to what it should do and what course the Minute would take after leaving Baltimore', but 'he was set straight by Mr Watts [a lawyer] and two or three others, and he moved, seconded by Mr Gillespie that the Minute be sent to the British Ambassador'. The motion was, however, withdrawn, and Captain Hayes saved the day by moving 'that the engrossed resolutions go direct to Lord Landsdowne to be laid before the King', a motion that was carried 'nem con'.[136] The business of empowering the Victoria Memorial Fund committee to pay over monies to the Druid Ridge Cemetery for an English plot proved uncontroversial by comparison. The plot was duly bought with a special fund and generous donations from Edwin Bennett, who also left the Society money in his will.[137]

The end of Edward VII's short reign in 1910 offered a moment of healing – one where members could mark the king's death in unison. Understandably, there was not the same sense of loss or of commemoration as there had been for Victoria. The annual report of the St George's Society of Toronto offered a heartfelt retrospective for the 'peacemaker' king and proven 'constitutional ruler'.[138] The Baltimore Society made plans to acquire fifty seats at a memorial service at St Paul's Church on 20 May, the date of the king's funeral, and a resolution of condolence was adopted. It included words of real feeling:

> Whereas it has pleased Almighty God, in His wise Providence, to take unto himself the soul of H.M. King Edward VII and thereby overwhelming in grief the members of the Royal Family of England and all His subjects throughout the world:

... that not only the British Empire, but the world at large has suffered an inestimable loss of a wise and pugnacious statesman, and his country a King who endeared Himself in a remarkable manner to the hearts of all His subjects ...;

The crux of its message was thus:

Therefore Be it further Resolved that the members of the St George's Society, at a special meeting called for the purpose on May 9th 1910, do hereby respectfully extend to H.M. George V, H.M. Queen Alexandra, and the other members of the Royal Family, in this, their hour of bereavement and affliction, their profound and heartfelt sympathy.'

This time there was no long debate about the etiquette of delivery. On this day in May 1910, the Society was English, not American, and so it was moved, seconded and passed that 'the resolutions prepared be handed to the British Consul in Baltimore'. It was additionally agreed '"that a message of sympathy be cabled to Lord Knollys, Buckingham Palace, London"'. This also was carried.[139]

Parades, galas and sports

St George's societies, the Sons of England and the OSStG were, by varying degrees, public as well as private organizations. Their public faces, however, extended beyond their presence among the poor and needy, and exceeded the open descriptions of their meetings, dinners and other events in the newspapers. The extent to which they were public in others ways depended partly on the country of origin, and partly on class and religion. While the American societies only intermittently formed up to walk or parade to their church services, this tradition was much stronger in Canada. The middle-class St George's societies might walk together to church on the Sunday closest to St George's Day, but they were not marching or parading organizations. The Sons of England and the OSStG made regular public appearances, forming up in pseudo-military style, with their uniforms of sashes and gloves, banners and other masonic para-phernalia. Like those of the Orange Order or early Freemasons, the marches of the Sons of England were often church parades, with planned routes taken through the streets, to church and back again. These events always involved a public collection of funds.[140] The *Record* encouraged these annual church parades. For the OSStG the hospital parade (raising funds for local care institutions) was a common vehicle for public expression, as were other gatherings. (Figure 4.1).

Marches were redolent of the Orange Order, as was the penchant for

Figure 4.1 Lincoln Lodge of the Sons of St George, 1895 (image courtesy of Michigan Technological University Archives and Copper Country Historical Collections, MS042-039-T-006)

masonic-style paraphernalia. In Baltimore in 1901, a special meeting was called purely to consider 'the advisability of adopting insignia for the Society for use as a seal, Coat of Arms, and Badge to be worn on special occasions', and also to arrange the year's St George's Day celebration.[141] The following month, W. Grant Daugherty informed the Society that its business would not be legal without a 'seal', and, amid some objections about adopting a badge, J. Collins Vincent explained how he had struggled to gain access to the memorial service for Queen Victoria at St Paul's Church – something he averred would not have happened if, like a member of their New York sister society, he had worn a badge denoting his membership. A committee was thus appointed to look into these accoutrements of membership.[142]

Like the badge, pin or visible insignia, public events were not simply a chance to raise funds: they offered 'the opportunity of publicly demonstrating that the bonds in which Sons of England are united embrace not only mutual material benefits and common love of Motherland, but acceptance of the Bible as the source of English power, and its teachings as the law by which man should govern himself'.[143]

Perhaps influenced by Orangemen, the St George's societies of Canada also walked in procession, which the Americans did not do. The men of Ottawa agreed to meet at their regular haunt, Macrow's Hotel, on 23 April 1860 'and from thence to walk in processions to Christ's Church'. The combining of a 'Dinner, Procession, &c. on the Anniversary of St George' necessitated a special meeting for organizing matters, which included securing the church, the right for the Society's own chaplain to preach, the opportunity to hold a collection for the Society's charity and the securing of the hotel for a dinner for numerous attendees at a shilling each.[144] St George's Day in Ottawa that year, 1860, was carried off to these plans, with a procession of eighty persons, a religious service and then a dinner. At the meal, the president received a telegram from the sister society in Montreal thanking the Ottawa brethren for their good wishes and reciprocating the desire for their 'health and prosperity'.[145]

The mid- to late- nineteenth century also witnessed an enormous increase in the importance of large-scale sporting events. Conflicts between amateur and professional codes were a feature of civic social life in these times, and they occasionally affected ethnic societies too. Even though their principles pointed to amateur participation by their own members, friends and families, they did sometimes sponsor professional elements. Thus, the OSStG included sporting fun for its members and families at Downer Landing, Massachusetts, in 1896, and this was run 'in addition to the regular professional athletics events'.[146] Historians have noticed that these ethnic groups were among the first to develop large-scale participants' sports. The Scots in the United States, Canada and New Zealand organized Highland Games under the auspices of Caledonian societies.[147] These large, lively, enjoyable summer-time events were significant civic events – among the largest in new colonial towns or fast-growing urban areas. Moreover, in Canada, 'the Scots who promoted and participated in the Games were a significant influence on the later development of track and field athletics', which, ironically, 'contributed to a decline in the popularity of Caledonian Games'.[148]

English associations were similar in principle and practice, though they had nothing as distinctive as tossing the caber and highland dancing to promote. Instead, they focused on general sporting events. The Scots were ahead of the English in organizing national sporting events, first organizing an event in New York in 1836.[149] Twenty-five years later, the St George's Society of Chicago organized its first annual picnic, which incorporated races and other fun.[150] In 1868, trains pulling over forty carriages, supplemented by over 100 private carriages, conveyed hundreds of St George's Society members, families and friends to Chicago's Haas Park.[151] Much smaller events of a similar nature were organized by the likes of the English Mission Lutheran Church of Wheeling, Ohio, which in 1875 needed nine train carriages to transport 200 or so folk to their annual picnic and party.[152] The serene enjoyment could occasionally be interrupted, as at Chicago in the same year, when 'several roughs managed to gain admission [to the St George's Society annual picnic] and made themselves obnoxious to a degree requiring the interference of the police'.[153] In 1884, the officers in charge of the OSStG picnic discovered gamblers hiding in the cars 'who had calculated running a skin game on the grounds ... They were given the choice of getting out of the cars or being thrown out'.[154]

These organizations thrived on committees. Sporting committees were founded by all these societies – especially, it seems, the less-common Albion Society – for the purpose of developing sports and games. For instance, Ottawa instituted a games committee, which agreed a series of races 'for amateurs only', with good prizes for winners: the one-mile race, with $4 for the winner and $2 for the runner-up, and an entrance fee of 75c.; the quarter-mile race for boys under fourteen, with prizes of $2 and $1 and a 10c. entrance fee; a half-mile race; a three-legged race; and both quoits and clog dancing. A silver medal awaited the winner of the velocipede race. Team games included seven-a-side 'La Crosse'.[155] A decade later, events in Ottawa had grown inordinately in size and complexity. The picnic and day out attracted so many people that the Society instituted a boat and ground committee, a sports and games committee, a music committee, a printing committee and a ticket committee.[156] Such committees were put to good practical use. The St George's Society of Kingston, Ontario, reported that the principal job of the general picnic committee, in 1887, was to collect pledges of prizes for the picnic day events: jewellery, an album, tin ware, a lamp, locket and other things such as a 'box of boots'. In 1881 the Albion Society held its eighth annual picnic and games at Jones' Wood Coliseum, where 'from the turrets of the building floated the American, English and Prussian flags'.[157] We get an insight into why so many committees and people were needed when we learn that the corresponding event in 1877 involved moving 1,500 people to Channel Grove, Simcoe Island, for the day out. The press may have known the organization behind it when commenting, 'the programme of entertainment laid down by the Society was a very good one, and was well carried out, everything going without the slightest hitch'.[158]

Identical forms of sociability were vital, too, for the Sons of England. Some of these activities operated on a small scale and were designed simply to provide entertainment. Smoke socials or smoking concerts were popular, at times, being intended too to bring together 'eligible Englishmen ... with the hope that they will eventually become members of the Society'.[159] Many lodges, for instance the Toronto-based Lodge Warwick, held annual excursions, with picnics often an integral part. In July 1896 lodge members thus left Yonge Street Wharf for Lake Island Park, Wilson, situated across Lake Ontario in the state of New York.[160]

A prominent larger-scale and public feature of the Sons of England's annual events calendar were church parades, the first having been held as early as 1876.[161] Parades provided an opportunity for the Sons of England to visibly demonstrate their presence in local communities large and small, but also to co-operate with other associations in their places of residence. Church parades were frequently held on St George's Day. In 1898, for example, members of various Toronto lodges and the Toronto St George's Society, totalling about 250, came together on Elm Street to march to St James' Cathedral.[162] While St George's Day was the most significant outlet for English sentiment, other annual holidays such as Empire Day also saw many a parade.[163] For the Sons of England too these holidays and anniversary days provided a readily usable hook for the celebration of their English heritage. In contrast to St George's societies – which enshrined such celebrations as a fundamental pillar for activities in their constitutions – the Sons did not formalize ethno-cultural pursuits in this way, but they certainly promoted them, seeking to be 'united by the bond of that fair land which was "home".'[164]

Things were hardly different in New York in 1882, when the Albion Society organized an annual picnic. Dashes, runs, hurdles, sack-races and various field events were part of the fun in July 1882 for the Society, its friends and its families, with good prizes given out and fields crammed with tents, marquees and stalls serving food, drink and sweets for kids.[165] Around a week later, the St George's Society in faraway Omaha, Nebraska, organized a huge picnic for over 500 people at Hansom Park. To begin proceedings, the crowd were reminded of the 'double relation' that Englishmen enjoyed with their homeland and adopted country, before food was enjoyed. In the afternoon a cricket match took place between Omaha and the Council Buffs club. Amid it all 'the English Jack and the stars and stripes hung side by side'.[166] In 1883, the Albion Society and the OSStG co-operated in what was dubbed 'the first Anglo-American picnic and fête day' at Suizer's Harlem River Park. Walks, runs, dashes and the sack-race were among the many elements.[167]

Some of the largest events were organized by the OSStG, whose lodges at the local, district and provincial levels were keenly aware of the need for social and cultural provision in order to retain the interest of members' families. The OSStG also had the financial clout to pay professional athletes. However, the focus was upon amateurs, as at Downer Landing, Hingham, Massachusetts, in 1896, when the Order's members put up against their own sons and daughters at a variety of races: running and swimming, short distances and long.[168] The New York OSStG hosted its fifth annual picnic at Brooklyn in 1883, with 'not less than 5000 people' present. An ox was roasted for ten hours, and dozens of open handicap races were accompanied by team games between the various lodges.[169] Two years later, the attendance figure was around 3,000.[170]

The Order's events continued to be large in the period that followed. In Massachusetts it organized an afternoon's sailing for 100 persons followed by a large dinner for 250 members and friends.[171] Waverley Lodge of the OSStG of Lowell, Massachusetts, in 1902, planned to celebrate its twentieth anniversary with a banquet and supper at the Odd Fellows' Temple. On that night, an additional twenty-four members were inducted.[172] In 1905, Syracuse OSStG needed ten special train cars to carry their members for a day excursion to Sylvan beach.[173] In 1910, as the picnic season reached its climax, many associations and societies were making for the beach. The Skaneateles OSStG went to Sylvan beach, a common destination for New York State members.[174] Also in 1910, it was reported the OSStG had revived cricket. At North Adam, where the Scots once had played the sport, the Order announced plans to play a match. 'Most townspeople of today have never seen the game. It ought to be a good one.'[175] Matches were common between cities close together. Thus Washington, Philadelphia and Baltimore often played each other, for example when, in 1910, the Englishmen of the capital defeated Baltimore's OSStG team.[176] Members of the 1913 convention were treated to music and an automobile ride around Boston.[177] At Washington's equivalent event in 1914, over 300 people attended a ball organized by the city's Columbia Lodge, lodge No. 396, where the room was characteristically decorated with United States and British flags.[178]

Identity, imperialism and 'Anglo-Americanism'

Questions of identity presented every possibility for division and chauvinism for these ethnic societies and strong and often impious views of the genius of their countries: in this, Germans, English, Irish and Scots were little different. All, however, stressed togetherness in the localities and regions in which they found themselves residing. A St George's Society dinner at Baltimore, in 1877, captured the local spirit well. Mayor Latrobe pointed out the English and Irish roots of place names about the city, before adding that 'whether Englishmen or Irishmen, they were all Marylanders and Baltimoreans'.[179] A year later in Kingston, Ontario, Mayor John McIntyre gave a remarkable speech, 'Old Albion', which the newspapers published in full. Presented by a man with Irish and Argyllshire roots, whose origins mixed 'cold, sinewy' restraint inherited from Scotland and 'stimulus' and 'ardour' from his Irish side, he was in a perfect position, he said, to be 'a disinterested and impartial judge' of the Society's success. Thereafter the speech mixed history and encomium: this was an Ulster-Scot whose veneration for England as the 'birthplace of liberty' was plain. What McIntyre did best, though, was to show in this exegesis what parts of England's identity comprised *his* British identity.[180]

If the argument has so far been made in favour of the ethnicity of the English, a note of caution also needs to be sounded. In the second half of nineteenth century, especially in times of tension between England and the United States, identity politics could be a tricky business – and some evidence of this we have already seen in the previous chapter. In the early 1840s, the members of Philadelphia's Sons of St George heard 'forcible and eloquent' words against conflict between the United States and Britain, and hopes for rapprochement from the vice-president. 'I am deeply convinced that the great majority of the people of Great Britain – the mighty mass – have the most friendly feelings, and the highest admiration for, the Government and people of this country' and so had no interest in war between them.[181]

Three decades later, the NAStGU, with aims of unifying continent-wide English societies around shared practical concerns, evinced the values and beliefs that may be described as ethnic and suffused them with appeals to a wider English origin that lies at the core of why historians of ethnicity in the United States have seen these societies as elitist parts of an Anglo-American identity, not an exclusively English one. There is some justification for this. Open declarations of Englishness were almost always laced with proud and commodious expressions of pro-American feeling since there was plenty of hostile opinion about England, Britain and the Empire, and not just from the Irish-American press. Consequently, the conventions always emphasize the cultural commonalities that connected them: the ties that bound. This was so because they took responsibility for their own poor and so prevented burdens from falling on Americans.

Such claims were, however, deliberate and political, since, in the 1860s and 1870s, these gatherings of Englishmen and Anglophile Americans clearly feared conflict between their nations – something that appalled and frightened them. At the Baltimore St George's Day dinner in 1878, Revd Dr Kirkus, a regular lecturer on politics, religion and other topics, followed the toasts with a response that mixed amity and defiance:

> ... for either England or America to go to war would be a calamity, and nothing short of absolute dishonor would justify either nation in engaging in strife. ... He believed the time had passed when Americans talked of John Bull as they did of old. Some people have a habit of saying every time England seeks mediation in the interests of peace that John Bull has pocketed his pride. The English bull is a rather formidable sort of dog, and when he don't get justice and is driven to extremities he generally takes a grip, and never lets go until he hears a bone crack [Applause]. If that bulldog be let loose may he never let go until he does hear that bone crack. [Applause and cheers.][182]

It was because of this underlying fear that both countries, Canada and the United States, and not just England, formed part of the toasting arrangements. For the United States branches the president, as well as the queen, was always toasted with a glass raised with gusto on St George's Day. Anglo-American connections and similarities were regularly stressed, for these men knew that, during the many occasions of diplomatic difficulty between England the United States, expressions of English loyalty could invoke criticism; indeed sometimes the reactions contained bile. Most of these organizations were very keen to stress the complementarity of their identities: many members were American- or Canadian-born; those who were English-born were often naturalized; and those who were neither were nevertheless keen to stress their loyalty to the United States. Indeed, English societies managed the Anglo-American hybridity in careful ways that never were necessary for immigrants of lesser national powers than England.

Canadian loyalty, being subservient to British imperial identity, carried no such risks and so required no public announcements of devotion. Remarking on the connections between England's constitution and those of both the United States and Canada, Revd Dr Kirkus was applauded when he referred to the friendship and trust between Britain, Canada and the United States.[183] The second vice-president, Edward C. Barber, stated how he felt as though he was 'speaking to men who were born and lived within the sound of Bow Bells'. Barber described the Union as honourable and selfless since there was no political gain to be had from travelling hundreds of miles to attend a convention with 'no prizes to offer'. Mr Lawson of Philadelphia then praised the development of civilization in Ottawa, the 'enterprise displayed by Canadians' and 'the success of Englishmen in every sphere of life'.[184] These meetings were indeed about formulating common policies for dealing with the indigent migrant English, and they were also about forging a group identity; as a result of both, they involved long encomia to the spirit, ideal and commonality of them all.

The NAStGU was no different from other ethnic organizations in stressing the commonalities of blood, history and mentality between the members of the nation it represented. At Hamilton in 1876, the focus was on animating common bonds between the 'two great English-speaking races'.[185] In his detailed historical lecture to the Washington convention in 1882, President Dawson focused on the north–south connection as well as the Atlantic one when he suggested that the gathering was a clear expression of the friendship from the United States and Canada which had played a vital role in this development in old country.[186] These emotions were wrapped up in celebratory aspects, for example co-operation with the British Association of Virginia concerning the queen's birthday celebrations. At Philadelphia in 1877, the fifth convention agreed basic principles, but to these was added official endorsement of 'amity between the English-speaking nations'.[187]

In 1881, the assassination of President Garfield created a national gloom. From its depths, however, emerged the opportunity to cement Anglo-American friendship through expressions of sympathy and grief. The St George's Society of New York adopted a lengthy resolution for dispatch to the widow. The opening lines captured the national mood:

> The St George's Society of New York, whose members are Englishmen or the descendants of Englishmen, desire, on the occasion of great gloom in the United States, to join in the universal expressions of sympathy and condolence with the countrymen and family of President Garfield on his death.

And then, in reflection upon English civilization and American political culture, the words continued:

> Like all who speak the English language we abhor assassination and respect the constitutional rules under who we live. We are, therefore, shocked at the violence, so cruel and wanton in a land where the frequent ballots of the people make and unmake the rulers, by which the late President has been hastened prematurely to his death.[188]

In 1881, just after President Garfield's assassination, Lionel Sackville arrived as British envoy. His posting would be severely strained by the effects of the Phoenix Park murders (1882) and the work of the Irish-American lobby, campaigning against British coercion in Ireland and British arrests of Irish-born American nations.[189] Nevertheless the early months included a cordial dinner arranged by the Sons of St George in Philadelphia, who advertised tickets for those wishing to join the new envoy.[190]

While 'English' and 'British' often were interchangeable terms for describing imperial, martial, economic and culture power, speakers at these English society meetings were quite precise in their association of Englishness with certain core values. Charles F. Benjamin, secretary of the Union from Washington, captured the essence well in a lecture to the NAStGU, an amalgam of English and wider British associations, when he described "'English-speaking communities'" as a 'group of political societies' which has 'for a common inheritance the language, literature, laws and habitudes popularly described as Anglo-Saxon'.[191] It was these common people whose numbers and range were expanded by mass migration, and who asserted their commonalities through shared history, ancestry, customs and values. In 1883, the delegates received a lecture from Lewis Abraham of Washington, an expansive, passionate treatise on the power, wealth and position of England and the United States. 'The immense sum of nearly £2,800,000,000 is now owing to England from foreign nations, and they are continually coming back for more.'[192] After a long description of territories, markets and cultures dominated by England, the speaker offered a lengthy quotation from Provost Paradal: 'two rival powers, but only one as to race, language, customs, and laws – England and the United States of America – are, with the exception of Europe, dominating the world'.[193] The reference to rivalry accompanied an acknowledgement that America was still rising, that the new English-speaking power would increasingly dominate the Pacific and the East. Underlying all this was an appeal for the kind of unity that was obvious to Englishmen and Anglophiles in North America, but which would not reflect foreign relations until at least two decades after this speech was made.

By the 1890s, the emphasis was increasingly on the principle of Anglo-American amity. Where geopolitical fears had caused the NAStGU's many earlier declarations of 'Anglo-Saxon unity', now it was possible to talk openly of Anglo-American friendship, interests and even reunion. Canadian newspapers reported the traditional St George's Day dinner at the Mansion House in London in 1894, at which the American ambassador, Mr Bayard, made a fulsome response to a toast offered in his honour by the lord major of London. Bayard reportedly said that

> He felt greatly embarrassed by the infinite hospitality of his English cousins. He was very conscious that the present occasion was a gathering of the clans. The chickens were returning to roost with the mother. He himself was in a way part of the branch broken almost 120 years ago. He met his fellow British men at the table with a sense of deep joy. He and his people were working with them to sustain the best hopes of the world's civilization and the progress of its better elements. All were members of a great voluntary committee charged with the traditions and heritages of their races, to insure the principles of liberty, both civic and religious, and to see that these principles should not be allowed to fail or deteriorate.[194]

Such words became common currency as geopolitical interests and national moments brought the two countries, and their zones of influence, closer together. At a meeting in 1902, President Alfred R. Wiggan explained that the recent death of Queen Victoria and assassination of President McKinley were unifying themes because of the 'spontaneous interchange of sympathy between the two nations upon both occasions'. These events called for 'stern, unfaltering determination … to fulfil the obligations of enlightened civilization in rendering justice and equality to all men'. Wiggan also broadened his theme to explain how the two countries were 'united in the same resistless [sic] manner the two countries will wage a relentless and successful war against the foul doctrine of anarchy as a dangerous menace to true liberty'.[195] Literature, politics, commentary and organizations such as the Atlantic League, founded in 1901 by the committed pro-American writer Walter Besant, all pointed to an intense consideration of the possibilities of Anglo-American unity. Indeed, the number of these Anglo-world organizations pointed strongly towards a growing Anglo-American comity in the wake of the 'great rapprochement', where commonality, not conflict, guided transatlantic relations.[196] Moreover, within this sphere of associational amity, the RSStG in London was by 1900 actively seeking to draw upon the global, not merely North American, frames of reference. This was the age of the Anglo-world, and as mighty as the United States was, it was, at that point, only one part of it. Partly as a consequence of such changes, the 1902 gathering of the NAStGU was to be its last such meeting. Practical pressures, such as falling membership, impinged directly on the NAStGU just as cultural diplomacy did in the political sense.

Conclusion

Unlike the Irish, English association members did not have a national struggle to focus their energies; however, that fact did not obviate, in their minds, the need for organized unity of the type described here. One ideal persistently defined these organizations and gave them shape and purpose, whatever age they were formed in or whichever period we explore: the desire to help their countrymen – whether as charities or friendly societies – provided the ultimate definition. From this financial, benevolent, charitable urge all other things flowed: sociability, celebration and discussion. Dinners raised money or awareness and made a civic mark; sporting and cultural events brought in income but also attracted members, who, in turn, paid their share.

Above mutualism and charity, a host of threads gave members common purpose. Monarchy and Empire in particular were repeated themes for celebration, discussion and veneration. These ideas of associational purpose were cast as Anglo-Saxon; England's role in the world was thought to be universally popular and always important. In these respects speeches and toasts reflected the un-self-conscious chauvinism of men – and they were mostly men – born in a world in which Britain – and for them, England – was a super-power. Social events were critical in this context, providing platforms for the public expression of these ideas. At the same time, however, these events often served a function aligned to charitable and mutual purposes. These were the pillars of English ethnic associations, and we explore their objectives and scope in the next chapter.

Notes

1 Anthony D. Smith, *Ethno-Symbolism: A Cultural Approach* (London, 2009), pp. 67–69.
2 The refutation was delivered at their annual St George's Day dinner by My Battersby. *Political Register*, 6 (1832), p. 229.
3 We see these most clearly denoted in the annual reports of the St George's Society of Toronto, e.g. TCA, Series 1093, StGS Toronto, File 26, Monthly Meetings Minutes, 1908–20, 78th Annual Report, 7 February 1913; 79th Annual Report, 6 February 1914, pp. 100–01, 122–23.
4 Peter Reitbergen, *Europe: A Cultural History* (London, 2005), p. 311; James R. Moore and John Smith, *Corruption in Urban Politics and Society: Britain, 1780–1950* (London, 2007).
5 MdHS, MS 1881, StGS Baltimore, Minutes, 20 January 1869.
6 *New York Herald*, 19 December 1844, 31 January 1845.
7 *Inter Ocean*, 30 December 1881.
8 *Rocky Mountains News*, 2 January 1887.
9 These were referred to assiduously in reports of the Toronto Society, e.g. St George's Society of Toronto, *Charter ... Report of the Committee of the St George's Society of Toronto ...* (Toronto, 1908), p. 7.
10 MdHS, MS 1881, StGS Baltimore, Minutes, 19 October 1908.
11 Ibid., 9 November 1909.
12 CTA, Series 1093, StGS Toronto, File 26, Committee of Management Minutes, 3 January 1860–10 May 1867, pp. 1–297. The Committee of Management was sometimes called the Committee of Officers.
13 ADOA], XM-72A, StGS Kingston, Minute Books, vol. 2, 5 October 1869, p. 4.
14 Any minute book details these officers; see also 'History of the Saint George's Society of Baltimore', in St George's Society of Baltimore, *Book of the St George's Society of Baltimore* (Baltimore, 1954), pp. 3–5, pamphlet in MdHS, MS 1881 files.
15 ADOA, XM-72A, StGS Kingston, Constitution, 6 April 1858, Article No. 7, p. 5.
16 'To The Members of the St George's Society and all Englishmen in Baltimore', 19 November 1873, MdHS, MS 1881, StGS Baltimore, Minutes, 19 January 1874.
17 Ibid., Secretary's Report, 17 January 1876.
18 Ibid., Secretary's Report, 15 January 1877; John L. Sanford, *History of the St George's Society of Baltimore* (Baltimore, 1929), p. 7.
19 MdHS, MS 1881, StGS Baltimore, Minutes, Secretary's Report, 17 January 1876.
20 Ibid., Secretary's Report, 15 January 1877.
21 Ibid., Minutes, 2 July 1883.
22 Ibid., 29 August 1883.
23 For example ibid., Minutes, Secretary's Report, 21 April 1893.
24 Ibid., 14 November 1894.
25 Ibid., 13 January, 27 January, 27 March 1896 [no minutes for the rest of 1896]; 23 April, 24 May 1897.

26 Ibid., 22 July 1897.
27 See Lesley C. Robinson, 'Englishness in England and the "Near Diaspora": Organisation, Influence and Expression, 1880s–1970s', unpublished PhD, University of Ulster, 2014, pp. 50–53.
28 Charleston, South Carolina, South Carolina Historical Society, StGS Charleston records, 1813–1977, RSStG Festival Dinner, 1905.
29 Ibid., Rules IV, VIII, pp. 7–8.
30 LAC, MG28-V3, StGS Ottawa, Minute Books, vol. 1, 30 April 1859, p. 1.
31 MdHS, MS 1881, StGS Baltimore, Minute Books, vols 1–3, 1866–1901; Members and Dues Book 1: 1900–50.
32 MdHS, MS 1881, StGS Baltimore, Minutes, Secretary's Report, 19 January 1871.
33 ADOA, XM-72A, StGS Kingston, Minutes, undated newspaper clipping [26 January 1860?].
34 ADOA, XM-72B, StGS Kingston, Minutes, 1874–82, 6 March 1877.
35 GMA, M-1659, Sons of England, United Roses Lodge, Minute Book, 1 August 1890; for Toronto see Record, 15 July 1896, p. 2.
36 St George's Society of New York, Annual Report of the St George's Society of New York, For the Year 1922 ... (New York, 1923), p. 24.
37 MdHS, MS 1881, StGS Baltimore, Minutes, 21 October 1872.
38 Ibid., 15 January 1877.
39 Ibid., 30 April 1877.
40 Ibid., President's Address, 21 January 1878.
41 MdHS, MS 1881, StGS Baltimore, Minutes, 9 April 1900; Baltimore Sun, 29 November 1900.
42 MdHS, MS 1881, StGS Baltimore, Minutes, 9 April 1900.
43 Ibid., Minutes, 16 January 1911, 17 April 1911.
44 R.J. Morris, 'Clubs, Societies and Associations', in The Cambridge Social History of Britain, 1750–1950, 3 vols (Cambridge, 1993), vol. 3: Social Agencies and Institutions, p. 412.
45 Philadelphia Inquirer, 12 August 1875.
46 CTA, Series 1093, StGS Toronto, File 26, Monthly Meetings Minutes, 1908–20, 4 Febuary 1915, pp. 174–76.
47 Morris, 'Clubs, Societies and Associations', pp. 412–13. Also see R.J. Morris, 'Urban Associations in England and Scotland, 1750–1914: The Formation of the Middle Class or the Formation of a Civil Society?', in Graeme Morton, Boudien de Vries and R.J. Morris (eds), Civil Society, Associations, and Urban Places: Class, Nation, and Culture in Nineteenth-Century Europe (Aldershot, 2006), pp. 139–58.
48 LAC, MG28-V3, StGS Ottawa, Minute Books, 13 vols, vol 1, 30 April 1859, p. 1.
49 Desmond Morton, 'Coffin, William Foster (1808–78)', Dictionary of Canadian Biography, vol. 10: 1871–1880, http://www.biographi.ca/en/bio/coffin_william_foster_10E.html (last accessed 10 August 2013). LAC, MG28-V3, StGS Ottawa, Minute Books, vol. 1, p. 1.
50 CTA, Series 1093, StGS Toronto, File 26, Monthly Meetings Minutes, 1908–20, 1 October 1915, p. 165.

51 Ibid., 3 March 1916, pp. 185; Capt. Ernest J. Chambers, *The Royal Grenadiers: A Regimental History of the 10th Infantry Regiment of the Active Militia of Canada* (Toronto, 1904), pp. 31, 35, 41, 49, 57, 77, 86–87, 126, 128.

52 Hanael P. Bianchi, 'St George's Day: A Cultural History', unpublished PhD thesis, Catholic University of America, 2011, p. 199.

53 He formed a 'limited co-partnership' with Jos. C. Yates of Bermuda in 1869: *Royal Gazette*, 8 June 1869.

54 MdHS, MS 1881, StGS Baltimore, Minutes, 21 January 1867, 30 January 1909. Also *Woods' Baltimore City Directory, Containing a Corrected Engraved Map of the City, A Business Directory, a Street Directory and Appendix …* (Baltimore, 1872), pp. 517, 925.

55 MdHS, MS 1881, StGS Baltimore, Minute Books, vol. 1, inaugural meeting and declaration, 3 December 1866.

56 Handbill in ibid., vol. 1, after 12 November 1877.

57 *Petersburg Index and Appeal*, 16 December 1876.

58 MdHS, MS 1881, StGS Baltimore, Minutes, 15 February 1909.

59 Ibid., 20 October 1912.

60 Ibid., 19 July 1875. Antoinette J. Lee, *Architects to the Nation: The Rise and Decline of the Supervising Architects Office* (New York, 2000), p. 81. Lind designed a number of the city's civic buildings, for example the First Presbyterian Church and manse: Nancy Capace, *Encyclopaedia of Maryland* (Baltimore, 1999), p. 230.

61 Robert M. Craig, *The Architecture of Francis Palmer Smith, Atlanta's Scholar-Architect* (Athens, GA, 2012), p. 8; Mary Ellen Hayward and Frank R. Shivers (eds), *The Architecture of Baltimore: An Illustrated History* (Baltimore, 2004).

62 MdHS, MS 1881, StGS Baltimore, Minutes, 25 March 1882. He was in turn replaced by Thomas G. Stowe, another stalwart: ibid., 18 October 1882.

63 Ibid., 2 July 1883.

64 Ibid., 20 April 1890.

65 For example ibid., 21 October 1872.

66 Ibid., Resolution, 10 September 1918.

67 *Daily Picayune*, 22 April 1866.

68 Robinson, 'Englishness in England', p. 179.

69 Bianchi, 'St George's Day', pp. 202, 203.

70 MdHS, MS 1881, StGS Baltimore, Minutes 20 April 1874.

71 *British Daily Whig*, 24 April 1878.

72 Muriel E. Chamberlain, 'Bulwer, (William) Henry Lytton Earle, Baron Dalling and Bulwer (1801–1872)', *Oxford Dictionary of National Biography*, Oxford University Press, 2004; online edn, January 2008, http://www.oxforddnb.com/view/article/3935 (last accessed 5 April 2014).

73 *The Argus & Democrat*, 13 April 1859.

74 Robert Ernst, *Immigrant Life in New York City, 1825–63* (1949; Syracuse, NY, 1994), p. 26.

75 CTA, Series 1093, StGS Toronto, File 26, Monthly Meetings Minutes, 2 April 1909, p. 22; also 'Seventy Fifth Annual Report of the Committee of Management of the St George's Society of Toronto, 1909', manuscript

contained with the minutes of StGS Toronto monthly meetings, 4 February 1910, pp. 34–35.

76 MdHS, MS 1881, StGS Baltimore, Minutes, 2 February 1882. The marriage of the Irishman Campbell Fair to Miss Mary Whitely Stone was reported in *New York Times*, 19 January 1883.

77 MdHS, MS 1881, StGS Baltimore, Minutes, resolution by the secretary A.B. Gillespie, 2 February 1924.

78 *Daily News*, 22 April 1878.

79 *British Daily Whig*, 24 April 1878.

80 CTA, Series 1093, StGS Toronto, File 26, Monthly Meetings Minutes, 1908–20, 1 May 1908, p. 5.

81 Ibid., 4 February 1916, p. 172.

82 MdHS, MS 1881, StGS Baltimore, Minutes, Secretary's Report, January 1873.

83 J.M.T. Finney, *A Surgeon's Life: The Autobiography of J.M.T. Finney* (1940; Whitefish, MT, 2007), p. 136.

84 MdHS, MS 1881, StGS Baltimore, Minutes, 20 January 1873.

85 ADOA, XM-72A, StGS Kingston, Minutes, 5 October 1869.

86 Bianchi, 'St George's Day', pp. 195, 209.

87 *New York Spectator*, 28 April 1841.

88 *Record*, 15 September 1896.

89 LAC, MG28-V3, StGS Ottawa, Minute Books, vol. 1, 22 May 1860, p. 26.

90 See also A. Radley, 'Artefacts, Memory and a Sense of the Past', in D. Middleton and D. Edwards (eds), *Collective Remembering* (London, 1990).

91 LAC, MG28-V3, StGS Ottawa, Minute Books, vol. 1, 23 April 1868; secretary's minute and press cutting [n.d.].

92 Ibid., 22 April 1870.

93 Ibid., 23 April 1872; *Sun* (Baltimore), 24 April 1872.

94 *Poulson's American Daily Advertiser*, 26 April 1814. Also confirm 1814 and in text.

95 *New York Spectator*, 28 April 1841.

96 *Calgary Weekly Herald*, 28 April 1849.

97 MdHS, MS 1881, StGS Baltimore, Minutes, 27 April 1867.

98 Ibid.

99 *Wisconsin State Journal*, 16 May 1865.

100 MdHS, MS 1881, StGS Baltimore, Minutes, 22 April 1870.

101 *Washington Post*, 24 April 1881, p. 1.

102 *Morning Herald* (Baltimore), 24 April 1896.

103 *Record*, December 1897, pp. 84–85.

104 *Lethbridge Herald*, 24 April 1930.

105 MdHS, MS 1881, StGS Baltimore, Minutes, 23 April 1929.

106 *Baltimore American*, 24 April 1872; MdHS, MS 1881, StGS Baltimore, Minutes, 23 April 1872.

107 *Manitoba Free Press*, 24 April 1894.

108 *Baltimore American*, 24 April 1878; *Baltimore Sun*, 24 April 1878; MdHS, MS 1881, StGS Baltimore, Minutes, 23 April 1878; Sanford, *History*, p. 8.

109 *Baltimore Daily Gazette*, 24 April 1879.

110 *Baltimore Gazette*, 24 April 1880.

111 *Baltimore Sun*, 24 April 1883.

112 *Manitoba Daily Free Press*, 24 April 1883, p. 8.

113 *New York Times*, 24 April 1883, p. 2.

114 *Albany Journal*, 25 April 1860.

115 See e.g. I. Allen Jack, *History of the St Andrew's Society of St John, New Brunswick, Canada, 1798–1903* (St John, 1903), menu, p. 103.

116 *Baltimore Sun*, 24 April 1884; Tanja Bueltmann, David T. Gleeson and Donald M. MacRaild, 'Invisible Diaspora? English Ethnicity in the United States before 1920', *Journal of American History*, 33:4 (Summer 2014), p. 22.

117 See also H.R. Diner, *Hungering for America: Italian, Irish, and Jewish Foodways in the Age of Migration* (Cambridge, MA, 2001).

118 Robert Waller, *A Sketch of the Origin, Progress and Work of the St George's Society, A.D. 1786–1886* (New York, 1887), p. 28.

119 Editor, 'What is the Value of the Oath of Allegiance?', *The Republic: A Monthly Magazine of American Literature, Politics & Art*, 3 (June 1852), p. 312.

120 This and the previous quotations from ibid.

121 LAC, MG28-V3, StGS Ottawa, Minutes, vol. 1, 26 April 1860, pp. 15–16.

122 Ibid., 12 May 1860, p. 21; 'Stewards Meeting', 19 May 1860, p. 25.

123 Ibid., 2 June 1860, p. 30.

124 Ibid., 'Stewards Meeting', 3 July 1860, pp. 32–33.

125 *New York Herald*, 25 May 1882, p. 3.

126 *Washington Post*, 25 May 1882, p. 1.

127 MdHS, MS 1881, StGS Baltimore, Minutes, 24 January 1901.

128 Ibid.

129 Ibid.

130 Ibid.

131 Ibid.

132 Ibid. The minutes appear virtually verbatim in the press: *Baltimore Sun*, 25 January 1901.

133 MdHS, MS 1881, StGS Baltimore, Minutes, 9 February 1901.

134 Ibid., 15 April 1901.

135 Ibid.

136 Ibid.

137 James Belden had similarly left a legacy to the Society when he died on 3 March 1877: in this case, a lot at the Mount Carmel Cemetery in O'Donnell Street. Sanford, *History*, p. 10.

138 CTA, Series 1093, StGS Toronto, File 26, Monthly Meetings Minutes, 1908–20, 3 February 1911, p. 60.

139 MdHS, MS 1881, StGS Baltimore, Minutes, 9 May 1910.

140 *Record*, May 1898, p. 143.

141 MdHS, MS 1881, StGS Baltimore, Minutes, 9 February 1901.

142 Ibid., 2 March 1901; Sanford, *History*, p. 12.

143 *Record*, June 1901, p. 1; July 1901, p. 3.

144 LAC, MG28-V3, StGS Ottawa, Minute Books, vol. 1, 7 April 1860, p. 8; 'Special Meeting', 13 April 1860, p. 9; also 'Stewards Meeting', 16 April 1860, p. 10.

145 Ibid.,vol. 1, 23 April 1860, p. 12.
146 *Boston Daily Globe*, 4 August 1896.
147 See, for example, G. Jarvie, *Highland Games: The Making of the Myth* (Edinburgh, 1991) on the Scottish origins and development; Gerald Redmond, *The Sporting Scots of Nineteenth-Century Canada* (Toronto, 1982); Tanja Bueltmann, *Scottish Ethnicity and the Making of New Zealand Society, 1850–1930* (Edinburgh, 2011), ch. 5.
148 Redmond, *Sporting Scots*, pp. 159–60.
149 Richard Blaustein, *The Thistle and the Brier: Historical Links and Cultural Patterns between Scotland and Appalachia* (Jefferson, NC, 2003), p. 74.
150 See e.g. *New York Times*, 1 August 1864; 27 July 1866; 24 June, 19 July 1867; 30 July 1869; 26 July 1871; 14 July 1872.
151 *Chicago Times*, 25 June 1868.
152 *Steubenville Daily Herald*, 19 June 1875.
153 *Chicago Daily Tribune*, 22 July 1875.
154 Ibid., 5 August 1884.
155 LAC, MG28-V3, StGS Ottawa, Minute Books, vol. 2, 5 August 1869, p. 1.
156 ADOA, XM-72A, StGS Kingston, Minutes, 13 July 1877, pp. 220–24.
157 *New York Times*, 26 July 1881.
158 ADOA, XM-72A, StGS Kingston, Minutes, extract from *Daily News*, dated August 1878, while the minutes date the preparations to July 1877, p. 235.
159 Moose Jaw Public Library, Archives Department, MJ-6.001, Moose Jaw Sons of England Benefit Society, Minute Book, 1904–07, 25 June 1904.
160 *Record*, 15 July 1896, p. 3.
161 Ibid., 15 December 1897, p. 78.
162 *Daily Mail and Empire* (Toronto), 25 April 1898.
163 See for instance *Record*, July 1901, p. 3.
164 *Daily Mail and Empire*, 25 April 1898.
165 *New York Times*, 25 July 1882, p. 1.
166 *Omaha Daily Herald*, 2 August 1882.
167 *New York Times*, 19 June 1883.
168 *Boston Daily Globe*, 4 August 1896.
169 *New York Times*, 31 July 1883.
170 *Chicago Daily Tribune*, 11 August 1885.
171 *Boston Daily Globe*, 7 October 1898.
172 *Lowell Sun*, 25 October 1902.
173 *Syracuse Post Standard*, 22 July 1905.
174 Ibid., 13 August 1910.
175 *North Adam Transcript*, 20 July 1900.
176 *Washington Post*, 11 July 1910.
177 *Lowell Sun*, 7 October 1913.
178 *Washington Post*, 19 March 1914.
179 MdHS, MS 1881, StGS Baltimore, Minutes, 23 April 1877.
180 Undated newspaper clipping (April 1878) in ADOA, XM-72B, StGS Kingston, Minutes.
181 *Philadelphia Inquirer*, 29 April 1842; *North American and Daily Advertiser*, 20 April 1842.

182 *Baltimore Sun*, 24 April 1878.

183 *Ottawa Daily Citizen*, 25 August 1880.

184 Ibid.

185 Details of all previous conventions, including Hamilton in 1876, were included in the president's address in Washington in 1882. See *Washington Post*, 20 May 1882; *Evening Critic* (Washington), 20 May 1882.

186 *Evening Critic* (Washington), 20 May 1882.

187 North America St George's Union, *Report of the Fifth Annual Convention*, pp. 12–16.

188 *New York Times*, 25 September 1881.

189 T. H. Sanderson, 'West, Lionel Sackville Sackville-, second Baron Sackville (1827–1908)', rev. H.C.G. Matthew, Oxford Dictionary of National Biography, online edn, October 2006, http://www.oxforddnb.com/view/article/35902 (last accessed 29 August 2015).

190 *Philadelphia Inquirer*, 2 November 1882, p. 5.

191 Charles F. Benjamin, *The future relations of the English-speaking communities; an essay read before the eleventh convention of the North American St George's union at Chicago, August 20, 1884* (Washington, DC, 1884), p. 1. Benjamin 'repeatedly declined' re-election as secretary. *Chicago Daily Tribune*, 22 August 1884.

192 Lewis Abraham, *Gloria Britan[n]ica and the Universality of Anglo-Saxonism. A Paper Read at the Convention of the North American St George's Union, at Toronto, August, 30, 1883* (Washington, DC, 1883), p. 6.

193 Ibid., p. 10.

194 *Manitoba Free Press*, 24 April 1894.

195 *Philadelphia Inquirer*, 11 September 1902.

196 Donald M. MacRaild, Sylvia Ellis and Stephen Bowman, 'Interdependence Day and Magna Charta: James Hamilton's Public Diplomacy in the Anglo-World, 1907–1940s, *Journal of Transatlantic Studies*, 12:2 (2014), pp. 126–48.

5

Charity and mutual aid:
the pillars of English associations

In late 1867 and early 1868 Maria Ray, a London-born tailoress thirty-three years of age, was a frequent visitor at the office of the Toronto St George's Society. As the Society's records reveal, Maria's husband, George, had left her a couple of years earlier, and her two children, a five-year-old girl and a boy aged two, were both sick. Maria was struggling to make ends meet. The Toronto St George's Society provided some temporary respite for her in the form of small cash payments. In several months to 3 January 1868 Maria had received $6.50. On her visits to ask the St George's Society for further support, Maria might have met thirty-five-year-old George Whatkins, another recipient of support on that winter's day. George suffered from a 'chronic disease of the bone', had a wooden leg and was, as the Society's records document, supporting 'himself by Begging'.[1] He was given 50c. The New Year had brought neither Maria nor George much luck or a change in their circumstances. They were not alone. On that same January day, Toronto St George's Society dealt with another eighteen cases, dispensing $32.00 in relief overall.[2]

Maria's and George's cases are of broader relevance, reflecting the founding principle of the North American St George's societies: the dispensing of brotherly love and charity to the poor and unfortunate. In the places where the English had settled in larger numbers since the early eighteenth century, the new local and national governments did not sufficiently address the social problems that poorer migrants encountered. This directly resulted in migrants – from, as we have seen, higher up the social ladder – seeking to fill the existing support void by setting up their own charities. These organizations had a clear ethnic remit, and not just as once-a-year sites of memory on St George's Day: they were practical dispensers of protection to the poor and unlucky English. Chapter 2 illustrated the idea that to provide support for fellow Englishmen and Englishwomen in need was paramount – and enduring. More than a century after the first St George's societies had been established, seeking to relieve some of that need, the newly formed Baltimore St George's Society, in December 1866, still trod firmly in these associational footsteps, having been set up 'for the relief of distressed English subjects'.[3] While sociability and camaraderie undoubtedly were important to these societies, ultimately they served to connect members for the purpose of carrying out benevolence. As article 1 of the New York St George's Society's constitution stipulated clearly in 1897, '[t]he property and income of the Society can only be expended in charity.'[4] So fundamental has been this charitable tradition that it continues to this day,[5] although it was clearly at its most profound during the nineteenth century, when, as a result of the mass migration across the Atlantic that we have traced in Chapter 1, the sheer volume of English migrants required robust systems of support. Within a wider context of expansion and growth, then, the first sections of this chapter explore the nature and extent of the charity provided by St George's societies throughout North America. The aim is to reveal not only the level of support offered, but also the regulations that governed it. Moreover, the chapter also interrogates the level of associational networking between organizations concerned with the provision of charity, and how this often transcended the ethnic remit of the associations involved.

The final section takes a different turn, since the charitable pursuits of St George's societies were only one dimension of several forms of community help that English immigrants provided. We thus move beyond the charitable elites and focus on the work of two large, ethnic mutual societies whose origins we discussed in Chapter 3 – the Sons of England and the OSStG. These two groups upheld the ethos of collective self-help and economic confraternity that typified not only the British World and European societies, both home and abroad, but also the United States, where, as Alexis de Tocqueville observed, citizens associated for a plethora of purposes, small and large.[6] The Sons of England and OSStG were large-scale mutual aid organizations and straddled the forms of fraternity noticed by the historian Beito: secret, ritual-bound societies; the sick and funeral clubs; and life insurance societies.[7] With their ceremonial form, sashes, pins and medals they owed something to the Orange Order, which, in turn, borrowed rituals heavily suffused with masonic mysticism and symbolism.[8] In collecting funds from members in set amounts and making payments for sickness, unemployment and death, and later running life insurance schemes, these English associations were a robust and long-lived representation of the wider range of North American ethnic mutualism.

We explore the operations and level of self-help offered by means of a case study of the Sons of England, for this Canadian-English association has left a wealth of archival records that permit detailed analysis of operations. There is every indication, however, that the OSStG, for which no comparable record base has survived, operated in very similar ways in the United States, with the Sons of England case study thus permitting broader conclusions. Ultimately, the critical point is to recognize that there were two distinct pillars of English ethnic associationalism: charity and mutualism – what Beito crisply denotes as 'hierarchical' and 'reciprocal' relief.[9] Each pillar must be understood clearly within the context of its respective and distinct function.

Types of charity

The disbursing of charity by St George's societies was a serious and highly organized enterprise. It was not a case of simply doling out a bit of money. Checks were made to prevent false claims. In Kingston, Ontario, in 1876 Major Barrow, the president of the local St George's Society, also warned of the risk of exploitation by professional beggars, the 'dead beats in Kingston and throughout the province'. As he went on, a clear disdain for the Irish was revealed:

> If the fellows cannot get relief from one society they change their nationality and try another – any dodge to get money. While the President was speaking three applicants for relief came forward, and in two cases the good done by the Society was practically illustrated, while in the third the applicant's inconcealable Gaelic betrayed him.[10]

One issue of concern for many societies was the type of aid to be provided, with many holding the view that cash disbursements were not the most suitable means of support. In fact, most associations sought to expressly avoid the payment of cash, offering instead such support as meal tickets, supplies of firewood or groceries. These moneyless offerings limited the possibility for abuse. Hence, in 1870, the Toronto St George's Society deemed it 'unadvisable to continue the system hitherto adopted of giving pecuniary assistance in all cases', instead making 'arrangements with several butchers, and bakers, in the City, to supply bread and meat, upon the orders of the visiting or general Committee'.[11] Not only did this alleviate pressure on the Society's almoner, but it was also an approach designed to limit the cases in which cash dispensed for relief purposes was used to meet other ends. Differentiations by the type of person seeking support were also common. While in Toronto in the 1930s and 1940s, families tended to receive provisions, milk or fuel, single men asking for relief were usually given temporary lodgings, meals or both.[12]

In Baltimore too, in the 1870s, the secretary reported a change in policy over relief, stating that for three months he had 'relieved [the poor] wholly by ticket instead of money'. The idea of giving those in need tickets that they could exchange for food and lodgings was 'commented on by many, but always with approval'.[13] This view was already evident at the Society's second quarterly meeting in 1867, when members questioned the principle of granting cash payments to those in need. Instead they turned to the 'propriety of having a house where, at a moderate price, a person could obtain a meal or lodging at his own expense, or, in extreme cases, at the expense of the society'. Moreover, it was unanimously agreed that the funds of the Society were not intended for those 'who had been many years in the country'.[14] As was noted by the Society's secretary, '[n] o English worthy of the name but will exult at the working of a Society which will help those that strive to help themselves and which will always help those who cannot help themselves.'[15] This later comment mirrored the words with which Samuel Smiles opened *Self-Help* (1859): 'heaven helps those who help themselves'.[16]

The Baltimore Society had a number of other regulations in place to ensure a systematic approach to relief provision. The maximum relief payable to recipients who had been thoroughly investigated was set at five dollars, 'except in special circumstances',[17] and further fine-tuning occurred. Overall, the number of cases in Baltimore was comparatively small. In his address of January 1880, the president spoke of sixty-eight cases of relief. One year later there were seventy-nine.[18] In January 1881, the Society began to minute separate meetings of the relief committee, with individual cases recorded. Donations of five dollars were normal. At the first meeting a destitute Englishwoman called Fletcher was granted enough for two weeks' accommodation at the city's Reid's Temperance Hotel.[19]

The New York St George's Society's relief system was particularly highly regulated to avoid abuse, and here too the preference was for cashless forms of relief.[20] From the late nineteenth century onwards, the Society thus began to utilize the so-called woodyard ticket. As Howard explains, a woodyard ticket entitled its holder 'to a woodyard shift, a night's lodging, and two meals'.[21] Such provision was designed, Howard continues, 'as a guilt-alleviating salve for urban dwellers uncomfortable at the sight of their suffering fellow city residents', but in New York the St George's Society was using the system widely and gave it more formalized approval. In 1910, for example, the Society handed out 487 woodyard tickets.[22] The breakdown of the Society's relief provisions for that year documents the varied nature of the support offered. In total the Society dealt with 1,415 new cases and 2,206 continued cases, refusing 426 cases. In only 525 of the cases that were supported did the Society dispense money – the vast majority of cases were supported by other means. In 33 cases the Society provided loans, while 125 received rent support. A total of 659 families received grocery supplies, and lodgings were offered to 3,635 transients who passed through New York. Moreover, the St George's Society provided nearly 3,000 pieces of clothing, as well as 155 pairs of shoes. Sixty-one people were sent to St Luke's Hospital, where the Society had exclusive access to a number of beds. The Society also helped with advice for those it could not directly cater for because of eligibility issues (e.g. non-English migrants), referring 186 cases to other societies. Finally, the Society also obtained 105 positions for people who were out of employment.[23] The latter was one of the most difficult forms of support to provide, particularly when jobs were genuinely scarce, but it was also an approach that many St George's societies regarded as particularly fruitful: it was the one deemed to be the best means for securing a person's long-term self-sufficiency. As noted by a New York St George's Society member,

[i]t has always been felt that the giving of alms to able-bodied men and women, while sometimes necessary and expedient, is on the whole demoralizing in its tendency and influence upon the recipients ... it has been thought that if the Society could aid such by helping them to procure the employment they seek, and thereby enable them to earn their own livelihood, a great deal of practical good would be done, more indeed than could be accomplished in any other way.[24]

Within the context of this ideal of self-help and enabling migrants to improve their situations, we find collaborations and support between English ethnic charitable organizations and English ethnic mutual associations. To achieve the goal of helping out-of-work immigrants find work, the New York St George's Society, for instance, supported the Order of the Sons of St George's new Labor Bureau, as well as other employment agencies.[25] In Toronto the St George's Society pursued similar objectives, stressing that '[e]very effort has been made to encourage self-reliance and to direct our applicants to some means of livelihood.'[26] In this respect the Society shared a common goal not only with fellow English in New York, but also with Toronto's St Andrew's Society, which had operated under the motto 'to help them to help themselves' ever since its establishment in the early nineteenth century.[27] The provision of clothing to relief seekers must also be seen in this context. As was noted in New York, '[m]any applicants [for relief] were in such a ragged and miserable condition, that they stood no chance of obtaining employment, but by enabling them to present a respectable appearance, several obtained good positions.'[28] The importance of this type of what we might call enabling support is also documented in a case from Baltimore. In that city the dying mother of two young children, Charles and Francis Ransome, children of a chemist and former Baltimore St George's Society member, Charles Ransome, passed into the care of the Society. The Society member and historian John L. Sandord reckoned the mother was 'made happy by the thought that her two boys for whom employment had been secured would continue to be looked after and guided right by the Saint George's'.[29] The social aspects that bonded men of common nationality, or individuals with strong English identifications, were secondary to this ongoing responsibility to the poor or unfortunate who followed them. Hence, the early members of the Baltimore Society remained concerned about the orphaned siblings, and 'occasionally visited and cared for' them in the asylum where they had been housed.[30]

Another common means of support in New York was the provision of return passages back to England or – increasingly from the late nineteenth century onwards – to destinations in the British Empire. In the 1870s and 1880s, well over a 100 return passages per year were by no means uncommon. For this system to work the New York St George's Society relied heavily on the support of various shipping lines, which offered reduced fares to the Society. In 1878, for instance, a total of 187 migrants were sent back to England, with 95 travelling supported by the National Line, 45 by the Inman Line, 22 by the Anchor Line, 14 by the White Star Line, 6 by the Cunard Line and 5 by the Williams & Guion Line.[31] Numbers decreased over time, but remained sizeable. In 1910, for example, 39 passages were offered, with 38 to England and 1 passage 'to the colonies'.[32] In Toronto too the local St George's Society was able to utilize the support of steamship companies, and still did so in the 1930s. In 1935, '87 families and 88 single persons ... have been repatriated' as a result of the companies' support – but it was offered only to those English migrants 'who had definite prospect of work in England or dependents who were going to relatives in England, who promised to care for them'.[33] It was, in all likelihood, the lack of such large-scale support from shipping companies that supplied one reason why the St George's Society of Ottawa regarded the provision of return passages as something that 'was entirely outside of [its] scope'.[34] Hence, at its quarterly meeting in early October 1900, the Society rejected the case of an Englishwoman who was keen to return to England and had asked for support to do so. However, thanks to the intervention of an individual St George's Society member who wanted to help, the matter could be resolved nonetheless, with funds for a return fare being collected by personal contributions.[35]

As the work of St George's societies progressed and as the age of mass migration passed, new types of charity were added. In New York increasing attention was given, for example, to working with pensioners, some of whom lived in old people's homes. In 1925, in fact, the majority of old people supported by the New York St George's Society were residents in the likes of the Home for the Aged and Infirm.[36] The tradition of aiding pensioners was, however, first established in the 1880s. In 1885, a 'list made up chiefly of aged men and women who from old age or infirmity are incapacitated from work, and who are dependent upon charity entirely for their means of subsistence' was drawn up. Classed as 'pensioners', these people received a maximum allowance of $4.00 per month. As the Society observed, this was 'in many instances ... their only means of support'. To ensure that only those in need of support were receiving pensions, the St George's Society 'inquired into [cases] every year, and great care is taken that only the deserving are retained upon the roll'.[37] In 1910 pensioners were described as ranging in age from sixty to eighty-two and 'mostly very infirm'.[38]

The Society also sought to provide support that served to enhance the lives of pensioners, including, for instance, the provision of invalids' chairs. In 1916 the breakdown of medical expenses further documents that spectacles and artificial teeth could be covered.[39] And, importantly, relief was not restricted to some form of financial support. In Baltimore an interesting measure of the extent of the local St George's Society's influence came in the case of Mr Horace R. Lutwyche, who in April 1901 wrote to thank the Society for its support. Lutwyche had stood charged with obtaining money by deception and was defended, at short notice, by a member and lawyer, P.B. Watts, with the result that 'the accused was vindicated of the charge and restored to the world with an unsullied name'.[40]

Table 5.1 offers an overview of the main expenses of the New York St George's Society for the period 1875 to 1954, documenting the provisions in a plethora of relief categories, some of which we have already seen for other locations. A number of developments over time are worth pausing over. The first notable point is that the provision of pensions or regular support for the elderly was an important pillar of the Society's relief operations: provisions made were consistently high when measured in absolute sums. The increase in expenses for Christmas presents provides further evidence of the importance of the Society's focus on supporting the elderly as, in New York, presents were primarily offered to them rather than families or children. At the same time, the types of relief the Society provided generally diversified over time. As a result, pension support, measured as a percentage of the total relief dispensed, became a less critical component as time went on: while in 1885, 50 per cent of the Society's total expenditure went to pension allowances, it was only 29 per cent in 1925, and 9 per cent in the mid-1950s. A second important observation is the rise in cash aids. These were, as noted above, not a preferred method of relief for many St George's societies in the mid-nineteenth century as they were seen to encourage dependence rather than facilitating self-help. In New York the increase in this type of support coincided with the outbreak of the First World War and, in the 1930s, depression and economic downturn. It appears that at these points of crisis the question of practicality was paramount: cash was the easiest to dispense. Moreover, these wider developments would have limited the availability

Table 5.1 *New York St George's Society: selected expenditure categories, 1875–1954*

	1875	1885	1895	1905	1915	1925	1935	1945	1954[a]
Pensioners/regular allowances	$1,718.60	$2,219.00	$2,347.00	1,801.00	$1,941.00	$3,180.00	$3,739.00	$4,776.00	$3,172.00
Sundry charity payments									$11,334.21
Rent aids				$348.40	$1,266.00	$755.00	$908.00	$134.00	$1,110.00
Allowances							$1,463.00		
Cash aids				$149.40	$1,222.98	$815.50	$3,215.00	$2,199.57	
Transients		$197.28	$303.00						
Meals & lodgings	$297.65	$724.45	$488.05		$758.10	$455.45	$268.10	$153.20	$1,032.45
Christmas presents			$59.00	$95.72	$153.00	$505.50	$323.00	$395.00	
Children's Christmas parties in England									$1,551.52
Clothing to England (freight cost)									$159.00
Groceries purchased			$25.07	$178.16	$707.35	$64.00			
Clothing purchased				$39.25	$48.67				
From pawn			$85.93	$33.50	$41.74		$4.25		
Bus/rail and carfares				$72.95	$151.45	$200.15	$27.15	$34.00	
Employment agency fees			$4.00		$211.34	$204.60			
Woodyard tickets			$21.00		$35.00				

Coal	$34.00	$11.15			$27.12			
Aid to England	$91.20	$48.51	$10.00					
Passages to England/colonies	$59.25			$280.50	$1,391.00	$324.75	$369.99		
Medical expenses					$209.95		$374.04	$95.00	$720.35
Telephone service (cardiac cases)									$143.15
Funeral expenses			$59.50			$261.00	$180.00		$595.15
Cemetery upkeep			$5.00					$111.06	$194.00
Office rent	$200.00	$250.00	$360.00	$332.88	$360.00	$870.00	$732.00	$780.00	$1,080.00
Almoner's salary	$350.00	$600.00	$960.00	$960.00	$1,440.00	$1,920.00	$2,400.00	$2,303.20	$4,402.32
Total expenditure as per annual report	$3,646.46	$4,431.53	$5,353.77	$8,060.83	$11,145.27	$10,789.58	$14,918.99	$14,702.82	$34,594.20

Source: St George's Society of New York, annual reports.
Note: [a]No report for 1955.

of alternatives, such as support for finding work, and are conceivably the principal reasons for this shift in thinking – although fees for employment agencies also increased for some of that period, documenting that the general desire to facilitate independence had not been undermined. In the 1890s and early twentieth century this ideal is also reflected in the money provided for taking the clothing of relief seekers out of pawn: in most cases the motivation for this was to ensure that people looked respectable when searching for jobs.[41] Noteworthy too is the provision of over $1,500.00 for Christmas presents for children in England in 1954 – an initiative that commenced after the Second World War and which we will explore in more detail in the next chapter.

In New York – as elsewhere – charitable relief was administered to both new and continued cases. In 1900, the New York St George's Society dealt with 754 new and 1,656 continued cases; there were also 435 calls from pensioners seeking support from the Society and 158 calls for information at its offices, and the almoner made 314 visits to applicants.[42] The extent of relief provisions is particularly well documented, however, for the St George's Society of Toronto, for which registers of relief recipients have survived. For the year 1868–69, a total of 1,539 cases were recorded; as 151 of them were listed without the name of the relief recipient, the usable number of cases for analysis is 1,388. Of them at least 218 were repeat cases. The age is recorded for 931 relief recipients, averaging 33.57 years. The vast majority of relief recipients were male – a fact reflective too of their status as heads of households – with only 68 women, or 4.9 per cent of relief recipients, receiving support. Between 3 and 24 January 1868, $250.26 was dispensed among 55 recipients, including Maria Ray and George Whatkins, who we have already heard about at the beginning of this chapter. On average the sum dispensed broke down to $4.55 per case, but in reality the relief received in cash was lower for most, there having been only a few cases where more substantial support was offered.[43] In 1870 the overall number of relief applications was similar, standing at 1,229, but the actual number of people applying was lower at 'about 400' because there were, on average, 'three applications from each person'.[44] This impact of repeat cases is important to consider when assessing the overall volume of relief requests and funds dispensed.

Apart from these general details about the level of relief, the Toronto St George's Society relief register also facilitates consideration of the origins of relief recipients, including details, in 1868–69, of the places of birth of 823 relief applicants. For some of them cities or villages were listed as the place of birth, but as the majority used county designations, these have been employed to trace overall patterns. To provide comparative context the origins of relief recipients for 1868–69 have been compared with the recipients of so-called 'Christmas Cheer' – about which more will be said below – as a list of recipients for 1878, including the origins for 448 cases, provides the best available comparator. Map 5.1 shows the overall distribution. For both samples London clearly stands out as the main point of origin of relief recipients, with the south of England generally supplying a good number. Distinct pockets of origin are also traceable, however, for Yorkshire and, especially in 1878, for Lancashire. These general patterns and concentrations were not specific to Toronto, as the assessment of relief records from the Sons of St George in Philadelphia documents for a similar time-frame (Map 5.2). But there were also discrete differences: among Philadelphia relief recipients, concentrations in some northern regions were more pronounced, while fewer hailed from the south of England when compared with those in Toronto.

While examples from Toronto and New York are particularly rich in documenting English ethnic associational activity, smaller operations are traceable throughout North America. In the eight years to 1821, for instance, the Philadelphia Sons of St George Society reported that it relieved 276 men, 362 females and 532 children, costing a total of $3754.87.[45] But the foci of associations gradually began to change over time – and this was often a result too of wider changes in society membership and societal developments. A century later, in 1910, for example, the charity dispensed by the Ottawa St George's Society stood at only $242.89.[46] Later reports suggest that one reason for the decrease in provisions in Ottawa can be found in improvements in the City of Ottawa's support for the poor. As was noted at the eighty-ninth annual meeting, '[o]wing no doubt to the excellent arrangements for relief organized by the city, the calls on our charitable fund have not been as heavy as was anticipated.'[47] The level of charity dispensed decreased further after the First World War. In 1923, for instance, only $20.60 was provided, with all other expenditure concerned exclusively with the annual banquet, hall expenses and the Society's annual church service.[48] This figure is a significant reduction compared with earlier in the century. This was a general trend. As was noted by the Toronto St George's Society, '[a]ny applicant who had resided in the city for one year or more, and for whom the City is responsible, was referred, except in a few special cases, to the House of Industry.'[49] But for the Ottawa St George's Society there are also clear indications that the changes in relief provision and focus were a reflection of changing membership: English migrants who now arrived in North America were more self-reliant and less in need of support than had been the case in the age of mass migration.

Cases of those that did receive support in the late 1920s provide further evidence of the changing nature in the provisions made. Between mid-December and mid-January 1928–29, for instance, the Ottawa St George's Society supported nine men. These included twenty-six-year-old Walter Jones from Liverpool, who had arrived in Canada in the spring of 1928 to farm in the west. He was robbed in Winnipeg, and was

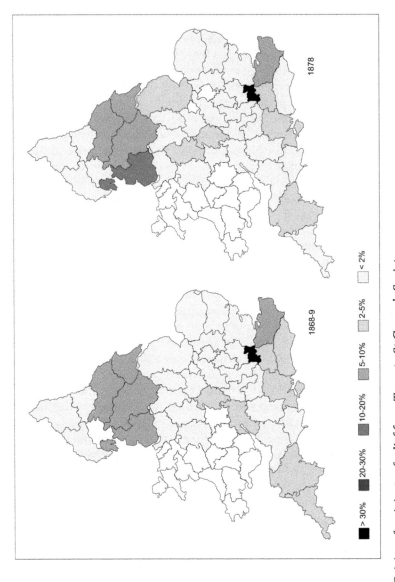

Map 5.1 Origins of recipients of relief from Toronto St George's Society

1878

1868-9

> 30%   20-30%   10-20%   5-10%   2-5%   < 2%

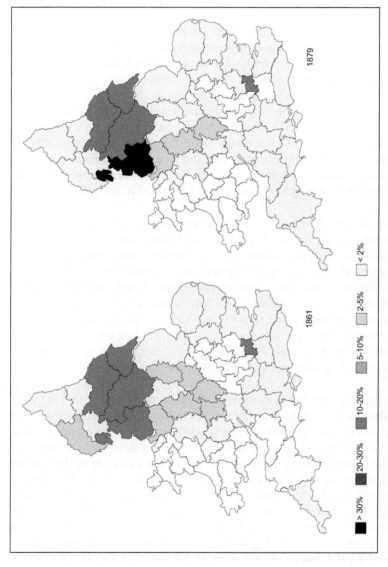

1879

1861

■ > 30%   ■ 20-30%   ■ 10-20%   ■ 5-10%   ■ 2-5%   □ < 2%

Map 5.2 Origins of recipients of relief from Philadelphia Sons of St George

now trying to get work in the east. Jones received an order for a bed for three days at the Salvation Army, and three days' board at the mission, soon securing his own way. And there was William Redmond, an ex-soldier who 'had been brought here to secure pension'. He had all the right provisions in place, but was in need of new clothes. Financial constraints may also have played a role in lower relief provisions. In several cases the recipients of support were warned that the provisions received were 'final', or were made to 'understand that this was all we could do'.[50] Finally, decreasing relief provisions came hand in hand with an increase in the Society's donations to other organizations, for instance to the Protestant Home for the Aged.[51]

The decrease in the relief provisions challenged the societies' very foundation of pursuing benevolence. In Baltimore, for instance, the early 1900s seemed to make few demands on the Society's funds: in 1912, it disbursed a little over $100 to assist forty cases 'including a number of men sent home to England on Cattle Boats'.[52] A few decades later, in Ottawa, the St George's Society's president noted to the point:

> At that time [1937] some of our members were strongly in favour of sur-rendering our charter, they felt we had outlived our usefulness. Other members and myself did not agree, we carried on under handicaps … In spite of the depression and 6 war years, plus deaths of our members, your society is an actual live organization for Service; the only English National Society in Ottawa or Eastern Ontario. We are not a Fraternal Society pro-viding sick benefits but a truly National Society which has served for over 100 years, with the Rose as our Emblem of Faith and the Union Jack as our Flag of Freedom, affiliating in 1941 with the Royal Society of St George, London, England with excellent and happy relationship.[53]

The issue of changes in membership was certainly critical, and not only in Ottawa. Records for Kingston highlight the impact that the departure of members had, and how many members failed to pay their dues.[54] And for all St George's societies one concern was a constant: the fact that Society membership never captured more than a fraction of the English in a particular locality. As was observed in New York, the St George's Society's membership there was 'wholly disproportionate to the number of English residents' in the city.[55] The sense of patrician benevolence so critical to the activities of St George's societies was not important to all English migrants or their descendants – nor was it one all could utilize, as the exploration of the activities of the Sons of England later in this chapter will further underline.

In New York, however, the St George's Society's operations contin-ued to be stable, a result, perhaps of its diverse base. Beyond providing the various types of relief (Table 5.1), the New York St George's Society was also able to use a number of beds to which it had exclusive access in St Luke's Hospital. These beds, members of the Society recognized, were 'a privilege the value of which cannot be over estimated'.[56] The origins of exclusive use of these beds lie in an agreement that was made between the Anglo-American church of St George the Martyr and St Luke's Hospital: wardens of the church 'were for a long time prominent and loyal members of St George's Society',[57] and hence when sick Englishmen came to the Society, arrangements were made to send them to a warden of the church to then be given a bed at the hospital. While that system worked well, a direct agreement between the church of St George the Martyr, St Luke's Hospital and the St George's Society was later put in place to allow the latter to send patients directly to the hospital. Originally, twenty beds were available in various hospital wards, but by the 1920s these were all held together in one ward. To enhance co-operation and facilitate the treatment of patients, two St George's Society members were elected annually as representatives to the board of managers of St Luke's Hospital.[58] The extent of provisions thus made is certainly significant. In 1925 alone, the New York St George's Society provided 755 hospital days in total for 53 patients. Beds were not, however, reserved exclusively for English migrants and their descendants. Of the 53 patients in 1925, only 22 were English. Moreover, while the majority of patients were that year were Protestant Episcopalians, there were also 9 Roman Catholics, 4 Presbyterians, 3 Methodists and 2 Congregationalists among them. Of those admitted under the aegis of the St George's Society, 17 were women, and 4 patients unfortunately died.[59]

Beyond life was the certainty of death, and many St George's societies thus viewed the provision of burial plots as important to their work. In Toronto, the local Society had plots at St James' Cemetery, while the New York Society offered plots at Cypress Hill Cemetery in Brooklyn. The plot that the New York Society had acquired in 1901 'bounded on either side by similar plots purchased by St Andrew's Society and St David's Society, for the internment of destitute English or Colonial peoples'.[60] By 1923, 108 people had been buried in ground owned by the New York St George's Society. The Society was pleased to be able to provide this final service to fellow Englishmen, not least because their 'remains would otherwise have been sent to Potters Field'.[61]

Regulated processes of assessment were critical in the decision-making for or against giving relief. In some instances this involved perhaps rather trivial matters. When the Ottawa St George's Society committee met in December 1894 to discuss the preparation of special Christmas relief, the committee discussed not only the fact that sixty families should be given food bags containing meat, bread, flour, rice, tea and sugar, but also the type of meat. It was decided where these goods should be purchased – flour had to come from McKay Milling Co. – and a Mr John Goodfellow was employed 'as butcher to cut up the meat' so as to resolve that matter properly. It was agreed 'to have two classes of relief, No. 1 to contain better cuts of meat and a little more in quantity than No. 2'.[62]

Almoners were employed by some of the larger, urban St George's societies for the day-to-day business of charity dispensation and administration, whether in the form of meal tickets or other provisions. In the 1870s, the almoner of the New York St George's Society was present at the Society's office at 432 Broome Street, room no. 9, every day between 1 p.m. and 4 p.m. to assess relief applications.[63] The almoner's salary was therefore, a critical expense, making up somewhere between 10 per cent in 1875 and 18 per cent in 1925 of the New York Society's total relief expenditure (Table 5.1). Toronto adopted a different system, and one that more closely involved all members. As was noted in the committee report for 1870,

[f]or some years past, it has been the practice for two members to be appointed each month to attend daily at the Office, and consider cases requiring immediate relief, and to visit all cases referred to them; but from the largely increased demands, it was found impossible for any two members to properly discharge these duties; and a system of Ward Committees has been adopted, which is found to be much more efficient.[64]

Smaller societies, such as the one in Baltimore, struggled to develop the kind of infrastructure that would allow for an almoner. There was discussion in the Baltimore Society in April 1890 about disbursing charitable funds either through the Charity Organization or else via paid almoner, but no conclusion was reached.[65] In 1893, the secretary once again raised the idea of a paid almoner, presumably because he and the treasurer came under the most administrative pressure over such matters. The secretary was also at pains to urge members to redouble their efforts to ensure that the many Englishmen who came to Baltimore knew about them.[66] The issue of an almoner was raised again in early 1894, with a suggestion that Mr Beveridge, who fulfilled the same role for the St Andrew's Society, be appointed.[67] This did not happen. In 1897 the secretary's report reminded members that 'No salaries of any kind are paid by the Society'.[68] By 1900, however, the Society had appointed an unpaid almoner who served as chair of the relief committee, an office filled by Henry W. Rowland.[69]

Assessing claims usually involved visits to individual homes by members of the societies' relief committees or their equivalents. Visits could take place in cases where those who were seeking support were too sick to come to a society's office, but were also utilized as part of the assessment of cases, particularly for the purpose of establishing whether an application was genuine and deserving of aid or not. Each society had at least one doctor affiliated, whose assessment was crucial. In 1875 the Kingston St George's Society did away with a registration office for those seeking relief and instead determined that 'personal applications for relief or work by members of the Society must be laid before the Committee at the Committee Room on each Monday evening at 8 o'clock'.[70] The change was agreed unanimously. The measures taken to ensure that funds were not wasted and only deserving cases were helped can be seen from just a few examples. In January 1876, when Henry Sole requested a loan to buy coal and Charles Litton applied for 'assistance or work', it was decided, in response, that Mr McLaren, presumably one of the stewards, should visit the two men.[71] The following year, however, another man, Mr Jones, had his request for a loan held over due to the Society's having insufficient funds.[72] Later that month the Society agreed that 'no monies be expended ... except by the relief committee in urgent cases, without the consent of the General Committee'.[73]

In Toronto too, records document that visits played a key role in the continuous assessment of the welfare of those who were sick. In May 1863, for instance, Toronto St George's Society members visited a Mr E. Curle, who had been in hospital, and received a doctor's note with details concerning the treatment. As the member who visited Mr Curle recorded in the Society's 'Visitors to Relief Recipients' register, 'I have given him an order for Bed and Board until Monday morning'.[74] The degree to which societies were able to look after existing cases depended not only on the availability of members to carry them out, however, but also on the overall volume of requests. The ebb and flow of claims reflected migration patterns and wider economic conditions. Thus the depression that affected the United States in the mid-1880s, for instance, made it difficult for an increasing number of people to find employment, and hence the number of aid seekers went up. At times, however, problems also arose from the types of migrants who arrived, and specifically as a result of their skills (or lack thereof). In the late 1860s, the Toronto St George's Society was particularly concerned because of this. Not only had the volume of migration increased significantly, leading to an 'increasing demand upon' the Society's funds, but there was '[a] marked difference ... in the character and class of those seeking relief'. These people, the Society went on, came to Canada 'with the vague undefined hope of improving their position'; but they 'are quite unsuited for laborious occupations, or from previous education or apprenticeship to some trade or calling peculiar to England, are without the ability to engage in the most ordinary kinds of work'. A related concern was that those who were fortunate enough to find work often had to 'unlearn all their previous experience',[75] as the jobs they found were not the ones they had been trained in. To address these issues, the Toronto St George's Society sought to find employment for as many relief seekers as possible as relief was considered less helpful. Instead the Society's committee was hoping to 'refer "the right man to the right place"', with 'situations' indeed found for many.[76] Problems amplified in the course of the 1880s. The Society's annual report for 1885, for instance, notes an increase in the number of relief seekers 'from those not used to manual labor, such as writers, clerks ... who find, on arriving in Canada, that the market is well supplied and vacancies few ... These cases are difficult to deal with'.[77] The same was true for the growing number of 'families, who arrived during the last summer, very respectable in appearnce [sic], yet entirely without means'.[78]

In 1885 just as much as in 1868, the Society was critical of the government and how it dealt with arriving emigrants. While, in 1868, the problem was a large one triggered by the Emigration Department's failure to classify new arrivals so as to give 'them information and advice as to where their labor and skill is most in demand',[79] the principal concern in 1885 was the overall provision for emigrants arriving in Toronto; these, the St George's Society argued, were 'either not available or ... unsuitable' and, in any case, temporary.[80] Partly as a result of these concerns over the failure of the government to deal appropriately with new arrivals, there was a strong desire to better inform migrants prior to their departure, with the St George's Society working together with other groups 'to aid by kindly counsel and advice'.[81] This was a strategy that St George's societies elsewhere in the world, as well as the associations of other ethnic groups, also pursued.[82] Thankfully the situation improved soon thereafter in Toronto as, in the 1890s, fewer emigrants arrived, and those who did come were 'generally of a more thrifty class than previous years'.[83] In Ottawa too there were fewer cases in the 1890s, with those reported largely supported by means of providing shelter. In particular, the Society was working with a Mr J. Burns of Navan House, York Street, who there honoured orders by the Society for a night's lodgings and meals.[84] Importantly, therefore, just as economic problems led to a marked increase in applications for relief, so did prosperity and availability of jobs result in the opposite. When relief numbers were especially low in Toronto in 1910 – there were only 174 recipients of relief – the St George's Society's annual report expressly notes that this was a direct result of '[t]he demand for men to work on railway construction, public works and private undertakings [which] largely exceeded the supply'.[85] This respite was, however, short-lived, as the outbreak of the First World War had an immediate impact, certainly in Canada, contributing to a significant increase in the demand for relief.[86] This upward trend continued in the immediate post-war period. But the character of relief recipients was changing, particularly in the course of the Great Depression. In New York in 1935, for instance, there was an increase in relief expenditure which, according to the Society, was 'caused by a change in the type of person requiring assistance – so many of our present applicants have been in good social position'.[87]

The provision of 'Christmas Cheer'

Distributing seasonal charity – 'Christmas Cheer' as they called it – was an important feature in the work of St George's societies, and one that began to increase in importance from the late nineteenth century, particularly in Canada. In Ottawa the St George's Society had a special Christmas fund, while members of the Kingston Society campaigned hard among their English compatriots to ensure a good Christmas box to spread their alms widely, also asking members 'to send in the names of recipients for "Good Cheer"'.[88] In 1886, that 'Cheer' consisted 'of beef, bread, tea, sugar and currant cake', and the payment of $1.00 entitled members 'to nominate a family for participation in the distribution'.[89] In 1880, ninety families received 'Cheer', representing 391 persons, at a cost of $97.93 – this compares with a total of $222.52 dispensed in relief that year.[90] Further south, in the city of New York, the idea of making available special Christmas provisions was also important, but it took a different form as the St George's Society there concentrated, as was noted above, primarily on offering Christmas presents for pensioners.

The most extensive 'Christmas Cheer' was provided by the St George's Society in Toronto. In 1876, a total of 559 households were supported on the recommendation of members, though another forty came without it. With the size of families varying significantly, including individuals, such as Maria Day, a sick nurse born in Suffolk, and small families like the family of four of John Terry, a labourer born in Norfolk, but also large households as that of William Robinson, a carpenter originally of Middlesex, who cared for a family of ten, the overall number of people aided was about 3,000. To offer 'Cheer' to them, the Society purchased 4,368 lb of meat, 767 loaves of bread, 121 lb of tea and 554 lb of sugar at a cost of $492.35 (Figures 5.1 and 5.2).[91] The items purchased were then

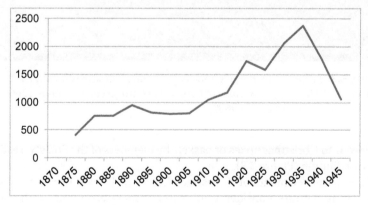

Figure 5.1 Overall 'Christmas Cheer' distribution expenses

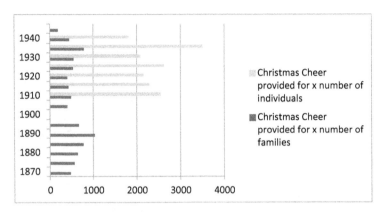

Figure 5.2 Number of 'Christmas Cheer' recipients

Figure 5.3 Toronto St George's Society preparing Christmas boxes, 23 December 1926 (image courtesy of City of Toronto Archives, Fonds 1266, Globe and Mail Fonds, Item 9680)

packed into Christmas boxes or baskets by members of the Society, ready for distribution (Figure 5.3).

The list of recipients of 'Christmas Cheer' in 1876 is worth pausing over as it permits consideration of their socio-economic profile in more detail. Of the 559 recipients listed in the Society's Christmas distribution register, the occupation is listed for 538. Of them, 48.8 per cent are listed as 'labourers'. This is a significant number and one that serves well to characterize the recipient of St George's Society support across the world: by and large recipients were at the lowest stratum. Other occupations include carpenter and blacksmith, and there were also a few clerks. The women listed were working primarily as laundresses, nurses and particularly as charwomen, and were hence often in some form of domestic service employment.[92] Moreover, by far the largest proportion of them, 39 per cent, hailed from London – a regional concentration in the south more broadly reflective of the background of most migrants to Canada.

Co-operation within and beyond the ethnic group

Critical to the charitable work of many St George's societies was the co-operation with other bodies – ethnic associations of other migrant groups as well as civic and government bodies. In Ottawa in the 1870s, the St George's Society frequently appointed special deputations to the mayor or other city officials to discuss cases of English migrants in distress, such as that 'of Mrs Knight and her helpless family of six children',[93] with a view to securing a grant from the Corporation of Ottawa. Children and women were recognized as obvious and necessary beneficiaries for charity and mutual aid when they were at risk if the breadwinning male died, suffered injury or abandoned them. Women's charities and asylums dated at least to the 1790s in the major sea-ports of America's east coast, and Presbyterians founded the Female Association for the Relief of Women and Children as early as 1800. These charities were not the same as the mutual aid organizations that gave them back the funds they, or their breadwinner, had invested, but the principle of supporting the family was long established.[94]

Towards the end of the century, there were a plethora of joint activities with the Sons of England – about who more will be said later – including annual church parades, but the two groups also joined forces for the good of English migrants. The Ottawa St George's Society did not customarily provide return passages for migrants, but in 1898 it 'co-operated with the Sons of England Lodges of the City in sending a distressed and invalid countryman, Mr C.H. Firth back to his home in England'.[95] The use of private funds – for return passages and other forms of relief – was by no means uncommon.[96] The tradition of co-operation between ethnic organizations and the amicable relations – documented too in the many toasts to 'sister societies' dispensed at annual celebrations such as St George's, St Andrew's or St David's Day – fostered strong bonds that extended beyond the immediate ethnic bounds of these organizations, further evidence of which we will see in the next chapter, where we compare English associationalism with that of other groups.

There also were more practical and substantial examples of co-operation, for instance in New York. It was in the city, in the 1860s and 1870s, that the St Andrew's and St George's Societies shared office space as well as their almoner. As was noted in the 1869 annual report, the then almoner, Mr James M. Munro, was 'a very correct and experienced person, well-adapted for the positions he holds; his holding these two positions prevents imposition on either Society, as has often occurred heretofore'.[97] The sharing of the almoner thus was the practical solution to attempted cases of fraud, when people either sought to acquire relief from both societies or were imposters altogether. We explore the level of co-operation in more detail in the following chapter.

Yet while all this charitable work was critical to the St George's tradition, it was, as we know, by no means the only avenue open to English migrants in need of support or keen to make a better life for themselves: next to it mutualism provided the second pillar. While the Order of the Sons of St George has left no extant archive (or none that has become apparent), the archives of the Sons of England are extremely rich and thus serve well for a coherent case study of the mutual aid dimension of English ethnic associational culture. Since the two organizations were almost identical, the insights obtained from the Sons of England may be more generally instructive. The remainder of this chapter will focus on the Sons and the multiplicity of mutualism that they offered their thousands of members.

The Sons of England and the development of English ethnic mutualism

Some time in the early 1870s a Toronto Englishman happened to witness the goings-on at a St George's Society Christmas distribution. Instead of feeling a sense of elation or perhaps pride in the good charitable work of his fellow countrymen, however, the observer was 'pained' by what he saw.[98] This applied not only to what he, according to a contemporary observer, viewed as a 'somewhat Poor-Law-Guardian haughtiness', but also because to this Englishman the English 'in Toronto were the only people out of all nationalities who had to parade their wants and sufferings to the gaze of others, and be made the recipients of charity in a public manner'.[99] For him the dispensing of food parcels and firewood was an annual public degradation 'no matter how excellent the intention' of the Toronto St George's Society.[100] It was on the basis of these sentiments that the foundations were laid for the establishment of the Sons of England. Set up in December 1874, the Sons were a mutual benefit society with the express purpose of providing a means for self-help: they sought to avoid compelling their fellow countrymen 'to [have to] solicit charity' as '[n]o man of fine feeling and high principle can receive charity without feeling humiliated', instead offering a means through which they could 'demand relief ... as a right to which we are justly entitled, from having, when in health and prosperity, provided against adversity'.[101]

In this view lies the principal difference between the St George's societies and the Sons of England: while a profound sense of patrician benevolence was foundational to the activities of the former, documenting the understanding of founders and members of St George's societies that there was a duty to aid countrymen in distress, this type of benevolence had no currency for those Englishmen who formed the Sons of England. Instead, they placed their organizational structures on mutualism – a focus that allowed them to actively shape their own future in a way that patrician benevolence could not. This was a direct result of their socio-economic position: those who joined the Sons of England were largely working class, and therefore they were more likely to be at the receiving end of patrician benevolence rather than being its agents. In that sense they had little to gain from it. While English residents of Toronto's big mansions would often seek to generate social capital from their involvement in the dispensation of charity, this would have been impossible for working-class men because of their inability to dispense funds for charity in the first place. For these working-class men, keen to establish a means that gave them agency in building their own lives and provide for the future, ethnic mutualism trumped ethnic associationalism. The background of the founding members provides important context here: all of them were working class, and five of them were, in fact, unemployed when the Sons of England's foundation meeting took place in December 1874, 'ready and anxious for a union of interests'[102] not least because of their own situation.

The principal initiator of the meeting, George F. Carrette, had arrived in Toronto in early September 1869, with the other founders for whom details are available making their way across the Atlantic around the same time. They also had in common their origins in England, as the majority hailed from London, and it is noteworthy that there were personal connections between them too – another founder, James Lomas, for instance, was married to a daughter of Carrette.[103] The start of activities was not straightforward, as the group initially struggled to recruit members. Fortunately, however, they found the support of Judge Duggan, who signed off the incorporation papers of the Sons of England early on in their formalization at the end of February 1875.[104] This provided a boost to the Sons' early endeavours, but so did the initiatives they pursued directly in support of growing membership.

As George Carrette explained in the Sons of England's *Record* at the time of the organization's twenty-fifth anniversary, '[w]e then went out on the highways and byways to get members. We left copies of the rules of the Society at the different hotels, railways stations, Y.M.C.A. rooms, and many other public places'; there was also a significant advertisement campaign in the press – though Toronto's *Globe* 'flatly refused to publish' the advertisement.[105] In their drive to recruit members the Sons emphasized an associational focus on mutualism, stressing that it thus had a remit 'entirely different' from existing English ethnic associations.[106] It was also this argument that the Sons began to increasingly utilize for advertisement purposes specifically among new English migrants who had recently arrived from England.[107]

Membership grew slowly but steadily. Organized in a lodge system, the Sons formed new lodges alongside the original one – Albion Lodge – and by the summer of 1876, four lodges existed: Albion, Middlesex, Kent and Essex. It was at this point that the idea of hosting a central annual meeting was first mooted. Subsequent to these discussions the first Grand Lodge of the Sons of England was held in Toronto on 30 October 1876, with George Carrette in the chair, supported by the wider executive of the organization and eleven delegates from all lodges, one delegate being absent.[108] Compare this scene with 1931. In that year, the fortieth session of the Grand Lodge was held in Windsor, Ontario, over four days from 11 to 14 August.[109] For that meeting 175 delegates and Grand Lodge officers came together from nearly as many lodges.[110] It is the history of this significant expansion, and the related development and growth in the Sons of England's mutual benefit provision, that the remainder of this chapter will explore, focusing on the two staples of the Sons' activities – the payment of sick and funeral benefits and the provisions of the beneficiary department.

Sick and funeral benefits

Provision for illness and support for families on a member's death lay at the core of the Sons of England's offering. These aspects defined their essential motto: 'not charity but fraternity'.[111] As outlined in its constitution, the organization was set up to offer 'assistance to members when sick, or unable to follow their employment', and to provide 'medical attendance and medicine to members, assuring lives of members on mutual principles, and assisting in defraying the funeral expenses of deceased members, members' deceased wives and children'.[112] To enable this mutualism the Sons, like other friendly societies, relied on a system of fee payments, comprising initiation fees and weekly or monthly subscription fees payable by members; levies were also

Table 5.2 *The cost of Sons of England membership, 1889*

Age	Initiation fee	Weekly subscription
18–30	$3.00	10c.
30–45	$4.00	13c.
45–50	$7.00	15c.
50–55	$10.00	20c.
55–60	$15.00	25c.

Source: Sons of England, *Constitution of the Sons of England Benevolent Society under the Supreme Jurisdiction of the Grand Lodge of Canada* (Belleville, 1889), p. 41.

charged (per member reported) for subordinate lodges to transfer to the Supreme Grand Lodge, which were used in support of general management costs as well as a permanent fund. Tables 5.2 and 5.3 document the costs to members. As is clear, this depended primarily on the members' age, with costs increasing the older a member was – a pattern clearly resulting from the assumption that with aging came a tendency to fall ill increasingly often. As a result of this thinking, there was an age limit for new members. While someone aged eighteen would thus have paid $3 for the initiation and 40 cents a month as subscription in 1889, someone aged sixty would have paid $15 for the initiation, and a monthly subscription fee of $1. By 1912, there were no standard rates for members over forty-nine years of age (Table 5.3). Generally the idea was that older men were more likely to claim than younger ones and so had to pay more to join for the first time.

Those keen on becoming members had to be proposed by an existing member with the support of at least one more, and were required to supply 'a certificate of good health from the Surgeon of the Lodge he wishes to join'; only after that a ballot on their application could take place.[113] Conducting medical examinations was only one of the duties of lodge surgeons, however. They were also required to attend to sick members and provide medicine for them – although only if the member lived in the designated catchment area of the lodge room.[114] Lodge surgeons were also the first to assess the state of health in cases of members seeking sick pay. If they were, on the basis of that assessment, found to be eligible for sick pay,[115] members, in 1889, received and allowance of $3.00 per week for thirteen weeks, thereafter reduced to $1.50 for a further twenty-six weeks. Should a member's wife die, the payment was $30.00, and if a child aged between five and fifteen died, it was $7.00.[116] Provisions were in place to prevent the payment of benefits in those cases where members were in in arrears more than six months – a rule later tightened to an immediate suspension from

Table 5.3 *The cost of Sons of England membership, 1912*

Age	Monthly payment
17	50c
18	50c
19	51c
20	52c
21	53c
22	54c
23	55c
24	56c
25	57c
26	58c
27	59c
28	60c
29	61c
30	62c
31	63c
32	64c
33	65c
34	66c
35	67c
36	68c
37	69c
38	70c
39	71c
40	72c
41	74c
42	76c
43	78c
44	80c
45	82c
46	84c
47	86c
48	88c
49	90c

Source: Sons of England, *Constitution of the Sons of England Benefit Society under the Supreme Jurisdiction of the Supreme Lodge* (Toronto, 1912), pp. 108–09.

benefits 'as soon as' dues were in arrears, though reinstatement was still possible.[117] Over time, and sometimes through by-laws of local lodges, the provisions changed in line with inflation and the rising cost of living. There were also, as is to be expected, significant differences between lodges. In the annual report presented at the 1888 Grand Lodge, for instance, details about the sick pay and medical expenses dispensed for all lodges then in existence ranged from $3,241.03 paid out by Albion Lodge to as little as $22.50 dispensed by Chelsea Lodge.[118] Overall, and particularly from the late 1890s, there was a steady increase in payments made for sick benefits and for medical attendance (Figure 5.4). This rise in the expenditure mirrored the rise in the Sons' membership, which, in the immediate period before the outbreak of the First World War, had reached over 35,000.[119] The war itself also had an immediate impact, resulting in a decline in requests for support – a direct effect of the fact that many Sons of England members were not at home in Canada to make claims, but had joined the Canadian troops sent in support of the British war effort. Unsurprisingly too, the post-war period then saw a rise in demand as soldiers returned, taking up ordinary employment again in Canada.

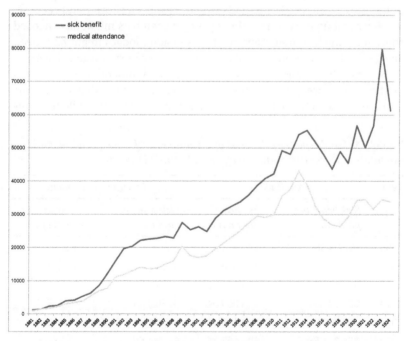

Figure 5.4 Total expenditure by the Sons of England on sick benefits and medical attendance, 1881–1924 (based on Sons of England, Supreme Lodge *Journal of Proceedings* for the period 1881–1924)

The juvenile branch of the Sons of England pursued essentially the same principles of sick pay provision, offering an organizational home for younger men. The express idea behind this was to offer the young an easy pathway to adult membership. As was noted in the *Record* in 1897, '[o]ur boys are the best and most reliable reserve possible from which to draw future reinforcements for the Society's ranks.'[120] To ensure the Sons' future prosperity, therefore, juvenile work was considered critical. This commitment is reflected in the general growth of the Juvenile Department. While there were an already respectable 531 members in 1895, by the First World War the overall membership of the Juvenile Department had risen to 2,285, and it peaked in the mid-1920s at around 4,000 members.[121] One general difference between the Juvenile Department and the adult operations was that, when it came to the difference between sick pay and medical attendance or surgeon's expenses, the Juvenile Department paid more for the latter than the former, while it was the reverse for the adult group (Table 5.4). While specific explanations are not provided for this difference, it is plausible to assume that the generally better health of the young members of the Juvenile Department was the principal reason, reducing the need for extended medical treatment or hospital stays. While accidents would have afflicted members regardless of their age, recuperation periods would have been shorter and recoveries faster among the young. Where younger members might have needed short-term medical treatment, members of adult lodges might have been affected by longer-term ailments because of their more advanced age.

Beyond the financial pay-outs of sick and funeral benefits lay a plethora of more practical means of mutualism provided in support of members who had fallen ill and their relatives. Hence, while the Sons

Table 5.4 *Funds spent by the Sons of England on sick benefit and medical attendance, 1885–1930: adult lodges and Juvenile Department*

Year	Adult lodge		Juvenile Department	
	Sick benefits paid out	Medical attendance	Sick benefits paid out	Medical attendance
1885	$2,578.28	$2,227.00	n.a.	n.a.
1895	22,083.38	$14,036	$426.91	$437.23
1905	$32,627.28	$23,278.82	$473.04	$921.77
1913	$54,105.54	$43,069.94	$1,970.23	$3,275.73
1924	$55,790.96	$29,463.43	$1,171.65	$3,410.40
1930	$55,271.78	$29,667.34	$1,264.55	$3,752.72

Source: Sons of England, annual reports; five-year intervals (or closest year with available data).

of England undoubtedly fulfilled functions of an insurance company, the more practical, often non-monetary, support provided most strongly reflected the ethnic remit of fraternal brotherhood that also underpinned the Sons of England's activities. In Toronto, for instance, a number of lodges were keen on offering 'ambulance classes' so as to better help patients in emergencies.[122] Further west, in Calgary in the spring of 1891, news of a fellow brother's sprained ankle prompted Bro. Thompson of the United Roses Lodge to note that 'he would hand the Lodge a pair of crutches'.[123] A more organized and centralized offering came by means of the Sons of England's journal, the *Record*, which began to run a 'situations wanted' column, in which '[a]ny Brother in good standing in his lodge in need of employment … [could] make known his requirements … without charge.'[124]

Visits to sick members were considered critical in ensuring the member's well-being and recovery, being considered a means 'to cheer him and distract his thoughts'. This was not a task reserved for subordinate lodge committee members: while it was their 'especial duty to discharge this service, there is nothing in the constitution to prohibit any member whose heart is true to his pledge, from calling upon a brother whom he knows to be sick'.[125] In Calgary this idea was certainly practised, and not only for members. In late 1892, for instance, Bro. Doughty of United Roses Lodge customarily went to visit the widow of another member recently deceased, and, in early 1893, the lodge minutes document the lodge's president reporting that the wife of a member was 'very ill', to which another brother replied that 'he would call and see her'.[126] In Toronto visits to members who had been admitted to hospital were a standard part of lodge activities. In fact, the Sons put in place a system to facilitate the visit of members at the city's hospitals, whereby a card was cut for each Sons of England member admitted to a hospital. This card was then entered into a Sons of England register containing all key details. The express purpose of this system was to ensure that lodges were aware, and could easily check, where the patient was located, so that they could visit.[127]

It is also in the category of visits that one might include that final farewell. As was enshrined in the Sons' constitution, it was their express purpose too to be part of members' funeral proceedings, and designated funeral regalia was adopted.[128] When Bro. William E. Muggridge died in July 1896, officers of his own Neptune Lodge conducted the funeral. Muggridge had been initiated to the lodge in September 1892. Of good health and character, he had died suddenly of a 'hemorrhage [sic] of the lungs'[129] when working as a fireman for the Canadian Pacific Railway. He left a widow and three children. While the Baltimore St George's Society decided to look after the orphaned children of a deceased member, the Sons of England formalized such activity in their constitution:

Should any member in good standing die, leaving children, and such children be without any competent relatives willing and able to provide for them, it shall be the bounden duty of the deceased member's Lodge to interest itself in their behalf, and to bring their case before the Supreme Grand Lodge with a view to have such children properly cared for.[130]

Another important element of the work of the Sons of England that went beyond their written constitution lay in the collection of funds for particular projects or people. Hence, in the early twentieth century a subscription was opened for a Sons of England cot in a Toronto hospital,[131] while, in the late 1890s, an appeal was launched on behalf of Bro. Robert Hurst, who had been 'disabled from the effect of typhoid fever since February, 1895 ... [and his] wife and four children are in destitute circumstances'.[132] In Calgary, in 1908, 'a subscription was being taken up' for a Mrs Osborne and family 'to enable her to return to the old country'.[133] It was in these cases of small-scale charity that, even among the Sons, a shred of patrician benevolence came through occasionally. But this was a shred that did not disrupt the focus on mutualism, as the wider context of the aid provided was the membership of Hurst and other individuals who were aided directly.

Overall, then, the Sons of England provided a fairly well-oiled organizational structure for the provision of sick benefits, but it was not one without its flaws and challenges, both internal and external. Internally a recurring concern for the Supreme Grand Lodge was the question of assessment, as it became a problem that some of the surgeons appointed to act as lodge surgeons were 'exceedingly lenient' in their 'reading of the constitution, and more than isolated cases have come to our knowledge where a strange coincidence has occurred between a brother's sickness and his lack of work'.[134]

Beyond such concerns, the Sons also had to deal with appeals. In Calgary, two members who had fallen ill did not receive their sick pay, for instance, because of a failure to submit the required paperwork properly. This was a fairly frequent occurrence and, in Calgary as elsewhere, often triggered discussions about the 'proper mode of procedure'.[135] In the early twentieth century, also in Calgary, a member 'reported negligence of Lodge surgeon in not attending him when called'.[136] The highest number of appeals were lodged, however, in relation to the funeral department, and often in relation to one problem: the failure, on the member's part, properly to register wives and children, making the payment of benefits impossible. In other cases members failed to report a marriage or the name of a new wife, leading to similar problems. All appeals made were lodged with the relevant committee and investigated thoroughly, not seldom deciding in favour of the member. J.M. Chant, for instance, had been suspended from Lodge Denbigh in

1902, but he should, soon thereafter, have been reinstated. Because his lodge secretary failed to submit the relevant paperwork, however, the claim made by his widow after his death was initially not paid, but, 'after some correspondence' was then paid out because it was discovered that the error had been made by the Lodge.[137] Elsewhere, Stockport Lodge, on opening, failed to send the names of members to the Supreme Lodge altogether – a management failure that probably explains too why the lodge did not exist for very long. In the case of Bro. Sickel, who was making a claim after the death of his wife, a discrepancy between the Sons of England's records, in which Sickel's widower was recorded as aged forty-eight, and the death certificate which stated fifty-nine, caused problems. Fortunately for Sickel, the 'difference of 11 years' was identified as 'a mistake of [the] doctor when examining at initiation', as he had 'put down [the] wrong age'. Consequently the claim was eventually paid.[138]

These cases of appeal, and the considerable administrative and management effort on the part of the Sons of England that they document, highlight that the association had grown, in many ways, into a fully fledged insurance company. What differentiated it from those in the open market were its lower rates,[139] and of course the ethnic remit pursued. Partly because of these offerings, external factors relating to the provision of insurance could impact upon the work of the Sons of England. This was the case in particular with respect to life insurance. '[B]ased upon mutual assessments, and so economically conducted', the offerings of the Sons of England were, as one member noted, 'an eyesore to the life line companies'. As a result, they made 'every effort ... to make it impossible for us [the Sons of England] to carry on our business'.[140] For a time, however, these efforts had little effect and the membership of the Sons of England continued to climb. Still there was scope for tension. In 1897, for example, the Quebec Medical Association was keen to adopt a new regulation 'forbidding doctors of that province to act as lodge surgeons under an arrangement such is at present in force'.[141] On a smaller scale, in Calgary, United Roses Lodge faced opposition from the local medical association after appointing a Dr George as lodge surgeon, and, in December 1890, '[c]onsiderable discussion regarding the attitude of the local doctors towards benevolent + secret societies took place.'[142] And, perhaps unsurprisingly, one of the most common external pressures came from those who simply sought to abuse the Sons of England's benefit system, coaxing funds for their own pockets without ever having paid in. As was recorded in the minutes of United Roses Lodge in November 1890, for instance, '[a] circular' had been received from the Supreme Grand Lodge, 'warning members against two men, W. C. Barrett + John Harrison, who were going about as members of our order + obtaining money under false pretences'.[143]

Table 5.5 *Sons of England Beneficiary Department contributions, 1889*

Age	For $1,000	For $500
30 years	.50c	.25c
30 and under 35	.55c	.28c
35 and under 40	.60c	.30c
40 and under 45	.70c	.35c
45 and under 50	.85c	.43c
50 and under 55	$1.10	.55c
55 and under 60	$1.50	.75c
Over 60	$2.00	$1.00

Source: Sons of England, *Constitution of the Sons of England Benevolent Society under the Supreme Jurisdiction of the Grand Lodge of Canada* (Bowmanville, 1889), p. 41.

Beneficiary Department

The Beneficiary Department, originally conceived as the Mutual Endowment Department, was a distinct branch of the Sons of England established in the summer of 1884.[144] Not every lodge member was also a member of this department, since membership required the separate payment of a fee, again depending on age, but also on the cover sought (Tables 5.5 and 5.6). Those keen on joining the Beneficiary Department had to be members of good standing in a Sons of England lodge. The purpose of the department was to provide financial support for widows and children of deceased members. As with the provision of sick benefits, the Beneficiary Department had age restrictions in place, also tightening them over time. By 1912, new beneficiary members aged over forty-nine were no longer accepted, but for those of that age who were already members of the department special rates were available.[145]

In comparison to the activities focused on the payment of sick benefits, the Beneficiary Department was less successful when measured in terms of its membership. Even by the mid-1890s, when Sons of England membership stood at 11,128, there were only 2,360 certificates for $1,000.00 in place in the Beneficiary Department.[146] Membership figures had increased over time, however, and continued to do so – and so did, therefore, the number of claims made. This can be seen, for instance, in the payments made for death claims, which, although always fluctuating, generally increased, certainly until the 1920s (Figure 5.5). From the early 1890s, it was potentially an option to pay out in disability claims instead, particularly when a workplace accident had been the cause.[147] Overall, it is clear, the underlying reason for the patterns are largely fluctuating death rates, which, in turn, were the result of natural developments (old age),

Table 5.6 *Sons of England Beneficiary Department contributions, 1912*

Age	Insurance cover $250.00	Insurance cover $500.00	Insurance cover $1,000.00
17	19c	37c	74c
18	19c	38c	76c
19	20c	39c	78c
20	21c	41c	81c
21	21c	42c	84c
22	22c	43c	86c
23	23c	45c	89c
24	23c	46c	92c
25	24c	48c	95c
26	25c	49c	97c
27	25c	50c	$1.00
28	26c	52c	$1.03
29	27c	53c	$1.06
30	28c	55c	$1.09
31	29c	57c	$1.13
32	29c	58c	$1.16
33	30c	60c	$1.20
34	31c	63c	$1.24
35	33c	65c	$1.29
36	34c	67c	$1.33
37	35c	69c	$1.38
38	36c	72c	$1.43
39	38c	75c	$1.49
40	39c	77c	$1.54
41	40c	80c	$1.60
42	42c	84c	$1.67
43	44c	87c	$1.74
44	46c	91c	$1.81

Source: Sons of England, *Constitution* (1912), p. 54.

but also of issues such as workplace safety. What is noticeable, however, is again the direct impact of the First World War, which undoubtedly was one factor in the consistently higher claims throughout the war years as well as the immediate post-war period.[148] By 1930 – a point by which

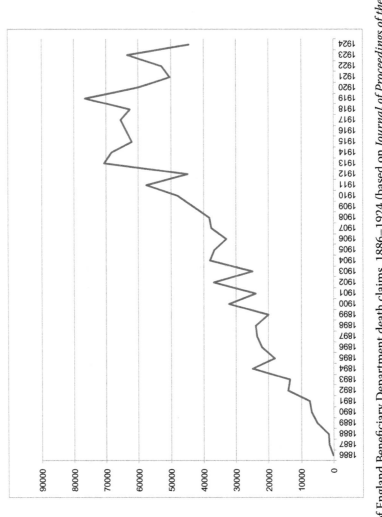

Figure 5.5 Sons of England Beneficiary Department death claims, 1886–1924 (based on *Journal of Proceedings of the Thirty-Seventh Session of the Supreme Lodge, Sons of England Benefit Society* (Toronto, 1925), p. 30)

the Beneficiary Department had been re-established as the Insurance Department – forty-seven death claims were made, resulting in a pay-out of $39,549.00.[149]

Beyond the financial metrics of contribution rates and claims fulfilled, the records of the Beneficiary Department provide another important insight by shedding light on immigrant health. In 1895, the oldest member of the Beneficiary Department who had died that year – of nephritis (inflammation of the kidneys) – was Richard Caddick of Toronto. Causes of death varied and included a number of accidental deaths, such as that of E.B. Axworthy, also of Toronto, who was forty-eight when he died after having been 'kicked by a horse'. In 1894–95 the average age of those who had died was 44.5 years.[150] In 1930, the oldest member of the by then renamed Insurance Department was ninety-three-year-old Joseph Rogers, whose cause of death is listed as 'senility'; the youngest person to die that year was Walter J. Creed who, aged forty-seven and thus already two-and-a-half years older than the average in 1895, died of cancer. By then, the year 1929–30, the average age at death for members was seventy-one, with most of the causes of death seeming to have been age-related, chiefly including sclerosis, heart conditions and cancer.[151] These calculations are, of course, just a snap-shot; but they do capture the plethora of reasons and circumstances that could contribute to a person's death, including the general standard of living and the level of medical care. The figures nonetheless offer an interesting pointer towards the changes in the Sons of England's membership – which generally had become older – and also towards the declining relevance of ethnic associations, in this case ethnic mutual benefit societies in particular. With the deaths of old members of mostly natural causes, the department was not, as in the past, reinvigorated with an equal number of new members.

The general rise in uptake and extended membership of the Beneficiary Department was also a result of co-ordinated advertising campaigns for the Beneficiary Department in the *Sons of England Record*. Most of these campaigns focused on highlighting the benefits of Beneficiary Department membership, and some were designed to achieve that not simply by listing benefits, but rather by invoking fear in potential members about what might happen to their families if they did not join the department, thus leaving their loved ones to fend for themselves. Even poetic language was employed to stir the sense of responsibility in Sons of England members:

> Excuse us for suggesting that a man is sure to die:
> 'Tis not a lively subject that would move a man to mirth;
> But we've seen the widow wailing, and we've heard the orphan cry,
> When a brother who was uninsured had shuffled off the earth.[152]

Other appeals stressed how the behaviour of members was critical to their family's well-being. Hence, while the *Record*'s editors noted in 1896 that they were 'not running a prohibition campaign', they nonetheless observed: 'wouldn't it be better to drop that glass of beer if keeping it up means a lack of even bread for those you are leaving behind?'[153] Their argument went that, when the choice was between a drink and the ability to contribute a monthly fee that would protect their family's future, the answer should be obvious. Yet other campaigns were more akin to shaming initiatives, directed at those who were members but had fallen behind with payments or thought about leaving the department. 'Did it ever strike you that a widow can't live on her deceased husband's unfulfilled intentions? You intend to get insured; do it now', one slogan went. 'Does your wife know you have neglected that last assessment? Better pay up at once', noted another.[154]

More powerful than such appeals to a member's conscience – or the invocation of fear in his wife – were financial considerations. As John S. King, a physician and member of the Sons of England, explained as early as 1885,

> [I]ts [the Beneficiary Department's] value when compared with the old system of insurance in Stock Companies, where immense outlays were made to support Agents and maintain a large staff of clerks and erect fine buildings, the money to do which came out of the pockets of those who were insured, will be so apparent, and the light payments at intervals so easy, that it is within reach of every member of the Society.[155]

Similarly, C.E. Martin described the Beneficiary Department's scheme as 'the best in the world', and one where 'there can be no embezzlements' as it was organized by the Sons themselves; for J.W. Clemesha it also served to 'strengthen the bond that binds us together'.[156] And indeed, the financial benefits in terms of the ratio between fees paid and claims paid out were clear. As was demonstrated in a calculation based on death claims paid in 1895–96,

> Has it ever occurred to the brethren to figure out just what the insurance for, say $1,000, really costs them in the Sons of England Benefit Society? … Take the experience of the brethren deceased since the first of this year … The brother who had been longest in the department joined in August, 1884, and was therefore seven years and eight months in membership; he paid during that time $109 into the department, and in return the department paid to his heirs $1,000. The brother who had joined most recently became insured in February, 1894, less than two years before his death, and had only paid $21.80 for the $1,000 his relatives received. The average membership of the eleven deceased brethren this year was about 4 years

and 6 months and the average amount they had paid for their $1,000 insurance was under $50.[157]

As with general membership of the Sons of England, the Beneficiary Department too relied on the work of existing members to attract new ones, with the former cast as ambassadors for the department's good work, and actively tasked to encourage others to join. In fact, '[w]hen you have an eligible Englishman never quit till you have brought him into the Order. ... Quality tells every time, be careful whom you propose, but never miss the right man.'[158]

A critical tool in the endeavour to extend the membership of the Beneficiary Department were the accounts of actual beneficiaries – accounts that served to highlight the Sons of England's good work. Hence we can learn of Sarah Thompson, whose husband had been a member of Prince Albert Lodge in Aylmer, Ontario. As Sarah noted in her letter to the lodge secretary, A.J. Elliott:

> I beg to acknowledge with thanks your letter of the 21st inst. Enclosing a cheque for one thousand dollars ($1,000) in payment of the beneficiary certificate upon the life of my late husband. ... The Sons of England Benefit Society is a noble institution, and I can only wish it God speed in the grand work that it is doing.[159]

A good year later another widow told the *Record* that 'had it not been for the Sons of England I should have been reduced to the greatest straits of misery, anxiety and want'.[160] Both women would thus presumably have agreed with Isabella Buller from Ridgetown, Ontario, who thanked Lancashire Lodge for the 'practical illustration of brotherly love which unites your noble Society, and leads me to believe that my dearly beloved husband made a wise choice in joining his national society. ... [M]ay God grant that your noble Society may go on increasing in numbers and usefulness.'[161]

Conclusion

Charity was a practical form of 'brotherly love'; as such, it was foundational to English ethnic associationalism, with the earliest societies established for the very purpose of dispensing relief to fellow Englishmen and Englishwomen in distress. From the origins of this tradition in the early eighteenth century developed a system of relief dispensation that, certainly in the large urban centres of North America, was well in tune with the activities of other ethnic groups from the British and Irish Isles. Relief provisions were extensive and ranged from small cash payments to regular monthly pensions, from the dispensation of 'Christmas Cheer' to covering medical and funeral expenses. At the heart of these activities was a profound appreciation of patrician benevolence: a feeling that those English better off abroad had a duty to look after those in need of support. This sense of patrician benevolence was the principal demarcation line between charity and ethnic mutual aid.

From the 1870s onwards the idea of offering sick and funeral benefits through a system of mutual insurance that rested on a person's ethnic origins began to eclipse the earlier St George's tradition. While lauding the activities of the many St George's societies, the Sons of England positioned themselves expressly against the idea of charity: critical to their foundation was the ideal of promoting self-help by enabling those of English descent to pay into an insurance system that would secure their livelihood – or that of their family – at crisis point. This ideal was born from the class background of the Sons – members were predominately working class – as well as economic pressures in the late nineteenth century: the idea of patrician benevolence, though noble, had no currency for them and they, therefore, sought to satisfy their desire for the provision of support prothrough an alternative form of associationalism. It was also in the late nineteenth century, however, that English associational culture generally changed in nature – a characteristic it had in common with other immigrant groups, which thus provide important comparative context. It is to this comparative focus that we now turn.

Notes

1 CTA, Series 1096, StGS Toronto Records, File 41, Relief Register 1868–69.
2 Charity in late nineteenth-century charity is explored in Mariana Valverde, *The Age of Light, Soap, and Water: Moral Reform in English Canada, 1885–1925* (Toronto, 2008), passim.
3 MdHS, MS 1881, StGS Baltimore, Minutes, 6 December 1866.
4 *Constitution of the St George's Society of New York*, contained in St George's Society of New York, *Annual Report for 1897* (New York, 1897), p. 40.
5 The New York St George's Society, while now more inclusive in terms of the people it caters for, still pursues benevolent activities through its scholarship programme, designed to support the education of outstanding students, and its beneficiary programme, which offers assistance to the elderly and disabled by means of rent support and the provision of help with home care expenses. In 2011, the total expense of programme services was $933,240.00 (see Financial Statement, St George's Society of New York, *2012 Annual Report*, p. 11). For further details see St George's Society of New York, http://www.stgeorgessociety.org/charity.html (last accessed 18 March 2016).

6 The literature on friendly societies and mutualism is enormous, but see Marcel van der Linden (ed.), *Social Security Mutualism: The Comparative History of Mutual Benefit Societies* (Berne, 1996); Alexis de Tocqueville, *Democracy in America*, 2 vols (New York, 2004), vol. 2:2, ch. 5.

7 David T. Beito, *From Mutual Aid to the Welfare State: Fraternal Society and Social Services, 1890–1967* (Chapel Hill, NC, 2000), p. 1.

8 Petri Mirali, *Freemasonry in Ulster, 1733–1813* (Dublin, 2007), passim, explores the many connections. The linkage was even stronger and more direct between Freemasonry and Catholic Defender ceremonials in 1790s Ulster: David Hempton, *Religion and Political Culture in Britain and Ireland: From the Glorious Revolution to the Decline of Empire* (Cambridge, 1996), pp. 69–70.

9 Beito, *Mutual Aid*, ch. 2, esp. pp. 18–19.

10 Report of annual meeting, *British Daily Whig*, 5 April 1876, contained as a clipping in the minutes: ADOA, XM-72, StGS Kingston, Minutes, n.d.

11 St George's Society of Toronto, *Charter ... Report of the Committee for 1870* (Toronto, 1871), p. 9.

12 St George's Society of Toronto, *Report of the Committee for 1940* (Toronto, 1941), p. 13.

13 MdHS, MS 1881, StGS Baltimore, Secretary's Report, 18 January 1875.

14 Ibid., Minute Books, 16 July 1867.

15 MdHS, MS 1881, StGS Baltimore, Minutes, 20 January 1868.

16 The comment sounds biblical, but is not; Smiles did not create it, but he popularized it beyond imagination. S. Smiles, *Self-Help; with Illustrations of Conduct and Perseverance* (London, 1886), p. 1.

17 MdHS, MS 1881, StGS Baltimore, Minutes, 31 December 1866.

18 Ibid., 17 January 1881.

19 Ibid., 26 January 1881, p. 29.

20 See for instance St George's Society of New York, *Annual Report for 1874* (New York, 1874), p. 8.

21 See Ella Howard, *Homeless: Poverty and Place in Urban America* (Philadelphia, 2013), p. 13.

22 St George's Society of New York, *Annual Report and Constitution: St George's Society of New York for the Year 1910* (New York, 1911), pp. 15–16.

23 Ibid. To help members to obtain employment, the Society spent $183.43 on 'fees for procuring positions for applicants' (ibid., p. 17).

24 St George's Society of New York, *Annual Report of the St George's Society of New York for the Year 1884* (New York, 1885), pp. 7–8.

25 See for instance ibid., p. 8.

26 St George's Society of Toronto, *Report of the Committee for 1935* (Toronto, 1936), p. 8.

27 It also used Scotland's motto, *Nemo me impune lacessit*, 'no one provokes me with impunity': *Constitution of the St Andrew's Society of the City of Toronto and Home District of Upper Canada* (Toronto, 1836), p. 5. For wider Scottish associational contexts, see Tanja Bueltmann, *Clubbing Together: Ethnicity, Civility and Formal Sociability in the Scottish Diaspora to 1930* (Liverpool, 2014), and Chapter 6 in this book.

28 St George's Society of New York, *Annual Report and Constitution: St George's Society of New York for the Year 1905* (New York, 1906), pp. 14–15.
29 John L. Sanford, *History of the St George's Society of Baltimore* (Baltimore, 1929), pp. 5–6. Sanford could find no other mention of the children in the record, though their well-being was reported annually after visits by officers of the Society. In the intervening years, however, the Society had lost touch with them.
30 We do not learn of this inspiration to associationalism until the secretary's report, 20 January 1868. MdHS, MS 1881, StGS Baltimore, Minute Books, vol. 1, 1866–77.
31 St George's Society of New York, *Annual Report of the St George's Society of New York, For the Year 1878* (New York, 1879), p. 6.
32 St George's Society of New York, *Annual Report and Constitution ... 1910*, pp. 15–16.
33 St George's Society of Toronto, *Report of the Committee for 1935*, p. 8.
34 LAC, MG28-V3, StGS Ottawa Minute Books, vol. 9, Minutes of a Quarterly Meeting, 2 October 1900.
35 Ibid.
36 St George's Society of New York, *Annual Report and Constitution: St George's Society of New York for the Year 1925* (New York, 1926), pp. 16–17.
37 This and the previous quotations from St George's Society of New York, *Annual Report ... 1884*, p. 7.
38 St George's Society of New York, *Annual Report and Constitution ... 1910*, p. 14.
39 St George's Society of New York, *Annual Report and Constitution: St George's Society of New York for the Year 1916* (New York, 1917), p. 18.
40 MdHS, MS 1881, StGS Baltimore, Minutes, 15 April 1901.
41 St George's Society of New York, *Annual Report of the St George's Society of New York for the Year 1895* (New York, 1895), p. 9.
42 St George's Society of New York, *Annual Report and Constitution, St George's Society of New York for the Year 1900* (New York, 1901), p. 17.
43 CTA, Series 1096, StGS Toronto, File 41, Relief Register 1868–69.
44 St George's Society of Toronto, *Charter ... Report of the Committee for 1870*, p. 8.
45 J. Thomas Scharf and Thompson Westcott, *History of Philadelphia, 1609–1884*, 3 vols (Philadelphia, 1884), vol. 2, p. 1467.
46 LAC, MG28-V3, StGS Ottawa, Ledger, Annual Financial Report for the year ending 23 April 1910.
47 Ibid., Minute Books, vol. 13, 89th Annual Report of the Executive, 17 January 1933.
48 Ibid., Minute Books vol. 12, Treasurer's Report for the Year 1923.
49 St George's Society of Toronto, *Report of the Committee for 1925* (Toronto, 1926), p. 8.
50 LAC, MG28-V3, StGS Ottawa, Minute Books, vol. 13, 85th Annual Report.
51 Ibid., 84th Annual Report of the Executive; also Treasurer's Report.
52 MdHS, MS 1881, StGS Baltimore, Minutes, 20 October 1912.
53 LAC, MG28-V3, StGS Ottawa, Records, vol. 18, Miscellaneous, President's Message, 1 December 1945.

54 Cf. ADOA, XM-72A, StGS Kingston, Committee of Management Minutes, 28 November 1879; also Attendance Roll for the Year 1880–81.
55 St George's Society of New York, *Annual Report of the St George's Society of New York, For the Year 1871* (New York, 1872), p. 5.
56 Ibid., p. 4.
57 St George's Society of New York, *Annual Report and Constitution: St George's Society of New York, For the Year 1922* (New York, 1923), p. 25.
58 Ibid., p. 26.
59 The breakdown of the remainder was: 15 from the British West Indies, 4 South Americans, 3 each from Ireland and India, 2 from the United States and one each from France, Australia, India, Canada and Norway. St George's Society of New York, *Annual Report and Constitution: St George's Society of New York for the Year 1926* (New York, 1927), pp. 25–26. For earlier evidence of the inclusion of non-English migrants see also St George's Society of New York, *Annual Report of the St George's Society of New York, For the Year 1869* (New York, 1870), p. 10.
60 St George's Society of New York, *Annual Report and Constitution: St George's Society of New York for the Year 1923* (New York, 1924), p. 23.
61 Ibid.
62 LAC, MG28-V3, StGS Ottawa, Minute Books, vol. 7, Meeting of the Committee, 18 December 1894.
63 St George's Society of New York, *Annual Report ... 1871*, p. 4.
64 St George's Society of Toronto, *Charter ... Report of the Committee for 1870*, p. 9.
65 MdHS, MS 1881, StGS Baltimore, Minutes, 20 April 1890.
66 Ibid., Secretary's Report, 20 April 1893.
67 Ibid., Minutes, 29 January 1894.
68 Ibid., Secretary's Report, printed sheets, January 1898.
69 Ibid., Treasurer's Statement, 17 January 1913.
70 ADOA, XM-72A, StGS Kingston, Committee of Management Minutes, 27 December 1875, p. 69.
71 Ibid., 3 January 1876, p. 70.
72 Ibid., 2 March 1877, p. 95.
73 Ibid., 28 March 1877, p. 97.
74 CTA, Series 1093, StGS Toronto, File 34, Visitors to Relief Recipients Book, 16 May 1863.
75 This and the previous quotations from St George's Society of Toronto, *Charter ... Report of the Committee for 1868* (Toronto, 1869), p. 16.
76 Ibid., p. 17.
77 St George's Society of Toronto, *Charter ... Report of the Committee for 1885* (Toronto, 1886), p. 6.
78 Ibid.
79 St George's Society of Toronto, *Charter ... Report of the Committee for 1868*, p. 16.
80 St George's Society of Toronto, *Charter ... Report of the Committee for 1885*, p. 6.

81 St George's Society of Toronto, *Charter … Report of the Committee for 1870*, p. 10.

82 See for instance Tanja Bueltmann and Donald M. MacRaild, 'Globalizing St George: English Associations in the Anglo-World to the 1930s', *Journal of Global History*, 7:1 (2012), p. 93; also Bueltmann, *Clubbing Together*, esp. ch. 3.

83 St George's Society of Toronto, *Charter … Report of the Committee for 1890* (Toronto, 1891), p. 7.

84 LAC, MG28-V3, StGS Ottawa, Minute Books, vol. 8, Report of the Committee of Management for the Year Ending 8 March 1898.

85 St George's Society of Toronto, *Report of the Committee for 1910* (Toronto, 1911), p. 8.

86 St George's Society of Toronto, *Report of the Committee for 1915* (Toronto, 1916), p. 7.

87 St George's Society of New York, *Annual Report and Constitution: St George's Society of New York for the Year 1935* (New York, 1935), p. 19.

88 For instance ADOA, XM-72A, StGS Kingston, Committee of Management Minutes, 28 November 1879.

89 Ibid., letter of St George's Society President and Secretary to members, 7 December 1886.

90 ADOA, XM-72B, StGS Kingston, Annual Report, 5 April 1881.

91 St George's Society of Toronto, *Charter … Report of the Committee for 1876* (Toronto, 1877), pp. 7, 9.

92 CTA, Series 1096, StGS Toronto, File 40, Christmas Distribution Register, 1876.

93 LAC, MG28-V3, StGS Ottawa, Minute Books, vol. 5, Monthly Meeting of the Committee of Management, 7 February 1871.

94 Robert A. Gross, 'Giving in America: From Charity to Philanthropy: From Charity to Philanthropy', p. 41, and Kathleen D. McCarthy, 'Women and Political Culture', p. 183, both in in Lawrence J. Friedman and Mark D. McGarvie (eds), *Charity, Philanthropy and Civility in American History* (Cambridge, 2003). Among the best book-length treatment is Jay Kleinberg, *Widows and Orphans First: The Family Economy and Social Welfare Policy, 1880–1939* (Champaign, IL, 2005).

95 LAC, MG28-V3, StGS Ottawa, Minute Books, vol. 8, Report of the Committee of Management for the Year Ending 8 March 1898.

96 In his address of January 1880, the president of the Baltimore St George's Society, for instance, noted sixty-eight cases of relief 'besides many others from their private purses'. See MdHS, MS 1881, StGS Baltimore, Minutes, 19 January 1880.

97 St George's Society of New York, *Annual Report … 1869*, p. 9.

98 Beito, *Mutual Aid*, ch. 3. Even the poorest and most at risk could express loathing of the 'indignity' of charity: Kleinberg, *Widows and Orphans First*, p. 93.

99 John S. King, *The Early History of the Sons of England Benevolent Society* (Toronto, 1891), p. 11.

100 Ibid., p. 12.

101 Sons of England, *Constitution of the Sons of England Benevolent Society*

under the Supreme Jurisdiction of the Grand Lodge of Canada (Belleville, 1889), p. 4.

102 King, *Early History*, p. 15.

103 Ibid., pp. 24–25.

104 Ibid., p. 32.

105 This and the previous quotation from *Record*, 15 December 1897, p. 78.

106 *Ontario Workman*, 7 January 1875, quoted in King, *Early History*, p. 32.

107 See *Record*, May 1905, p. 7.

108 Ottawa, Archives of Ontario, F 1155 – MU 2864, Sons of England, Minutes of the Grand Lodge of the S.O.E. held Oct. 30th 1876.

109 It was only the 40th meeting because, from 1900, the Grand Lodge –by then called the Supreme Grand Lodge – was held bi-annually, and the First World War had resulted in a change from holding it in even years to uneven years.

110 Sons of England, *Journal of Proceedings of the Fortieth Session of the Supreme Lodge, Sons of England Benefit Society, held in the City of Windsor, Ontario, Tuesday, Wednesday, Thursday, and Friday, August, 11th, 12th, 13th, and 14th, 1931* (Toronto, 1931), p. 12.

111 *Record*, May 1905, p. 7.

112 Sons of England, *Constitution of the Sons of England Benevolent Society* (1889), pp. 7–8. As the organization's early history shows, these were essentially the same rules as those first stipulated in early 1875; see King, *Early History*, p. 28.

113 See articles 59 and 60 in Sons of England, *Constitution of the Sons of England Benevolent Society* (1889), p. 28.

114 Ibid., pp. 39–40.

115 Members in more remote areas that lay outside the jurisdiction of a designated lodge surgeon could get the relevant certificates from their local doctor.

116 Sons of England, *Constitution of the Sons of England Benevolent Society* (1889), p. 42.

117 Sons of England, *Constitution of the Sons of England Benefit Society under the Supreme Jurisdiction of the Supreme Lodge* (Toronto, 1912), pp. 68–69.

118 Secretary's Report, in Sons of England, *Report of the Thirteenth Annual Meeting of the Grand Lodge, Sons of England Benevolent Society* (Ottawa, 1888), p. 23.

119 See figures for 1913 in Sons of England, *Journal of Proceedings of the Thirty-Second Session of the Supreme Lodge, Sons of England Benefit Society, held in the City of Niagara Falls, Ont., Tuesday, Wednesday, Thursday, and Friday, August, 10th, 11th, 12th, and 13th, 1914* (Toronto, 1914), p. 29.

120 *Record*, 15 October 1897, p. 52.

121 Figures extracted from Grand Lodge and Supreme Lodge reports.

122 *Record*, 15 March 1897, p. 2.

123 GMA, M-1659, Sons of England, United Roses Lodge, Minute Book, 2 April 1891.

124 Ibid., 15 September 1897.

125 Ibid., 15 May 1897.

126 Ibid., 1 December 1892 and 19 January 1893.
127 *Record*, March 1905, p. 5.
128 Sons of England, *Constitution of the Sons of England Benevolent Society* (1912), p. 173.
129 *Record*, 15 August 1896, p. 2.
130 Sons of England, *Constitution of the Sons of England Benevolent Society* (1889), p. 46.
131 *Record*, January–February 1904, p. 7.
132 Ibid., April 1898, p. 135. For details on some subscriptions received, see *Record*, June 1898, p. 6.
133 GMA, BD.I.U58A V.2, Lodge Calgary Records, Minute Book, 18 May 1908.
134 *Record*, 15 November 1896, p. 5.
135 GMA, M-1659, Sons of England, United Roses Lodge, no reference number, 19 December 1895.
136 GMA, BD.I.U58A V.2, Sons of England, Lodge Calvary, Minute Book, 3 February 1908.
137 Sons of England, *Journal of Proceedings of the Twenty-Eighth Annual Session of the Supreme Lodge, Sons of England Benefit Society, held in the City of Chatham, Ontario, Tuesday, Wednesday, Thursday, and Friday, August, 14th, 15th, 16th, and 17th, 1906* (Toronto, 1906), p. 21.
138 Ibid., p. 22.
139 See table in *Record*, 15 September 1898, p. 39; also Sons of England, *Journal of Proceedings of the Twenty-Eighth Annual Session of the Supreme Lodge*, p. 30, where reference is made to the 'co-operative principle' of the Sons of England, and the fact that, therefore, premiums charged were for those insured rather than for profit, preventing 'excessive rates'. The rates offered by the Sons of England were generally much lower than those offered by insurance companies, as well as some other mutual benefit societies, and, at times, were lowered even further. In 1897–98, for instance, special jubilee rates were available in celebration of Queen Victoria's Diamond Jubilee. See *Record*, 15 March 1898, p. 121.
140 *Record*, 15 July 1808, p. 15.
141 Ibid., 15 October 1897, p. 57.
142 GMA, M-1659, Sons of England, United Roses Lodge, Minute Book, 4 December 1890.
143 Ibid., 20 November 1890.
144 The first report of 'the first seven months of its existence' was presented at the Tenth Grand Lodge meeting in Lindsay, Ontario, in early February 1885. Sons of England, *Report of the Tenth Annual Meeting of the Grand Lodge, 1885* (Belleville, 1885), p. 20.
145 Sons of England, *Constitution of the Sons of England Benefit Society* (Toronto, 1912), p. 56.
146 Sons of England, *Report of the Twentieth Annual Meeting of the Supreme Grand Lodge, 1895* (Toronto, 1895), p. 74.
147 See Sons of England, *Journal of Proceedings of the Twenty-Eighth Annual Session of the Supreme Lodge*, p. 36.

148 Though it is important to note that 1913 already saw a significantly higher rate. There is no clear reason for this.

149 Sons of England, *Journal of Proceedings of the Fortieth Session of the Supreme Lodge*, p. 99.

150 Based on statistics included in 1895, pp. 84–85. The average age of death of Beneficiary Department members that year was almost the same as that of the Sons of England membership as a whole, which stood at forty-three.

151 Sons of England, *Journal of Proceedings of the Fortieth Session of the Supreme Lodge*, p. 100.

152 *Record*, 15 March 1897, p. 1.

153 Ibid., 15 October 1896, p. 2.

154 Ibid., p. 2, and 15 November 1896, p. 5.

155 Sons of England, *Report of the Tenth Annual Meeting of the Grand Lodge*, p. 22.

156 Ibid., pp. 23–24.

157 *Record*, 15 July 1896, pp. 1–2. There is an obvious miscalculation in the membership length of the longest-insured member. This was F.W. Turner of Lodge Albion, and he had joined the Beneficiary Department on 1 August 1884 and died 20 April 1896, hence was a member for eleven years and a good eight months, not seven years and eight months. Turner was a resident of Toronto and died of heart disease. See *Record*, 15 June 1896, p. 2.

158 Ibid., 15 July 1896, p. 3.

159 Ibid., 15 August 1896, p. 2.

160 Ibid., 15 July 1897, p. 14.

161 *Record*, 15 October 1896, p. 8.

6

English, Scots and Germans compared: British and continental perspectives

New York, the greatest immigrant hub in North America, has long been home to a great many ethnic clubs and societies. The city's St George's Society was founded comparatively early, in 1770, though the Scots beat the English to it when a St Andrew's Society was established over a decade earlier.[1] Despite smaller, informal activities, the Germans and Irish formalized associations in the city only after the American War of Independence. In 1784, both the German Society (Deutsche Gesellschaft) and the Irishmen's Friendly Sons of St Patrick came into being. From then on the activities of ethnic clubs and societies in New York increased and associational culture proliferated, soon catering for most if not all immigrant groups. At the same time as immigrant numbers from Britain and Ireland increased in the 1840s and 1850s, larger numbers of continental Europeans also began to arrive. By the century's end, eastern and southern Europeans – Italians, Poles and others – outstripped the older northern European flows. Since they faced many similar problems, it comes as no surprise that leaders of these communities and their various societies did not exist, or act, in isolation. Representatives of many different national associations commonly joined each other for celebrations of national days or annual balls; civic activities, such as celebratory parades, also brought together diverse ethnic groups.

As might be expected, links were especially strong between organizations from the British Isles. With language no major barrier – though Gaelic speakers need to be remembered – and a shared history and similar customs, cultural traditions and norms, this is understandable. What is more, this strength in links was not simply a social one, expressed at annual gatherings through speeches and toasts. It also came in very practical forms of co-operation. As we have seen in Chapter 5, for example, in New York the St Andrew's and St George's societies worked together closely in the 1860s and 1870s – so closely, in fact, that they shared the same lodgings at 3 Broadway and an almoner for a time in the 1870s.[2]

Such practical co-operation extended to other groups, and, critically, it did so within a wider civic context. The formation of the New York Board of United Charities was a key milestone. The Board's roots lay in the Bureau of Charities founded in 1874 as a 'confederation of a large number of the [charitable] Societies' of New York.[3] The establishment of the Board was part of a concerted effort to regulate charity work, including immigrant aid, on a city-wide basis, helping to oversee and streamline the activities of charity organizations.[4] One of the first initiatives of the New York Board of United Charities was the compilation of a directory of charities. Published annually, the directory gave the residents of New York a tool they could use to establish 'year after year the financial and general condition of the principal Benevolent Institutions of New York',[5] also enabling them to ascertain whether an organization was genuine, and to learn about the type of work it was carrying out.

The Board represented organizations with a broad range of foci, including those catering exclusively for women in need of medical treatment; specifically excluded from the directory were organizations operating under the aegis of churches, though this changed in later charity directories. Importantly, ethnic associations were included, and this identified them as one key part of New York's social support system for the poor. In fact, ethnic societies were critical to the Board's operations. Shortly after its establishment, the Board's executive committee comprised eight members, five of them being the presidents of ethnic societies, including Henry E. Pellew, the president of the St George's Society, Robert Gordon, president of the St Andrew's Society, and Willy Wallach from the German Society. Through their roles on the Board, these men were also in contact with various New York commissioners who were concerned with charitable and immigration matters, including, for instance, James Lynch, president of the Irish Emigrant Society, and Frederick Shack, president of the German Society, who both sat on the State Board of Emigration.[6]

The directory of the Board of United Charities offers useful context for our comparative exercise here, providing detailed information on the work of ethnic associations in the city of New York (Table 6.1). A comparison highlights that while the English made important contributions to the provisions for immigrants, in monetary terms theirs were smaller than those of other groups in relation to the number of immigrant arrivals, or, when looking at the Scots, relative to the two groups' respective population ratios at home in the United Kingdom. In terms of overall spending, in 1875, the St George's Society spent $4,960.42, and the St Andrew's Society $3,916.20; the Society of the Friendly Sons of St Patrick and the Irish Emigration Society together spent $12,110.00, and the German Society $21,000.00.

Table 6.1 *Expenditure and income of ethnic associations in New York in the mid-1870s*

Name	Year established	Objective	To whom to apply for relief	Income (1875) ($)	Expenditure (1875) ($)
Société Belge de Bienfaisance	1869	The relief of Belgian citizens in distress	To secretary at the office	n.a.	n.a.
French Benevolent Society	1809	The relief of poor of French nationality	At office during particular times	7,814.63	6,710.74
German Society	1783	To assist German emigrants and to relieve distressed Germans and their descendants	At office	28,000.00	21,000.00
Irish Emigrant Society	1841	To afford aid, advice, protection, and information to Irish emigrants	At office	10,506.56	9,100.00
Società d'Unione e Fratellanza Italiana	1857	Mutual aid to Italians	n.a.	n.a.	n.a.
New England Benefit Society	1805	To afford relief to poor persons of New England origins	To president	6,180.00	4,600.60
St Andrew's Society	1756	To aid Scotchmen and descendants in distress	At office	c.4,000.00	3,916.20
St George's Society	1786[a]	The relief of indigent English people	At office daily at 1 p.m.	5,569.50	4,960.42
Society of the Friendly Sons of St Patrick	1827	The relief of poor Irish people	To any member	3,026.89	3,010.00
Swiss Benevolence Society	1851	To relieve needy persons of Swiss origin	To president	3,846.53	3,084.93

[a]Although 1786 was, for a long time, listed as the year in which the New York St George's Society first operated, it was actually founded in 1770; the year 1786 was often listed because that was when records were first kept.

Source: Amended from Tanja Bueltmann, *Clubbing Together: Ethnicity, Civility and Formal Sociability in the Scottish Diaspora to 1930* (Liverpool, 2014), table 2.6, p. 83.

These figures bring out three critical explanatory contexts for our comparative assessment of ethnic associations that must accompany us through the chapter. First, the differences in the numbers of immigrants in particular groups are important: clearly there is a case to be made that the sizes of ethnic communities, in terms of both the proliferation of ethnic associations and also the provisions they then made, were critical. The second context is the timing of the migrants' arrival and their geographic dispersal: both can help explain ethnic associational patterns and activities. And finally, we also need to bear in mind the types of migrants who arrived: were they, for example, from poorer backgrounds, workers without employment, or rather those bringing some capital with them? In order to fully appreciate these contextual questions, we must briefly consider here the general migratory patterns of the English in comparison to the other groups we are primarily interested in, before we move on to our assessment of the associational culture of these groups. While it is not possible to replicate, in one chapter, as detailed an assessment for a number of groups as we offer for the English throughout this study, we are confident that highlighting the principal patterns for Scots and Germans in particular will help us better understand the English case.[7]

Migratory pathways and the persistence of ethnic ties: a comparative view

The key purpose of this comparison is to explore how the English fitted in within other immigrant groups, to ask: could they be described as ethnic like other national groups? We have already outlined our theoretical considerations, and the evidence we have presented so far documents clearly a strong English ethnic behaviour. Such ethnic behaviour, the persistence of ethnic ties, is reflected to this day in the American Community Survey, which documents the numbers of people claiming particular ancestries. Measured in this way, the 2009 survey documents that the Germans are by far the largest group; with over 50 million people claiming German roots, we are looking at a figure that is nearly double that for English ancestry, which is claimed by almost 28 million people. The Irish sit at nearly 37 million, while the Scots and Scotch-Irish (two separate categories in the survey) together make up a little over 9 million (Table 6.2). The survey highlights a number of important issues, including qualifications within groups, for example Scotch-Irish vs. Scottish, or, in later surveys, the distinction between German and Pennsylvania German. Moreover, the survey also explores the question of how many ancestries respondents feel they have – a single one or multiple ancestries. In all cases of the ancestries we are concerned with, the majority of respondents in the 2013 American Community Survey

Table 6.2 *Population by selected ancestry group and region, 2009*

	English	Scottish	Scotch-Irish	Welsh	British	Irish	German
2009	27,658,000	5,847,000	3,570,000	1,987,000	1,172,000	36,915,000	50,708,000
Per cent distribution by region							
North-east	17	17	12	20	16	24	16
Mid-west	21	20	17	23	17	24	39
South	37	37	51	30	38	32	26
West	25	27	20	27	29	18	19

Source: United States Census Bureau, 2009 American Community Survey, table 52, 'Population by Selected Ancestry Group and Region', http://www.census.gov/compendia/statab/2012/Tables/12s0052.pdf [last accessed 18 June 2015].

claimed multiple ancestry, with the exception of those claiming 'British', where a narrow majority claimed it as their single ancestry (Table 6.3).

Of particular interest to us is the regional spread of migrants: as we have already seen for the English, there is an immediate correlation between settlement patterns of immigrants and the development of ethnic associations. Those claiming English, Scottish and Welsh ancestry are spread fairly similarly, with the majority claiming ancestry in the south (37 per cent each for English and Scottish; 30 per cent for Welsh). Scotch-Irish ancestry lies primarily in the south (51 per cent). Patterns for the Irish are not dissimilar to those of the English and Scots, but there are fewer respondents in the west, and slightly more in the north-east and Mid-West. More significant are the differences, and this does reflect ethnic association development patterns, in the German community: here the majority of respondents claimed that ancestry in the Mid-West at 39 per cent, and hence a figure nearly double that of the English and Scots for that region (Table 6.3).

Ancestry responses clearly reflect historic regional settlement patterns.[8] Detailed data for the period before the American War of Independence are limited for all the groups we explore – a problem we have already seen for the English. Prior to the mid-seventeenth century, as few as around 200 Scottish settlers crossed the Atlantic to English plantations.[9] In fact, overall, the number of Scots emigrants at this early juncture was falling.[10] This changed as a result of the Union of 1707, which officially opened the now British Empire for Scots – although numbers remained low for some time, with an estimated 30,000 Scots arriving in North America in the period from 1700 to 1760.[11] By the time of the first United States census in 1790, all groups we are concerned with had seen a growth in numbers, though, at that point, the English (in this calculation these included the Welsh) clearly dominated with over 2 million; Scots, Irish and Germans still constituted only a relatively small fraction of the overall arrivals at this point (Table 6.4).

Regional settlement patterns show marked differences between the groups. While the English could be found in all states and territories, although they were clearly stronger in some states than others as a result of overall migration patterns, they were strongest in Massachusetts. The Germans, on the other hand, were strongest by far in Pennsylvania, where nearly 80 per cent of them were based (Table 6.4). Critically, early figures must be looked at with some caution, particularly those for the Scots and Germans. For these two groups figures are best considered as showing a minimum of migrants, given that a number of factors, including the placing of Ulster-Scots in the categorization, or the fact that the category 'German' did not refer to a unified nation state prior to German unification in 1871, will have had an impact. The general settlement pattern of Germans, however, is appropriately reflected and goes back

Table 6.3 *Ancestry reported in the 2013 American Community Survey*

	English	Scottish	Scotch-Irish	Welsh	British	Irish	German
Single ancestry	9,141,283	1,679,586	1,401,794	366,233	631,100	9,492,676	15,876,190
Multiple ancestries	16,017,853	3,694,909	1,673,241	1,410,425	619,164	24,503,808	30,905,304
First ancestry	17,118,568	3,383,270	2,342,780	887,977	935,413	21,129,676	32,581,769
Second ancestry	8,041,994	1,991,295	732,357	888,734	315,025	12,868,127	14,209,738

Source: Based on data extracted from United States Census Factfinder, http://factfinder2.census.gov/faces/nav/jsf/pages/searchresults.xhtml?refresh=t (last accessed 20 July 2015).

Table 6.4 *State and territory settlement patterns by nationality of main ethnic groups, 1790 (numbers of residents)*

State	English & Welsh	Scotch	Irish	German
Connecticut	223,437	6,425	1,589	4
Maine (territory)	89,515	4,154	1,334	436
Maryland	161,011	12,441	4,550	11,246
Massachusetts	351,698	13,375	3,793	53
New Hampshire	132,726	6,648	1,346	0
New York	245,901	10,034	2,525	1,103
North Carolina	220,901	29,829	6,206	7,422
Pennsylvania	249,656	49,567	8,614	110,357
Rhode Island	62,079	1,976	459	33
South Carolina	115,480	16,447	3,576	2,343
Vermont (territory)	81,149	2,562	597	35
Virginia	108,859	9,114	2,591	6,277
TOTAL	**2,042,412**	**162,572**	**37,180**	**139,309**

Source: University of Virginia, Geospatial and Statistical Data Center Historical Census Browser (2004), http://mapserver.lib.virginia.edu/collections/stats/histcensus/index.html [last accessed 30 May 2015].

to the earliest German migration to the American colonies, which in the early 1680s brought a small number of Quaker and Mennonite families to Pennsylvania, where they then founded Germantown – today a part of Philadelphia – on 6 October 1683.[12] But let us turn to explore the Scottish case in more detail first.

Scottish ethnic associationalism: from philanthropic roots to caber tossing

Wherever they settled, and whether they were English, Germans or Scots, ethnic groups marked their attachments through associations, and they began to do so soon after arrival. The first incursion by the Scots was the Scots' Charitable Society of Boston, established in 1657, which significantly pre-dated any English group.[13] It clear that the Boston Society was modelled on the London-based Royal Scottish Corporation, which had been founded in the early seventeenth century to support impoverished Scots resident in the English capital, since they were not entitled to parish poor relief. The Scots' Charitable Society of Boston's objectives reflect this ideal, offering 'benevolence ... for the releefe of our selves being Scottishmen or for any of the Scottish nation whome we may see cause to helpe'.[14] After this start, the Society had a somewhat shaky early history. This was primarily the result of its relatively low membership and the financial problems this brought with it. Consequently, the Society was re-organized in the mid-1680s, and then continued to flourish.[15] As with the English, a benevolent ideal underpinned the Scots' ethnic associationalism at foundational level.

In the Scottish community St Andrew's societies were the principal carriers of this ideal. The first St Andrew's Society was set up in Charleston, South Carolina, in 1729; next followed Philadelphia (1749), Savannah, Georgia (1750), and New York (1756). That the birthplace of the St Andrew's tradition was Charleston is worth pausing over because Charleston was also where the first recorded St George's Society was founded in 1733. In part the explanation for this lies in the fact that Charleston was a principal early colonial centre for trade, not least as a result of the relative proximity to the Caribbean.[16] It also is plausible to suggest, however, that competitive ethnicity – or, at a minimum, an awareness of ethnic community activism among other migrant groups – prompted the English to form clubs and societies, thus following their northern neighbours.[17] The importance of this context is underlined by the subsequent geographical spread of Scottish groups: while this was not entirely synchronized with that of other migrant communities, organizations generally spread up the eastern seaboard cities of the original thirteen colonies.

We saw in Chapter 2 how tensions were raised by English associations during the American Revolution, but many Scottish groups also halted their activities during the conflict. In New York, where the St Andrew's Society was formed at the end of November 1756 for the purpose of providing 'charitable relief of those fellow-Scotsmen, resident in New York, who might be in want or distress',[18] little happened during the war years – though the Society was 'immediately reorganized' after the war's conclusion.[19] Then, the Society's constitution was adapted to fit the new political set-up in the American republic. This constitution confirmed the benevolent focus as '[w]hen people fall into misfortune and distress in any part of the world, remote from the place of their nativity, they are ever ready to apply for relief to those originally from the same country.'[20]

Also like the English, Scottish St Andrew's societies provided support in diverse forms, ranging from cash payments to meal tickets, onward rail tickets to other cities where relatives lived or employment was available, or even return passages to Britain.[21] In New York the St Andrew's Society also supported migrants, particularly the elderly and the sick, by visiting them in order to establish their needs and look after them.[22] Many Scottish associations favoured a system of support that had a long-term outlook. Supporting migrants in gaining employment, for example, was seen by many as the best way to ensure the migrants' welfare beyond their most immediate needs. This type of philanthropy reflects, perhaps, a desire for some social engineering, but also a broader mind-set: whether it was a deliberate choice or not, many societies followed Smilesian notions of self-help among those in need.[23]

Support for the elderly – an activity that the English also pursued in an organized form – became a key concern for Scottish groups in a number of cities. The principal example comes from Chicago, where the local St Andrew's Society set up a Scottish Old People's Home in 1901. While it was first housed in a rented building, the Society soon built its own house outside Chicago, in Riverside, to provide a home for elderly Scots; men had to be sixty-five years or older, and women sixty years or older, to be eligible as residents.[24] That men and women could live in the same home in the first place was a marked departure from established practice, as was the fact that the home permitted married couples to remain together.[25]

A 1929 assessment of homes for the elderly in the United States run by national groups established that the Scottish home in Riverside had a capacity of fifty, though the average number of residents was thirty-seven; its annual operational cost was $25,685.[26] These details relate to the second home in Riverside, as the first had been destroyed by a fire in March 1917.[27] In total, the 1929 assessment documented that there were thirty-seven homes for old people of particular 'national groups' in the United States; many were sponsored by fraternal organizations.[28] The charity offered by ethnic associations, as the Scottish case confirms when read together with the examples we have already explored for the English, was often very practical. Other examples include the New York St Andrew's Society's provision of beds at the city's St Luke's Hospital and the Presbyterian Hospital,[29] as well as the provision of burial plots.

Yet while such philanthropic activities were a critical pillar of Scottish ethnic associationalism in North America, it was changing – and changing in a way that clearly set it apart from the activities of the English. Although the English also saw a diversification of their associational culture – primarily, as we have seen, through the late nineteenth-century establishment of a mutualist strand – the Scots diversified their associational culture even more. In Canada, the Sons of Scotland provided mutualism, while in the United States the Order of the Scottish Clans was particularly important, with an estimated total of 250 branches.[30] A new range of cultural activities was sponsored by the proliferation of Caledonian societies; and on top of that came a growth of organized Highland (or Caledonian) Games. All these changes meant that St Andrew's societies were, by the early twentieth century, heavily outnumbered.

A search for Scots mutualism compels us to make a brief detour to Canada, where the Sons of Scotland showed strong similarities to the Canadian Sons of England and the American OSStG, which we examined in Chapters 3 and 5. The Sons of Scotland was founded as a mutual aid society in Toronto in 1876 and – very much like the Sons of England – was designed to provide insurance to members.[31] Its prime organizational unit was the Grand Camp, with branch camps established as either subordinate or juvenile camps. The Grand Camp was headed by a Grand Chief, who provided leadership for the Sons as a whole, while other grand officers were in place in designated roles. For instance, the Grand Physician had overall responsibility for questions concerning the medical examination of membership applicants.[32] Annual – later biennial – roving conventions of the Grand Camp, similar to the Grand Lodge meetings of the Sons of England, brought together delegates from camps from throughout Canada to discuss annual reports and financial statements, as well as to elect officers. Among the Sons of Scotland's more socially oriented pursuits was the annual celebration of the birth of Scotland's national poet, Robert Burns.[33] Burns was 'the epitome of Scotland', and therefore served as 'a particularly potent connector, symbol, and point of contact for memorialisation … and effective site of memory for Scots'[34] across the Scottish diaspora.

One of the Sons' subordinate camps was Inverness Camp, No. 54, in Goderich, Ontario. Apart from having to pass eligibility assessments, including nationality and health checks, prospective new members had to pay an initiation fee based on their age: for those aged 18 to 30 it was $8, for ages 30 to 40 it was $9, and for ages 40 to 50 it was $10; fees included the required medical examination and the issuing of the Beneficiary Certificate. Once someone was accepted for membership, payment of a monthly due of 35 cents was required.[35] All members who had been members for at least six months and were not more than three months in arrears with their monthly dues received a sick benefit of $1 per week for thirteen weeks in cases of illness. Prior to any payments, however, the member's state of health had to be checked, and their illness 'verified by a physician and the chairman of the Sick Committee'.[36] Good behaviour was expected, and there could be sanctions if members failed to comply, particularly if it was poor conduct, such as 'drunkenness, immoral or disorderly conduct', that was the cause of sickness.[37]

The ethnic mutual focus was not the only commonality between the Sons of England and the Sons of Scotland. Both organizations used a basic lodge or camp system similar to that adopted by the masonic lodges or the more clandestine Orange Order.[38] Rituals played a role, and for the Sons of Scotland too there was an element of secrecy. As the by-laws of the Inverness Camp stated, 'no member shall make known out of this Camp any proceedings, decisions, or business of any kind transacted ... to any person not a member of the Camp'.[39] At the heart of the Sons of Scotland members' activities lay, however, such pursuits as 'music, singing, lectures and storytelling'.[40]

The combination of social and cultural pursuits was also an important aspect in the work of the many Caledonian societies that were founded in North America from the mid-nineteenth century onwards. What made them different was, however, that their principal associational hook was very specific: the promotion of Highland Games. While other activities, such as celebrating St Andrew's Day, were pursued, the organization of annual Highland Games and the promotion of associated traditional sports were their main focus. In the United States the first Caledonian society was established in Cincinnati as early as 1827. While this society, in its rules, continued to focus on benevolence too, seeking 'to relieve such of our countrymen as may arrive among us in distressed circumstances, and to give them information and advice for locating themselves in the western country',[41] it soon changed to concentrate more exclusively on social and sporting pursuits. Some Caledonian societies were founded as an offshoot of – or at least were in some way connected to – an established St Andrew's Society. What this indicates is that there were, on occasion, rifts in the Scottish community. Similar to the English St George's societies, St Andrew's societies were elite organizations. While they too catered for a much broader, and more socially diverse, migrant cohort than this, their own members generally came from a comparatively high socio-economic background. Caledonian societies, with their focus on sports and competitions, offered earthier activities and were concerned not so much with elite dinners – although these did often take place – than with leisure. Generally, however, the rise of Caledonian societies was not only about providing a platform for leisure pursuits: it more broadly reflected a gradual decline in the relevance of philanthropy. In short: the need for it waned. A number of reasons are forthcoming. First, there were wider political and societal developments that were important, including the tightening of immigration regulations by the state and a more stringent monitoring of new arrivals – a shift epitomized by the opening of the immigration centre on Ellis Island. Changes were also the results of more positive developments, particularly the improvements made in the support systems provided by the state, as well as a competitive private market. However, secondly, more community-specific factor were also critical. They included both a diversification of the migrant body and generational shifts – the priorities changed. The balance hence tipped in favour of mutualism and sociability, and in the Scottish case more specifically in favour of leisure; these were given precedence over philanthropy.

Some established societies sought to buck this trend by adjusting their focus and offering new services, as did the St Andrew's Society of

Philadelphia, which resolved 'to establish a Library of Scottish Literature' in late February 1910.[42] Moreover, many associations were keen to make their business meetings more interesting, also offering entertainment. In urban centres, the focus on entertainment was taken to a completely new level with the proliferation of large-scale annual balls – although they usually still had a clear link to benevolence in that they commonly served to raise funds for charity.

The most visible change in Scottish associational life in North America remains, however, the proliferation of Highland Games from the mid-nineteenth century onwards (Figure 6.1). In this the Scots were much more dynamic and distinctive than the English, with their cricket matches, picnics and day-trips. While there is disagreement over whether the Highland Society in Glengarry, Ontario, hosted full Highland Games or simply a piping contest, we can say with certainty that activities common to Highland Games crossed the Atlantic in the early nineteenth century. There are early references to Highland Games, such as those hosted in New York in 1836 by the Highland Society of New York.[43] Understandably, the Civil War put a stop to such leisure activities, and hence it was only after the war that the Games grew more significantly. Zarnowski suggests that, across the United States and by 1875, there were at least eighty Scottish associations that organized annual Games.[44]

Figure 6.1 Caledonian Games of the Caledonian Club of New York, Jones's Wood, 2 September 1869 (from *Frank Leslie's Illustrated Newspaper*, 18 September 1869)

These Games were very popular – in fact, their expansion was a result too of a significant increase in spectator numbers.[45] By the 1870s, the Highland Games hosted by the Brooklyn Caledonian Club could easily have up to 5,000 spectators; in Detroit there could be 6,000; Boston saw as many as 8,000; the Toronto Games witnessed the arrival of nearly double that number with 15,000 spectators; and New York boasted an impressive total of 20,000.[46] And even that number was small compared with the Games held in New York two years later, when the crowd swelled to 25,000; this was, in all likelihood, one of the largest groups of spectators, if not the largest, at any Highland Games in the world – the proliferation of Highland Games was not restricted to North America.[47] Nor were the Games confined to the east coast there, as they soon spread to the Mid-West and then all the way to California. Shell Mound Park in San Francisco was a common venue where the San Francisco Caledonian Club, which had been established in 1866 primarily for the purpose of providing 'encouragement and practice of the Games',[48] held its events. Thousands also visited the Sacramento Games organized by the Sacramento Caledonian Club.[49] One reason why Highland Games did so well was that they were opened up beyond the Scottish ethnic group and appealed to a broader segment of society. Despite their ethnic and national origins, Highland Games were soon cast as among the principal sporting events in the annual events calendars of many communities. This was the case not least because the Games began to attract well-known athletes. Pat Donovan, 'the marvel of the 56 pound weight', competed, for example, at the San Francisco Games in 1913,[50] while, a decade earlier, even athletes from Australia were invited.[51] Star athletes were in themselves an attraction[52] – and not just for Scots.

Within the Scottish immigrant community in North America the proliferation of Highland Games was important for another reason: it served to facilitate collaboration through the North American United Caledonian Association. Established in 1870 for the purpose of standardizing rules for the Games,[53] the organization was, as the writer of the history of another Scottish organization aptly noted in 1895, 'the Grand Lodge, so to speak, of the Caledonian Clubs of the United States and Canada'.[54] The Association oversaw regulations, checking that they were adhered to by member societies, and it was concerned with the question of who was allowed to compete at Highland Games in the first place; at times there were tensions, for example, with respect to whether competitors would have to be members of an associated Caledonian society; whether they could, perhaps even should, be professional athletes; or whether amateurs sportsmen were still wanted.[55]

One of the Association's presidents was William Burns Smith. Born in Glasgow in November 1844, Smith had made his way to Philadelphia with his parents in the early 1850s, and became a member of the local

Caledonian club in 1863.[56] Smith, like many of the English migrants we have already encountered, was a serial associationalist: he was also a member of the Philadelphia St Andrew's Society, the Scots Thistle Society and the Burns Association, as well as a charter member of the Caledonian Lodge, No. 700, and other masonic lodges. Smith was first elected president of the North American United Caledonian Association at the organization's meeting in 1875. He was re-elected a year later when it met in his home town. Much like the conventions of the Sons or England and the Sons of Scotland, the North American United Caledonian Association brought together delegates from different places – and, as was the case with the NAStGU, did so transnationally from throughout North America. In one way, this was simply a reflection of what, on the sports ground, had already been happening for a few years: American and Canadian athletes had been competing at Highland Games in each other's countries for some time.[57] Still, in the Scottish community this federation under a head society marked an important milestone as it was driven not simply by Scottish ethnic identity as such, but rather by sports. This had practical implications: in many ways the Association was more concerned with maintaining the standard of Games rules and sporting activities than with Scottish ethnic identity.[58] But what this meant, on the other hand, was that the Scots managed to permeate a much wider section of society than the English ever did – more, in fact, than they ever could, as they did not have a pursuit that could match, in terms of wider community appeal, the Highland Games of the Scots. This marks an important point of difference from the ethnic associational life of the English. While they too pursued certain traditional sports, such as cricket, these were always English sports. Scottish Highland Games, on the other hand, were very much transformed into community sports while maintaining their Scottish character – so much so, in fact, that they played an important role in the development of athletics and sporting culture, and not just in North America. Even greater champions of this wider community-focused ethnic associationalism, however, were the Germans – at least until the First World War.

German ethnic associationalism: strength in number, diversity and intensity

Philadelphia was, as one early twentieth-century writer observed, the 'cradle of the German colonization in America'.[59] The same can be said of German ethnic associational life, since the first German association to be established in the United States, in 1764, was the Deutsche Gesellschaft (German Society) in Philadelphia. It was born out of very specific problems concerning the arrival of new German immigrants in

Pennsylvania rather than a broader desire to bring them together as a group. According to the association's history, the terrible circumstances of the Atlantic crossing, particularly how shipping companies dealt with the migrants' luggage and organized arrival procedures, were critical concerns. As was noted by the Gesellschaft, it was common practice that the luggage of those emigrating via England was unloaded there, and the newly created free space filled with goods instead – a procedure that some shipping lines and captains had found to be very profitable because it allowed merchants to save taxes, as emigrant ships carrying German migrants bound for the colonies were not heavily controlled. The migrants' luggage was then sent on at a later stage, but this delay did, of course, have negative consequences for them as they found themselves in a new world without their clothes and other essential items. There were also reports of migrants having to sleep on deck as there was not enough space below, and one captain was accused of packing the poor passengers like sardines ('die armen Passagiere wie Heringe zusammen zu packen').[60] For many of these early German immigrants the start to their life in the United States meant indentured servitude; of course this was by no means uncommon, but a lack of English language knowledge made it more difficult for Germans to understand the terms of their con-tracts.[61] It was as a result of this situation that sixty-five men from the German community in Philadelphia came together to take action, plan-ning a system of support for new arrivals. While there had been a number of earlier support initiatives in the 1760s, these men were responsible for giving them an organized and formalized framework by establishing the Deutsche Gesellschaft at the end of December 1764. As they explained:

> We, His Majesty of Great Britain's German subjects in Pennsylvania, have, as a result of the pity-inducing circumstances of many of our compatriots who have arrived in Philadelphia on the last ships from Europe, been compelled to think of means that would ease the foreigners' situation ... This has led us to conclude, as we have come together, to establish a society for the aid and support of the poor foreigners of the German nation in Pennsylvania.
>
> (Wir, Seiner Königlichen Majestät von Großbritannien Deutsche Unterthanen in Pennsylvanien, sind bei Gelegenheit der Mitleidswürdigen Umstände vieler unserer Landleute, die in den letzten Schiffen von Europa in dem Hafen von Philadelphia angekommen sind, bewogen worden, auf Mittel zu denken, um diesen Fremdlingen einige Erleichterungen zu verschaffen ... Dies hat uns zum Schluß gebracht, so wie wir zusammen gekommen sind, eine Gesellschaft zur Hülfe und Beistand der armen Fremdlinge Deutscher Nation in Pennsylvanien zu errichten.)[62]

It was agreed that quarterly meetings would take place, and that those of German blood ('von Deutschem Blut entsprossen') who wanted to become members could apply, and their application would then be put to the vote at a quarterly meeting; a majority was needed for someone to be approved as a member.[63] Initially, it was stipulated the meetings should not be held in an establishment that served alcohol, with rules also explicitly stating that no alcohol should be consumed, but as an annotation in the Society's history documents, this rule was done away with promptly.[64]

In terms of its initial motivation to support new immigrants and help by improving their journey and arrival circumstances, the Deutsche Gesellschaft moved quickly, lobbying local politicians to ensure that changes were made. It had some success, as a law was passed on 18 May 1765 that required that more space be given to passengers aboard ships, and that each ship have a doctor and medical supplies on board. It was also stipulated that more controls were required to avoid any abuse of luggage, and it was agreed that a translator would be present to support migrants upon arrival as needed.[65]

As for many other ethnic associations, the War of Independence marked a caesura for the Deutsche Gesellschaft, not least in that it essentially halted German migration to the United States. Consequently, as the Society explained in a pamphlet celebrating the 100th year of its incorporation in 1881, the Society had effectively lost the reason for its existence.[66] The situation became all the more difficult during the British occupation of Philadelphia between late September 1777 and June 1778, with no meetings of the Society taking place until Christmas 1778. When the war was over and the United States had become a republic, however, the Deutsche Gesellschaft was quick to respond to the new political climate, devising a new charter to accommodate the new circumstances. Moreover, it also recognized that it had to extend its original focus. When the Gesellschaft was incorporated in 1781, therefore, the support of new German immigrants was only one of a number of objectives, and education had also become a key aim:

> such as to teach and improve poor children, both in the English and German languages, reading and writing thereof, and to procure for them such learning and education as will best suit their genius and capacities, and enable the proper objects to receive the finishing of their studies in the University ... Likewise to erect a Library, and to do any other matter or thing which, without any prejudice to other inhabitants of this State, in charity they might do for the relief and benefit of their countrymen.[67]

The Society was growing steadily, with over 250 new members signing up between 1791 and 1800, though, as was the case for other organizations, its vitality always depended on the ebbs and flows of migration streams. But generally all went well, and so well, in fact, that the Society, in 1806, built its own hall; this hall was extended in 1821, and a new and much bigger building was erected in 1866, the latter being a direct reflection of the Society's revival – in terms of membership – in the wake of new waves of German immigrants who started arriving in the late 1840s.[68] This, as the development of other organizations will confirm later in this chapter, made the 1848–49 revolutions in Germany a watershed in terms of not only immigrant numbers, but also the expansion and diversification of German ethnic associationalism.

The Deutsche Gesellschaft remained popular among new arrivals, a fact that is also reflected in the expansion of its library, which, by the end of the nineteenth century, held 20,000 books, and the introduction of new services. These included an agency that provided legal advice for immigrants ('Agentur zum Rechtsschutz') and also served as an employment agency for both German migrants looking for work and local employers.[69] Both services were expressly designed to aid the integration of German migrants, a focus that became all the more pronounced, as Pfleger shows, in the lead-up to and the period after the First World War, when the Society offered designated naturalization classes for immigrants.[70]

Yet while this suggests a success story and good provisions for German immigrants through ethnic associational structures in Philadelphia, Kazal argues that there were many divisions in Philadelphia's German community at the turn of the twentieth century, with class, religion and gender being the critical forces.[71] One contributing factor was certainly the resurgence in migration from Germany after 1848. Not only did this bring a large and diverse new wave of migrants, but it also heralded the birth of a broad range of new associations. We will explore these in more detail later in this chapter; suffice it to say here that organizations like the Deutsche Gesellschaft, which, in terms of their social make-up, activities and functions were very much of the same ilk as St George's and St Andrew's societies, no longer represented fully the needs or wants of the German immigrant community as a whole.

Still, the Deutsche Gesellschaft of Philadelphia had been a critical pillar in the ethnic associational life of Germans in the United States, not least because it also served as a model for other groups. In New York, a Deutsche Gesellschaft was founded two decades after the Philadelphia one, in 1784. Its role too was that of providing support for German immigrants, and it still pursued such work in the late nineteenth century. As the New York charity directory stipulated in 1888, the Society 'assists all needy Germans by furnishing medical advice and medicines, food, clothing and money'. By that stage it also had 'two out-door physicians to visit German families', and the number of people assisted in 1887 was 3,199.[72] The Society also took it upon itself to provide advice for intending migrants, publishing a booklet, which it distributed free of charge, entitled

Praktische Rathschläge und Mittheilungen für deutsche Einwanderer
('Practical Advice and Information for German Immigrants').[73] The motivation for the production of the booklet stemmed from two intertwined
problems: that those Germans who made their way to America often did
not speak English, and hence struggled after arrival in terms of getting
practical information, and that much of the existing literature for them
was produced by people with rather self-serving interests at heart, which
made those brochures misleading and harmful ('geradezu irreführend
und schädlich').[74] The booklet contained thematic chapters, starting with
advice concerning the transatlantic crossing and arrival in New York,
and going on to details about newspapers and how to find employment.
Separately, there was also advice on legal matters in the United States, as
well as on how land was purchased. On an even more practical level, the
booklet ended with a list of the costs of the most commonly needed food
items, goods, clothes, furniture and other things that immigrants might
require, such as those needed for setting up a farm. There was also a list
of locations that were considered particularly relevant to immigrants,
that is, those to which they might consider moving from New York,
including details of travelling times as well as ticket prices and the costs
of transporting luggage. Finally, the Deutsche Gesellschaft of New York
included a map of Castle Garden, presumably to make it more familiar to
the arriving immigrants, showing where luggage could be deposited and
the location of the customs office.[75]

By 1916, the New York German Society's work concentrated on six
areas: (1) the traditional relief work it had pursued since its founding
days; (2) a medical service maintained by nine physicians; (3) a Labour
Bureau, which was run jointly with the Irish Emigrant Society; (4) the sta-
tioning of officers on Ellis Island to provide support and comfort to new
arrivals; (5) a business department that was responsible for all sorts of
business matters, also serving as an information office, answering letters
and queries concerning immigration to the United States; and (6) services
to represent clients in German courts.[76] The Society's office on Fourth
Avenue was open daily from 9 a.m. to 5 p.m. except on Sundays and
public holidays. In 1916, when the Society had 704 members, $15,844.75
was dispensed in cash to 4,453 cases of poverty after prior inspection
('Armenfällen nach vorhergegangener Untersuchung'); $983.00 in cash
was given to 2,015 unemployed people; $169.65 was used for 1,562
meal tickets for unemployed young males; $36.85 was used for lodging
tickets for unemployed young males; $1,977.25 for 584 half-tons of coal;
$2,285.45 for medical services; and $885.00 for the seamen's mission,
with $100.00 given to the German seamen's home in Hoboken. Beyond
these dispensations, the Society's physicians also carried out 3,336 sick
visits; the Labour Bureau dealt with 2,832 applications; and 1,558 new
immigrants were supported at Ellis Island.[77] The Deutsche Gesellschaft

in Baltimore, founded in 1817, pursued similar work, also securing, in 1841, that German translators were used at courts.[78]

What the activities in New York highlight, and as is emphasized in the Society's active engagement in the United Board of Charities and its later work on Ellis Island, is that the Deutsche Gesellschaft saw its function as a not exclusively ethnic one. While the immediate recipients of the philanthropy dispensed were German, there was a much wider civic purpose to the association's work. As much was made clear at a celebratory dinner in 1902 when a speaker noted that the Society had cast itself from the beginning as an association of the citizens of New York, enabling them to exert their united power in civic matters ('die Gesellschaft hat sich ... von Anfang an als eine Vereinigung der Bürger dieser Stadt zum Zwecke der Bethätigung ihrer geeinten Kraft in öffentlichen Gebieten kund getan').[79] This civic focus was emphasized too by many of the other German benevolent associations in New York. Among them were the German Ladies' Society for the Relief of Destitute Widows, Orphans and Sick Persons, founded in 1844 and providing support for 2,974 cases supported in 1887; the German Legal Aid Society, established in 1876 and offering legal aid to those of German birth who could not afford a lawyer, supporting 3,485 cases in 1887; and also the German Poliklinik, set up in 1883 to provide free medical treatment for sick and disabled, chiefly German, citizens in New York and treating over 11,000 in 1887.[80]

In the south too German associations soon spread, for instance in Charleston, South Carolina. Critical to the German Society's formation there was Johann Andreas Wagener. Born in Hanover in 1816, he arrived in Charleston in 1833 and soon became involved in the community. He was responsible for establishing a German fire brigade in the aftermath of the 1838 fire, and supported the establishment of a new German congregation in 1840. He founded the German newspaper *Der Teutone* and was also heavily involved in Freemasonry, founding Walhalla Lodge as well as its Turnverein (gymnastics club – we discuss this separately later in this chapter). Even more actively, Wagener was, together with about sixty other Germans, responsible for the founding of the settlement of Walhalla. This was a direct result of the 1848 revolution in Germany, in the aftermath of which the number of German arrivals in the United States increased significantly.

Another key supporter was Philipp Tydemann. Born in Charleston to a German father and a Scottish mother, Tydemann lived for a time in Scotland, where he studied medicine. He eventually returned to Charleston, however, and became an important contributor to association activities, also contributing financially – so much so, in fact, that he stated in his will that the Society should receive $5,000 upon his death, to be used to support new German arrivals who could not make ends meet.[81]

In New Orleans there was a clear trail of organized initiatives in support of German migrants, but these were few and for specific purposes only, as the German migrant population in the city was small until the mid-nineteenth century.[82] Eventually the impetus to formalize activities on a permanent footing came as a result of reports about poor conditions in Germany, which, some Germans in New Orleans argued, would contribute to increased levels of emigration and therefore, an increase in the number of needy German arrivals in the United States.[83] Consequently, a meeting was called by a number of German men for 5 May 1847, and less than two weeks later the new organization reportedly had 397 members and a newly accumulated foundation fund of $3,075.[84] With hindsight we can say that these men showed great foresight: as the Society's first annual report documents, 17,548 Germans arrived in New Orleans in the first year of the Society's operations. Of these, 6,001 German emigrants were supported by the Society to travel to St Louis, while another 3,892 were sent up the Ohio River, and 317 received funds to go to Texas; another 1,423 were supported to gain employment in New Orleans. The first year of operations, therefore, provided proof that the Society was addressing a real need.[85] This was all the more obvious when a Yellow Fever epidemic hit New Orleans in the summer of 1847.

Over the years the Deutsche Gesellschaft continued to support migrants as it had done in its first year (Table 6.5). In the first fourteen years of operation, that is until the Civil War, 240,000 Germans arrived in New Orleans, the majority of whom made use of the support or advice of the Gesellschaft; specifically, 38,523 were supported in gaining employment, and there were also ninety orphans for whom homes were found, in either local families or public institutions.[86] In 1852, the Society also looked after seventy-five women who either had lost their husbands during the journey across the Atlantic or were travelling on their own. It was undoubtedly as a result of their status as single women that a few of them, once they had arrived, found themselves in the city's red light district – or, as the Society's history couched it, in a house with a poor reputation ('einem übelberufenen Hause').[87]

Following the same path as all other immigrant groups examined here, German ethnic associationalism had philanthropy as only one facet of its activities: for the Germans too mutualism provided a critical further pillar. Here we concentrate on the two largest German organizations: the Order of the Sons of Hermann (OSH) and the German Order of Harugari (GOH).[88] The two orders were set up at similar times – in 1840 and 1847 respectively – and it appears that there was even an overlap in founding members. The timing of the organizations' establishment is critical as it documents that they were founded as a direct result of anti-German sentiment prevalent in the United States in the mid-nineteenth century, specifically that expressed by those active in the Know-Nothing movement, who eventually formed the Native American Party: Germans,

Table 6.5 *Deutsche Gesellschaft of New Orleans: the number of German arrivals in New Orleans compared with the number of Germans supported by the Society, and types of support received, 1847–61*

	1847 –48	1848 –49	1849 –50	1850 –51	1851 –52	1852 –53	1853 –54	1854 –55	1855 –56	1856 –57	1857 –58	1858 –59	1859 –60	1860 –61
German arrivals in New Orleans	17,548	19,166	12,707	13,029	25,264	32,703	35,965	27,010	10,752	12,642	13,912	6,549	6,125	7,535
Onward travel to St Louis	6,001	7,142	4,806	6,418	8,717	14,996	16,976	11,038	6,046	8,476	9,796	4,557	4,018	4,358
Onward travel up the Ohio River	3,892	4,655	2,921	3,362	4,791	5,157	6,155	3,524	1,016	660	1,259	602	446	723
Onward travel to Texas	317	277	86	366	1,209	1,504	1,566	1,290	190	417	111	63	–	238
Support for gaining employment	1,423	1,636	1,909	2,169	3,552	7,068	3,832	3,755	2,445	2,255	1,648	1,929	3,107	1,795

Source: J. Hanno Deiler, *Geschichte der Deutschen Gesellschaft von New Orleans: Festschrift zum Goldenen Jubiläum der Gesellschaft* (New Orleans, 1897).

like Catholic Irish, were key targets. As was explained in a *New York Times* article recounting the history of the GOH, '[t]he antagonism of the native element had the effect of cementing the Germans in this land into strong brotherhoods.'[89]

Both the OSH and the GOH were making historic connections to Germany through their choice of name: 'Harugari' refers to early traditions in Germanic paganism, describing those who worshipped in a sacred grove.[90] But the name is also connected with the old Germanic tribe of the Cherusci; the leader of the Cherusci, who led his tribe into the Battle of the Teutoburg Forest (9 AD) and defeated a number of Roman legions there, was Arminius – a name that, from the sixteenth century onwards, has been commonly regarded as the Latinized version of Hermann.[91] In light of the threats that they faced from the Know-Nothing movement, the founders of the OSH, as one speaker at an early meeting observed, 'again need a Hermann under whose mighty guidance we may be enabled to trample upon our enemies'.[92] This sentiment was confirmed decades later, in 1909, by a lodge of the OSH in California at a celebration commemorating the Battle of the Teutoburg Forest:

> By choosing the proud name of 'Sons of Hermann' an association of German lodges in our adoptive fatherland at once makes its initial purpose and goal apparent. Bringing together, like Hermann the Cheruscan, the German tribes in a protective and defence union.
>
> (Indem eine Vereinigung von deutschen Logen in unserm Adoptivaterlande den stolzen Namen 'Hermannssöhne' sich beilegte, ist damit gleichsam eine Andeutung des anfänglichen Zweckes und Zieles dieser Gesellschaft gegeben. Denn wie Hermann der Cherusker die deutschen Stämme zu einem Schutz- und Trutzbündnisse einte.)[93]

It was perhaps this idea of establishing a union that would serve to defend against and protect from external threats that explains, in part, why the OHS and GOH were set up as secret societies.[94]

So potent was Hermann as a symbol of unity that he became an enduring anchor of Germanness throughout the United States, and not only at celebrations such as those held in California. In New Ulm, Minnesota, which had been founded in 1854 by the Chicago-based German Land Company and was supported, with money and settlers, by the Settlement Association of the Turnverein, a Hermann monument was erected in the late nineteenth century.[95] Inspired by the Hermannsdenkmal (Hermann Monument) in Detmold, Germany, which was unveiled there in 1875, members of the New Ulm lodge of the OSH decided that they too wanted to have a monument dedicated to Hermann in celebration of the city's German roots. Julius Berndt, president of the New Ulm Lodge but at the time also the national secretary of the OSH, was chiefly responsible for

the design and financing of the monument, which was eventually dedicated in 1897.[96] The 106th United States Congress, in 2000, designated
the monument 'a national symbol of the contributions of Americans of
German heritage'.[97]

By then, the OSH had come quite a long way since its foundation in
New York in 1840. A key leading figure among the founders was Philip
Merkel, who would later also be chiefly involved in setting up the GOH.
Merkel was born in Frainshaims in 1811. Initially a student of medicine,
he switched to theology at his father's request, studying at the University
of Heidelberg. It was there that Merkel was imprisoned in relation to
political activities associated with the 1832 uprisings that he pursued.
As a result of this conviction, he was unable to find work in Germany
and decided to emigrate to the United States, becoming a pastor at the
German Lutheran Church in Newark. He then moved to New York and
held several church posts there before being appointed as special examiner of drugs for New York; a number of other city posts followed. He was
also politically active as a member of the general committee of Tammany
Hall and as a Freemason, hence exhibiting the characteristics of a serial
joiner and man of political activism also shown by so many of the English
we explore throughout this study.

From these early days the OSH had a positive trajectory, albeit one
that did not initially offer comprehensive mutual benefits, but focused
more – undoubtedly also in light of the Know-Nothings – on securing the
maintenance of the German language and customs.[98] Still, a first Grand
Lodge meeting in New York in 1849 cemented these foundations, and
the founding national Grand Lodge meeting was held in Rochester eight
years later. Correspondingly, the mutualism of the OSH's work grew. By
the end of the nineteenth century, the total membership of the OSH was
estimated at 90,000.[99]

This growth was also the result of the geographical spread of the
association, with groups now being set up beyond the borders of New
York. The first OSH lodge established outside New York was founded in
Milwaukee in 1848.[100] The new association had a clear vision of its role:

> We shake the hand of brotherhood and establish this union of friendship.
> Together we will sow the seed and hope that we can also harvest together.
> We want to promote German customs, the German spirit, German
> knowledge ... We all embrace the individual, and the individual embraces
> us all.
>
> (Damit nun diese grosse und würdige Arbeit gefördert werde, reichen
> wir uns die Bruderhand und stiften diesen Freundschaftsbund. Gemeinsam
> wollen wir säen und hoffen auch gemeinsam zu ernten. Wir wollen die
> deutsche Sitte, den deutschen Geist, das deutsche Wissen fördern ... Wir
> alle umschliessen den Einen und der Eine umschliesst uns Alle.)[101]

The spirit of unity expressed in Milwaukee was not, however, one that endured nationwide. As lodges of the Sons of Hermann spread to new locations throughout the United States, several of the already established state lodges left the national Grand Lodge. One of them was that of Wisconsin. The lodge had abandoned one basic objective of the Order, the promotion and maintenance of the German language,[102] and was unwilling to change its view. Consequently, it could no longer be part of the OSH.

This also highlights the fact that language had, since the arrival of the first German immigrants, been a key concern in the settlement process of Germans in America. Language is also a critical point of difference between migrant groups from the British Isles and Germans. While language was not uniform among the former either – there were migrants who spoke only Gaelic – speaking a foreign language was a key marker of differentiation for Germans. It could be a significant difficulty for them while, at the same time, being the most potent force of unity between the national group within associational contexts and beyond. A whole industry – the newspaper industry – capitalized on this, and German newspapers proliferated with the arrival of German migrants.[103] But there is another critical point relating to language that we need to bear in mind: prior to the unification of German in 1871 and the establishment of the German Empire, and hence before the existence of a German nation state, language was the sole marker available at macro-level to express belonging in terms that went beyond a migrant's regional or local background. But what this also meant, prior to 1871, is that the definition 'German-speaking' encompassed people who were not actually German, for instance Swiss or Austrians. This overlap is clearly reflected in ethnic associational culture, with Swiss and Austrian groups often listed in directories that nominally covered German associations.

For the OSH language was, however, not the only cause of dissent. Another state lodge that went its own way, and from the start, was that of Texas. Jakob Goll was the founder of the first group there, in San Antonio, when John Lemnitzer, a member of Genesee Lodge No. 10 in Rochester, New York, visited San Antonio in 1860.[104] As in New York, initially the support provided for members was not formalized in the same mutualist terms that we saw right from the outset with the Sons of England: when a Mr Werner died in late September 1861, the Society simply paid for his coffin and grave, and 'his widow is referred to in many succeeding meetings as receiving attention and assistance'.[105] The lodge received its charter in August 1870, and it was shortly after that incorporation that, in 1873, the idea of providing life insurance through the lodge was mooted; this was eventually introduced in September 1876. Still the San Antonio Lodge remained the sole lodge in Texas until Eintracht

Lodge No. 2 was founded, in Austin, in 1890. This was also the year of the first Grand Lodge in the state, and from then onwards a significant increase in activities could be seen: 'in little more than a year the hundredth lodge was established when Jubel Lodge No. 100 was installed at Caldwell, Texas'.[106] By the 1920s the Order in Texas also had a number of sister lodges, as well as one mixed lodge, Pershing Lodge No. 160, established on 1 April 1920.[107] At the height of business impressive numbers had been achieved: there were 217 OSH lodges in Texas with a total membership of 34,000.[108]

One person heavily involved in the Sons in Texas was Leo M.J. Dielmann. He was born in San Antonio in August 1881, but travelled to Germany – his parents' homeland – to study architecture, before making his way back to Texas, where he eventually set up his own business as architect. He was president of the Sons of Hermann Harmonia Lodge in 1940 and also sat on the committee of the Sons' Home for the Aged. This had had been founded near the town of Comfort, Texas.[109] Completed in 1915, the home offered sixty single rooms and was open for Order members who were over sixty-five, 'the only prerequisite for such admission [being] the conveyance of the insurance certificate of such a member to the Home, for its use and benefit'.[110]

Despite the internal frictions that existed among the Sons of Hermann concerning national and state organization, the OSH had grown steadily and made significant inroads in the provision of mutual benefits for Germans across the United States. This is evidenced strongly in records of insurance commissioners and other statistics pertaining to insurance provision by ethnic societies. In Connecticut, in 1906, for instance, the OSH disbursed $11,812.00 in death claims, $250.00 for permanent total disability claims and $4,079.12 for sick and accident claims.[111] To enable it to payment of such benefits, the OSH, like the Sons of England for example, relied on its membership paying fees that were graded by age. In Connecticut there were 1,828 members in total, with 341 aged 18–29, 462 aged 30–39, 567 aged 40–49 and 330 aged 50–59; the figures dip to 121 for those aged 60–69 and to 7 for those aged over 70.[112] A comparison of mutual aid provisions across a select number of ethnic groups based in Illinois (Table 6.6) reflects general patterns nationwide, documenting the scope of German mutualist provision. This was highest among the groups compared – a result too of overall migrant ratios – and had a strong women's auxiliary in the OSH's Sisters of Hermann. This had also grown significantly and, by 1910, had 2,480 benefit certificates in force, with a total income of $8,374.01 and $4,040 paid out in death claims.[113]

While there is only a little manuscript material for the German Order of Harugari, it is clear that it had also done well: according to the *New York Times* in 1895, it had 'a larger number of members than any other

Table 6.6 *Ethnic associations in Illinois: mutualist provisions compared, 1911*

	Number of benefit certificates in force	Total membership dues ($)	Total income ($)	Death claims paid ($)	Number of death claims	Total disbursements ($)
German Beneficial Union (national)	16,087.00	255,305.45	287,232.91	60,940.56	152	203,558.48
Grand Lodge of the German Order of Harugari, Illinois	1,841	36,857.00	41,959.19	23,500.00	51	35,632.83
Grand Lodge, Order of the Sons of Hermann of Illinois	303	2,498.69	2,667.45 (from members only)	700.00	7	2,536.81
Grand Lodge of the State of Illinois, Order Sons of St George	2,601	361.00	24,253.92	15,500.00	24	20,015.24
Hibernian Life Insurance Association	2,997	1,360.28	28,008.87	24,859.59	33	13,796.30
Order der Hermanns Schwestern, Illinois	2,480	5,641.28	8,374.01	4,040.00	22	25,404.15
Order of Scottish Clans	13,753	118,659.55	140,845.71	95,500.00	105	127,367.79

Source: Fred W. Potter, Forty-Third Annual Insurance Report of the Insurance Superintendent of the State of Illinois, Part III: Casualty and Assessment Insurance and Fraternal Societies (Springfield, 1911).

German secret order in America',[114] with about 31,000 members in 1895, 8,000 of whom were women, and the last Grand Lodge, held in Denver in 1894, documented a total of 370 lodges in twenty-five states.

Finally, it is also worth mentioning the German Beneficial Union. Incorporated in 1892, it expressed concern for the

> German-American element [which] was facing a state of disintegration, frittering away its strength [as] thousands of our German countrymen joined the ranks of the flourishing American mutual insurance orders, which were exercising a great attraction by their alluring promises. To counteract this disintegration and decomposition of the German-American element was the principal motive in founding the German Beneficial Union.[115]

Its stance was clear: it argued that established German mutual benefit societies, such as the GOH and the OSH, did not offer good enough provisions when compared with insurance providers without an ethnic anchor, and hence Germans were choosing them instead. The Union sought to counter that, highlighting what became an increasing dilemma in a lot of immigrant communities: that when it came to mutualism, ethnic mutualism was only one option for migrants, and one that was easily outdone by the Woodmen, Foresters and other friendly and benefit societies that were not restricted by ethnicity.

Still neither the German mutual benefit societies nor the other groups we have considered here were by any means small in their operations, and it is important to recognize the impact they had within and beyond their respective communities. What was characteristic of German ethnic mutualism, certainly when compared with that of the English, was its diversity and earlier timing: it rested on a number of organizations rather than just one as English ethnic mutualism in the United States did, and it developed earlier and not only as a result of German immigrants being keen to provide for themselves at times of sickness, but also because of the immediate threats the German immigrant community was facing as a result of the Know-Nothing movement. Despite these threats, German ethnic associationalism was by no means defensive or shaped primarily through external factors: it also comprised a number of distinctively German characteristics through distinct associational strands, each of which had a clear focus on one specific activity.

One of the associational strands that Germans established was the Gesangsverein – a singing society – also frequently referred to as a Liederkranz or Liedertafel (literal translation: 'song wreath' or 'song table', essentially meaning a singing circle). Its roots go back to Pennsylvania, where the first such societies were founded in the early nineteenth century. Among these were the Philadelphia Männerchor (a male choir), the oldest Gesangsverein in the United States, which was founded in 1835. But the tradition spread quickly, with singing societies soon established in Baltimore (Liederkranz, 1836), Cincinnati (Deutsche Gesangverein, 1838 or 1839) and New Orleans (Liederkranz, 1845). Louisville in Kentucky was another early centre, with a Liederkranz set up in 1848. Its founder, Fritz Volkmar, suggested the establishment of a federal umbrella organization to bring together singing clubs in a more structured way.[116] The suggestion was well received, and the Nordamerikanischer Sängerbund (North American Singing Federation) was established in Cincinnati in 1849, though there were some frictions with another Sängerbund set up shortly thereafter.[117] The Sängerbund's principal activity was its annual Sängerfest (singer festival), the second of which was held in Louisville in 1850. Like other ethnic associational activities we have discussed here, many singing clubs suspended their operations during the Civil War, but soon resumed their work when the war had come to an end. This was also a time when, as a result of the growing popularity of singing societies, some new ones were founded as offshoots of existing associations, for instance the Harugari Men's Glee Club in New Orleans.[118]

Records relating to the Deutscher Liederkranz of New York provide details of its membership and activities. Founded in 1847 not only for sociability but also for patriotic reasons, the club soon flourished.[119] By 1881, it had 818 members, though the vast majority of them – 700 – were, as the annual report explains, passive members. The Liederkranz had a female choir, but the women active in it, fifty-one in number, were not full members of the Liederkranz. In 1880–81, it organized, along with a few smaller events, three concerts, two musical evenings, seven social evenings, one masquerade ball, a festival for children and a summer festival. Finally, there was also a celebration for the laying of the foundation stone for the Society's new hall.[120]

The Liederkranz's president at the time was William Steinway, son of the founder of Steinway & Sons, Henry E. Steinway. William had arrived in the United States together with his father and brothers in 1850, and his father established Steinway & Sons in 1853. A music gene clearly ran through the family – in fact, all Steinways were actively engaged in the New York Liederkranz – and it was perhaps that gene, coupled with Steinway's prominent name, that explains how he came to be president of the Liederkranz for consecutive periods: so often, in fact, that 'the entire period from 1867 to 1896 could be called "William Steinway era"'.[121] Steinway certainly had a lasting impact and contributed to making the Liederkranz popular and well received beyond the borders of New York – a fact that is reflected too in the rise in the number of members.[122]

By the time of the Nordamerikanischer Sängerbund's golden jubilee in 1899, it welcomed 120 clubs and 2,757 singers at its Cincinnati meeting. The annual festival that brought these singers together, like festivals that had gone before, included prize concerts that were open to the public and solo performances. Yet while singing was by no means restricted to men – there were female and mixed choirs – it too was an associational domain where men were prominent in the early period. Moreover, for a long time, and even after the first female choirs had been established, there were some official gender restrictions, including, for instance, the fact that at the Sängerbund festival 'the competition of prizes [was] restricted to the Männerchöre'.[123] This focus on performances by male choirs supplies one reason why they played a particularly important role in the spread of singing circles. The number of male choirs, and the prominence of German male choirs among them, is certainly impressive, also documenting the critical contribution that they made to the development of choral singing in the United States.[124] A related factor for its spread, however, was a much simpler one: singing was popular, and the Germans were visibly at the helm of promoting it. What Highland Games were for the Scots, singing festivals were for the Germans. Like the Scots, they used a tradition that had established roots in their home nation, transferred it to America and made it an activity that appealed to the community as a whole. In this way the Germans too championed their ethnicity in a civic way. This becomes particularly clear when we look at early twentieth-century singing festivals. Milwaukee, Baltimore, Philadelphia and New York were among the cities that were glad to host them, with 'representative officials of the state and city ... lend[ing] a hand at welcoming and entertaining' because they were well aware of the popularity of the events.[125] One such festival was held in Indianapolis in 1908 and provides insights into how the federation saw its role:

Significant are the achievements of the Nordamerikanische Sängerbund, invaluable its influence on the development of culture ... The German song has conquered the world, and we have every right to be proud of this precious good which we ... have brought from the fatherland to enrich the new homeland. German song, German language and German customs are things that we need to maintain without infringing upon our duties as American citizens.

(Gross sind die Errungenschaften des Nordamerikanischen Sängerbundes und unschätzbar dessen Einfluss auf die Kulturentwickelung dieses Landes ... Das deutsche Lied hat sich die Welt erobert, und wir haben ein Recht stolz zu sein auf dieses kostbare Gut, das wir ... mit herüber gebracht haben vom alten Vaterland zur Bereicherung der neuen Heimath. Deutsches Lied, deutsche Sprache und deutsche Sitten sind die Dinge, die wir uns erhalten müssen, ohne dass wir unsere Pflichten als gute amerikanische Bürger verletzen.) [126]

The idea of using German customs in support of enriching and developing not only the German immigrant community, but expressly also the new homeland, was paramount in another German associational strand that developed in the mid-nineteenth century: the tradition of the Turnverein, which translates as gymnastics club. That translation does not represent well, however, what Turnvereine were about. While gymnastics were foundational to them, the establishment of Turnvereine rested on the ideas of Friedrich Ludwig Jahn – commonly referred to as 'Turnvater Jahn', the father of gymnastics – who had started the German gymnastics movement in the early nineteenth century. Jahn believed that gymnastics could develop a person's physical as well as mental capacity.[127] But there was another important element to the Turnverein ideal: the clubs operated, to some extent, in the political sphere. In Germany, many members, seeing their liberal views well represented in Jahn's ideas, took part in the revolution of 1848. Consequently, the gymnastics movement was suppressed in Germany thereafter, and this was a contributing factor in the decision of many of its followers to emigrate, with the United States being a principal destination – a fact that explains why many of the new arrivals were keen to establish the gymnastics tradition in the United States as soon as possible, and did indeed manage to get it off the ground very quickly.[128] Cincinnati was the home of the first society (1848), and New York (1848) and Philadelphia (1849) followed soon thereafter.[129] Despite the speedy progress there were problems at first, however – a result, again, of 'the influence of the Know-Nothing party, narrow minded, puritanical and opposed to everything foreign'.[130] It was partly as a result of anti-German sentiments that those engaged in Turnvereine sought to strengthen their position with an umbrella body, the Nordamerikanischer Turnerbund (North American Gymnastics Union), which was founded soon after the formation of the first clubs.[131] Similar to the uniting efforts we have seen for the Scots' Highland Games federation, the Gymnastics Union's role related to maintaining uniformity in rules and activities. It also, however, began to develop its role as a voice for the integration of gymnastics in school curricula, and it established the Normal College of the North American Gymnastics Unions, 'the oldest American institution for the education of teachers of physical training'.[132] Moreover, the Union's newspaper, *Der Fortschritt* (meaning 'The Progress'), served the more political vision of the gymnastics movement, not only reporting on activities, but also acting as a platform for ideas.[133]

Clubs offered gymnastics classes and trained regularly, often coming together to exhibit their skills at an annual Turnfest (gymnastics festival); the first such Turnfest was held in Philadelphia in late September 1851. While the gymnastics movement was initially a purely German endeavour, people from other backgrounds soon became interested in joining, a trend that resulted too from the underpinning philosophy of the gymnastics movement, that it was not just about physical exercise, but also the education of the mind. As the *New Yorker Volkszeitung* explained, 'there is a strong urge to show one's good performance, thereby showing the well-being of the body' ('Man ist stark bestrebt, gute Leistungen zu zeigen und dabei das Wohlbefinden des Körpers vor Augen zu führen'). This was always the well-being of the body as a whole, hence the establishment of committees responsible for 'mental endeavours' ('geistige Bestrebungen').[134] This was also why, in the 1880s, there were grave concerns that most clubs were not devoting enough time to developing the intellect of gymnasts, and were failing to offer sufficient stimulating educational input. As was explained, in 1879, only 213 clubs – a fraction of the clubs that existed – together hosted a meagre eighty such educational events.[135]

At about the same time, questions were raised too, however, as to the standard and standing of gymnastics. The St Louis club reported in 1879, for instance, its dismay that a parade hosted as part of a Turnfest was far too long, taking a good two hours as opposed to the thirty to forty-five minutes that had been planned for it. As a result, time was taken away from the actual gymnastics programme. This, the club thought, was not a good trend. Regardless of such tensions, the Nordamerikanischer Turnerbund continued to grow and, by 1908, had 40,021 members, 5,368 of whom were classed as 'active gymnasts', with a range of other classes, including classes for women, older gymnasts and learners described as 'Turnschüler'.[136] The fact that women were increasingly prominent in the movement (Figure 6.2) makes the Turnverein one of the few associational outlets in which women could participate without too many barriers – though, as we have seen, this did not automatically extend to competitions.

While gymnastics was favoured by a good many German-Americans, another activity that can be classed as a sport and was largely shaped by the German immigrant community soon took off: rifle clubs, or, to use the German term, Schuetzenvereine.[137] As with the Turnvereine, the name does not convey all that the associations focused on. While shooting activities were their principal pursuit, they were customarily embedded in a broader range of social activities and annual celebrations,[138] the latter often including balls and dances. In Springfield, Massachusetts, for example, the local Schuetzenverein customarily hosted an annual ball and masquerade dance. In 1894, when the event was organized for the twelfth time, the evening began at 8 p.m. with a concert by the Springfield Orchestral Club. This was followed by a dance, which included a 'grand march' comprising the leaders of the Schuetzenverein and a good fifty couples. All those participating in the march were dressed in colourful costumes and, as a local newspaper reported, 'the whole effect of the

Figure 6.2 Turnverein Society, Anaheim, c.1900 (image courtesy of Anaheim Public Library, Accession #P489)

dresses and masks was pretty'.[139] Given the timing of the event – in early March – it is plausible to assume that the idea of hosting a masquerade ball was connected to the German custom of carnival, in which dressing up is a key element.[140]

The most traditional event that Schuetzenvereine in the United States organized, however, was the Schuetzenfest – an event that continues to be celebrated in Germany and abroad to this day. The Washington Schuetzenverein started hosting these annual celebrations in 1866. Of the 1878 event the *Daily Critic* had only good things to say and was full of praise, noting that 'great preparations without regard to expense were made for the event'. As in previous years, proceedings commenced with a street parade, with 'nothing [being] left undone to make the pageant what it proved to be – a splendid affair'. This was the result too of the association's new uniform, the cadets making 'a fine appearance' and carrying 'small rifles and bouquets'.[141] A delegation from the Baltimore Schuetzenverein was present, and the parade also included several coaches, one decorated to resemble a throne for the 'Schuetzenking' and 'Schuetzenqueen' and drawn by four horses. Shooting activities were an intrinsic part of the celebrations, with prizes awarded for the best shooters.[142] In other parts of the country Schuetzenfeste were organized beyond the local level,[143] and sometimes by two or more shooting clubs together; there was some co-operation with clubs of other groups, notably those of the Swiss, who also had a long tradition of forming rifle clubs.[144] Eventually such co-operation was largely channelled through the National Rifle Association. Founded in 1871, the Association soon became an umbrella for anyone interested in guns and shooting, and thus provided and important engagement structure also for German Schuetzenvereine. Members of the Schuetzenvereine were active in the Association, and activities of German associations were reported regularly.[145]

The impact that Germans had through their ethnic associational-ism, then, was significant. This cannot be overstated as it extended into a number of other strands for which we do not have sufficient space here to explore in detail. Suffice it to provide some headlines and overall figures. One such strand was that of ethnicity-based German trade organization and unionism. Throughout the United States a plethora of organizations existed in support of workers' rights, whose members were solely of German origin. As Kazal argues, 'its backbone was the United German Trades' labour federation', and the federation's newspaper reflected its relevance with a circulation of over 40,000.[146] In some ways these organizations intersected directly with the associational strands we have explored above – only with a distinctly working-class twist: there were workingmen's male choirs and gymnastic clubs, and while the mutualist groups we have examined already were more working class in terms of their membership, some German trade organizations offered their own 'Arbeiter-Kranken- und Sterbekasse' (workingmen's sickness and death insurance). The *New Yorker Volkszeitung* had a special column entitled 'Aus unseren Arbeiterorganisationen' ('From our Workingmen's Associations) which covered news from German labour organizations.[147] One of them was the Journeymen Bäcker-Union No. 1 (a bakers' union).[148] What is more, the ethnic-based solidarity that German workers were expressing through this distinct associational strand operated transnationally. When a flood of the Rhine and Danube in the winter of 1882–83 threatened the livelihoods of many Germans, it was working-class organizations, for instance in Chicago, that led support initiatives, though the Order of Harugari and other German societies were involved too.[149] As with other associational pursuits in the German community, working-class women were active in the same ways as their male counterparts, setting up their own unions, such as the Gewerkschaft der Shopschneiderinnen, which Ortlepp has examined in more detail.[150]

Like other groups, Germans had fully recognized that being well organized in associations meant being stronger as a group. In fact, according to the editors of the address book of German associations, organization was the 'Zauberwort' (magic word).[151] If we look at

California as a small case study, we see this exemplified in the directory of German associations for 1915. In that year alone 181 ethnic associations were listed. The majority of them, well over forty, were singing societies, including the Harmonie Club in San Francisco or the Damen Chor (women's choir) in Oakland. There were also a good forty organizations with a benevolent or mutualist focus; groups with a regional anchor, such as the Bayern Verein in Los Angeles; and a good number of Turnvereine and rifle clubs. The final type of association documented – and one that we have not explored in detail here but that is worth mentioning – was that with a military link. Such groups existed in other immigrant communities; one might think, for instance, of Scottish regiments. But among Germans they had one distinct characteristic that is worth noting: they included associations for German veterans of not only German wars, but also American wars.[152] Again the aim of celebrating and maintaining Germanness while also expressing Americanness comes through strongly.

Prolific and important though they were, integrated and generally well regarded, Germans in North America, and by extension their associations, faced their greatest challenges with the two world wars. Wartime saw the English and others in the wider world echoing the prejudices of their kinsmen at home. Where once Germans and other foreign nationals would happily band together with English, Irish, Scots and Welsh for dinners and dances organized by each of their own national societies, this ceased to be possible in the course of the First World War. All over the world, Germans (and Italians) faced violence, prejudice and imprisonment.[153] In Melita, Manitoba, the local Sons of England lodge went so far as to send a letter to Major General the Hon. Sam Hughes to voice its concerns about what it described as the threat of German saboteurs on the Canadian railway. Given that so many of German birth were working on the railway, members of Lodge Milford believed there to be a great 'menace' as these workers 'of enemy birth' were employed in key positions.[154] The relevant military district officer did not, however, see an issue, noting that 'as a rule the track men referred to are a faithful, hard-working class. While it is possible that some dangerous men might occasionally be employed, the same thing might occur no matter what the nationality of the track men was.'[155] Acts such as the sinking of the *Lusitania*, in 1915, exacerbated national prejudice.[156]

Germans clearly felt the impact. In the United States, German orchestras and concerts by singing circles were banned; Sauerkraut was suddenly called 'liberty cabbage'; and many German associations, on their own accord, suspended annual events such as German Day celebrations. There were also direct threats. The Patriotic Sons of America, for example, threatened Germans, sending a postcard to the German Society in Philadelphia:

> If the sympathy of your Society is with the United States, place the stars
> and stripes outside of your building, as you did of the German colors. This
> is a friendly tip. The Society of the Patriotic Sons of America is only one
> short square from your building ... So get the flag out at once. If you do not
> do so and anything happens you know you have been warned.[157]

And this happened despite the Society's making it very clear that it did
not support Germany. In fact, in an attempt to prove its loyalty to the
United States, the Society even began helping the police and government
officials to register non-citizen Germans as enemy aliens.[158] Elsewhere,
the National German-American Alliance agreed, in early 1917, to donate
a recent collection to the American Red Cross.[159] It took some time for
German associations to bounce back after the First World War, but most
did and continued their work – which, in the case of a good number of
associations, included a strengthening of focus on America, for instance
through the offering of English language classes to help Germans with
the naturalization process.

Conclusion

This examination of the associational history of the Scots and Germans
confirms our main argument in this study: that the English behaved every
bit as ethnically as other groups; that they utilized and exhibited their
ethnicity in similar ways; and that the strategies they actively employed
to do so through ethnic associations were, in essence, the same as those
used by other groups.

Yet while all of this holds true, and in fact strengthens our case, we
have also seen critical evidence of how the English story differed and
was distinct from others. Importantly, the differences in ethnic associational history between groups that we have unravelled here supply some
reasons that help to explain why English ethnic associationalism and the
idea that the English were a diaspora have been largely dismissed thus
far: it is fair to say that, on the whole, English ethnic associationalism was
weaker than that of several other groups. Why was that so?

Figure 6.3 provides a systematic representation of the main strands
of English, Scottish and German ethnic associational culture. What is
immediately apparent is that the English had the fewest strands. In fact,
essentially their associationalism rested on only two: philanthropy and
mutualism – or what we have previously described as its two pillars.
While associations with a local homeland referent, such as Yorkshire
societies, provided an additional hook for associational activity in the
English community, all of these societies, even if, as we have argued, they
partly served a civic role, catered primarily for the English immigrant

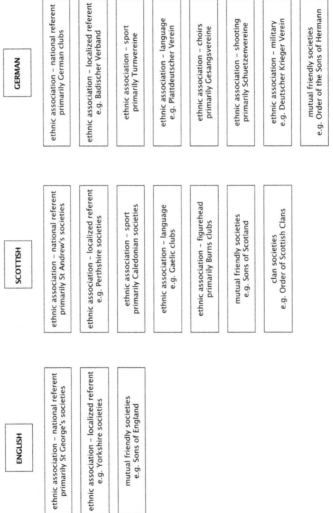

ENGLISH

ethnic association – national referent primarily St George's societies	
ethnic association – localized referent primarily Yorkshire societies	
mutual friendly societies e.g. Sons of England	

SCOTTISH

ethnic association – national referent primarily St Andrew's societies	
ethnic association – localized referent e.g. Perthshire societies	
ethnic association – sport primarily Caledonian societies	
ethnic association – language e.g. Gaelic clubs	
ethnic association – figurehead primarily Burns clubs	
mutual friendly societies e.g. Sons of Scotland	
clan societies e.g. Order of Scottish Clans	

GERMAN

ethnic association – national referent primarily German clubs	
ethnic association – localized referent e.g. Badischer Verband	
ethnic association – sport primarily Turnvereine	
ethnic association – language e.g. Plattdeutscher Verein	
ethnic association – choirs primarily Gesangvereine	
ethnic association – shooting primarily Schuetzenvereine	
ethnic association – military e.g. Deutscher Krieger Verein	
mutual friendly societies e.g. Order of the Sons of Hermann	
ethnic–based unionism e.g. Deutscher Metzger Verein	

Figure 6.3 Ethnic associational strands for the English, Scots and Germans

community. In that sense their focus was inward-oriented. That was, in itself, not a problem and is a characteristic that we also find in some associations of the other groups examined. The critical difference is that the English only had such associations: what they lacked was an associational anchor that could give their associationalism broader appeal.

The Scots achieved this with their Highland Games, and more specifically through the popularity of the Games as a sporting event. Scots thus shaped American sporting culture in ways that significantly transcended their own ethnic group boundaries. The German case is even stronger in this respect than that of the Scots – partly because there simply were more Germans present to have an impact, but primarily because it was not just one event that they placed on that broader footing, but several activities. Although these were initially born out of an ethnic associational culture that was more exclusive by default – simply through the use, by most groups, of German as the associational language (certainly in the early days) – Germans managed to establish three associational strands that eventually shaped American culture more broadly while also being popular, namely their singing clubs, their gymnastics clubs and, to a lesser extent, their rifle clubs – until the First World War, that is, for this was a critical caesura in the German case and an important qualifier in terms of their impact that we must bear in mind.

Still, the strength that German associational culture derived from these different strands cannot be denied, and it was significantly enhanced through the comparatively well-integrated and strong associational culture of German women. While other groups offered platforms for women in some ways, essentially all the organizations that made up German associational life had a branch or outlet for women that was formalized, from female benefit societies to female Turnvereine. This was not the case for the English or Scots.

Ultimately, then, what united all immigrant groups that we have explored here is that they found themselves at a watershed in terms of their ethnic associationalism in the mid- to late nineteenth century. But while the English at that caesura added only mutualism as another pillar to their associational endeavours, both the Scots and the Germans diversified their associational activities, a trend fuelled too by the arrival of new migrants. While this did not do away with divisions among Germans, or with different views in terms of their identity – for instance, this was also the time when Pennsylvania Germans began seeing themselves as a distinct group, eventually founding their own association in 1891 – the diversification of German ethnic associational culture contributed to its strength and visibility. The Scots were particularly good at maintaining a 'popular momentum' with the wider public, and their Highland Games still attract thousands in a number of locations around North America to this day. The English failed to achieve anything of this kind in terms of their ethnic associationalism. While this does not diminish the importance of their ethnic associationalism, which, in itself, was profound, this difference supplies one reason for the assumption held by many that English ethnicity was weak. It was, however, everything but that, as our final chapter, in which we explore English associational culture in global perspective, confirms.

Note

1 George Austin Morrison, *History of Saint Andrew's Society of the State of New York, 1756–1906* (New York, 1906).
2 St George's Society of New York, *History of St George's Society of New York, from 1770–1913* (New York, 1913), pp. 75, 322. See also Board of United Charities, *Hand Book of the Benevolent Institutions and Charities of New York for 1876* (New York, 1876), p. 54.
3 Board of United Charities, *Hand Book* (1876), Preface.
4 In 1894, the Chicago Bureau of Charities was founded with the object of creating general standards. K. Cmiel, *A Home of Another Kind: One Chicago Orphanage and the Tangle of Child Welfare* (Chicago, 1995), p. 54.
5 Ibid.
6 Ibid., p. 9.
7 We do not, however, consider the Irish in detail. They occur amply elsewhere on account of the regularity of conflict between them and the English. Besides, Irish associational culture was complicated by religious and political factors, particularly separate strands of political organization, which were focused on the likes of Fenians and Clan na Gael. Our study concentrates mostly on non-political forms of association, and German and Scots serve as suitable comparators for that.
8 For details see also University of Virginia, Historical Census Browser, http://mapserver.lib.virginia.edu (last accessed 5 August 2015). The browser permits filtering by a number of filters, including ethnic origins.
9 David Dobson, *Scottish Emigration to Colonial America, 1607–1785* (Athens, GA, 1994), p. 33; Alexander Murdoch, *Scotland and America, c. 1600–c. 1800* (Basingstoke, 2010), p. 24.
10 Ned C. Landsman, *Scotland and its First American Colony, 1683–1764* (Princeton, NJ, 1985), p. 134.
11 See T.C. Smout, Ned Landsman and T.M. Devine, 'Scottish Emigration in the Seventeenth and Eighteenth Centuries', in Nicholas P. Canny (ed.), *Europeans on the Move: Studies in European Migration* (Oxford, 1994), p. 98.
12 Today 6 October is celebrated as German-American Day, an idea mooted by Ronald Reagan in 1983 in celebration of the tercentennial anniversary year of the German settlement of America that was approved by Congress in 1987. See Celeste Ray, *Ethnicity* (Chapel Hill, NC, 2007), p. 47.
13 One suggestion has been that this early formation relates to the fact that at this point many of the Scottish indentured servants who had been

transported to America as prisoners of war after the Battle of Dunbar were at the end of their term, and struggled to make ends meet. *Boston Evening Transcript*, 30 November 1907.

14 'Laws Rules and Orders of the Poor Boxes Society (1657)', in Scots' Charitable Society of Boston, *The Constitution and By-Laws of the Scots' Charitable Society of Boston (Instituted 1657) with a List of Members and Officers, and many Interesting Extracts from the Original Records of the Society* (Cambridge, MA, 1878), p. 25. Quotation accessed via the Scots' Charitable Society of Boston website, http://scots-charitable.org/about/ (last accessed 18 March 2016).

15 Dobson, *Scottish Emigration to Colonial America*, p. 81.

16 See also Douglas J. Hamilton, *Scotland, the Caribbean and the Atlantic World, 1750–1820* (Manchester, 2005).

17 See Tanja Bueltmann and Donald M. MacRaild, 'Globalizing St George: English Associations in the Anglo-World to the 1930s', *Journal of Global History*, 7:1 (2012), p. 86.

18 This and the previous quotation from George Austin Morrison, *History of the Saint Andrew's Society of the State of New York, 1756–1906* (New York, 1906), p. 7.

19 Ibid., p. 10.

20 Ibid., pp. 10–11.

21 See for example J.H. Easterby, *History of the St Andrew's Society of Charleston, South Carolina* (Charleston, 1929). For details on provisions across the United States and Canada, see Tanja Bueltmann, *Clubbing Together: Ethnicity, Civility and Formal Sociability in the Scottish Diaspora to 1930* (Liverpool, 2014).

22 Harlan D. Whatley, *Two Hundred Fifty Years, 1756–2006: The History of the St Andrew's Society of the State of New York* (New York, 2008), p. 32.

23 For Smiles, see for instance R.J. Morris, 'Samuel Smiles and the Genesis of Self-Help', *Historical Journal*, 24 (1981), pp. 89–109.

24 City of Chicago, *Department of Public Welfare: Social Service Directory* (Chicago, 1915), p. 92.

25 Florence Evelyn Parker, *Care of Aged Persons in the United States* (Washington, DC, 1929), p. 179.

26 Ibid., p. 175.

27 *The Caledonian*, 17 April 1917, p. 38.

28 Parker, *Care of Aged Persons in the United States*, p. 175.

29 See certificates listed in Morrison, *History of the Saint Andrew's Society*, p. 177.

30 *Scottish Canadian*, October 1897 and December 1900. Celeste Ray argues that the Sons of Scotland had 5,000 members, while the membership of the Order of the Scottish Clans stood at about 16,000. See Celeste Ray, 'Scottish Immigration and Ethnic Organization in the United States', in Celeste Ray (ed.), *Transatlantic Scots* (Tuscaloosa, 2005), p. 67.

31 Sons of Scotland Benevolent Association, *Constitution of the Grand and Subordinate Camps* (Belleville, 1892), p. 8.

32 Ibid., p. 17.

33 See for instance *Morning Leader* (Regina), 27 January 1919; *Edmonton Journal*, 24 January 1920.

34 Tanja Bueltmann, *Scottish Ethnicity and the Making of New Zealand Society, 1850–1930* (Edinburgh, 2011), p. 179.

35 *By-Laws and Rules of Order of Inverness Camp, No. 54, S.O.S.* (Goderich, 1893), pp. 3–4.

36 Ibid., p. 5.

37 Ibid., p. 6.

38 See also Bueltmann and MacRaild, 'Globalizing St George'; also Donald M. MacRaild, *Faith, Fraternity and Fighting: The Orange Order and Irish Migrants in Northern England, c. 1850–1920* (Liverpool, 2005).

39 *By-Laws and Rules of Order of Inverness Camp*, p. 5.

40 Ibid.

41 1827 Constitution of Caledonian Society of Cincinnati, quoted in Addison H. Clipson, 'The Caledonian Society of Cincinnati', available at Caledonian Society of Cincinnati, http://www.caledoniansociety.org/societyhistory.html (last accessed 28 May 2015).

42 Robert B. Beath, *Historical Catalogue of the St Andrew's Society of Philadelphia: With Biographical Sketches of Deceased Members* (Philadelphia, 1913), p. 28.

43 See also Stephan Thernstrom, Ann Orlov and Oscar Handlin (eds), *Harvard Encyclopaedia of American Ethnic Groups* (2nd edn, Cambridge, MA, 1980), p. 915; and R.J. Blaustein, 'Scottish Americans', in J.H. Brunvand (ed.), *American Folklore: An Encyclopedia* (New York, 1996), pp. 652–55.

44 Frank Zarnowski, *All Around Men: Heroes of a Forgotten Sport* (Lanham, MD, 2005), p. 14.

45 For useful wider context and some specific references to the role of Caledonian Games in the growth of organized sports, see also Nancy B. Bouchier, *For the Love of the Game: Amateur Sport in Small-Town Ontario, 1838–1895* (Kingston and Montreal, 2003).

46 Zarnowski, *All Around Men*, p. 14.

47 Still other variants could be witnessed in Australia and New Zealand. For details, see Bueltmann, *Clubbing Together*.

48 From the Society's by-laws, quoted in Emily Ann Donaldson, *The Scottish Highland Games in America* (Gretna, 1986), p. 32.

49 As reported in the *Los Angeles Herald*, 4 June 1899.

50 *San Francisco Call*, 25 May 1913.

51 Ibid., 20 March 1904.

52 See also Ted Vincent, *The Rise and Fall of American Sport* (Lincoln, 1994), p. 56.

53 See Gerald Redmond, *The Sporting Scots of Nineteenth-Century Canada* (Toronto, 1982), p. 188.

54 Peter Ross, *The Book of Scotia Lodge: Being the History of Scotia Lodge, No. 634* (New York, 1895), p. 110.

55 See Redmond, *Sporting Scots*, pp. 190, 193.

56 Biography of Burns Smith in John H. Campbell, *History of the Friendly Sons of St Patrick and of the Hibernian Society for the Relief of Emigrants from Ireland* (Philadelphia, 1892), p. 523.

57 Ray, 'Scottish Immigration and Ethnic Organization', p. 78; Redmond, *Sporting Scots*, p. 299.

58 William Wood, *The Laws of Athletics* (New York, c.1880), pp. 47ff.

59 William G. Bek, *The German Settlement Society of Philadelphia and its Colony Hermann, Missouri* (Philadelphia, 1907), p. 1. For more on early works on Germans in the United States, see Library of Congress, *A List of Works Relating to the Germans in the United States* (Washington, DC, 1904).

60 Oswald Seidensticker, *Geschichte der Deutschen Gesellschaft von Pennsylvanien, 1764–1917* (Philadelphia, 1917), p. 32.

61 Ibid., p. 34. See also Georg von Bosse, *Das deutsche Element in den Vereinigten Staaten unter besonderer Berücksichtigung seines politischen, ethnischen, sozialen und erzieherischen Einflusses* (New York, 1908).

62 Seidensticker, *Geschichte der Deutschen Gesellschaft*, p. 40.

63 Ibid., p. 57.

64 Ibid., p. 58.

65 Von Bosse, *Das deutsche Element*, p. 57.

66 *Hundertjährige Feier der Incorporation der Deutschen Gesellschaft von Pennsylvanien* (Philadelphia, 1882), p. 3.

67 English in the original; *Hundertjährige Feier der Incorporation der Deutschen Gesellschaft*, p. 8.

68 Birte Pfleger, 'German Immigration to Philadelphia from the Colonial Period through the Twentieth Century', in Ayumi Takenaka and Mary Johnson Osirim (eds), *Global Philadelphia: Immigrant Communities Old and New* (Philadelphia, 2010), p. 127.

69 More about the role of the society – and other ethnic groups – in Priscilla Ferguson Clement, *Welfare and the Poor in the Nineteenth-Century City: Philadelphia, 1800–1854* (London, 1985).

70 Pfleger, 'German Immigration to Philadelphia', p. 138.

71 Russell A. Kazal, *Becoming Old Stock: The Paradox of German-American Identity* (Princeton, NJ, 2004), p. 18.

72 Board of United Charities, *Hand Book of the Benevolent Institutions and Charities of New York From 1877* (New York, 1877), p. 158.

73 *Praktische Rathschläge und Mittheilungen für deutsche Einwanderer* (New York, 1883).

74 Ibid., from the preface.

75 Ibid., pp. 44, 47–49.

76 See Deutsche Gesellschaft der Stadt New York, *Jahresbericht für 1916* (New York, 1917), p. 2 (English summary of the Society's annual report for 1916), and also p. 7.

77 Ibid., p. 7. Details about many of the members, as well as Germans in New York more broadly – including those who were involved in other associations – can be found in Otto Spengler, *Das deutsche Element der Stadt New York: Biographisches Jahrbuch der Deutsch-Amerikaner New Yorks und Umgebung* (New York, 1913).

78 Von Bosse, *Das deutsche Element*, p. 238.

79 *Bericht über das Festessen zur Feier des 118-jährigen Bestehens der Deutschen*

Gesellschaft der Stadt New York am 8. März 1902 im Waldorf-Astoria, New York (New York, 1902), p. 9.

80　*New York Charities Directory* (New York, 1888), pp. 154–59.

81　Von Bosse, *Das deutsche Element*, p. 234.

82　J. Hanno Deiler, *Geschichte der Deutschen Gesellschaft von New Orleans: Festschrift zum Goldenen Jubiläum der Gesellschaft* (New Orleans, 1897), p. 51.

83　Ibid., p. 52.

84　Ibid., p. 53.

85　Ibid., p. 54.

86　Ibid., p. 87.

87　Ibid., p. 69.

88　The GOH and OSH were the largest orders, but there is very little scholarship on either of them, particularly the GOH given the paucity of source material. Gerhard Wiesinger, 'Orden der Hermanns Söhne and Deutscher Orden der Harugari: Two Antinativist Fraternal Orders in the United States', *In Their Own Words*, 3:2 (1986), pp. 135–57.

89　*New York Times*, 25 August 1895.

90　Ibid.

91　For details see Dieter Timpe, *Römisch-germanische Begegnungen in der späten Republik und frühen Kaiserzeit: Voraussetzungen – Konfrontationen – Wirkungen* (Mnich, 2006), esp. ch. 14. In popular culture Arminius or Hermann is often referred to as 'Hermann the German'.

92　Quoted in Albert C. Stevens (ed.), *The Cyclopedia of Fraternities* (New York, 1899), p. 283.

93　*Neunzehnhundertste Jahresfeier der Schlacht im Teutoburger Walde: Gedenkblätter an das Fest der Deutschen von Californien* (San Francisco, 1909), p. 35.

94　See also James M. Berquist, *Daily Life in Immigrant America, 1820–1870* (Westport, CT, 2008), p. 149.

95　For details on the history of New Ulm, see Daniel J. Hoisington, *A German Town: A History of New Ulm, Minnesota* (Roseville, 2004).

96　See also Hans A. Pohlsander, *National Monuments and Nationalism in Nineteenth-Century Germany* (Bern, 2008), p. 158.

97　106th Congress, 2d Session, Report 106-482, 'Hermann Monument and Hermann Heights Park' p. 1.

98　*Neunzehnhundertste Jahresfeier der Schlacht im Teutoburger Walde*, p. 39.

99　All quotations above from Stevens, *Cyclopedia of Fraternities*, p. 283.

100　Anke Ortlepp, '*Auf den, Ihr Schwestern!': Deutschamerikanische Frauenvereine in Milwaukee, Wisconsin, 1844–1914* (Stuttgart, 2004), p. 240; see also Julius Tengg, Carl C. Wurzbach and Emmett Whitsett (eds), *90th Anniversary Harmonia Lodge No. 1 Order of the Sons of Hermann, San Antonio, Texas, July 6, 1951: A Short History from the Documents of Harmonia Lodge No. 1 from 1861 to 1951* (San Antonio, 1951), p. 35.

101　*Neunzehnhundertste Jahresfeier der Schlacht im Teutoburger Walde*, p. 41.

102　Ibid., p. 43.

103 Their proliferation is reflected, for instance, in the Balch Collection held at the Historical Society of Pennsylvania, which includes a significant number of ethnic newspapers from Germans and other groups.
104 Tengg, Wurzbach and Whitsett, *90th Anniversary Harmonia Lodge No. 1*, p. 17.
105 Ibid., p. 61.
106 Ibid., p. 37.
107 Ibid., p. 55.
108 Ibid., pp. 21, 39.
109 San Antonio, Daughters of the Republic of Texas Library, Leo M.J. Dielmann Papers, Drawings, and Photographs, Col 883.
110 Tengg, Wurzbach and Whitsett, *90th Anniversary Harmonia Lodge No. 1*, pp. 77, 79.
111 *Forty-Second Annual Report of the Insurance Commissioner, 1907 (Business of 1906), Part III: Fraternal Societies – Twelfth Annual Report* (Hartford, 1907), p. 18.
112 Ibid., p. 19.
113 Fred W. Potter, *Forty-Third Annual Insurance Report of the Insurance Superintendent of the State of Illinois, Part III – Casualty and Assessment Insurance and Fraternal Societies* (Springfield, 1911). For a more detailed assessment of the Sisters of Hermann, see Ortlepp, *'Auf den, Ihr Schwestern!'*, ch. 6; and Mary Ann Clawson, 'Nineteenth-Century Women's Auxiliaries and Fraternal Orders', *Signs*, 12:1 (1986), pp. 40–61.
114 *New York Times*, 25 August 1895.
115 From the preface in Louis Volz, *German Beneficial Union and German Beneficial Union of Pittsburgh* (Pittsburgh, 1917). There is also a German version with the title *Deutscher Unterstützungs-Bund und Deutscher Unterstützungs-Bund von Pittsburg*.
116 John F. Kleber, *The Encyclopedia of Louisville* (Lexington, 2001), p. 338.
117 For details on the rival organization and the early history of singing clubs, see Albert B. Faust, *The German Element in the United States, with Special Reference to its Political, Moral, Social, and Educational Influence*, vol. 2 (Boston, 1909), pp. 271ff. See also Von Bosse, *Das deutsche Element*, p. 423.
118 John F. Nau, *The German People of New Orleans* (Leiden, 1954), p. 104.
119 For details on its early history, see Hermann Mosehthal, *Geschichte des Vereins Deutscher Liederkranz in New York. Im Auftrag seines 50-jährigen Bestehens am 9. Januar 1897* (New York, 1897).
120 Details from *Jahresbericht und Mitglieder-Liste des Deutschen Liederkranz für das Vereinsjahr 1880–81* (New York, 1881), pp. 3ff.
121 See Edwin M. Good, 'William Steinway and Music in New York, 1861–1871', in Michael Saffle and James R. Heintze (eds), *Music and Culture in America, 1861–1918* (Abingdon, 2013), pp. 10ff, quotation on p. 11.
122 By 1906 the society had 1,074 members, and ten years later the figure still stood at nearly 1,000, though– and this is important to note – the number of active members who sang remained steady at around 100. See *Jahresbericht und Mitglieder-Liste des Gesangs-Vereins Deutscher*

Liederkranz der Stadt New York für das Vereins-Jahr 1905–1906 (New York, 1906), p. 4; and *Jahresbericht und Mitgliederliste des Gesangsvereins Deutscher Liederkranz der Stadt New York für das Vereinsjahr 1915–1916* (New York, 1916), p. 4.

123 Faust, *German Element*, p. 274.
124 For New York and New Orleans this is documented in Mary Sue Morrow, 'Somewhere between Beer and Wagner: The Cultural and Musical Impact of German Männerchöre in New York and New Orleans', in Michael Saffle and James R. Heintze (eds), *Music and Culture in America, 1861–1918* (Abingdon, 2013), pp. 79–110; see in particular table 1 and table 2, pp. 81–82. See also Ann Ostendorf, *Sounds American: National Identity and Music Cultures of the Lower Mississippi River Valley, 1800–1860* (Athens, GA, 2011), pp. 120–21.
125 Faust, *German Element*, p. 276.
126 32nd National Saengerfest N.A.S.B., Indianapolis, June 17–20, 1908. Official Souvenir (Indianapolis, 1908), p. 4.
127 See Heikki Lempa, *Beyond the Gymnasium: Educating the Middle-Class Bodies in Classical Germany* (Lanham, MD, 2007).
128 For a list of the earliest Turnvereine, see *Jahresbericht des Vororts des Nordamerikanischen Turnerbundes* (Indianapolis, 1909), p. iii.
129 For New York see *Zur Feier des Fünfzigjährigen Jubiläums des New York Turn Vereins in der New York Turn-Halle* (New York, 1900).
130 Henry Metzner, *A Brief History of the North American Gymnastic Union* (Indianapolis, 1911), p. 23.
131 Von Bosse, *Das deutsche Element*, p. 123.
132 Metzner, *Brief History*, p. 59.
133 See for instance the mission statement in the first issue, *Der Fortschritt*, 18 December 1887. A similar role, as well as that of chronicling activities, also fell to annual yearbooks; see for instance the first volume of *Jahrbücher der Deutsch-Amerikanischern Turnerei* (New York, 1890).
134 This and the previous quotation from *New Yorker Volkszeitung*, 29 November 1931.
135 *Jahres-Bericht des Vorortes des Nord-Amerikanischen Turner-Bundes* (Milwaukee, 1880), p. 18.
136 *Jahresbericht des Vororts des Nordamerikanischen Turnerbundes* (1909), pp. v–vi.
137 The word should be spelled 'Schützenverein', but it was commonly written with 'ue', which is an alternative representation of the umlaut ü. It was also frequently spelled 'Schuetzen-Verein'.
138 This tradition continues in Germany to this day.
139 *Springfield Republican*, 3 March 1894.
140 While there is no uniform tradition, carnival is celebrated in Germany during Lent and, in some regions, costumes that contain masks are a key feature.
141 This and the previous quotes from *Daily Critic*, 29 July 1878.
142 See for instance *Daily Inter Ocean*, 28 May 1879.
143 For instance *New Yorker Volkszeitung*, 27 May 1900.

144 *Neunzehnhundertste Jahresfeier der Schlacht im Teutoburger Walde*, pp. 15 and 19.

145 See for instance *Report of the National Rifle Association of America, 1905* (New York, 1906), p. 112.

146 Kazal, *Becoming Old Stock*, p. 31.

147 *New Yorker Volkszeitung*, 29 November 1931.

148 Ibid., 20 September 1918.

149 Hartmut Keil and John B. Jentz (eds), *German Workers in Chicago: A Documentary History of Working-Class Culture from 1850 to World War 1* (Chicago, 1988), pp. 184–85.

150 Ortlepp, '*Auf den, Ihr Schwestern!*', pp. 215–34.

151 *Deutsch-Amerikanisches Vereins-Adressbuch fuer das Jahr 1914-15* (Milwaukee, 1914), p. 5.

152 Figures and details above from ibid., entry for California.

153 The classic work is P. Panayi, *The Enemy in Our Midst: Germans in Britain during the First World War* (Oxford, 1991); for New Zealand, see Andrew Francis, '*To be Truly British we must be Anti-German': New Zealand, Enemy Aliens and the Great War Experience, 1914-1919* (Oxford, 2012).

154 LAC, Department of National Defence Records, R.G. 24, vol. 2018, Sons of England Lodge Milford to Major General the Hon. Sam Hughes, 25 June 1915.

155 Ibid., vol. 2018, District Officer Commanding Military District No. 10, 19 July 1915.

156 Tilman Dedering, '"Avenge the Lusitania": The Anti-German Riots in South Africa in 1915', *Immigrants and Minorities*, 31:3 (2013), pp. 256–88; Panayi, *Enemy in Our Midst*, esp. ch. 8.

157 Quoted in Pfleger, 'German Immigration to Philadelphia', p. 141.

158 Ibid., p. 143.

159 Ibid., p. 141.

7

The making of a global diaspora

It is, perhaps, in the due order of things that the 'predominant' partner in the British Empire should have been content for so long to merge his identity in the wider and more composite citizenship associated with the word Briton. And at a time when we are seeking to emphasize the fact that the United Kingdom is merely the centre of a much vaster system, it may seem inconsistent to urge the individual claims of England for some tangible expression of devotion from her sons and daughters ... But intensity of love for the component part is by no means at variance with the patriotism that is required of all British subjects ... (*North China Herald*, 29 April 1910).

This strident appeal for Englishmen in Shanghai to join together in promoting the tenets of national patriotism fell into line with the prevailing desires of the London headquarters of the RSStG, whose annual report inspired the epistle in the first place. It is revealing too since, once more, the identity of the English was subsumed within that of Britain, the United Kingdom and the Empire. Alongside this sublimation resides a concomitant failure by the English-born to match the Scots, Welsh or Irish in extolling their particular components of the federal whole. Thus we see, at a stroke, the essence of the problem of English identity, one that has remained a live issue for over a century. Diffidence or indifference marked the English in the later nineteenth century as geopolitical threats heightened concerns for the position of Britons. The same detachment from ethnic identity remains prevalent today in an age of fracturing identity politics closer to home.

This chapter shows, however, that the English around the world offered one last hurrah and, in so doing, promoted not merely imperial unity or British patriotism, but also their own increasingly attuned Englishness. As the journalist of the *North China Herald* suggested in respect of English identity, 'the spirit of comedy has given place to a serious mood when great problems and overwhelming passions have to be grappled with'.[1] Gilbert and Sullivan were being placed in perspective by ethnic and patriotic societies, fired up by strong national sentiments and features of social imperialism, like the Navy League, in expressing increasingly bellicose and racialized national identities before the First World War. After the war, the power of identity remained, and, if anything, was strengthened. Thus, the RSStG avowed its nationality, denying strongly that nationalism 'was the curse of Europe', as Lord Hugh Cecil had claimed in 1921. Instead, the Society reckoned it was 'chauvinism', not 'love of country', that had caused Germany to go to war in 1914.[2]

In the United Kingdom, English folk paid far less attention to ethnic identity politics than their neo-British colonial cousins, prompting J.R. Seeley to declare that 'the history of England is not in England, but in America and Asia'.[3] R.J.C. Young shared this view, arguing that English ethnicity was made not in England, but in the Empire.[4] As Seeley implied, distance enhanced visions of identity, but, more importantly, being of English descent was a stronger impulse than simply being born in England. While Englishness abroad was always more powerful than at home, it did not matter since Englishmen all over the world were united, for Seeley, by their membership of the Anglo-Saxon race.[5] Moreover, for Seeley, the British Empire was 'an extension of English nationality', with 'Greater Britain' no more than a 'vast English nation'.[6] The development in London of the RSStG offered a sign that concomitant connections were being made – that England, at home, was connecting with modes and methods of Englishness in Empire and the colonies. RSStG members were determined to act as a centripetal focus for an otherwise scattered collective – a fact that aligns with modernist notions of English nationalism. In the early decades of the twentieth century anything from ten to more than fifty active branches existed in England, Wales and Ireland (Scotland had none). A global Anglo-Saxonism and the language of racial difference and superiority were certainly very much part of the new and pronounced English identity. By the time of the Great War, local societies in England and the Dominions were fully aware of each other. When members of 'the English Society' (i.e. the RSStG) in Todmorden got wind of some anti-English slander uttered by a Canadian senator in 1916, they wrote to their peers in Toronto, who forwarded the complaint to the appropriate authority and informed Mr W.E. Percy, secretary at Todmorden, of 'the steps we have taken'.[7]

The following discussion explores the globalization of associational English culture. It is not, however, limited to the RSStG, important though it is. We focus on three overlapping themes. First comes the rise of societies and associations that spread beyond the territory of their first formation. While Australasian St George's societies developed at about the same time as those in the Mid-West of America, and thus reflected the internal colonization of both British and American worlds, they were not in any sense joined up until the RSStG was set up and provided the adhesive to bond all the Anglo-world's English societies. Secondly, the chapter focuses on the way in which monarchical celebrations acted as glue for transnational and global activity.[8] Queen Victoria and the Empire were important and enduring foci for Englishmen, Englishwomen and their offspring wishing to evince patriotic support for the country of their birth or descent. The third feature of the chapter is the post-1918 world, in which the RSStG became yet stronger, its degree of integration became more noteworthy, and the concept of an Anglo-Saxonist Anglo-world became more prevalent in the citizen diplomacy of determined middle-class operators functioning below the political level who were keen to stress the shared cultural characteristic of the English, British, Americans and neo-Britons in Empire. It was within these shifting contexts, underpinned by the risks and effects of world wars, that the St George's tradition, and wider English ethnic associationalism, passed from its roots as a gentleman's benevolent society set up for poor English settlers in colonial America to a global network evincing shared Anglo-Saxonist visions of superiority and togetherness.

From local to global expressions of organized ethnicity

The growth and development of the RSStG reflected particular visions of English national identity. Neither a charity nor a friendly society, the RSStG was an active cultural association that 'exists primarily to foster the English race sentiment' located within 'a sense of the wider imperial citizenship'.[9] Indeed, that identity, as evinced in the nation's emigrant associational culture, conformed to what Kumar identifies as an imperial nationalism. In one sense, how could it not? The overseas lodges were founded and staffed by Britons serving overseas – as civil servants, businessmen, military personnel and teachers, and in a plethora of other functions which together constituted the practical operation of Empire. Beyond the Empire's confines, branches in places such as Japan suggested a role for expatriates, rather than imperialists, but generally the Empire was the setting for such expressions of patriotic sentiment. For most nations, the homeland was the unit of remembrance, memory and articulation; for the English, it was a global Empire of neo-Britons. This is why the RSStG at home, with its fifty or so branches in England and Wales, and in Ireland, was relatively feeble, while its overseas equivalent, with hundreds of branches and lodges in at least three different English ethnic organizations, was so much more impressive.

If rather limited at home, the RSStG was the key component in the globalization of English associational culture. No other attempt at English ethnic associationalism spread so far and wide. Chapter 2 illustrated that dozens of St George's societies in Canada and the United States, in the 1870s, tried, for thirty years, to integrate their organizations, but with limited success. The Sons of England in Canada and OSStG in the United States developed into huge enterprises with thousands of members and millions of dollars invested, but never succeeded in their ambition to unite. The Sons did, however, spread to southern Africa, albeit on a small scale. A few sources exist to verify this, including a South African government report of 1964 into the activities of the Afrikaner-Broederbond, which, in the interests of impartiality, had its terms of reference extended to include the Freemasons and the Sons of England.[10]

Established in 1881 at Uitenhaye, Cape Province, the Sons seven years later numbered only seven lodges in South Africa, which fell to four in 1891, the other three being marked as defunct.[11] A small recovery occurred in 1892, and the South African English founded a Grand Lodge of the Sons of England, following discussions as to how difficult it was effectively to run an organization whose headquarters was in Canada. In view of the minority status of the English, Scots, Irish and Welsh there – pressed as they were between more numerous Boers and the native African populations – it is no surprise the Sons of England in South Africa allowed 'male British subjects ... whose ancestors shall have been born in the United Kingdom of Great Britain and Ireland' to join.[12] In 1896, the Sons of England Grand Lodge discussed accepting members whose mothers were English 'no matter what nationality their fathers are, provided the candidates declare themselves to be Englishmen'.[13] Generally, South Africa's Sons of England had between sixteen and ninety members per lodge, amounting to 381 members in 1894.[14] The president revealed that year why lodges came and went. One of them, Albion Lodge in East London, fell into disagreement with other lodges about the nature of the Order; Union Jack Lodge, in Cathcart, ceased because the key active members had to leave town; and Salisbury Lodge, Coleberg, went into demise because the railway employees who set it up had to move on too.[15] In 1896, the president also appealed for the lodges not entirely to sever their connections to Canada.[16] The outbreak of the Second Anglo-Boer War emphasized this point: not only were some Canadian Sons of England fighting in imperial regiments in Africa, but solidarity was profound, as the war was effectively 'a lesson in' it.[17] Hence, Sons of England lodges in Canada were active not only in expressing that solidarity verbally, casting the war as a 'struggle for the maintenance of the common rights and privileges of all free-born subjects of our Most Gracious Majesty the Queen',[18] but also through their financial contributions to relief funds. During the twentieth century the Sons spread to Northern and Southern Rhodesia, reaching a total of seventy-nine lodges with 1,937 members.[19] This was not a mass membership society in southern Africa.

The English societies creating this collective splash formed part of a formidable associational world: Freemasons, Orangemen, the Navy League, the Magna Charta Association and English county associations – all of them shared, to some degree or other, the imperial ideal. Against the backdrop of the Second Anglo-Boer War, masculine groups such as those analysed here were matched by a flowering of female loyalist and imperial organizations, including America's Order of the Daughters of St George, New Zealand's Victoria League, Canada's Imperial Order of the Daughters of Empire and the South African Guild of Loyal Women.[20] However, the first flowering of this associational culture had occurred in the American colonies, not in England; and even in the nineteenth century, the colonies were quicker to organize than the imperial heartland at home.

The emergence of a global St George's culture did not coincide precisely with the timing of emigration. Quite often, some additional spur was needed over and above the simple arrival of a number of English immigrants. The shaping of organized ethnicity in the English diaspora was not helped by the fact that the English at home did not easily recognize far-flung developments of this type, and certainly did not see any importance in them. In this respect, they contrasted as fully as possible with the Irish. Thus, there were English societies in many parts of the world long before the RSStG emerged, in 1894, to play the type of central, organizing role that arguably should have been in place decades previously.[21]

We have already noted that Charleston, Philadelphia, and New York had founded societies named for St George in the eighteenth century. While these were middle-class charities, they also were drinking and toasting clubs and were expressly concerned to evince patriotism as well as charity. In the 1870s serious attempts were made for American and Canadian branches through the NAStGU to work in concert, while a less successful attempt at a full-blown merger was discussed by the OSStG and the Sons of England. Matters in the colonies were slightly slower to develop. New South Wales and Victoria, for example, were populated numerously with English people long before St George's societies cropped up. The colonial English were certainly much tardier than their English American cousins in developing such expressions of Old World identity.[22] The likeliest reason is that the degree of ethnic competition that, from an early point, marked both the United States and Canada was less apparent in Australia, where 'English' and 'establishment' were unchallenged and hegemonic; this was despite occasional bravado, such as that offered in Melbourne, in 1884, at the inaugural dinner of the Caledonian Society, 'that wherever one looked a Scotchman or an Irishman was found at the head of colonial affairs in this colony [and] the Englishmen were only looking on'.[23] It is interesting that in South

Africa, where an ethnic edge was matched by a racial one, the types of ethnic organization which occurred were more like that of the United States, being marked by hostility in a way that was not true of ethnic relations in Australia or New Zealand.[24] We catch faint markers of this after the Second Anglo-Boer War was over, for example, at a Johannesburg banquet for St George's Day, when the Earl of Selbourne appealed to Englishmen to respect the Dutch language.[25]

Competitive ethnicity underpinned such developments, and in Africa such matters were much more discordant. There was certainly significant English associational activity in parts of Africa – for example, Salisbury, Rhodesia, and Cape Town, South Africa – where elites and settlers blended together in English associations.[26] In Blantyre, in modern-day Malawi, notables spent late 1904 and early 1905 establishing a RSStG branch.[27] Within a year, 150 members and friends gathered for St George's Day. Middle-class elements established *conversazione* (polite, intellectual discussions and debates).[28] In South Africa, Durban and Harrismith fostered Sons of England lodges that reported their saint's day celebrations to RSStG headquarters. Bloemfontein, Klerksdorp and Potschefstroom had RSStG branches, and Pretoria and Ladysmith had plans to found them. At Stanger, the English celebrated in the St George's Patriotic Society.[29] While all these groups tended to organize dinners for the saint's day in April, at Blantyre the RSStG put on cricket matches, 'old English glees, games, and dances' and fancy dress balls.[30] Further progress was made, as Salisbury, Rhodesia, inaugurated a branch in 1912; a year later, Mombasa, Kenya, experienced similar developments.[31] By 1914, the Mombasa branch was capable of organizing a large and successful dance that plainly had become a society event.[32] The English repeatedly talked about setting up a branch of the RSStG in Kampala, Uganda, but in the absence of one, they still organized a fine saint's day dinner, dance or fancy dress ball at the Entebbe Club.[33] After similarly lengthy discussion, but this time with a different outcome, a branch appeared in Gwelo, Bulawayo, in 1918.[34] During the First World War the societies were full of concern for the mother country and for its small size as a community shaped by the background of war.

The RSStG's heart was in England, but its lifeblood thus flowed most strongly in the colonies and Empire. In March 1924, for example, the RSStG's journal, *The English Race*, listed just ten 'home' branches, and only one for Ireland.[35] At various other times, however, Ireland had branches in Dublin, Belfast, Derry, Cork and Limerick. Wales regularly returned information on one branch in Cardiff.[36] Despite the partition of Ireland, the Irish lodges were listed under the category 'home', suggesting a curious ability to ignore the tide of history.

By sharp contrast, the 1924 data included numerous branches overseas, and these were impressively widely spread in geographical terms.

There were forty-six in Australia, thirty-one of them in Queensland alone. The African continent had eight, two of which were in Southern Rhodesia, one in British East Africa (Kenya) and five in South Africa. The earliest newspaper reference to an African branch of the RSStG dates to 1903.[37] Canada had five, as had China, and both Malaya and Japan had two, while Malacca and Penang had one each. The Sons of England organized similar cultural events to the RSStG in both Canada and southern Africa. In 1909 and 1910, at Beira, in the Portuguese but British-dominated colony of Mozambique, it was the Sons of England, not the RSStG, that organized a dinner and dance in the Drill Hall.[38] The presence of the RSStG and Sons of England was by no means a sign of division. They came from different traditions, as Chapter 4 shows, and were thoroughly capable of sharing a platform, as they did in the 1920s, in Salisbury, Rhodesia, in celebration of their saint.[39]

The growth of English societies in South Africa was shaped primarily by tensions with the larger Afrikaner population. Many societies there were transplanted directly from England; others were introduced from Canada,[40] which explains the existence of the Sons of England in only Canada and South Africa. In Canada and the United States the English clubbed together against Irish and French threats, but in South Africa, where the Irish were sparse, Boer nationalism was the enemy. Lambert in particular has done much to recognize the flowering of various societies and associations in South Africa as focal points for expressing British identity in an increasingly hostile environment.[41] While certainly not as numerous as in other Dominions, St George's societies and the Sons of England were more important in South Africa than has been recognized, especially when added to the county societies which proliferated there, as they did in New Zealand.[42] Like their peers elsewhere, members in South Africa serviced social and cultural needs, laced occasionally with politics.

In one sense, we might wonder why an Englishman in Australia or New Zealand needed to form an ethnic society. The position of the English was strong and relatively unchallenged; and the essential apparatus of colonial governance was, if not English, then certainly British. There is, however, another angle. The timing of the first St George's Society in Australia, which was set up in Melbourne in 1847,[43] is instructive. The previous year had seen a spate of outbreaks of Ribbon-style violence, which caused protracted legal wrangling and political disagreement due to the way the authorities had handled the matter. It could be a coincidence; but it is more likely that a degree of English anxiety promoted the idea of a St George's society at that moment.[44] Adelaide Englishmen claimed that they mooted a society in early 1845, but it took until 1850 to set one up.[45] By the turn of the century, numerous larger St George's societies could be found across the country, from Kalgoorlie and Perth in Western Australia to Hurstville and Sydney in New South Wales; from Scottsdale and

Figure 7.1 St George's Society celebrations in Barcaldine, Queensland, c.1905 (image courtesy of Picture Queensland, State Library of Queensland, image number 46735)

Launceston in Tasmania, and Warrnambool in Victoria, to Toowoomba and Brisbane in Queensland.[46] The RSStG became the headquarters of many new branches. Local papers reported instances of St George's societies and published RSStG annual reports, thereby ensuring that branch societies knew of each other. In neighbouring Australia, Sydney Englishmen formed a branch in 1900;[47] further north, in Queensland, a branch was established in Barcaldine (Figure 7.1).

New Zealand proffered fewer instances of English national associations than other countries with such associations.[48] Contemporaries shared the view that 'for some unexplained reason, St George's Day has never been observed in New Zealand, except as a bank holiday'; but it was not strictly true.[49] Auckland had a society, but it appeared mostly to offer advice to potential immigrants from England, outlining 'the peculiar advantages the Province of Auckland possesses as a field of emigration', and organized saint's day events between 1859 and 1861.[50] New Zealand experienced only flickering English associational culture in this period – a fact that may reflect the colony's comparatively small, concentrated populations, or, as Fairburn characterized it, the lack of communal and associational cohesion.[51] St George's Day did, however, become a bank holiday in 1870s New Zealand and was, by the 1890s, filled with sporting activities as part of a national culture of annual sports days and festivals.[52] Equally, when Edwardian Englishmen in the town of Thames considered establishing a branch of the RSStG, readers of the local newspaper were reminded that '[i]t has long been a reproach to New Zealand that in this Dominion there exists only one branch of the Royal Society of St George.'[53]

English associations also extended to the remoter Pacific colonies and to the mercantile empire in Asia, where developments were not supported by large-scale immigrations. Hawaii hosted a St George's Society;[54] and, in 1869, the St George's Society in the Sandwich Islands made headlines when the Duke of Edinburgh, Prince Albert, offended members by refusing an official dinner hosted by the Society.[55] The sense of being connected to a global community expanded as the RSStG grew and spread, ensuring that branches in places such as Singapore, which assiduously reported the wider Society's activities, were connected to the global community.[56] Thus, in 1907, China newspapers carried news of the annual address of the RSStG secretary, Howard Ruff, in which he praised 'the observance of "England's Day," not only at home, but in the colonies, the United States of America, and abroad', which 'will be on a much more extended scale than even that of last year'.

Hence, while a journalist of the *North China Herald* wondered 'why St George's Day is so neglected in Shanghai and Hong Kong as well as the smaller ports of China',[57] this was to change. Gradually, in the early 1900s, numerous RSStG branches were noticed in south-east Asia: Singapore, Kuala Lumpur, Negri Sembilan, Malacca and Shanghai. In 1903, the St George's Society in Shanghai organized a fancy dress ball for November, with the press emphasizing that for a decade or so the English had not reciprocated the hospitality that the Irish and Scots, and others, had showed to them.[58] The Shanghai Society did not become affiliated to the RSStG in London until 1906, when the move was unanimously supported at its annual meeting.[59] In Shanghai, the climate presented a problem for the English, which was not faced by the Scots celebrating St Andrew's Day at the end of November: the weather was too wet in April for outdoor events, but too warm for large indoor ones. However, the local RSStG branch committee 'will ... do their best to see that the day does not pass totally unobserved'.[60] Three years later, the members in Shanghai were still complaining at the lack of effort for the saint's day.[61]

During the inter-war period, the associational culture of the English became more firmly planted in Asia, where societies and clubs tended to be the preserve of elite administrators and military personnel rather than a popular movement.[62] Events organized throughout the Anglo-world, such as the visit of the 'Heir-Apparent and Prince-Consort' to Singapore,[63] were not for the hoi polloi. In Shanghai for example, as in Baltimore and other places, the Consul-General was a key player. In this case, Sir Pelham

Warren served as president and hosted fetes, balls and meetings at his official residence.[64] In 1911 the presidency was filled by Sir Havilland de Sausmarez, a high-ranking judge who served in various imperial postings.[65] Such officials received support from expatriate businessmen such as the real estate magnate E. Jenner Hogg.[66] The high-ranking leadership clearly created some issues, with de Sausmarez offering to resign at the annual general meeting of 1913 before eventually the members voted to extend the committee and reduce the term of office to one year.[67]

These societies were amalgamations of settler self-help and elite benevolence and sociability. In other words, they ran the gamut from American- or Canadian-English friendly-society activity to the high-society events held in New York, Philadelphia and London by bankers, politicians, aristocrats and millionaires. If nothing else, this demonstrated the broad range of possibilities such societies could encompass, with all members at least united by their love of the homeland, if not by the power of their purses. Charitable concerns, though not of interest to the London RSStG, united those abroad. In Shanghai, from the earliest point, members were reminded that they were both a national and a benevolent grouping. In 1911, the Shanghai RSStG teamed up with other ethnic societies, charities, and churches to discuss founding an Associated Charities headquarters to share the burdens of administration and disbursement; twenty-two societies for Americans, English patriotic societies (male and female), Germans, Protestants, Catholics, Jews, the Seamen's Mission, the St Vincent de Paul Society and schools of all types for all beliefs and creeds were present.[68]

Additionally, English societies were strongly in favour of improvement schemes. Education was, like welfare and hardship, a common and preferred direction for support. In 1912, the RSStG in Shanghai, for example, introduced two scholarships of $100 each – one for a boy, one for a girl – to be used at any local school. An examination was to be set to test English subjects and arithmetic, and eligibility was restricted to children whose fathers qualified for membership of the society by birth. Later on it was reported that pupils from the Public School of Shanghai took both of the prizes in the first year.[69] Branches in other countries also offered scholarships, such as that at Barcaldine, Queensland.[70]

Later Asian branches of the RSStG still drew upon smaller populations than those in the colonies of settlement, with the consequence that branches generally were not large. They seemingly ran steadily on membership numbers of 150–300.[71] They organized a variety of events and activities in what were primarily expatriate, rather than colonial, communities, in which the turnover of English men and women was high. Moreover, while the lodges in the colonies of settlement and the United States could stick rigidly to a clear-cut membership rule, based on English birth or descent, such matters were much more complicated in the Far East. Consequently, there was enlightened realism in interpreting such rules. In Malaya, a world where sojourners and natives inevitably produced children, the RSStG was praised in a letter, written under the nom de plume 'Justice' in 1941, for allowing entry to Anglo-Malayans. Despite being controlled 'by the bluest blood', the Society decided to 'open its doors to any person who has one parent of English blood'.[72]

Generally, Malaya had branches in Kuala Lumpur, Malacca, Negri Sembilan and Ipoh.[73] In Malacca, in 1923, St George's Day was celebrated with a cricket match, with the England XI playing a World XI, followed by a fancy dress ball.[74] The Malacca Society had a membership of 143 in 1925, while the Selangor membership stood at 231 in 1927.[75] At Kuala Lumpur, in the mid-1920s, there was clear concern at a membership of just 143. While the Malaya members were somewhat in the doldrums, the press nevertheless reported branches opening at the same time in Swansea, Wales, Singapore, Canton and Nairobi.[76] Ten years later, the Kuala Lumpur organization was still going strong, and was in much better shape. Thus, in 1933, in Selangor, a pyjamas dance was 'among the suggestions for celebrating the day of England's patron saint', while, in 1937, 300 loyal followers of St George came together for the annual gathering at the Eastern Hotel, where they 'were a chorus of merry-makers'.[77] In 1926, the newspapers contained a lengthy article about the St George's Society's latest win over the St Andrew's Society in a charity golf match.[78] In the same year, the St George's Day dinner appears to have been especially sumptuous. The Imperial Hotel was resplendently decorate, and an interesting innovation – one also adopted elsewhere in the twentieth century – was the presence of 'Beef-Eaters'. They 'put in their processional appearance, led by Major Bourne and carrying platters of the Roast Beef of Old England as well as making time to the tune played by the cruiser's [HMS Vindictive] orchestra.'[79]

As with all overseas ethnic associations, Asian variants too were social clubs, patriotic gatherings and charities 'to relieve distressed and deserving Englishmen', as the Singapore RSStG declared.[80] In 1929, this branch had $1,000 in the bank and another $1,000 in investments – funds dedicated to the purpose of relief.[81] During the Depression of the 1930s, a lot of these funds were 'taken over by the European unemployment committee appointed by the Government' in Kuala Lumpur, in order to help Westerners suffering in the eastern colonies.[82] The travails of these times certainly brought people together. As Mr H. Bowery, president of the Singapore RSStG, stated in 1932, 'there cannot be anything seriously wrong with the Empire when you can get seated round the same table Englishmen, Scotsmen, Welshmen and Irishmen discussing amicably how best to make money for the unfortunate unemployed'. The words were not idle ones, for the Society donated $1,500 that year to the government fund.[83] Later on, during the 1930s, the wealthy of the colonial world turned their benevolence towards the sufferings of the unemployed in Britain and Europe, with Kuala Lumpur and Singapore making considerable donations.[84] Like their American counterparts many years earlier, the Shanghai RSStG warned 'about the increasing number of unemployed Englishmen arriving in Shanghai in search of work'.[85]

In 1933, a mannequin parade and cabaret netted $100 for the fund, this time from the Kuala Lumpur branch.[86] Later that year, Singapore contributed $175 to hard-up fellow nationals and it continued the good work in the following year, though this was difficult with members not always paying their dues. Under such circumstances members were very wary about having a lavish dinner for St George's Day, though in Singapore a modest affair was agreed to for 1933 and the following two years.[87] By 1937, however, things were looking up, with over 300 present at the annual St George's Day event in Kuala Lumpur, though the branch still advertised regularly for new members.[88]

All of these developments – from North America to Asia, Africa and the Antipodes – predated the formation, in London in 1894, of the Society of St George, which later achieved monarchical patronage and became a 'royal' society. Bianchi argues that the London-based tradition owed its initial impetus to American developments, and there is some evidence of this.[89] Certainly, Walter Besant, who spent time in the United States, was involved in an earlier St George's society that first appeared in 1879, according to Bianchi, and drew in some significant high-society support. Besant certainly fostered appeals to Englishmen at home to copy their brethren in America who successfully utilized St George's Day to promote national 'sentiment'.[90]

The real power behind the first St George's society in 1870s London was Harry W. Christmas, who, in the late 1880s, was campaigning for a global St George's society, a fact that had come to the attention of the press in India.[91] Besant was an honorary vice-president of the RSStG, but hardly played a major role.[92] By the 1890s, and until his death in 1902, Besant was the founder and principal promoter of another type of organization, the Atlantic Union, a forerunner of the English-Speaking Union, and an early example of the associational dimension of the emerging 'special relationship', promoting as it did Anglo-American comity.[93]

Besant was correct about the power of tapping national consciousness to evoke an individual's or nation's patriotism. It was, however, the British World at war, not at play, which provided the main driver for this. The English ethnic tradition inevitably also came into conflict with the Dutch in South Africa, against whom a war erupted. Lasting three years (1899–1902), this conflict resulted in a wave of patriotic organizations and a spurt of growth for existing societies, including the Sons of England and the St George's societies. A new harshness was also noticeable in the language of English associations, especially in southern Africa, as sociable ethnicity was overtaken by political events. Indeed, the St George's platform was regularly given over to expressions of political support for Britain's war in South Africa.[94] In Rhodesia, strident language suggested a firmly racial viewpoint. In 1900, at the formation of the Society of St George in Salisbury, the secretary described it as part of a 'mighty Zollverein of the Anglo-Saxon race'.[95] The politicization of the St George's tradition in South Africa, which was a function of the context of a brutal war, was demonstrated by the clear support given at meetings for Lord Alfred Milner's aggressive stance on how to tame the Dutch republics.[96]

By 1900 the same wave of activity washed over the country. In London, Covent Garden flower-sellers were doing a roaring trade in roses as the authorities 'gaily decorated' the West End for the national saint's day. Immense crowds watched the mounting of the guard at St James's Palace as the Coldstream Guards relieved the Scots Guards and 'played a number of stirring and patriotic English airs'.[97] With the Second Anglo-Boer War as the context, the intensity of national feeling was heightened. The relationship between war and St George was even more marked in Southampton that year, when a smoking concert at the Philharmonic Hall attracted 400 persons who contributed heavily to the mayor's war fund.[98] In Colchester's Trinity Church, the Revd J.R. Early noted the growth of national feeling at that time, reminding his flock that 'those of our race who inhabited the Colonies of Great Britain' were 'wont to mark the recurrence of St George's Day with special regard'. The newspaper reporting these events in Essex noted how initial hostility to the saint's day had diminished and that celebrations thus were growing.[99]

All this pointed to opportunities and responsibilities for the RSStG, a group which provided the clearest example of the transnationalism of Englishness. Forming such a society confirmed middle-class domination of ethnic societies, but also marked a significant imperial turn – from economic collectivism or simple sociability to a staunch defence of Empire. Glorification, celebration and an urgent form of identity replaced the more gentlemanly credo of the eighteenth century. Crucially, this was an example, *pace* Young, of the English at home responding to Englishness in the colonies.[100] The essence was captured well in a message by Howard Ruff, honorary secretary of the RSStG, London:

> ... it is now generally conceded ... that a day of celebration in the interests of Empire is a pressing necessity of our times, and there is a general consensus of opinion that St George's Day, 23rd April, is the most suitable day in every way for that purpose – and one which all members of our glorious Empire, irrespective of creed or party, could adopt.[101]

Certainly, the people of Ceylon, whose newspaper reported this speech, were told in no uncertain terms that the League of Empire in

Ceylon had no intention of proposing Trafalgar Day as such an occasion, since there are 'a plethora of holidays in Ceylon already'.[102] The Sons of England in Canada did not wish to suggest a further bank holiday for Trafalgar; however, they demanded in strong terms that the anniversary be marked, not simply because defeat for Nelson would have been disastrous for the outcome of war with France, but because 'the Empire must ever maintain her naval supremacy'. Nelson, then, encapsulated national prestige and a glorious history, but he also reflected contemporary anxieties about military competition in the world.[103] The English of Durban, Cape Town and Salisbury persistently marked Nelson's greatest triumph.[104] However, the greatest energy was expended in 1905 to mark the centenary of the victory at Trafalgar. The Sons of England in Canada held dozens of celebrations across the continent, with their newspaper containing several pages of quotations, poetry and reports on how they 'belted the earth with patriotic melody on Oct. 21st'.[105]

It was also at this time that regional and county groups also became more prominent – something we can also notice among the Irish community. In the United States, Ridge, who explores the New York dimension, explains that while ethnic organizations based on village or local-level affinities 'faded out in subsequent generations as provincial loyalties gave way to broader national or religious associations',[106] county associations thrived.[107] Perhaps sport – especially cricket – shaped English county organization too. New Zealand, with its English population generally drawn from small numbers of counties, made up for its lack of English *national* societies with English *county* societies.[108] In many cases, these societies were surrogates for national associations, taking responsibility for festivities on the national saint's day and other patriotic events. In Wellington, a Yorkshire Society was established in 1895.[109] The Society's inaugural dinner was held in January the following year, complete with 'sheep's trotters, stewed tripe and onions' and Yorkshire pudding. 'The object of the society', stated its president, the Revd J.C. Andrew, 'was to promote social feeling among Yorkshiremen, to aid in charitable work, and ... to read and receive papers upon the antiquity of the county'.[110] Settlers from Lancashire, Cheshire, Dorset, Kent, Northumberland and Durham made similar efforts.[111] In 1901 the Association of Lancastrians in China also was announced with a soirée that involved good music and much dancing.[112] Three years later, Lancastrians in Shanghai were gathering regularly, on this occasion to mark St George's Day.[113]

Shanghai was, by this time, regularly reporting London St George's Society activities. The RSStG's honorary secretary, Howard Ruff, captured the essence well in 1904 in a widely reported annual address:

> there is [now] ample evidence that Englishmen in the outlying portions
> of our world wide Empire are beginning to give outward expression to

that inborn love of Country which henceforth will no longer be regarded exclusively as the special attribute of the Scot or the distinguishing characteristic of the sons of Erin.[114]

Such words were doubtless met approvingly by the Shanghai St George's Society, which celebrated the saint's day that same year in fine style.[115] By 1906, the Society, which had by now affiliated to the RSStG, could draw 800 persons to its annual dinner.[116]

While these developments were critical in facilitating the diversification of English ethnic associational culture, the accretion of the prefix 'Royal' to the London Society following sanction from the Privy Council, in 1902, meant that a very careful line had to be trodden.[117] This was especially so when what might be perceived as a political point was being formulated. In supporting the principles of rearmament in 1936, the editor of *The English Race* declared: 'The Royal Society of St George is non-party and non-sectarian and draws no distinction in the matter of creed or party. For this we have to tread warily when contemplating an incursion into the field of politics.' The members feared royal disapproval; they did not wish to embarrass a non-partisan monarch; but they had to be wary of 'lynx-eyed members [who] keep a sharp eye on editorial delinquencies'.[118] When the Order of Crusaders affiliated to the RSStG in 1936, the latter's periodical reported that the Order was 'not hampered by politics or sectarianism', and was 'composed of men with pledged patriotic motives'.[119] Moreover the local branches maintained the mantra of freedom from such biases. The branch in Edmonton, Alberta, for example, mixed independence starkly with patriotism. The Society, it declared, 'is non-political, unsectarian and upholds the same ideals for which so many soldiers of the British Empire made the supreme sacrifice during the Great War'.[120] Thirty years later, and across the world, the essence remained. In 1951, the branch in Palmerston North, New Zealand, wrote in its rules: 'the Branch shall be unsectarian and independent of party politics'.[121] Such an expression would gain more than murmurs of approval among the council today. Equally, its 'primary objects' included the obligation 'to encourage and strengthen the spirit of patriotism, Loyalty and Service to the British Crown and Constitution among all persons of English birth or origin throughout the world, irrespective of creed or party'.[122]

Global celebrations of monarch and Empire

We saw in Chapter 4 how the English in North America celebrated royal and imperial connections. Unsurprisingly monarchy was a strong universal adherent for Britons and neo-Britons all over the world. The attachment to queen and country was not, however, unique to the English: it would be hard in most cases to separate flag-waving Britons from the cheering English as a royal carriage passed down a thoroughfare in Toronto or Melbourne. In all sites of settlement, monarchical loyalty was a requirement, though few went as far as the wealthy Philadelphia Sons of St George Society, which commissioned a portrait by William Sully to mark Queen Victoria's accession.[123] In 1862, Sully's portrait was flanked by a bust of Nelson and engravings of Victoria and Albert,[124] and, in 1887, the Society sent it to the American Exhibition in London.[125] In New York, a statute of Queen Victoria by the sculptor Stout was commissioned and put on display in the city's Stuyvesant Institute.[126] In 1879, the St George's Society of Baltimore was presented with a painting of Queen Victoria by the Canadian artist O.H. Ireland.[127] Another portrait of Queen Victoria, this time by the Baltimore artist George D'Almaine, was revealed at the 1881 St George's Day banquet at the Eutaw Hotel. Two decades earlier a society ball held in New York in honour of the Prince of Wales was adorned with many decorations including 'a magnificent oil painting of the Queen', which belonged to the St George's Society.[128]

Although Anglophilia was deeply ingrained in antebellum America,[129] the Civil War loosened the seams of such adherence. With Britain accused of pro-Confederate sympathies and actions, reverence for the queen could result in accusations of divided loyalty by the English and Anglophile Americans. In 1862, the Philadelphian Englishmen carefully included 'England' and 'America' in their programme of toasts, but pointedly not the queen. Sometimes the order of toasting placed the queen ahead of the president; at other times, not.[130] Contrastingly, Canadian loyalists raised glasses, without fear of criticism, to both the queen and the Governor-General.[131] The St George's Society of Hawaii toasted the president, the queen and the king of Hawaii.[132] It is, however, the growth in the monarchy during Victoria's reign, at a time when Britain's reach extended beyond that of any modern nation, which strikes the observer today. As King states in his study of Victoria's court in her Diamond Jubilee year, 1897, 'people thought they knew Victoria. For most of her subjects, scattered across the globe, she was a distant, majestic figure, but also a human one, whose joys, sorrows, and worries they recognized in their own lives.'[133] Her lengthy mourning of her consort, Prince Albert, shaped this personal connection.

The popularity of monarchy was hard-won. The Hanoverians enjoyed none of Victoria's public support, and the people were, during the early part of Victoria's reign, sceptical about monarchy and unsure about Empire. It was not just radicals who felt this way; the popular view in the country became nearly universally monarchical only as attitudes shifted and grew in time with Victoria's entwining within the nation's heart. 'During her reign', King argues, 'the British Empire reached its zenith, the queen's influence reaching across the globe, from Canada to Australia, South Africa and India to the exotic mysteries of Hong Kong and encompassing 400 million subjects.'[134]

Monarchical ceremony was a strong feature of the London society calendar during Victoria's reign. In 1877, however, marking monarchical milestones became imperial events. In that year, the visionary opportunist and Conservative prime minister, Benjamin Disraeli, united queen and Empire through the orchestration of her fortieth anniversary celebrations on the throne.[135] On 1 January, Victoria was proclaimed Empress of India – something she had pressurized Disraeli for. The Royal Title Bill, which Disraeli framed as central for British imperial policy in the East and as a slap to Russian aggression, took some effort to push through, and was a personal triumph for the prime minister.[136] The imperial title elicited sometimes strong Liberal opposition, for it smacked of absolutist governance, with Robert Lowe MP leading the charge. The poet Ben Johnson appealed to the title of queen, not empress, when he asked: 'Who so great as India's Queen?'[137]

Victoria herself had pushed for the title of 'empress'. Empires were greater than nations, and kings and queens smaller and more contained in every way than emperors and empresses. Disraeli initially was unconvinced and expressed unease at what he knew would be looked upon as aloof, dictatorial and un-British. Nevertheless, once persuaded, he was a dogged and charismatic advocate. His commitment was based on the concept of mystery, and he declared somewhat typically, and patronizingly, that 'you can only act upon the opinion of Eastern nations through their imagination'.[138] So it was the enormous stage-managed durbar in Delhi that capped her new status. The durbar took a classic meeting of Indian rulers and those they ruled and integrated it into a medieval European-style pageant, which 'made "manifest the sociology of India"' and cast 'their South Asian empire as a "feudal order"'.[139] That may have been so; but the monarch also was able to exert considerable psychic impact upon an imperial 'imagined community' that included British administrators, immigrants and their offspring, as well as upon Indian princes or Maori and African chiefs. From now on she would sign herself 'Victoria, Regina et Imperatrix' ('Victoria, Queen and Empress').

'Empress of India' and its Latin version were quickly cast in poetry, song and popular exchange, thus confirming the awe, gravity and seeming permanence of the bestowal.[140] G.F. Savage-Armstrong used it in a song for Ireland in 1887, the year of the Golden Jubilee. Ada Barker, and Thomas Jenner, members of the China Society, acted likewise in their poems for the Diamond Jubilee ten years later.[141] However, Richards argues that the Golden Jubilee 'had been a domestic spectacle' and 'had transformed Victoria into a domestic article'. Most importantly, 'what little charisma she possessed in 1887 she derived from the regard lavished on her by the various institutions' that utilized the reluctant queen 'to further their own interests'. Here Richards is thinking of the commodities cast for the occasions: cups, plates, wallpapers and so many others. Moreover generally, by the 1880s, royal jubilees, coronations, funerals and visits had become inherently imperial occasions.[142]

Although what they organized in 1887 could not match the events of ten years hence, there still was a strong intention to mark the golden anniversary in good style, and the RSStG certainly demonstrated no little commitment. In April that year, the British societies of Los Angeles, for example, which included the St George's Society, were marshalled by the British pro-consul, with a committee formed.[143] Similarly, the massive immigrant entrepôt of New York played a full part, with a general committee in which 'all classes and conditions of English, Irish, Scotch, and colonial residents, are represented' formed under Erastus Wiman, the elected 'permanent Chairman'.[144] In London, the gala dinner for members of the Order of St Michael and St George, held traditionally at St James's Palace, was dedicated both to the national saint and to the queen's jubilee.[145] In June 1887, a jubilee gathering of celebrating English, Scots and Canadian immigrants in Chicago was captured under the heading 'The Exiles Rejoice'.[146] In Cairo, it was reckoned, 'never before have so many members of the British community ... assembled in such numbers as came together to-day to express unswerving loyalty to their Queen-Empress'. British officialdom, the Khedive's ministers, all churches and ordinary folk packed a variety of functions and religious services. At Alexandria, the story was similar, while the same lengthy newspaper article reeled off further celebrations including English, Scots and those of many other nationalities, and both individuals and associations, in Vienna, Berlin, Constantinople, Oporto, Perth, Melbourne, Brisbane, Chile, Freetown and Gibraltar.[147] The press in Bermuda reported many of the events in these same places, but also offered closer detail of the great array of activities organized by the British, and their societies, in the United States, from Washington and Albany, where the St George's societies featured prominently, to Chicago, where both 'British and Orange societies formed in procession and marched through the principal streets'.[148]

While the monarchy had enjoyed ceremonial power before the age of Empire, the imperial context provided significantly greater potential for expressions of adoration. This was cemented, according to Richards, by the events of the later 1880s and early 1890s that saw continued imperial expansion consuming vast territories in Africa. Consequently, 'the image of Victoria lost its home-and-hearth quality and became a transnational and transcendental absolute', with, by the same turn, monarchical charisma 'obliterating the old image of the melancholy widowed queen'.[149] The blackness of queenly mourning was replaced by vivid imperial spectacles drawing upon the colour and costumes of hundreds of the Empire's peoples.

The efforts of English societies for the Queen-Empress's Diamond Jubilee in the summer of 1897 required no official prompt and no orchestration from opinion-savvy imperialist prime ministers. What occurred that year very much suggested that Disraeli's vision had been realized, with monarchy and Empire inseparably intertwined. Evidence for the vitality of Disraeli's vision took many forms as government officials, imperial officers, members of the armed forces, civic leaders, indigenous dignitaries, schools and organizations proffered adoration for their queen and empress in manifold public and private ways. In Australia, the St George's Society demonstrated clear patriotic intent, in November 1904, by asking the Australian prime minister to adopt the reigning monarch's birthday as Empire Day.[150] This was duly adopted for the following year.

Canada's Sons of England took a strong and forceful lead in 1897: for them the events of that year were inherently about celebrating the queen as the embodiment of their transnational nation, their federation of Britons, their multitude of connected nations. In a situation where claims were made for the unity of peoples of diverse colour, creed, religion and geography, the unifying singular – the Queen-Empress – was the vital lodestar. This is why the Sons of England encapsulated their own globe-wide celebrations in terms of the monarch's place in their transnational world. 'Summoned by the magic call of the Empress Queen, "Greater Britain" has suddenly stepped forward on the field as an actual and integral part of her Realm and Empire.'[151]

Behind this statement was an utterly extraordinary act of organization. As Queen Victoria approached the end of her sixtieth year on the throne, the Sons of England in Canada evoked this 'Greater Britain' by co-ordinating a sustained global celebration, appealing to kindred associations around the globe, including the Orange Order and the St George societies, to mark the jubilee with 'a scheme that is at once novel [and] patriotic'.[152] The Sons wanted to 'be first in any movement to commemorate' the jubilee.[153] In February 1897, the Sons had not alighted on their grand plan. This was to be left to the upcoming Grand Lodge in Brantford. Meanwhile, the Sons' official organ asked members and officers to come up with proposals for marking the celebration.[154] Meeting on 9–12 March 1897, the twenty-second annual session of the Supreme Grand Lodge discussed the jubilee in depth and issued a circular, No. 2. The Supreme Grand President, Barlow Cumberland, wrote to require all lodges attend Divine Service on Sunday 20 June. 'These services shall be conducted so that the National Anthem shall be sung, and prayer for the Queen said by the Sons of England in one continuous strain around the world.' It was asserted that the celebrations would begin with the lodges in South Africa and 'so follow the sun westward', and 'upon the sun having crossed the ocean and reached the Continent of America, the brothers in St John's, Newfoundland, will commence the anthem'. The impressive thought going into the jubilee included an astronomical timetable that was to be drawn up from Meteorological Department data and sent to lodges so that timings could be precise.[155]

The Sons' aim was for 'the *Jubilee Service of a continuous anthem around the world*, to take place on Sunday, the 20th of June, the actual anniversary of Her Majesty's accession',[156] engaging 'one people, the citizens of Empire'.[157] However, the Sons were restricted to southern Africa, Newfoundland and Canada. It would take a little more than that for 'Greater Britain' to rise as one to sing the national anthem at around 4 p.m. local time. The press furnished some of the required effort, with the scheme quickly gaining traction through the *Mail-Empire* and *Globe* titles. By May 1897, the scheme was widely known in Canada and had spread overseas, and the Sons themselves continued to do their best to spread the word: as records after the event document, 2,600 letters were sent, and 60,000 copies of the circular distributed.[158] They ensured that Buckingham Palace was aware of the plan,[159] and when Sir George O'Brien, the newly appointed Governor of Fiji and High Commissioner for the Western Pacific, happened to pass through Canada en route to his new home, 'he was furnished with a copy of the Jubilee circular of the service'.[160] The Anglican Church also provided effort by spreading the word of the Sons' plans through its worldwide diocesan system. In the same month, the Sons' organ had published the timetable of an order of service, which in turn was liberally distributed throughout the world via churches, the St George's societies and other associations. Events were to begin at sunrise in the Pacific. The Sons hoped 'to manifest the intense, all-pervading affection and reverence felt for out glorious Empress Queen' and show 'the immensity, magnificence, solidity, and power of the Empire'. The whole episode was to be 'an object lesson to other nations of the earth, which it is unnecessary to add will have an inestimable effect upon them'.[161]

Despite 'the many doubts ... expressed as to the possibility of its being actually accomplished', averred the Supreme Grand President of the Sons of England after the event, the desired outcome was achieved: the services had followed 'the sun westward', traversing 'the world in one unbroken line through the colonies of the Empire of the Union Jack'.[162] Englishmen in Fiji, New Zealand and Australia, the Straits settlement of Singapore, elsewhere in Asia, Arabia, Egypt, South Africa, Europe, West Africa, the mid-Atlantic and North America and even on board British ships in the Pacific Ocean joined the 'Wave of Song'.[163]

The local press and the *Sons of England Record* document the extent of the celebrations in detail. First in line were the inhabitants of Levuka, Fiji Islands. As a letter from Dr Garner Jones, headmaster of the Levuka public school, to *The Globe* explained, "'[o]wing to geographical position ... the inhabitants of Levuka, Fiji Islands, enjoyed the unique honor of initiating the 'Wave of Song' that hailed the Jubilee ... The service was an open air one, being held in the Government school grounds, Rev. W. Floyd, vicar of the Episcopal English Church, officiating.'"[164] Following on from these remotest climes came New Zealand, where Dunedin, Balclutha, Lawrence, Riversdale and Waiau, all in the South Island, conformed to the plan.[165] In Launceston, Tasmania, people of all denominations sang the anthem together; in Adelaide, the singing took place after a fine tea, while in Melbourne, at 4.20 p.m. – precisely the time listed by the Sons – the national anthem rang out at the Augustine Congregational Church.[166] In Perth, Western Australia, where the Anglican bishop and the local St George's Society joined forces, 'one of the most striking features of the service' was a large number of young children singing the anthem, being fully 'in accordance with the wish of the Sons of England Society'.[167] In North America 'our own brethren in Newfoundland and Canada and patriots in the United States took the service up with energy and enthusiasm'.[168] British Americans in Milwaukee followed suit, as did British subjects in Galveston, who accompanied the anthem with cricket and other sports.[169] In Charleston, South Carolina, the anthem was sung in the afternoon, and a dinner, jointly organized by St Andrew's and St George's societies, was held in the evening.[170] And a hint of the inclusivity of English imperial values was given as Jews and Christians, both Catholics and Protestants, were involved in the celebrations.[171] A circular had gone out, for example, from the Revd Monsignor Farrelly to the pastors of churches in the Archdiocese of Kingston, Canada, calling for Catholics to ensure that 'the day be properly honoured, enthusiastically celebrated, and marked in the calendar'.[172]

The Sons' own celebrations in Canada were staggering. Brockville, Campbellford and other places declared that they organized the largest parades ever seen in those towns. Unity with other friendly societies was noted in Sherbrooke and Richmond, Quebec, Fredericton, New Brunswick, in Cornwall and Ottawa, Ontario, and in many other places besides. Gatherings in the thousands were commonplace. Most interestingly, the Sons' journal reported the precise time at which the 'wave of song' broke out in each Canadian town: '8:12 in Charlottetown, Prince Edward Island, 8:14 in Halifax, Nova Scotia, 9:03 in Brockville, Ontario', and so on for each and every town listed.[173] The Sons of England in South Africa received grateful thanks from the queen for their 'loyal address' to mark the event.[174]

The newspaper also received a letter from a Sons' member, Mr Frank Vipond, who was on board the *State of California*, 'four days' run from Ireland'. The captain had received the jubilee instructions from the president of the Sons and so participated fully with a service, party and prizes.[175] Elsewhere, the commander of the SS *Catalonia* reported that 'it was a great disappointment to me that we could not hold the service I had intended, but all classes of passengers were so sea-sick'.[176] Further east, those shipwrecked on the *Aden* of the P & O line, which had left Yokohama and struck a rock off the island of Socotra, celebrated the jubilee on the wrecked ship by singing 'God Save the Queen' – as was noted in the *Record*, '[a]n Englishman is loyal, courageous and cheerful even with one foot in the grave.'[177] Perhaps the most remarkable story, however, comes from Alfred French, lighthouse keeper at Wailagilala lighthouse, Fiji, who wrote the following:

> A doubt being expressed about the proper day and as a good action could not be performed too often, I observed both the 20th and the 21st of June in the same way, I also had a bonfire lit on both nights so that ships passing either eastward or westward could see that the Anniversary was kept to suit either contingency.[178]

A mere fifty-four minutes west of the Meridian, French thought that this approach to the wave of song was the most suitable.

So it was that the Sons of England had mobilized powerful networks of church and confraternity in veneration of one of the strongest icons of identity in the Empire and at home: the monarchy.[179] The August issue of the Sons' newspaper contained even more information on just how 'The Circle of Song [was] Completed'.[180] Politicians capitalized on this wave of great British devotion, with a conference of premiers from all of the colonies attending a meeting in London, dubbed an 'historical gathering of imperialists in old London', at which they were addressed by Joseph Chamberlain, Imperial Secretary for the Colonies, a man well versed in the global community of 'Greater Britain', as he had himself called it, in the 1880s, during a speech to the Order of the Sons of St George.[181]

The intensity of the celebrations was, in one sense, stirred by the fact there would be no other decadal anniversary. In 1901, the death of the queen, after sixty-three years on the throne, left many Britons bereft. All but the oldest of her subjects could not remember a world before her. Moreover, her death came during the Second Anglo-Boer War, at a time when the British World was in conflict with itself. It is little wonder that, with the queen eliciting such displays of devotion as were shown in 1887 and 1897, these ethnic associations would seek to do something to memorialize her. We have seen what the American and Canadian groups did: memorials, graveyard plots, hospital beds and so on. Those in the Empire did likewise.

One feature of the queen's death was the emergence of what one newspaper called 'the Empire Day movement', headed by Lord Meath since 1896, though originated by the RSStG's own Walter Besant.[182]

Remarking how curious it was that the queen's birthday had been the only day officially marked by the British, the item pressed the claim hard. It suggested that 13 million British citizens around the world had fallen in behind the idea. The aim was to appeal to children and 'young folk'. Indeed, Empire Day was also known as 'Children's Day', and was meant to focus on creating the next generation of imperial patriots.[183]

Like the 'wave of song' for Victoria's Diamond Jubilee, the idea with Empire Day was, at heart, a simultaneous, global demonstration of unison and togetherness. The proposal was tied to a series of observable days when 'the Union Jack shall be ceremoniously hoisted in all British schools, and saluted by all boys and girls, and also that upon the King's Birthday, and any other notable dates, the National Anthem and Empire songs shall be sung'. The movement floated on the currents of the time and responded to contemporary challenges, within the Empire and beyond, as a result of war, the queen's death and the loosening federation of the Dominions. Its motto fitted, too, into the growing militarism of that time: 'One King, One Flag, One Fleet, One Empire'.[184]

Lord Meath was concerned that Empire Day should not be seen as belligerent or jingoistic. It was aimed to convey a Christian spirit of global togetherness. Meath cannot have been anything other than moved by the enthusiasm and alacrity with which his proposal was taken up. Canada (1901), Australia (1905), New Zealand and South Africa (both 1901) and India, in 1912, formalized the deceased queen's birthday, 24 May, as Empire Day one by one. In Australia, branches of the RSStG reckoned that they were principally organizers of Empire Day events.[185] In Canada, Empire Day quickly developed 'a martial spirit with the additional of rifle drills and cadet parades'. It was, overall, 'an unabashed celebration of Anglo-Saxon superiority, a day on which Anglo-Canadians ... gloried in their membership in the Master Race'.[186] Certainly, the English around the world would have heartily concurred with Governor-General Earl Grey, who reminded Britons that Empire Day was a festival where 'the British Empire stands out ... as the fearless champion of freedom, fair play and equal rights', even if such claims rather missed the supremacist point.[187]

Under constant pressure from patriotic organizations such as the RSStG, the United Kingdom was last in line, adopting the day in 1916 and upholding it until 1958, when it became Commonwealth Day.[188] Empire Day also was celebrated with gusto in the West Indies and other colonies.[189] Richards demonstrates how important music was in the celebration of Empire Day, with popular papers, such as the *Daily Express*, and sporting occasions, such as football matches, promoting tunes such as 'Land of Hope and Glory', thus suggesting continuity with the musical celebration of Queen Victoria's Diamond Jubilee.[190] Central, too, was the British Broadcasting Corporation, which, as well as hosting many Empire

Figure 7.2 Royal tour, arch in Ottawa, 1901 (image courtesy of McCord Museum, VIEW-6740)

Day events, also broadcast St George's Day lectures.[191] To Webster, Empire Day was a prominent example of how 'generations of schoolchildren encountered the empire through a growing body of publicity and propaganda'.[192] In the RSStG journal, a letter-writer named 'Æ Triplex' made strong case for Empire Day, and many other days besides, as key training for good, loyal, God-fearing citizens.[193] Of course, such appeals had less truck in Lord Meath's own Ireland, where only Belfast truly succumbed to its attractions.[194] Among the English abroad, however, Empire continued to be celebrated frequently, with visits of members of the royal family also providing important opportunities to do so (Figure 7.2).

If Victoria's birthday gave Britons Empire Day, the new monarch, her son, saw his birthday also marked as a moment of celebration. In November 1903, for example, in Shanghai, King Edward VII's birthday was celebrated in 'royal weather' with the harbour's vessels highly decorated in streamers and bunting. The RSStG there sent a telegram of good wishes to Sandringham, and the king's private secretary, Mr Knollys, wired back: 'The King thanks you for loyal congratulations'; in 1909, the same message went out and came back, using the same formulation; and in 1916, a new king and a new secretary at the palace still conveyed formal thanks – not just to the St George's societies, but also to the societies of the Welsh, Irish and Scots.[195] The level of communication was such that the men of Shanghai knew that the London headquarters moved their annual dinner from what would have been Easter Sunday to the following Wednesday. The usual greeting was sent to the London folk.[196] Yet the RSStG also campaigned furiously for the date of Empire Day to be moved from the 'meaningless' date 24 May, which was associated with a long-dead queen, to 22 June, the date of the current monarch's 'official birthday'.[197]

Likewise, when a new monarch came to the throne, the coronation was an event English associations chose to mark in style. At Shanghai, in 1911, for instance, the RSStG branch planned to mark the accession of George V with a fine dinner.[198] The event was used by the Society to impress upon the citizens of the city that it was untrue to claim that 'the St George's Society is apt to become somewhat torpid as compared with its sister societies in Shanghai'. The coronation celebrations, allied to the saint's day feast, high turnouts, 'terse and patriotic' and menus printed in English, all pointed to a strong, if focused, little piece of England in faraway Asia. The only thing that grated somewhat was 'the use of the Union Jack and of the Red, White and Blue for the decoration of the menu cards', though this was explained by the fact that the event, incorporating celebrations of the coronation, was 'to be not only English, but in all senses British and Imperial'.[199]

Such connections were endlessly cemented by grand dinners and lavish events organized by far-flung St George's societies for visiting politicians, writers, admirals or clerics, and by telegraphic communications from headquarters to the branches. Many rose to approving applause at dinners around the world, as for instance when Admiral Sir George Fowler addressed the Sydney branch in 1913. News of the event reached New Zealand.[200] When the London group sent St George's Day greetings around the world via cable, the branch in Launceston, Tasmania, responded, 'your England is our England'.[201] In 1911, the Shanghai branch of the RSStG sat down to a fine dinner in the Astor Hotel and announced that good wishes had come in from London, Queensland, Yokohama and Adelaide.[202]

Queen-Empress and the god of war

Monarchy provided a binding for the British World; war was another adhesive. In Baltimore, the effect of the outbreak of the First World War was immediate, even though the United States was not a belligerent. The treasurer of the city's St George's Society reported in December 1914 a year of 'unusual demand' for help. He continued,

> our heaviest item was for 1130 meals and lodgings caused by the large number of Englishmen who have come here trying to get home for the war. We have been instrumental in this and other ways of getting over 100 men

back to England and feel the expense was more than justified, in a time like the present, when England needs all the men she can get.[203]

By contrast, war initially passed over the St George's Society of Toronto. No mention was made in its annual report of 1914. A year later, things had changed, and a grave tone was adopted. It was moved and accepted that the Society should not hold its annual St George's Day dinner that year, 'when many of our members and fellow citizens may be torn with grief and anxiety on account of the war'. Instead, it was proposed and agreed that the church service, a more appropriately solemn occasion, be moved to 23 April itself, with the Sons of England, 'other public and patriotic societies', MPs, the Lieutenant-Governor and a host of other big-wigs invited. This policy hardened, and dinners, but not church services, were cancelled for each year the war raged.[204] That year, Toronto's annual report reflected on how the Board of Control and the Board of Education had arranged for flag-flying and for 'patriotic addresses to the school children, impressing on them that in honouring Saint George's Day they were honouring the Empire ... to which Canada's sons + daughters have given and are continuing to give such undoubted evidence of their loyalty'.[205]

The Toronto English were, by 1915, more in line with the perceived wider role of St George's societies as sites of patriotism and charity. Such was never more apparent than during wartime and, as we have already seen in Chapter 6, this had an immediate effect on the German community, as previous co-operation quickly turned into suspicion and open animosity. Such animosity was heightened by specific events. The Baltimore St George's Society suffered in a personal way, for instance, when the *Lusitania* went down. A long-standing Society member of seventeen years' service, Montagu Tassel Grant, and his wife Christina were killed on the ship.[206] Christina's body was never recovered but Grant himself was buried at Brockley, near Deptford in London.[207]

These associations also demonstrated transnational loyalty during times of war and crisis. In doing so, they were part of a dizzying effort made by people of all classes and creeds throughout the entire Empire.[208] All the while, the RSStG's journal, *The English Race*, hammered home the importance of making that contribution, consciously focusing on the whole Empire and not just the metropolitan hub. Such messages had their effect. The Hong Kong English sold First World War bonds to raise funds for the imperial war effort. Posters and brochures depicting St George attacking a German soldier (Figure 7.3) brought the themes of Englishness and war together – an effort also supported by the Patriotic League of Britons Overseas. In January 1916, the League wrote to the Charleston St George's Society asking whether it would assist in setting up a branch of the League, which 'now has 129 branches in various parts of the world, all of which have been established in the last nine months'.[209] Baltimore St George's Society organized a fund-raising drive to supplement the 'Prince of Wales Fund', monies from which were intended for widows and orphans of 'British soldiers and sailors killed in the disastrous war now being waged'.[210] Also in 1916 the Baltimore St George's Society received from Buckingham Palace a letter thanking the Society for a donation of £10 to the National Relief Fund – a fund which, the letter explained, had accrued £6 million.[211] $300 in donations was recorded in January 1915; $500 was sent to London in April; a further $250 was sent in July. Collections went on throughout, with another $211 recorded.[212]

To this latter end it was reported that the Shanghai folk had raised £760 for the Prince of Wales war fund – something that their American peers were also contributing to simultaneously.[213] Donations garnered at dinners or association meetings had been firmed up by 1916 as the war dragged on. The press in Shanghai reported the opening of a St George's War Fund, which would be funnelled into the War Loan, with any funds being used 'for the assistance of any member of the Society or his family, who may have been injured or killed in the war'. The president of the RSStG there, Mr Sausmarez, then wrote to every Englishman in the city via the press.[214] It was noticeable that the women of the Society were tasked to collect funds from groups of English folk, something they also did, going from table to table, at the St George's Day dinner that year. The result was $2,000 collected.[215] RSStG branches all over the world contributed quantities of money to various war funds: the prince's fund in England, or schemes organized in their home jurisdictions or colonies. For instance, £38 7s. 6d. was sent from the Monmouth branch in Wales and £88 from Southend-on-Sea in Essex in May 1915; Melbourne raised £300 in August of the same year.[216]

Toronto's St George's Society captured the general mood in 1916, when the tercentenary of Shakespeare's death and the seemingly remorseless threat of war caused the Society to mark its national saint's day, which also was the precise anniversary of Shakespeare's death, with a celebration.[217] The Society also sent a cablegram to the king, which focused on monarchical loyalty and imperial patriotism, expressing 'continued loyalty and devotion' and 'express[ed] the fervent hope that the war which the Empire is now engaged in for the maintenance of its honour, and the preservation of civil and religious liberty may be brought to a successful issue resulting, as they feel sure it will, in the permanent good of mankind'.[218] Its 'fervent hope' for the war's conclusion would not be realized for nearly three more years.

In 1917, the Hong Kong English, who were pointedly singled out for their tardy display, surprised the local press by forming a branch of the RSStG. The war obviously fired their patriotism, and as the news of their initiative filtered out, so too did the news that the famous Hong Kong

Figure 7.3 'Every Ticket Helps', war bond drawing organized by the Hong Kong St George's Society (image courtesy of Imperial War Museums, Art. IWM PST 12271)

Races, in 1917, raised an impressive £5,000 for the war effort, a figure matched by donations from the RSStG in the same city in 1918.[219] The selling of war bonds was a key means for the raising of funds in Hong Kong (Figure 7.3). The 1917 annual general meeting of the Association of Lancastrians dovetailed war, savings, sacrifice and patriotism, and gave them all a redoubtable Lancastrian spin. Lancashire's contribution to the war effort, to the war fund and to war bonds, and the efforts of its folk to learn the value of saving as a way of investing in the war effort, were fulsomely detailed. A highlight was the reference to Lancashire's £98 million war savings certificates, which the members in Shanghai greedily gobbled up as prejudicial to their interests.[220] Also in 1917, St George's Day in Cape Town was an occasion for celebration and for the archbishop to make an 'earnest appeal for recruits'.[221] Charitable donations were not only sent home for the war effort, however, but also sometimes passed on to locations abroad where battles took place, or wounded soldiers were being treated. In 1918, the matron of the General Hospital in Cairo, which treated many troops involved in the Gallipoli campaign, sent a letter of thanks to the St George's and St Andrew's societies for donating the proceeds of a charity golf match.[222]

In each period of their existence, these associations were shaped by the context. In 1915, Howard Ruff, in a wide-ranging speech on Empire Day, among the many features of 'Organized Patriotism' on which he spoke, the chase for 'Chairs of Patriotism at the Universities' – in both the United Kingdom and the Empire – was the most extraordinary. For him, education in Britain and the colonies had 'unfortunately been of a character too cosmopolitan'.[223] When the conflict was over, wartime bellicosity did not diminish quickly. As late as 1919, with the taste of war still on the tongue, the RSStG in Shanghai was talking not merely about 'having nothing to do with Germans', but also of 'exerting a certain amount of pressure to in certain directions … [to] get rid of the enemy in their midst'.[224] The English in Australia also wished to rub the noses of their vanquished foes in the dirt. The RSStG in South Australia petitioned the state government to make cheap land available for returning servicemen at the expense of 'Germans', 'enemy aliens' and 'disloyalists' who had not supported the war.[225]

The inter-war decades were marked by revulsion at the horrors of the First World War. This helped promote pacifist ideologies and a desire to make peace – aims that were underpinned by geopolitical integration for the English-speaking peoples. A heightened concern for the togetherness of Empire and an emphasis on patriotic, imperial and militaristic already pervaded journals, such as the *Sons of England Record*, as a mere glance at any issue from the late 1890s onwards would show. Things, however, intensified in the 1920s and changed tack. Imperialism was, by then, fundamentally shaped by the idea that the Anglo-world could stand together: gone was a focus on the Empire alone; now the Americans had to be included. Standing together, it was averred, they would guarantee force by their overwhelming strength. These imperatives saw long-standing English and British ethnic organizations, such as the St George's societies, the OSStG and the Sons of England, becoming more political. In 1919 the OSStG founded a newspaper, *The English-Speaking World*, as the organ for communication for a variety of broadly Anglo-Saxonist organizations and activities.[226] Organizations such as the Society for American and British Friendship, the Canadian Club, the Order of the Daughters of Empire, the Magna Charta Dames and the Ulster League of America (which mixed fund-raising for the Ulster Volunteer Force with pro-imperial rhetoric) commanded space in the organ because they were practical deliverers of an Anglo-Saxonist, Anglo-world mission. The organizations were numerous; the active non-state actors within them were many; and they overlapped in terms of membership and ideology. Within their ranks the British World and the Anglo-world became increasingly coterminous.

German opinion in the United States briefed against Anglo-world comity, but *The English-Speaking World* gave them short shrift and suggested that 'if Germany is sincere in her desire for a lasting peace ... the combination of the English-speaking nations will insure for them a peaceful condition' wherein to redevelop their commercial prestige.[227]

The essence of the RSStG penetrated deeply into the organization. Speaking in the 1930s, Councillor Hampson of the branch in Salford captured what every office-holder across the world would have known and agreed with: 'The Royal Society of St George was founded ... to encourage and strengthen the spirit of patriotism and pride or race amongst Englishmen of every class and creed. Its branches exist all over the English-speaking world'.[228] Everywhere their branches emerged, the RSStG members and officers, in discussions and toasts, repeatedly mentioned the idea of being part of the 'English-speaking world'. This entity had taken on much greater importance in the wake of a brutal, global conflagration.[229] This was strikingly the case in James Hamilton's speech on the desirability of celebrating Magna Carta as a global icon of the Anglo-Saxon world in a two-page article which stressed the common dangers faced by the Americans and the British Empire, using the term 'English speaking' nine times; in another piece of similar length, the term appears ten times.[230]

If war had provided a dramatic focal point and an opportunity for the associations to show sympathy, patriotism and generosity to their homeland, the inter-war years offered a mix of freer social intercourse, dramatically more expansive sporting and cultural events, dances and lectures.[231] Images of the poor of England trudging to dole offices, or peopling unemployed protests, are nowadays iconic reminders of those hardships; but the Depression was global and it threw ordinary Europeans out of work in the eastern colonies too. Although in Shanghai and Hong Kong, members had a further opportunity for showing financial power and acuity in the face of Depression, they also had to look to the unemployed Europeans and beachcombers on their own doorsteps.

During the Second World War, the RSStG once more opened up a variety of patriotic funds. In the East, of course, this was particularly tense, with the Malay Peninsula, where various such groups existed and raised money, eventually falling to the Japanese. In the early years of the war, it certainly was fund-raising business as usual.[232] In 1941, for example, the Singapore branch of the RSStG raised $1,431 and distributed it to the RSStG: $200 each to the Loyal and Manchester Regiments, with the remainder disbursed by the Command Welfare to isolated units. Requests were also made to spread these funds to units stationed elsewhere on the peninsula, such as the appropriately named East Surreys (St George's Regiment).[233] Then, of course, the lights went out on Britain's Asian Empire, and the RSStG there fell into darkness too.

The most significant English associational activity during the Second World War – and one that directly linked diaspora and old homeland – came from St George's societies in North America, particularly those of Toronto and New York. Both organizations, as those in Asia and elsewhere, supported the war effort with donations. As is documented in a 1945 report for Toronto, for instance, $3,200.00 had been spent for that purpose since 1939.[234] Such financial support took varied forms, but often comprised a mix of funds taken from contingent funds as well as special subscription lists to which members were invited to contribute. This was an established tradition, as war had long since provided an impetus for contributions. The Second Anglo-Boer War, for example, led to a big push to raise funds for widows and orphans. Hence, at the meeting of 15 December 1899, Baltimore's St George's Society agreed to further meetings and produced a fund-raising handbill which was sent out to members urging them to contribute to 'the fund being raised under the auspices of the St. George's Society for the benefit of WIDOWS AND ORPHANS of soldiers and sailors in the South African War'.[235] In the final meeting of the year, with new members signing up in comparatively large numbers, the Society heard that the fund for South Africa had reached $1009.90, which became £250. A draft for that amount was handed to the Lord Mayor of London, who was treasurer of the Mansion House Fund. During the First World War the Society continued these efforts, raising large amounts of money for the 'Prince of Wales Fund' to help widows and orphans of 'British soldiers and sailors killed in the disastrous war now being waged'.[236] Elsewhere, in the 1920s, the Toronto Society supported the United British Relief Committee, while, in 1940, a contribution was made to the Lord Mayor of London Fund for Relief of War Victims.[237] More pertinently, however, and by the Toronto Society's own assessment, the sums thus dispensed 'by no means represent[s] our full effort, the major contribution having been the taking of children into members' homes'.[238]

This initiative was born in the summer of 1940, when a special sub-committee was appointed in late June 1940. At that point thirty-one English evacuee children were already placed in homes, but the new sub-committee was meant to give the initiative a clear organizational voice within the Toronto St George's Society, also formalizing processes and adequately recording decisions.[239] In particular, the sub-committee was concerned with locating homes for children – customarily doing so, in the first instance, by writing to members to see if they could host a child – and the children's welfare while in Canada. This involved regular reporting on each child's progress and well-being, and the provision of financial support. Moreover, the Toronto Society also informed the RSStG in London of these plans, asking 'if we could do anything to assist them'. It was as a result of this offer that 'some English boys' were 'placed

in excellent homes of our members'. As a number of the children arrived
with their mothers, and evacuee women were generally also seen as vulnerable and victims of the war, the Society extended its remit and also
began aiding a number of Englishwomen. As was explained, 'and though
originally we had only children in mind, our policy has been broadened
to include adults, as it was felt this would be the wish of the members'.
This was the case in particular because these women were not to blame
for their own situation – most were 'in financial distress, on account of
government restrictions on sending of money to Canada'.[240] One such
case was that of a Mrs Blanche Richards. While keen to make ends
meet herself, she was plagued by a number of illnesses that prevented
her from working. As was reported, a medical assessment revealed that
Mrs Richards a 'suffers from varicose veins and bunions which interfere
with her walking and standing for long periods ... Her general health
is also affected by worry and uncertainty of the future.'[241] The Society
also co-operated with other organizations, most notably the Imperial
Daughters of the Order of Empire, agreeing, for example, to share the
relief costs in certain cases.[242] This extended remit lay in the fact that
the Society could not cater for quite as many children as it had hoped
because of the ban by the British government on sending children.[243]

The sub-committee's work was well received by Society members,
many of whom made special contributions in support of the initiative. In
1940, donations for the evacuee fund amounted to $270.00; this sum was
augmented with another $200.00 transferred from the Society's General
Fund.[244] Particularly notable in these early days of operations were the
donations made by a Mr Charles E. Watson: he was not actually a Society
member, but, in August 1940s, sent his British pension cheque of $18.00
to the Society for the second month in a row, advising that it should be
credited to the evacuee account that the Society was keeping. As was
quite adequately noted in the sub-committee's minutes, '[t]his is a most
touching contribution', and to express that appropriately 'a special letter
was sent to him.'[245]

Some of those who offered homes for evacuee children had received
them via organizations such as the Children's Aid Society, but the
St George's Society still provided support at times of need, for instance in
cases where there was a lack of funds such as that of Mrs Orpwood, who
looked after a fifteen-year-old girl. The Society sent a member to 'ascertain not only the immediate but also future requirements'.[246] Another
common form of support – and one less concerned with the basic
provisions of life than with the bringing of some happiness to evacuee
children – was the provision of Christmas presents for them.[247] John
Gomme, who resided with a Mr W.H. Leak, thus received two books,
and a hockey stick and puck; and for Barbara Willmore, who lived with
a Mrs Haslem, a velocipede was acquired. A card from the St George's

Society was prepared for each present, and, presumably to instil a personal touch, was delivered 'by a member of the sub-committee'.[248] Of one recipient of Christmas presents, John Gomme, we can later learn that he turned eight in October 1941, and that he was 'in excellent health' and, together with Mr Leak's own son, 'attends the Village school'.[249] Gomme stayed with the Leak family for all his time in Canada, and eventually returned home to England in the summer of 1945.[250]

One of the most interesting cases of evacuee children whom the Society looked after was set in motion by a request from England, before drawing on associational networking. It was in the early days of operations that the then president of the RSStG in London, Almeric Paget, Lord Queenborough, sent a cablegram to Toronto, asking if a home could be found for 'two boys, sons of an architect'; so important was this case considered to be that the Toronto Society's president looked after it himself.[251] The two boys in question – Trevor and Peter Morgan – arrived in Toronto in August 1940, and made a temporary home with Judge Coatsworth.[252] Coatsworth, already an old man at that point, was only ever meant to host the boys for a short time, but it seems that something between them just clicked. As was reported in late May 1941, '[t]he boys ... have become in a real sense members of the Coatsworth family. They participate in the Family Worship morning and evening and are keen to take their turn in reading the lesson of the day.'[253] So even at times when it was difficult for Coatsworth to still accommodate the Morgan boys, he eventually always decided to keep them – the bond that had developed was strong, or, in the words of the Society, '[t]he attachment between the family and the boys is mutual and spontaneous.'[254] This remained so even after Judge Coatsworth's death in 1943: while the plan had been to then find a new home for Trevor and Peter, one of Coatsworth's daughters decided it was best for the boys to stay with them.[255] After all, they 'came to Canada to be as free as possible from the hazards of War',[256] and constant moves would hardly have made them feel well looked after. This instance of great care was recognized by the RSStG president in London, who sent a letter of thanks.[257] By 1944 there was talk of the boys returning home to their father in London, but this was not to be as the home 'had been bombed and could not be repaired at present'. And again they remained with the Coatsworth family.[258] This changed only in the summer of 1945. With the end of the war in sight, Trevor Morgan – the younger brother – was first to return home to England. For eighteen-year-old Peter this seems not to have been such an appealing thought, however: he did not wish to return. So concerned were the Coatsworths about his views, believing firmly in the need for Peter to be reunited with his father, that they contacted the Toronto St George's Society to ask for help. After that the Society's chairman 'had a heart to heart talk with Peter', and while he still was not keen to leave, he 'was coming round to the idea that he would have to'. Peter eventually made his way home in September 1945, and 'expressed the thanks of Trevor and himself to St. George's Society of Toronto for what had been done for them'.[259]

When the war was over, almost all evacuees returned home. Having supported evacuees, the Society believed, was not only of benefit to the members who provided a home for them; there was also a wider relevance:

> We know that our members who received children into their homes extended to them the same care and guidance as they gave to their own and this will have benefitted them materially and spiritually. It is our belief that on their return home these children have carried a good report of our Dominion. Several of the boys have stated they intend to return and make this their adopted country.[260]

Homeland and diaspora connections were also exemplified by the activities of the New York St George's Society, which, after the Second World War had ended, sent '[m]ore than TWELVE THOUSAND TOYS and thousands of pounds of candy'[261] across the Atlantic to provide a different type of 'Christmas Cheer'. This was carried out together with mayors in a number of 'industrial cities', including Stoke-on-Trent and Liverpool, though poor parishes in London were also sometimes included, with 'the presents being distributed by the Vicars to their poorest little parishoners'. [262] Moreover, the Society had sent a remarkable 'ONE HUNDRED TONS of clothing … this helping about SEVENTY-FIVE THOUSAND indigent persons over there. Many families of invalid War Veterans have been helped in this way.'[263] Prior to the war's end this type of activity was matched, albeit on a much smaller scale, by initiatives in New York, including, for instance, a co-operation between the New York St George's Society and the city's OSStG lodge. For this the former provided the latter with funds to hold a Christmas party at which seventy British children were entertained, including twenty English refugee children who had been sent to New York by the Edith Gould Foundation.[264]

An 'imagined community' made real

St George's Day celebrations anywhere in the world usually offered a moment for impressive displays of communication between English associations. In 1939, with war against Germany looming and comments made about the ever-growing need for patriotism, over 250 attended the St George's Day dinner at the Raffles Hotel in Singapore. 'Ye Sire-Loin of Olde Englande' was served up to a contingent of notables including the bishop of Singapore, the General Officer Commanding Malaya,

Major-General W.G.S. Dobbie, and the United States Consul-General, K.S. Patton. The American presence prompted the bishop to say that 'all British people wished to include within their family their American cousins',[265] thus showing the emphasis on comity spreading far beyond the Atlantic sphere. Whether an exotic branch, such as this, or a local branch in Huddersfield or Barnsley, messages of goodwill, via cards and telegrams, were received. The archives that exist in Australia and New Zealand and the pages of the RSStG journal reveal that such messages criss-crossed the world in impressive style. Clearly, secretaries in one country noted the names and addresses of secretaries in others, and, as of right, posted out dozens, if not hundreds, of messages of goodwill in remembrance of St George. As well as cards and telegrams of good wishes on St George's days, however, the RSStG also received visitors in London from elsewhere in England, the United States, the Empire and former colonies and many other countries where the English settled and founded St George's societies. Hence, while an 'imagined community' was maintained through messages of goodwill, and while shared beliefs cemented relations between people who never met, there were more direct personal engagements. For a minority did travel and connect; for them diaspora and homeland connections became tangible.

Holidays, business trips and deliberate acts of roots-tourism, as well as official trips made by officers of the RSStG and other associated organizations, ensured a significant degree of personal interaction.[266] And associationalism played a critical part in its facilitation. In 1910, for example, an impressive party of around 700 generally well-to-do Canadian Sons of England and their families embarked on a three-week trip to Britain, where they travelled from London and Bristol through the Midlands and north to Edinburgh, taking in sites of historic interest. These were wealthier folk, whose desire for cultural enrichment and reconnection with the old land were coupled with an attempt to encourage migration to their new homeland. As the *Times* explained, 'each member of the party will try to induce one resident of Great Britain to come to Canada'.[267] Such encouragement was shaped by fears at being overrun by 'a vast influx of foreign emigration', and must therefore be viewed as another instance of Anglo-Saxonist thinking and action.[268] The objective of promoting migration was, it seems, of less importance in the 1920s, when trips were still made. In 1926, for instance, 250 Sons of England left on the Cunard liner *Ascania* from Montreal; their excursion included a tour of London, but also the French and Belgian battlefields.[269] Travellers also came, for reasons of cultural importance, from the further-flung colonies in the southern oceans. For instance, in 1930, James Barrett, RSStG member and president of the International Magna Charta Day Association in Australia, led a tour back home. The travellers were guided under the auspices of the RSStG but were primarily going to take part in celebrations of the charter on 15 June at Runnymede.[270] In 1937, when Mr Quo Tai-chi, Chinese ambassador to the Court of St James in London, gave an address to the RSStG, praising the unity revealed by its existence, his words were reproduced in full in Malaya because the country was a meeting place for Chinese and English.[271] This age of mass and speedy communication, via telegraph and ever-shortening sailing times, made the web connections more obvious and easier to manage.

Less lofty men and women than the Chinese ambassador also made the pilgrimage to the St George's London headquarters. Moreover, not all trips were organized *en masse* like those of the Sons of England. Fortunately, the RSStG maintained a partial and rather haphazard visitors' book, which survives for the period of the 1950s. This shows that members and associates from all over the world had occasion to check in with headquarters in these years. Australia, New Zealand and Canada predominated, with members from Mexico, Brazil, Ireland and Northern Ireland also well represented. Visitor numbers were not large, and it is plausible to surmise that these were sojourning officers from elsewhere who stopped by to meet the London officers. They certainly did not only appear around St George's Day. In fact, those from the Antipodes tended to arrive in August when it was winter Down Under. Of the seventy-eight visitors listed for the years 1952–54, most came from England, with five from Canada, thirteen from Australia and seven from New Zealand, and other more exotic travellers came from Brazil (five), the United States, Mexico, Persia, Tanganyika and Singapore.[272]

Small, distant branches, such as that of the New Zealand town of Palmerston North, tell us much about the way a global society such as the RSStG functioned. Close communication was maintained with headquarters in London. This branch was set up according to the strictest reading of the RSStG rules and regulations, and obeying conventions relating to claims to royal patronage, the new society, in 1951, received official permission to use the 'Royal' prefix from the Governor-General, and also received official sanction from Godfrey Laws, General Secretary in London.[273] Within its archive, the neatly typed 'rules and bye-laws' included a list of dates, which were clearly intended for dutiful observation:

St George's Day – 23 April
Empire Day – 24 May
Battle of Britain Day – 15 September
Magna Charta Day – 15 June
Trafalgar Day – 21 October 21
Remembrance Day – 11 November

This branch also maintained personal connection to the London centre. The Palmerston North branch sent someone to the London headquarters five or six times in the 1950s and 1960s. In 1954, it was Mrs Betty Jessop, the wife of a society councilman, Stuart Jessop, who signed the book.[274] In 1960, the branch's long-serving president, Mr C.W. Teppett, a close associate of Mrs Jessop's husband, also signed in with the Society in London.[275]

Such personal interactions undoubtedly forged bonds, but they also provided inspiration for the expression of common views. Empire was first celebrated during the Edwardian period; but, as an official event, it was only beyond Britain's own shores. The population at home began to mark the day, 24 May, the anniversary of Queen Victoria's birthday, only in the 1920s and 1930s. It is unsurprising that those who were in Empire should have marked it with most purpose. To the members of the RSStG in 1950s New Zealand, it marked the fitting union of monarchy and Empire, since 'the Throne had always been the unifying factor'. Interestingly, the Palmerston North RSStG president, Mr C.W. Teppett, also saw Empire Day as part of the education of the colonies of the Commonwealth 'in one of the vital essentials of independence, the fundamentals of government'.[276]

Conclusion

The global St George's tradition was, and remains, part of an international network of kindred organizations declaring a common patriotism and national identity alongside a larger interest in the English-speaking world. The network of organizations was not restricted to the RSStG, though that was the most impressive and persistent in the twentieth century. Indeed, great strength and durability was found in the ability of the RSStG to unite with the Sons of England, the Order of St George and unaffiliated individual St George's societies, such as New York's, and to find common cause with the Anglican Church, the English-Speaking Union and the International Magna Charta Day Association and others. Like iron filings attracted to a magnet, the forces of a global Englishness drew the constituent elements together from the Victorian period when the Empire, facing both internal and external threats, simultaneously witnessed possible strength through unity with the Americans in what became an English-speaking world rather than a British world. The RSStG thus was one of a number of organizations that might be presented as loyalist, patriotic and imperialist but also pro-American. Indeed, the RSStG was primarily concerned with the idea of Englishness and the fomentation of a value system and shared beliefs that could be called 'English'; it was not concerned with charity and mutual aid, though it sometimes raised funds, applauded others for doing so and happily carried advertisements and stories to this effect in its publication.

Whether they were charities, mutual aid societies or cultural organizations like the RSStG, there was shared ground. Unity of purpose at the level of pro-English propaganda and campaigning brought groups together, something that was operationalized through the structures provided globally by these associations. The monarchy, certainly at the end of Victoria's reign and prior to the outbreak of the First World War, remained a crucial anchor in this global world. Particularly potent for the generation of a common goal was, however, war. It was during the two world wars that English associations generated unprecedented levels of transnational connection around the world through their efforts to contribute to war relief, linking Englishmen and Englishwomen overseas back to the old homeland in very direct ways. This, there can be no question, is a fundamental characteristic of a diaspora, and an active one at that.

Notes

1 *North China Herald*, 29 April 1910.
2 *The English Race*, December 1921, p. 6. Cecil was Unionist MP for Oxford University and supporter of various inter-war pacifist movements. He lined up, in 1922, as principal speaker at the Lord Mayor of Belfast's Empire Day demonstrations. David H. Hume, 'Empire Day in Ireland, 1896–1962', in Keith Jeffery (ed.), *An Irish Empire?* (Manchester, 1996), p. 159.
3 J.R. Seeley, *The Expansion of England: Two Courses of Lectures* (London, 1883: Chicago, 1971), p. 13.
4 Robert J.C. Young, *The Idea of English Ethnicity* (New York, 2008), pp. 1–2. Declan Kiberd ascribes similar powers to Irish-America: *Inventing Ireland: The Literature of the Modern Nation* (London, 1995).
5 Krishan Kumar, *The Making of English National Identity* (Cambridge, 2003), pp. 170ff discusses Seeley extensively.
6 Seeley, *The Expansion of England*, pp. 40, 63; Kumar, *Making of English National Identity*, p. 189.
7 CTA, Series 1093, StGS Toronto, File 26, Monthly Meetings Minutes, 1908–20, 5 May 1916, p. 189.
8 For the most recent study, see Charles V. Reed, *Royal Tourists, Colonial Subjects and the Making of a British World, 1860–1911* (Manchester, 2016).
9 *The English Race*, February 1908, 'A Foreword for Englishmen', p. 3.
10 London, The National Archives, NA/FO/37/1182/137, RP no. 20/1965, *Report of the Commission of Enquiry in the Secret Organizations*, part II, 13-30, pp. 2–4.
11 Ibid., 12, p. 2. See also Sons of England, *Proceedings of Conference held at Grahamstown, October 1888* (Grahamstown, 1888), p. 3; Sons of England, *Minutes of the Conference of Delegates held at Graham's Town, Cape Colony, November 24 and 25, 1891* (King William's Town, 1891), pp. 1, 5.
12 Sons of England, *Proceedings of Conference held at Grahamstown, October 1888*, p. 5.

13 'M. W. Grand President's Report', in Sons of England, *Report of the Sixth Annual Meeting of the Grand Lodge Sons of England Benevolent Society (South Africa). Held in Council Chamber, Port Elizabeth, Wednesday, Thursday and Friday August 25th, 26th and 27th, 1897* (Port Elizabeth, 1897), p. 4.

14 Sons of England, *Report of the Fourth Annual Meeting of the Grand Lodge, held in the St Alban's Lodge Room, Grahamstown, Thursday and Friday, Aug. 8th and 9th, 1895* (King William's Town, 1895), p. 4.

15 'President's Report', in Sons of England, *Report of the First Annual Meeting of the Grand Lodge Sons of England Benevolent Society, South Africa, held in the Town Hall, Port Elizabeth, Thursday, Friday and Saturday, October 21, 22, 23, 1892* (King William's Town, 1892), p. 4; lodge information, p. 10.

16 'MW Grand President's Report', in Sons of England, *Report of the Fifth Annual Meeting of the Grand Lodge (South Africa) Sons of England Benevolent Society, held in the Jubilee Lodge Room, King William's Town, Wednesday, Thursday and Friday August 20th, 21st and 22nd, 1896* (King William's Town, 1896), p. 3.

17 *Record*, 16 October 1899, p. 4.

18 Ibid., 15 November 1899, p. 7.

19 London, The National Archives, NA/FO/37/1182/137, RP no. 20/1965, *Commission of Enquiry*, 13, p. 2. Roman? See above.

20 Joanna Trollope, *Britannia's Daughters: Women of the British Empire* (London, 1983), and Julia Bush, *Edwardian Ladies and Imperial Power* (London, 2000); Eliza Riedi, 'Women, Gender, and the Promotion of Empire: The Victoria League, 1901–1914', *Historical Journal*, 45:3 (2002), pp. 569–99; Katie Pickles, 'A Link in "the great chain of friendship": The Victoria League in New Zealand', *Journal of Imperial and Commonwealth History*, 33:1 (2005), pp. 29–50, and Katie Pickles, *Female Imperialism and National Identity: Imperial Order Daughters of the Empire* (Manchester, 2002); E. van Heyningen and P. Merrett, '"The Healing Touch": The Guild of Loyal Women of South Africa, 1900-1912', *South African Historical Journal*, 47 (November 2002), pp. 24–50.

21 See Lesley C. Robinson, 'Englishness in England and the "Near Diaspora": Organisation, Influence and Expression, 1880s-1970s', unpublished PhD thesis, University of Ulster, 2014, ch. 2 and passim for the foundations.

22 It is important to note, however, that ethnic associationalism was generally slower to develop in Australia. The Scots took their time too, and the earliest associational formations they established, such as the St Andrew's Society of South Australia, were short-lived; see Tanja Bueltmann, *Clubbing Together: Ethnicity, Civility and Formal Sociability in the Scottish Diaspora to 1930* (Liverpool, 2014), ch. 3. It was only in the second half of the nineteenth century, and when Caledonian Games emerged as a critical activity, that the Scots established enduring ethnic associational roots in Australia.

23 Letter from 'An Englishman' to *The Argus*, 24 December 1884.

24 Sons of England, *Proceedings of Conference held at Grahamstown, October 1888*, p. 5.

25 *Grahamstown Journal*, 25 April 1908.

26 *Madras Mail*, 20 April 1888; *Rhodesia Herald*, 24 April 1890; *Pioneer*, 13 June 1900.

27 *Central African Times* (Blantyre, Malawi), 12 November 1904, 14 January; 11, 12, 25 March; 1, 29 April 1905; 14 April 1906; 3 April 1907.

28 For example *Central African Times*, 29 April 1905; *Bulawayo Chronicle*, 2 May 1903.

29 Royal Society of St George, *Annual Report and Yearbook of the Royal Society of St George* (London, 1906), pp. 46–54.

30 *Central African Times*, 12 November 1904, 14 January; 11, 12, 25 March; 1, 29 April 1905; 14 April 1906; 3 April 1907.

31 *Rhodesia Herald*, 1 April 1912; *East African Standard*, 19, 26 April 1913;

32 *East African Standard*, 25 April 1914.

33 *Uganda Herald*, 27 March, 24 April 1914.

34 *Bulawayo Chronicle*, 30 August 1918.

35 *The English Race*, March 1924, p. 48. There were 57 branches in 1906, including four in Ireland: Cork, Limerick, Dublin and Londonderry. Royal Society of St George, *Annual Report and Yearbook of the Royal Society of St George* (London, 1906), pp. 21–44. The Society's journal listed 21 branches in 1930 and 1931, and 22 in 1933. *The English Race*, March 1930, p. ii; July 1931; 55 January 1932, p. iii. We thus see considerable fluctuations.

36 For example *The English Race*, July 1932, p. ii; also January 1933, p. ii.

37 Reporting events in Cape Town: *Bulawayo Chronicle*, 2 May 1903.

38 *Beira Post*, 5 May 1909, 27 April 1910.

39 *Rhodesia Herald*, 25 April 1919, 28 April 1922.

40 John Lambert, 'Maintaining a British Way of Life: English Speaking South Africa's Patriotic, Cultural and Charitable Associations', *Historia*, 54:2 (2009), pp. 55–76.

41 John Lambert, 'South African British? Or Dominion South Africans? The Evolution of an Identity in the 1910s and 1920s', *South African Historical Journal*, 43:1 (2000), p. 206; John Lambert, '"An unknown people": Reconstructing British South African Identity', *Journal of Imperial and Commonwealth History*, 37:4 (2009), pp. 599–617.

42 Gary B. Magee and A.S. Stewart, *Empire and Globalisation: Networks of People, Goods and Capital in the British World, c.1850-1914* (Cambridge, 2010), pp. 87–88.

43 *Argus*, 19 March 1847. Though Mr Booth, an early English settler noted that St George's Day was marked as early as '1842 or thereabouts'. *Herald* (Melbourne), 2 July 1897.

44 There certainly is evidence of such triggers for the formation of English ethnic associations elsewhere: see Gillian I. Leitch, 'The Importance of Being English: English Ethnic Culture in Montreal, c.1800–1864', in Tanja Bueltmann, David T. Gleeson and Donald M. MacRaild (eds), *Locating the English Diaspora, 1500–2010* (Liverpool, 2012).

45 *South Australian Register* (Adelaide), 18 January 1845; *Courier* (Hobart), 23 April 1851, 16 May 1851.

46 *Sydney Morning Herald*, 9 December 1893; *West Australian* (Perth), 24 June 1898, 28 April 1900; *Brisbane Courier*, 25 October 1904, 1 February 1913; *Camperdown Chronicle*, 1 May 1913.
47 The Australian version still exists: http://www.royalsocietyofstgeorge.com.au/ (last accessed 18 March 2016).
48 See for example *Colonist* (Nelson), 24 April 1903.
49 For example announcements in the press: *Colonist*, 19 April 1887; *Star* (Auckland), 24 April 1903.
50 *Nelson Examiner and New Zealand Chronicle*, 7 May 1859; *Daily Southern Cross*, 28 February 1860, 17 April 1860, 23 April 1861.
51 Miles Fairburn, The Ideal Society and its Enemies: Foundations of Modern New Zealand Society, 1850–1900 (Auckland, 1989). For an opposing view, see Tanja Bueltmann, *Scottish Ethnicity and the Making of New Zealand Society, 1850–1930* (Edinburgh, 2011).
52 *Wellington Independent*, 22 April 1872; *Colonist* (Nelson), 19 April 1887; *Poverty Bay Herald* (Gisborne), 14 April 1896.
53 *Thames Star*, 29 October 1907.
54 *Hawaiian Gazette*, 29 April 1868.
55 *Madras Mail*, 14 October 1869.
56 *Straits Times*, 12 April 1904. The *North China Herald* reported receipt of these each year. See e.g. 28 April 1905.
57 *North China Herald*, 24 April 1901.
58 Ibid., 2 October 1902.
59 Ibid., 5 October 1906.
60 Ibid., 15 April 1907.
61 Ibid., 26 April 1910.
62 Robert Bickers, *Britain in China: Community, Culture and Colonialism, 1900–49* (Manchester, 1999), passim.
63 *Ceylon Observer*, 25 April 1901.
64 *North China Herald*, 30 May 1908.
65 Obituary, *Times*, 27 May 1941.
66 H. Lu, *Beyond the Neon Lights: Everyday Shanghai in the Early Twentieth Century* (Berkeley, 2004), p. 141; e.g. officers listed in *North China Herald*, 14 April 1910.
67 *North China Herald*, 15 March 1913.
68 Ibid., 16 December 1911.
69 Ibid., 1 June 1912; 28 December 1912.
70 *The English Race*, February 1908, p. 45; or from the Shanghai branch, December 1919, p. 50.
71 Though the Singapore branch went on a concerted recruitment drive when only sixty-two members paid their 1930 subscriptions. *Straits Times*, 11 February 1930; 12 March 1930.
72 Ibid., 27 June 1941.
73 For example ibid., 28 April 1930; *Singapore Free Press*, 29 April 1931.
74 *Straits Times*, 9 February 1923.
75 Ibid., 9 February 1925, 3 February 1927. Also *Singapore Free Press and Mercantile Advertiser*, 4 February 1935.

76 *Straits Times*, 9 February 1925; 10 June 1925.

77 Ibid., 13 February 1933, 24 April 1937.

78 *North China Herald*, 1 May 1926.

79 Ibid., 1 May 1926.

80 *Straits Times*, 9 February 1926.

81 Ibid., 22 January 1929.

82 Ibid., 19 February 1932; *Singapore Free Press*, 27 April 1932.

83 *Straits Times*, 9 February 1932.

84 *Singapore Free Press and Mercantile Advertiser*, 9 December 1930; *Straits Times*, 8 November 1932.

85 *Singapore Free Press and Mercantile Advertiser*, 15 November 1932.

86 *Straits Times*, 16 September 1933.

87 *Singapore Free Press*, 7 November 1933; *Straits Times*, 2 March, 16 November 1934.

88 *Straits Times*, 24 April 1937, 14 October 1937.

89 Hanael P. Bianchi, 'St George's Day: A Cultural History', unpublished PhD thesis, Catholic University of America, 2011, p. 223.

90 Ibid., p. 222.

91 *Madras Mail*, 20 March 1888.

92 Loughton, Essex, RSStG Headquarters, RSStG, minutes 1896–1901, 5 February 1901; Robinson, 'Englishness in England'.

93 W. Besant, 'The Atlantic Union', *The Forum*, October 1900, pp. 245–56; also W. Besant, *Autobiography of Sir Walter Besant: With a prefatory note by S. Squire Sprigg* (New York, 1902), p. 270.

94 *Mafeking Mail*, 15 May 1901; *Rhodesia Herald*, 18 May 1910.

95 *Rhodesia Herald*, 24 April 1900.

96 Sir George Sprigg at consecutive St George's Society events in Cape Town: *Pioneer* (Allahabad), 13 June 1900; *Mafeking Mail and Protectorate Guardian*, 15 May 1901. K.T. Surridge, *Managing the South Africa War, 1899–1902* (London, 1998), ch. 4.

97 *Morning Chronicle*, 24 April 1900.

98 *Hampshire Advertiser*, 25 April 1900.

99 *Essex County Standard*, 28 April 1900; *West Suffolk Gazette, and Eastern Counties Advertiser*, 28 April 1900.

100 Young, *Idea of English Ethnicity*.

101 *Ceylon Observer*, 10 April 1902.

102 Ibid., 26 October 1905.

103 *Record*, 15 October 1897, p. 51.

104 *Grahamstown Journal*, 22 October 1922; *Bulawayo Chronicle*, 16 October 1914; *Rhodesia Herald*, 16 October 1914; 8, 22 October 1915.

105 *Record*, November 1905, pp. 1–3.

106 John T. Ridge, 'Irish County Societies in New York, 1880–1914', in Ronald H. Bayor and Timothy J. Meagher (eds), *The New York Irish* (Baltimore, 1996), pp. 275–300 (quotation p. 275).

107 Ibid., pp. 277, 279, 287ff. County associations among the Irish were initially the work of relatively comfortable immigrants, for instance the Sligo Young Men's Association (1849), but their appeal broadened as time passed. By the

1870s, New York Irish county associations represented eighteen of the thirty-two counties. While Irish politics drove much of the mid-nineteenth-century effort, the later period focused strongly on sporting rivalries – something we strongly associate with Irish counties today.

108 English regional migrant legacies are briefly discussed in Jock Phillips and Terry Hearn, *Settlers: New Zealand Immigrants from England, Ireland and Scotland, 1800–1945* (Auckland, 2008), pp. 167–68. See also Raewyn Dalziel, 'Popular Protest in Early New Plymouth: Why did it Occur?', *New Zealand Journal of History*, 20:1 (1986), pp. 3–26; Brad Patterson, 'Cousin Jacks, New Chums and Ten Pound Poms: Locating New Zealand's English Diaspora', in Bueltmann, Gleeson and MacRaild (eds), *Locating the Hidden Diaspora*.

109 *Evening Post* (Wellington), 2 November 1895. On county societies, see James Watson, 'English Associationalism in the British Empire: Yorkshire Societies in New Zealand before the First World War', *Britain and the World*, 4 (2011), pp. 84–108.

110 *Evening Post*, 16 January 1896; also 2 July 1898, 23 December 1913.

111 Ibid., 19 October 1909; 31 January 1933; 22 February, 3 April 1936; 28 April 1936; 25 November 1937, 16 December 1937; 24 April 1939.

112 *North China Herald*, 16 January 1901.

113 Ibid., 15 April 1904, 1 December 1905, 9 November 1906, 19 April 1907, 22 November 1907, 14 November 1908, 27 February 1908, 13 November 1909, 1 April 1910, 24 April 1911; they resumed post-war and the press continued once more to report at least one event each year, e.g. *North China Herald*, 4 April 1922.

114 'England's Day', *Straits Times*, 12 April 1904.

115 *North China Herald*, 5 August 1904.

116 Ibid., 16 November 1906.

117 Robinson, 'Englishness in England', ch. 2.

118 *The English Race*, December 1936, p. 5.

119 Ibid., p. 13.

120 Ibid., 33 (December 1921), p. 45.

121 Wellington, Archives New Zealand, NZ, AEFZ/W5727/22620/171, RSStG Palmerston North, 1951–52, 'Rules', 11'December 1951, Rule 1 (b).

122 Ibid., Rule 3, I Primary Objects (a).

123 *The original painting of Her Majesty, Queen Victoria the First, painted by Mr. Thomas Sully, expressly for 'The Society of the Sons of St. George' Philadelphia* (Philadelphia, 1839). The painting was mentioned as being placed behind the president's chair in the City Hotel, Philadelphia; see *Philadelphia Inquirer*, 29 April 1842. Also see J. Thomas Scharf and Thompson Westcott, *History of Philadelphia, 1609–1884*, 3 vols (Philadelphia, 1884), vol. 2, p. 1048. Elisa Tamarkin, Anglophilia: *Deference, Devotion, and Antebellum America* (Chicago, 2008) discusses the art-historical and psycho-sexual dimensions of the painting.

124 *Philadelphia Inquirer*, 24 April 1862.

125 *Anglo-American Times*, 19 November 1886, p. 6.

126 *Southern Literary Messenger*, 5 (1839), p. 525.

127 MdHS, MS 1881, StGS Baltimore, Minutes, President's Address, 3 February 1879, p. 1.
128 *Royal Gazette*, 6 November 1860.
129 See Tamarkin, *Anglophilia*, passim, for a rich study of this phenomenon.
130 *Philadelphia Inquirer*, 24 April 1862.
131 For example *Montreal Gazette*, 24 April 1878.
132 *Hawaiian Gazette*, 29 April 1868.
133 Greg King, *Twilight of Splendour: The Court of Queen Victoria during her Diamond Jubilee* (London, 2007), p. 2.
134 Ibid., p. 4; Reed, *Royal Tourists*, pp. 35–76.
135 Clarissa Campbell Orr, 'The Feminization of the Monarchy, 1780–1910: Royal Masculinity and Female Empowerment', in Andrzej Olechnowicz (ed.), *The Monarchy and the British Nation, 1780 to the Present* (Cambridge, 2007), p. 92.
136 Helen Rappaport, *Queen Victoria: A Biographical Companion* (Santa Barbara, CA, 2003), p. 135.
137 Richard Koebner, *Imperialism* (Cambridge, 1964), pp. 119, 120.
138 Ian St John, *Disraeli and the Art of Politics* (London, 2005), p. 187.
139 David Cannadine, *Ornamentalism: How the British Saw their Empire* (London, 2001), p. 46.
140 This permanence would already be breaking down by the 1920s and was removed in a new bill in the 1950s, with the accession of Queen Elizabeth II. Cannadine, *Ornamentalism*, p. 159.
141 George F. Savage-Armstrong, *Victoria, Regina et Imperatrix: A jubilee Song from Ireland, 1887* (London, 1887); Ada Barker, *Victoria Regina et Imperatrix, June 20, 1897* (London, 1897); and Thomas Jenner, *Victoria Regina et Imperatrix: A Diamond Jubilee Ode in Sixty Lines* (London, 1897).
142 Thomas Richards, *The Commodity Culture of Victorian England: Advertising and Spectacle, 1851–1914* (Stanford, CA, 1991), p. 116.
143 *Los Angeles Times*, 6 April 1887.
144 *New York Times*, 22 January 1887.
145 *Leeds Mercury*, 25 April 1887.
146 *Chicago Times*, 22 June 1887.
147 *Times*, 24 June 1887.
148 *Royal Gazette*, 28 June 1887.
149 Richards, *Commodity Culture*, pp. 115–16.
150 Canberra, National Archives of Australia, A2/1904/2695, RSStG, letter from secretary, J.C. Langley, to the prime minister, 26 November 1904.
151 *A sketch of how 'the diamond anthem' was sung around the world through the colonies of the empire on the 20th June 1897. Being an extract from the annual report of the supreme grand president of the Sons of England, given at St Catherine's, Canada, 8th March 1898* (Toronto, 1898), p. 1.
152 *Daily Mail and Empire* (Toronto), 15 April 1897.
153 *Record*, 15 December 1896, p. 10.
154 Ibid., 15 February 1897, p. 4.
155 Ibid., 15 April 1897, pp. 1, 4.
156 *A sketch*, p. 1.

157 *Record*, 15 July 1897, p. 15; large item in *Daily Mail and Empire*, 15 April 1897, illustrating that plans had passed beyond the confines of the Society itself.
158 *Record*, 15 December 1897, p. 78.
159 Ibid., 15 May 1897, p. 1.
160 Ibid., 15 June 1897, p. 9.
161 Ibid., p. 2.
162 *Evening Telegram* (St John's, Newfoundland), 4 May 1897.
163 Sons of England, *Diamond Jubilee of Her Majesty Queen Victoria, Sunday, 20th June, 1897: Sons of England Service to be Held in Continuous Succession through the British Colonies around the World* (n.p., 1897).
164 *Record*, 15 August 1897, p. 27. Later the Sons of England helped to raise money for a 'Diamond Jubilee Memorial Church' there in celebration of Levuka, having marked the starting point of the anthem; see *Record*, January 1901, p. 2.
165 *West Coast Times* (Hokitika), 21 June 1897; *Otago Witness* (Dunedin), 24 June 1897; *Clutha Leader* (Balclutha), 25 June 1897; *Tuapeka Times* (Lawrence), 23 June 1897; *Mataura Ensign* (Gore), 24 June 1897; *Star* (Christchurch), 25 June 1897.
166 *Mercury* (Hobart), 21 June 1897; *Argus* (Melbourne), 21 June 1897.
167 *West Australian*, 1 and 21 June 1897 (quotation from the latter); *Western Mail* (Perth), 4 June 1897.
168 *A sketch*, pp. 2–3.
169 *Milwaukee Sentinel*, 20 June 1897; *Galveston Daily News*, 23 June 1897.
170 *Weekly News and Courier* (Charleston), 30 June 1897.
171 For instance *Forth Worth Register*, 14 May 1897.
172 *Daily Mail and Empire*, 17 June 1897.
173 *Record*, 15 July 1897, pp. 15–17, 20–21, 24.
174 'MW Grand President's Report', in *Report of the Sixth Annual Meeting of the Grand Lodge Sons of England Benevolent Society (South Africa). Held in Council Chamber, Town Hall, Port Elizabeth, Wednesday, Thursday and Friday, August 25th, 26th and 27th, 1897* (Port Elizabeth, 1897), p. 4.
175 *Record*, 15 July 1897, p. 24.
176 Ibid., p. 15.
177 Ibid., 15 June 1898, p. 3.
178 Ibid., 2:15 December 1897, p. 78.
179 See Paul Ward, *Britishness since 1870* (London, 2004), ch. 1.
180 *Record*, 15 August 1897, pp. 27–29, 36.
181 Ibid., 15 September 1897, pp. 39–40.
182 According to members of Scottsdale, Tasmania that claimed their own Walter Besant was behind the day. *The English Race*, February 1908, p. 53; and in an article, 'Mr Asquith and Empire Day', *The English Race*, September 1913, pp. 5–6.
183 Susan Fisher, *Boys and Girls in No Man's Land: English-Canadian Children and the First World War* (Toronto, 2010), pp. 62, 82–89, 128.
184 A lengthy two-page item in *North China Herald*, 13 March 1909.
185 A claim made by the Barnsley and Warnambool, Victoria, branches, *The English Race*, August 1913, pp. 28, 43–44.

186 Ibid.
187 Daniel Francis, *National Dreams: Myths, Memory and Canadian History* (Vancouver, 1997), p. 66.
188 Details from Jeffrey Roberts, *Imperialism and Music: Britain, 1876-1953* (Manchester, 2002), ch. 5, esp. p. 165; J. English, 'Empire Day in Britain, 1904-1958', *Historical Journal*, 44:1 (2006), pp. 247-76. Examples of RSStG pressure for the day to be marked officially include an essay 'St George for England's Empire', *The English Race*, September 1913, pp. 13-14.
189 Anna S. Rush, *Bonds of Empire: West Indians and Britishness from Victoria to Decolonization* (Oxford, 2011), pp. 38, 56, 59, 61, 156.
190 Roberts, *Imperialism and Music*, pp. 166ff.
191 Simon J. Potter, *Broadcasting Empire: The BBC and the British World, 1922-1970* (Oxford, 2012), pp. 16, 28, 52, 63, 69, 70, 75, 100, 161, 169.
192 Wendy Webster, 'The Empire Comes Home: Commonwealth Migration to Britain', in Andrew Thompson (ed.), *Britain's Experience of Empire in the Twentieth Century*, Oxford History of the British Empire Companion Series (Oxford, 2012), p. 149. J.A. Mangan, '"The Grit of our Foregathers": Invented Traditions, Propaganda and Imperialisms', in John M. MacKenzie (ed.), *Imperialism and Popular Culture* (Manchester, 1986), pp. 113-39.
193 *The English Race*, April 1908, p. 23.
194 Hume, 'Empire Day in Ireland', pp. 149-68.
195 *North China Herald*, 13 November 1903, 13 November 1909, 10 June 1916. The same paper reported similar notes of congratulations and thanks on 9 and 16 June 1917 and 16 November 1918.
196 Ibid., 12 May 1905.
197 For example 'Empire Day', *The English Race*, April 1914, p. 10. Indeed, they had deprecated the use of Victoria's birth date since 1905, they claimed.
198 *North China Herald*, 15 April 1911.
199 Ibid., 22 April 1922.
200 *Ashburton Guardian*, 24 April 1913.
201 *Sydney Morning Herald*, 27 April 1904; also *New York Times*, 24 April 1901.
202 *North China Herald*, 29 April 1911.
203 Treasurer's Annual Report, MdHS, MS 1881, StGS Baltimore, Minutes, 18 January 1915.
204 Examples for 1915 and 1916: CTA, Series 1093, StGS Toronto, File 26, Monthly Meetings Minutes, 1908-20, minutes of the 84th and 85th Annual General Meetings, 5 March 1915, 4 February 1916, 11 May 1917, pp. 155, 171, 224-25.
205 CTA, Series 1093, StGS Toronto, File 26, Monthly Meetings Minutes, 1908-20, 'Committee and Stewards Report', 14 May 1915, p. 158.
206 MdHS, Minutes, vol. 4, n.d. [26 July?], pp. 78-79.
207 John L. Sanford, *History of the St George's Society of Baltimore* (Baltimore, 1929), p. 14.
208 J. Saxon Mills, *The Gathering of the Clans: How the British Dominions and Dependencies have Helped in the War* (London, 1916).
209 In StGS records, Charleston, South Carolina, South Carolina Historical Society, 1124.00.

210 MdHS, MS 1881, StGS Baltimore, letter from Alexander B. Gillespie, secretary and treasurer of the Society, to Mr James Holland, 11 January 1915, in the leaf of Minutes, 18 April 1901.

211 Ibid. letter from Walter Peacock, Buckingham Palace, to A.B. Gillespie, 1 December 1916, in the leaf of Minutes, 18 January 1909.

212 MdHS, MS 1881, StGS Baltimore, Minutes, 18 January, 19 April, 26 July 1915; letter from Walter Peacock to A.B. Gillespie, 1 December 1916, list of members and their contributions to the Prince of Wales Fund.

213 *North China Herald*, 20 March 1915.

214 Ibid., 15 and 29 April 1916.

215 *North China Herald*, 6 May 1916.

216 *The English Race*, May 1915, pp. 36, 38; also August 1915, p. 26.

217 Something with wide resonance beyond the English ethnic group: Monika Smialkowska, 'An Englishman in New York? Celebrating Shakespeare in America, 1916', in Bueltmann, Gleeson and MacRaild (eds), *Locating the English Diaspora*); and Monika Smialkowska, 'Conscripting Caliban: Shakespeare, America, and the Great War', *Shakespeare*, 7:2 (2011), pp. 192–207.

218 CTA, Series 1093, StGS Toronto, File 26, Monthly Meetings Minutes, 1908–20, 5 May 1916, p. 188.

219 *North China Herald*, 7 April 1917; *The English Race*, December 1918, p. 15. *North China Herald*, 6 May 1916.

220 Ibid., 7 July 1917.

221 *Mafeking Mail*, 24 April 1917; *Rhodesia Herald*, 27 April 1917.

222 *North China Herald*, 3 August 1918.

223 *The English Race*, May 1915, p. 45.

224 *North China Herald*, 8 March 1919.

225 Extract of a resolution of a meeting of the RSStG, Adelaide, 29 September 1919, Canberra, National Archives of Australia, /1919/10401/A2487.

226 *English-Speaking World*, 3:5 (May 1920), p. 15.

227 Ibid., 3:1 (January 1920), p. 16.

228 *The English Race*, January 1934, p. 36.

229 For example at the 25th festival dinner, of the RSStG in Toowoomba, Queensland, *The English Race*, August 1934, p. 34.

230 *The English Race*, January 1935, pp. 9–10; also September 1936, p. 17. For Hamilton's career, see Donald M. MacRaild, Sylvia Ellis and Stephen Bowman, 'Interdependence Day and Magna Charta: James Hamilton's Public Diplomacy in the Anglo-World, 1907–1940s, *Journal of Transatlantic Studies*, 12:2 (2014), pp. 126–48.

231 *Straits Times*, 9 February 1926, 17 February 1927.

232 Ibid., 25 April 1940.

233 *Singapore Free Press*, 23 April 1923.

234 St George's Society of Toronto, *Report of the Committee for 1945* (Toronto, 1946), p. 14.

235 MdHS, MS 1881, StGS Baltimore, Minutes, 15 December 1899; handbill to members, dated 21 February 1900; also Minutes, 24 February 1900.

236 Ibid., letter from Alexander B. Gillespie to Mr James Holland, 11 January 1915.

237 St George's Society of Toronto, *Report of the Committee for 1940* (Toronto, 1941), p. 31.
238 St George's Society of Toronto, *Report of the Committee for 1945*, p. 14.
239 CTA, Series 1093, StGS Toronto, File 39, Minutes of Meetings of the Sub-Committee on Evacuee Children, 1st Report, 28 June 1940.
240 This and the previous quotations from St George's Society of Toronto, *Report of the Committee for 1940*, p. 13.
241 CTA, Series 1093, StGS, Toronto, File 39, Minutes of Meetings of the Sub-Committee on Evacuee Children, 15th Report, 28 February 1941.
242 See for example ibid., 20th Report, 11 June 1941.
243 St George's Society of Toronto, *Report of the Committee for 1940*, p. 14.
244 Ibid.
245 CTA, Series 1093, StGS Toronto, File 39, Minutes of Meetings of the Sub-Committee on Evacuee Children, 3rd Report, 15 August 1940.
246 Ibid., 5th Report, 27 September 1940.
247 Ibid., 10th Report, 10 December 1940.
248 Ibid., 11th Report, 31 December 1940.
249 Ibid., 24th Report, 17 October 1941.
250 Ibid., 57th Report, October 1945.
251 Ibid., 2nd Report, 16 July 1940.
252 Ibid., 3rd Report, 15 August 1940. Later reports also reference the case of Mrs Morgan, the boys' stepmother, and her nineteen-month-old baby—for them too the president of the RSStG 'cabled to know if we could find temporary accommodation'. This proved problematic, but the sub-committees' accounts document that the Toronto Society tried to do so and supported Mrs Morgan over an extended period.
253 Ibid., 19th Report, 28 May 1941.
254 Ibid., 24th Report, 17 October 1941.
255 Ibid., 39th Report, 3 June 1943.
256 Ibid., 42nd Report, September 1943.
257 Ibid., 44th Report, December 1943.
258 Ibid., 52nd Report, October 1944.
259 Ibid., 57th Report, October 1945.
260 St George's Society of Toronto, *Report of the Committee for 1945*, p. 14.
261 St George's Society of New York, *Annual Report and Constitution St George's Society of New York for the Year 1955* (New York, 1955), p. 11.
262 Ibid.
263 Ibid.
264 St George's Society of New York, *Annual Report and Constitution St George's Society of New York for the Year 1944* (New York, 1944), p. 22.
265 *Straits Times*, 6 May 1939.
266 For Scottish roots-tourism, see Tanja Bueltmann, '"Gentlemen, I am going to the Old Country": Scottish Roots-Tourists in the Late 19th and Early 20th Centuries', in Mario Varricchio (ed.), *Back to Caledonia: Scottish Return Migration from the 16th Century to the Present* (Edinburgh, 2012).
267 *The Times*, 7 July 1910.

268 Goldwin Smith, *The Schism in the Anglo-Saxon Race: An Address delivered before the Canadian Club of New York* (New York, 1887), p. 25; see also Tanja Bueltmann, 'Anglo-Saxonism and the Racialization of the English Diaspora', in Bueltmann, Gleeson and MacRaild (eds), *Locating the English Diaspora*.
269 *Wetaskiwin Times*, 8 July 1926.
270 *Argus* (Melbourne), 4 April 1930.
271 *Straits Times*, 4 January 1937.
272 CTA, StGS Toronto, Visitors to Relief Recipients Book, pp. 1–3, to December 1954.
273 Wellington, Archives New Zealand, NZ, AEFZ/W5727/22620/171, RSStG Palmerston North, 1951–52, letter, 11 January 1951, from M.C. Adams, registrar of Incorporated Societies, Wellington, to John Combe, Palmerston North; letter, 14 August 1951, to John Combe, Palmerston North, from Godfrey W. Laws, London.
274 Palmerston North, New Zealand, Mathieson Archive, RSStG (Inc.), Series 1, 'newspaper cuttings book', in which Stuart Jessop is listed in a newspaper article [n.d., c.early 1950s].
275 CTA, SStG Toronto, Visitors to Relief Recipients Book, 20 August 1960.
276 Palmerston North, Mathieson Archive, newspaper clipping, 'Empire Day. Royal Society of St George' [n.d., c.early 1950s].

Conclusion

On Friday, 5 November 1915, members of the St George's Society of Toronto gathered at their regular monthly meeting. Amid discussions of mundane business matters members heard the obituary of one of their more prominent and active members, the past president James Cooper. Cooper had made his way to Canada in 1845, arriving there from Gainsborough in Lincolnshire as a pioneer – and at a time 'when Canada had hardly emerged from its forest stage'. He rose to be a 'prominent merchant', deciding on his retirement 'to spend his remaining years in the old Land'. Despite his return to England, however, Cooper was still 'deeply interested in all that pertained to the well-being and progress of the city [of Toronto]'.[1] Cooper was a genuine transnational actor in a world that was characterized by the continuous movement not only of goods and people, but also of ideas and culture – there were a multitude of connections crossing the Atlantic even, as Cooper's case shows, beyond death.[2]

Associational culture gave a certain structural order to the transnational and migratory lives of Cooper and his countrymen. The ethnic clubs and societies that English emigrants established in new lands provided critical points of reference in this mobile world, yet the permanence such associations implied could be misleading. The fluidity of migration, trade and social communication across the oceans ensured that these organizations were never fully divorced from the homeland. Transatlantic population flows brought English migrants to the New World but, crucially, worked both ways, also taking a proportion of them back again. Most came with the intention to stay; others used the United States or Canada as an extension of their homeland economic sphere. The miner or engineer, the trader or businessman, went back and forth across the Atlantic and other oceans. Culturally, even in the early days of settlement, English associations continued to connect English migrants, but also their descendants, with England. It was within this structural context that Cooper personified the closeness of the two worlds in the immigrant's life, the old and new homelands, with his personal narrative contextualizing the transnational connections framing our study.

Migration is the lifeblood of our story. While the English who made it to the original thirteen colonies prior to American independence were fundamental to the English story in North America, vastly larger waves came from the 1840s onwards. Spurred by the demand for labour in the ever-expanding United States, builders and skilled workers, but also farmers, were chief among those crossing the Atlantic. They arrived in three distinct waves: the first in the mid-nineteenth century; the second following the American Civil War; and the third between the 1880s and the economic crash of 1893. Thereafter new immigration policies had an impact on numbers. However, even when quotas were introduced, based on existing numbers of each nation's immigrants already in the country, the United Kingdom's allowance fell but was entirely filled on only two occasions in the 1920s (1923 and 1924).[3]

North of the border in Canada large-scale migrations from England generally occurred later. In the early nineteenth century less than 10 per cent of English migrants went to Canada; only after Confederation in 1867 did this begin to change. This pattern was a reflection of the later development, urbanization and settlement expansion in Canada, a fact underscored by the significant increase in English migrant arrival numbers in the early twentieth century. With the westward expansion into the prairie states in these decades came a wave of new arrivals from England. While the First World War generally slowed migration down, political initiatives, such as the 1922 Empire Settlement Act, contributed to a continuing flow.[4]

Migrants to the United States and Canada came from diverse backgrounds. Among them were well-to-do migrants keen to seize business opportunities. Others were from the working class but highly skilled, and thus generally sought after. Some were English, Scottish and Welsh tradesmen, including engineers, instrument-makers, mechanics, toolmakers and many more. But there was also a third group, those with neither skills nor luck: the jobless and poverty-stricken; vulnerable women and children and the old or infirm; others were those who had fallen on hard times and workers in the dying handicrafts, such as handloom weaving. These migrants did not always find better lives abroad, and instead struggled to make ends meet. It was sufferings of the poor within these waves that prompted the establishment of English ethnic associational culture in colonial North America.

From these early days English ethnic associations never operated in isolation. In fact, it is unsurprising that gatherings of Englishmen in different urban centres in North America – and later also beyond it – should have acted in concert. Societies like theirs faced common issues

in accommodating the needs of their countrymen; and so they communicated with each other – between towns, and across state and territorial
borders – to establish co-operative principles and to share knowledge.
A shared sense of patrician benevolence was paramount here: it was
viewed as a duty to help fellow English migrants who were in distress, and
exchange between associations was considered a tool to better enable
organizations to carry out this work. In the late nineteenth century the
NAStGU offered a means to formalize collaboration, seeking inroads
into durable, practical unity by linking local societies transnationally
through its annual, roving conventions. But the tyranny of distance
impacted heavily on the ambition to bring all societies together in this
way. Consequently, the fact is that most attendees at these conventions
came from a quadrant which, if drawn from a compass point in Toronto,
would stretch east as far as Boston, passing south through New York to
Baltimore and then westwards to Chicago. Even then, most attendees
were from Pennsylvania, New York State and Ontario: there was a clear
geographical skew, though this does not mean that Californian societies, for instance, were not part of the federation. They were, but in a
loose way. They communicated their congratulations and best wishes on
St George's Day; and all these societies read out telegrams of fraternity
at their annual dinners. However, getting members across 2,500 miles of
territory into one place in the Mid-West or north-east was never realistic. We must point, then, to the existence of an 'imagined community',[5]
kept together by modern communications and print culture; but not a
community of individual personal connections beyond the core region
described here. In fact, in some ways the concentration of players in that
core region in the east quite appropriately reflects the geographic proliferation of societies there: English ethnic associations were first founded,
and spread most numerously, in that area of North America despite the
general trend of westward expansion that we have seen taking place from
the mid-nineteenth century onwards.

Other weaknesses were also apparent. The St George's societies,
with their emphasis on charity and benevolence disbursed by those
who could afford it, were socially limited. The New York Society, the
Charleston variant (run as it was by a tiny English-born community and
wealthy Americans of English birth) and the larger Sons of St George in
Philadelphia touched upon wider membership bases at times, but were
for the most part socially exclusive. What is critical though is that despite
this clear caveat, these organizations catered for a wider immigrant body
through the aid they dispensed. So while there was a significant level of
social exclusivity and some elitism among members, the work they did
had much wider currency.

What these relief provisions and charity also highlight is that there
were elements of English life in North America that contradict ideas of

easy assimilation. Within the United States in particular scholars have, for too long, assumed the synonymy of American and English cultures and the straightforward assimilation of the immigrant into the host group. But there could be underlying tensions for Englishmen too. Even the wealthy and privileged felt something of it, as Henry E. Pellen, president of the New York St George's Society, implied in 1875, when he wrote to the Earl Dufferin, Governor-General of Canada, to invite him south for St George's Day. Pellen touched on the balance of ethnic expression and assimilation affecting the English. 'The English colony in New York', he told the Governor-General, 'is not so influential as it ought to be: many men out here seem rather afraid of being known as Britons, while others marry into American families and become merged in the single genus.'[6]

Moreover, for ordinary workers the balance of integration, assimilation and ethnic pillarization was delicate. And this is a fact that explains, in part, the emergence of a second strand of English ethnic associationalism, one that was distinctly working class and founded on principles of mutualism; and it was to become the much larger English associational variant in terms of membership and reach. For when faced with the indignity of workingmen extending the cap for charity from elites in the St George's societies, the independently minded English workingmen of Toronto, steeped in the friendly-society traditions of the old country, formed the Sons of England. And when English workers on the Pennsylvanian coalfields came under pressure from Irish proto-trade unionists and secret society members, in the 1860s and 1870s, they responded with their own popular, but initially clandestine, ethnic organization, the Order of the Sons of St George. The English could call upon Welsh and some American support, but were hopelessly outnumbered by the Irish. The Irish, in turn, showed a superior drive to naturalization and a concomitant bulking of their votes in favour of the Democrats. This, in turn, created strong local, Irish political influence, and an impressive communal coalescence and shaped by economic hardship, anti-English/British feeling and growing political nationalism. The English could not match this; but instead of disappearing into the mass of the host population (who in any case had their own reasons for hostility to the British Empire), they tried to counter Irish power and, in so doing, retained a clearly Protestant, English, sectarian ethnic identity that was remarkably durable across the decades. Still, unlike the Irish, these English association members did not have a national struggle to focus their energies.

What persistently defined English organizations, what gave them shape and purpose, whatever age they were formed in or whichever period we explore, was an ideal framed around the desire to help their countrymen, whether as charities or friendly societies. Behind it often lay, most explicitly for mutual societies, the idea of promoting self-help too. But even among the charitable St George's societies this was critical for many: while ad hoc relief in pressing cases was most likely of a monetary kind, many society rules stipulated a preference for more long-term solutions, and for this support that enabled migrants to help themselves. Hence, as well as doling out charity and 'Christmas Cheer', these societies sought out labour-market intelligence, shared news on employment conditions between their towns and warned the press in England when conditions were unsuitable for labour migration. Despite these similarities in outlook, and while the ideal of helping fellow English in distress provided the ultimate definition, it was not sufficient to bind associations together in union: not even the OSStG and Sons of England could fully combine. Although attempts were made to unify the two, in the end they got no further than a few joint meetings and invitations for each other's officers to attend functions.

All other associational activities stemmed from this ideal of benevolence: sociability, celebration, and discussion. Social aspects, which were various, occupied an important position. The sports, excursions, trips, dinners, and other aspects of their activities underpinned the basic financial meaning of these groups, whether elites, middle class or working class. Great store was set by ensuring attendance at dinners and officials functions. Not only did these bind members, but they also inculcated friends and acquaintances with the likely benefits of joining up. Ultimately, celebrating St George was a near-religious event, with the structures of social etiquette and civic profile matched by the pious attendance at a church on the day, or an adjacent Sunday, to reflect upon the Godly, Protestant, nature of what they stood for. Dinners raised money or awareness and made a civic mark; sporting and cultural events brought in income but also attracted members, who, in turn, paid their share. And loyalty to the crown, even in the republican United States, provided critical glue that served to connect not only an association with the Crown, but also with each other. The Sons of England's 'Wave of Song' is the most remarkable example of global, transnational communication fostered by one group, in Toronto, through the networks of English associations and the Anglican Church, with the effect that an orchestrated singing of the national anthem took place from sun-up in Fiji to sun-down on vessels, also in the Pacific. What this rolling celebration that traversed the globe highlighted was that, for all their differences, these English folk shared a common culture, regardless of whether they were an architect recently off the boat, like Edward G. Lind of Baltimore, or the scion of an old colonial-age loyalist family, such as William F. Coffin of Kingston, Ontario. English-born, or of English descent, members of these societies together raised their glasses to toast the Empire, sang 'God Save the Queen' or lines from Gilbert and Sullivan with gusto. But their city, province and land of adoption – their America or Canada – also received due deference. These were civic societies as well as ethnic ones, and their work and their sentiment cut across the simple divisions of birthplace and extended over generations. In combination, the social, benevolent and mutualist activities of the English were impressively wide-ranging. They were a critical feature of civic, associational and ethnic life in the United States and Canada that united different organizations – and this was a feature repeated wherever these English formed their associations.

In Chapter 6 we undertook a comparative assessment of English with Scottish and German ethnic clubs and societies. This exploration confirmed the principal argument made in this study: that English immigrants behaved in the same ethnic ways as other groups; that they did so by employing and exhibiting their ethnicity in similar ways to those adopted by other immigrant groups; and that the strategies English immigrants actively utilized through ethnic associations in order to do so were essentially the same as those of other groups. This significantly strengthens our case that there was an English diaspora when measured in these types of ethnic criteria. Still our comparisons show how the English story could also differ and in what ways it was distinct.

The critical differences between the English and the comparator groups examined – which go some way to explain why the English have been perceived as invisible and weak in many existing studies – is that their ethnic associationalism rested on the fewest number of strands: it was less diverse than that of the Scots and Germans, being based principally on philanthropy and mutualism. This gave English ethnic associations a narrower footing, effectively preventing it from having a more broad-based community appeal. This does not mean that English societies played no civic role – they certainly did so: particularly with respect to charity provisions in support of new migrants. The key difference from other groups was that the English lacked a cultural anchor that could give their associationalism broader appeal. The Scots achieved this with their Highland Games, more specifically through their popularity as a sporting event and the role the Games played in the development of field athletics and sport more broadly. In so doing Scots shaped American sporting culture in ways that significantly transcended their own ethnic group boundaries. The German case is even stronger in this respect than that of the Scots – partly because there simply were more Germans to have an impact, but primarily because it was not just one event they placed on that broader footing. Although initially born out of an ethnic associational culture that was more exclusive by default – simply through the use of German as the associational language by most groups (certainly in the early days) – Germans managed to establish three associational strands that eventually shaped American culture more broadly while also being popular, namely their singing clubs, gymnastics clubs and, to a slightly lesser extent, their rifle clubs. Until the First World War, these German clubs and societies played central roles in communities large and small throughout the United States in particular.

Although English ethnic associationalism failed to achieve this broader appeal, English clubs and societies too increasingly cut across national boundaries: while there generally was a proliferation of English associations around the world, in tune with migratory pathways we find a distinct global turn in the late nineteenth century. This was, in no small part, the result of a heightening of English consciousness at home, undoubtedly partly because of the work of men like Walter Besant, who had lived in the United States and so witnessed the work of St George's societies first hand.[7] His associates, men like H.W. Christmas and Howard Ruff, would take up the cause in the following decade, when, in 1894, the Royal Society of St George was formed. Its immediate intent was to join together a plethora of English associations like these – groups in the United States, Canada, Australasia and South Africa, which had for years joined in marking their distinct national culture. The RSStG never resulted in a true global federation. In fact, it instead became still another component of a perhaps more federated system. However, it brought the English homeland into the equation for the first time, succeeded in rallying some existing societies to its own banner and generally provided a strong colonial and imperial dimension to what had been, until that point, a North American phenomenon.

Our study has found Kumar's concept of imperial nationalism useful when describing the global efflorescence of English societies.[8] Indeed, our research shows the formation and spread of a series of ethnic societies that were fundamentally reliant on imperialism for impetus. Unity of purpose persisted long beyond the halcyon days of Empire. Some of the smallest indicators could speak volumes, for example the connections made through simple logistical efficiencies such as those demonstrated in Wellington, New Zealand, in 2000, when the local RSStG branch was in the habit of meeting as part of the Combined Commonwealth and Kindred Societies. Along with the RSStG itself could be found the Commonwealth Trust, the Early Settlers Association, the English-Speaking Union, the Commonwealth Trust, the Victoria League and the New Zealand Founders Society. Altogether, these represented the perfect encapsulation of New Zealand, its origins and its connections across the world of English-speaking peoples.[9] The global St George's tradition was, and remains, part of an international network of kindred organizations declaring a common patriotism and national identity alongside a larger interest in the English-speaking world. The network of organizations was not restricted to the RSStG, though this was the most impressive and persistent in the twentieth century. Indeed, great strength and durability were found in the ability of the RSStG to unite organizations.

The global turn of the late nineteenth century offers a suitable opportunity to return to the idea of an English diaspora, summarizing our findings about the role of English ethnic associations within a diaspora framework (Figure C.1). English associational culture offered a valuable prism through which to cast light on the English immigrant community because its structures facilitated a sense of community and helped the new arrivals, and those of English descent, to maintain a collective identity.

In practical terms, the study of associations captured the actions of immigrants as active agents. Admittedly, this active agency applied only to those who were consciously and demonstrably English – thus only to those who joined these societies, or were helped out by them in difficult times. Either way, the member or the charity case stepped forward with a declaration of nationality or roots. While we recognize that the association-forming English were a particular group, we also suggest that mapping of associational activities, especially the provision of relief and the development of impressive mutual insurance funds, shows the wide reach of associations.

Our work has recognized that not all of the societies were the same. Indeed, they fell into two quite distinct strands: the first was built on 'hierarchical' charitable aid; the second asserted connection through 'reciprocal' aid, through economic mutualism.[10] Each strand had distinct agents and recipients, which revealed lines of demarcation corresponding to the class backgrounds of those involved. While middle-class migrants were the agents of ethnic charity, working-class migrants usually were the recipients. St George's societies were socially limited charities, and there were hierarchical dimensions in the way middle- and working-class migrants were thus connected. The funds of these associations were dispensed according to decisions beyond the recipient. English mutual benefit societies, on the other hand, were distinctly working class in their origins, although middle-class members were clearly there. Class did not demarcate English mutual aid societies, since both working- and middle-class members were both agents and recipients of this associational formation. Moreover, the connection between the members was reciprocal because agreed, constitutional rules, not the moral whims of individuals, governed access to funds; moreover, the rules were known when members joined and could not be changed arbitrarily by individuals.

Importantly, both these types of English ethnic associations operated in three distinct communities. First, and most immediate to them, was the immigrant community: their members came from it, as did those St George's societies which sought to help. Then came the New World host community. The degree to which associations connected with it varied – some, such as the lodges of the Sons of England, for example, were quite secretive about certain aspects of their operations. But there

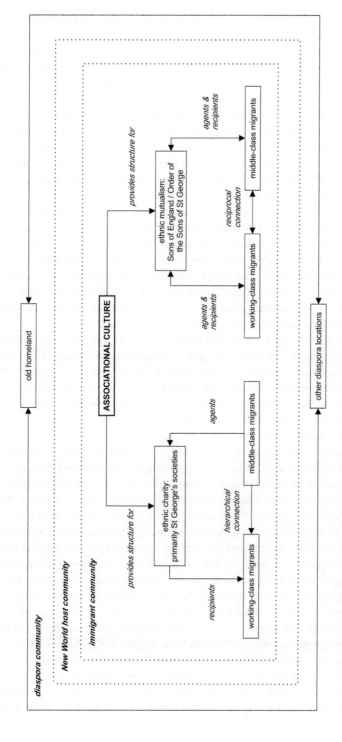

Figure C.1 English associational culture as a measure of diaspora

usually was a direct link as, after all, these associations operated at least partly in the public sphere. Connections were strongest when activities that were ethnic at the outset – for instance the relief for migrants in distress – became civic. Examples of how English ethnic associations were recognized as critical providers of charity, as in New York, or of insurance, best document the extent of this civic reach. Finally, all these activities sustained the English diaspora community, with associations connecting not only back to the old homeland, but also to other diaspora locations. Across all three communities this was largely a world without barriers in which communication was critical in underpinning exchange.

English immigrants actively developed ethnic associations shortly after they first arrived in the New World. In so doing they behaved in very much the same way as other ethnic groups, displaying behaviours and carrying out activities that have been described as critical elements of a diaspora for others, but have been largely ignored for the English. There are no grounds on which that view can be sustained. The instances of ethnic associationalism and ethnic mutualism documented here are not isolated, but are examples of a profound culture that was integral to life in many places, particularly where it connected ethnic activities with wider civic purposes, such as in the provision of immigrant aid.

There was a high level of communication between the various types of societies explored, and a degree of awareness at home in England concerning their activities in the United States and the colonies. By the later nineteenth century, the English at home were demonstrating a type of national pride, focusing on their saint's day. Such behaviour was in keeping with activities pursued in the English diaspora since the early eighteenth century. There was a significant level of exchange and a transnational diasporic consciousness, crossing the border between the United States and Canada and reaching all the way back to England and the wider world. We have offered explanations as to why we believe English ethnicity has been overlooked or underplayed, stressing that limitations in the conception of diaspora have led to the exclusion of the English in North America from consideration alongside other European migrant groups. A nuanced picture of North American immigration history requires recognition that ethnic groups, wherever they come from, express national pride below the level of national or state identity. English immigrants in North America cannot be viewed simply as a synonym for Anglo-American culture or as a simple case study in the ease of transfer of English culture from one side of the Atlantic to the other and in persistent imperial ties. At times, when Anglo-American relations were uneasy, which in our period they often were, the results could be fraught for the ordinary English immigrants on the streets of American cities. Englishness in North America involved an exchange between immigrant group and host community, and facilitated processes of associating, mutualism and self-expression that were, by any measure, both ethnic and diasporic.

Notes

1 CTA, Series 1093, StGS Toronto, File 26, Monthly Meetings Minutes, 1908–20, 15 November 1915, p. 164.
2 Gary B. Magee and Andrew Thompson, *Empire and Globalisation: Networks of People, Goods and Capital in the British World, c.1850-1914* (Cambridge, 2010); Desley Deacon, Penny Russell and Angela Woollacott (eds), *Transnational Lives: Biographies of Global Modernity, 1700-Present* (Basingstoke, 2010).
3 William E. Van Vugt, 'British and British Americans (English, Scots, Scots Irish, and Welsh), to 1870', in Elliott R. Barkan (ed.), *Immigrants in American History: Arrival, Adaptation, and Integration*, 4 vols (Santa Barbara, CA, 2013), vol. 1:1, p. 241.
4 Freda Hawkins, *Critical Years in Immigration: Canada and Australia Compared* (Kingston, Ont., 1991), pp. 23, 26, 27; Keith Williams, '"A way out of our troubles": The Politics of Empire Settlement, 1900-1922', in Stephen Constantine (ed.), *Emigrants and Empire: British Settlement in the Dominions between the Wars* (Manchester, 1990), pp. 22–44, and most other essays in the volume.
5 Benedict Anderson, *Imagined Communities: Reflections on the Origins and Spread of Nationalism* (London, 1983).
6 Letter from Henry E. Pellen to the Right Honorable, the Earl of Dufferin, 4 March 1875, Belfast, Public Record Office, Northern Ireland, Dufferin Papers, PRONI DIO71/H/B/P/155/4, Canada 1872-78. We are grateful to Lady Dufferin for permission to cite this item.
7 Besant was behind the first attempt at a modern St George's association in 1880s London; see W. Besant, *Autobiography of Sir Walter Besant: With a prefatory note by S. Squire Sprigg* (New York, 1902); Lesley C. Robinson, 'Englishness in England and the "Near Diaspora": Organisation, Influence and Expression, 1880s-1970s', unpublished PhD, University of Ulster, 2014, ch. 2; Hanael P. Bianchi, 'St George's Day: A Cultural History', unpublished PhD thesis, Catholic University of America, 2011, pp. 222, 230-31.
8 Krishnan Kumar, *The Making of English National Identity* (Cambridge, 2003), p. 34.
9 Wellington, Archives New Zealand, C344 831, Misc + RSStG, Minutes of the Combined Commonwealth and Kindred Societies, meeting, 3 February 2000, Wellington.
10 David T. Beito, *From Mutual Aid to the Welfare State: Fraternal Society and Social Services, 1890-1967* (Chapel Hill, NC, 2000).

Appendix 1 North American cities and towns with St George's societies and other English associations

United States

Albany, NY	St George's Society
Auburn, NY	St George's Society
Augusta, GA	St George's Society
Baltimore, MD	St George's Society
Baltimore, MD	British Association of Virginia
Bay City, MI	St George's Society
Boston, MA	St George's Society
Bridgeport, CT	St George's Society
Buffalo, NY	St George's Society
Charleston, SC	St George's Society
Chicago, IL	St George's Society
Cleveland, OH	St George's Society
Cohoes, NY	St George's Society
Detroit, MI	St George's Society
Indianapolis, IN	St George's Society
Little Falls, NY	St George's Society
Newark, NJ	St George's Society
New York, NY	St George's Society
New York, NY	Albion Society
Onondaga, NY	St George's Society
Oswego, NY	St George's Society
Philadelphia, PA	Sons of St George
Richmond, IN	St George's Society
Rochester, NY	St George's Society
Savannah, GA	St George's Society
Schenectady, NY	St George's Society
Skaneateles, NY	St George's Society
South Cleveland, OH	St George's Society

Syracuse, NY	St George's Society
Toledo, OH	St George's Society
Utica, NY	St George's Society
Washington, DC	St George's Society
Waterloo, NY	St George's Society

Canada

Belleville, Ont.	St George's Society
Brantford, Ont.	St George's Society
Clifton, Ont.	St George's Society
Coburg, Ont.	St George's Society
Guelph, Ont.	St George's Society
Hamilton, Ont.	St George's Society
Kingston, Ont.	St George's Society
London, Ont.	St George's Society
Montreal, Que.	St George's Society
Ottawa, Ont.	St George's Society
Peterboro, Ont.	St George's Society
Prescott, Ont.	St George's Society
St Catharines, Ont.	St George's Society
Stratford, Ont.	St George's Society
Strathoy, Ont.	St George's Society
Toronto, Ont.	St George's Society

Note: This list shows societies which were represented at the NAStGU or for which we have archive data.

Sources: Handbill: a report by members of the delegation at the 'St George's Convention, 1878 to St George's Society, Kingston', ADOA, XM-72B, StGS Kingston, Minutes, 1878. An additional list of towns with lodges can be found in *Philadelphia Inquirer*, 10 September 1877.

Appendix 2 Lodges of the Order of the Sons of St George, 1885

Connecticut

Ansonia	Lord Nelson Lodge
Hartford	Capital Lodge
New Britain	Hearts of Oak Lodge
New Haven	Redcross Lodge
Portland	Freestone Lodge
Thompsonville	Rowland Hill Lodge
Waterbury	Hawthorn Lodge

Illinois

Braidwood	Start of the West Lodge
Chicago	Good Samaritan Lodge
Chicago	Red Rose Lodge

Iowa

Des Moines	Princess Alice Lodge

Maine

Sanford	Pioneer Lodge

Massachusetts

Boston	Albion Lodge
Boston	James A. Garfield Lodge
Boston	Admiral Nelson Lodge
Boston	Cromwell Lodge

Cambridgeport	Harvard Lodge
Clinton	Rose Lodge
Dedham	Royal Oak Lodge
Fitchburg	Shakespeare Lodge
Holyoke	Pioneer Lodge
Lawrence	Friendship Lodge
Lowell	Waverly Lodge
Lynn	Lord Beaconsfield Lodge
Northampton	Victoria Lodge
Shelburne Falls	Nelson Lodge
Springfield	Leopold Lodge
Waltham	Anglo-American Lodge
Worcester	Prince Consort Lodge

Michigan

Ann Arbor	Chatham Lodge
Detroit	Britannia Lodge

New Jersey

Camden	Albion Lodge
Elizabeth	Pride of Elizabeth Lodge
Gloucester City	James A. Garfield Lodge
Hoboken	Raglan Lodge
Jersey City	Dean Stanley Lodge
Paterson	Wilberforce Lodge
Paterson	Shakespeare Lodge
Trenton	Sir Charles Napier Lodge
Trenton	Royal Oak Lodge
Trenton	Chatham Lodge

New York

Brooklyn	Heart of Oak Lodge
Brooklyn	Mistletoe Lodge
Brooklyn	Anglo-Saxon Lodge
Brooklyn	Shakespeare Lodge
Brooklyn	Commonwealth Lodge
Brooklyn	London Lodge
Brooklyn	Longfellow Lodge
Brooklyn	Ivanhoe Lodge
Brooklyn	Holly Lodge
Buffalo	Queen City Lodge

Jamestown	Chautauqua Lodge
n.a.	Anglo-American Lodge
New York City	Charles Dickens Lodge
New York City	Wellington Lodge
New York City	Nelson Lodge
Troy	Britannia Lodge
Troy	King Harold Lodge
Williamsburg	Magna Charta Lodge
Yonkers	Columbia Lodge

Ohio

Alliance	Wellington Lodge
Canton	Montgomery Lodge
Cleveland	Britannia Lodge
Cleveland	Albion Lodge
Cleveland	Prince Albert Lodge
Cleveland	Livingstone Lodge
Cleveland	Nelson Lodge
Massilon	Abraham Lincoln Lodge
Niles	Pride of Niles Lodge
Steubenville	Milton Lodge
Youngstown	Star of Albion Lodge

Pennsylvania

Altoona	Lincoln Lodge
Banksville	Loyal Rose Lodge
Bradford	Bradford Lodge
Chester	Nelson Lodge
Conshokocken	Wellington Lodge
Creighton	Union Jack of England Lodge
Erie	George Stephenson Lodge
Fall of Schuylkill	Shakespeare Lodge
Frankford (Philadelphia)	Prince of Wales Lodge
Germantown (Philadelphia)	William Penn Lodge
Girardville	Girardville Lodge
Harleton	Dragon Lodge
Homestead	Commonwealth Lodge
Houtzdale	Royal George Lodge
Irwin	Perseverance Lodge
Jermyn	Mayflower Lodge
Luzerne	Lord Beaconsfield Lodge
Manayunk	Admiral Collingwood Lodge

Mansfield Valley	Victoria Lodge
McKeesport	Welcome Stranger Lodge
n.a.	Lord Byron Lodge
n.a.	Peabody Lodge
n.a.	Robin Hood Lodge
n.a.	Sir Henry Havelock Lodge
n.a.	Centennial Lodge
n.a.	William Pitt Lodge
Nanticoke	Friendship Lodge
Oil City	Crown Lodge
Philadelphia	Anglo-Saxon Lodge
Philadelphia	Albion Lodge
Philadelphia	Britannia Lodge
Philadelphia	Victoria Lodge
Philadelphia	Alfred the Great Lodge
Philadelphia	Sir Robert Peel Lodge
Philadelphia	Pickwick Lodge
Philadelphia	Southwark Lodge
Philadelphia	Beaconfield Lodge
Phillipsburg	Richard Cobden Lodge
Pittsburgh	English Standard Lodge
Pittsburgh	Central Lodge
Pittsburgh	Lincoln Standard Lodge
Pittston	Keystone Lodge
Plains	North Star Lodge
Pleasant Valley	Rose of Valley Lodge
Plymouth	Lord Raglan Lodge
Reading	Cavendish Lodge
Reading	Braddock Lodge
Rockdale	Charles Dickens Lodge
Scranton	St George's Lodge
Shenandoah	Shenandoah Lodge
Stockton	Franklin Lodge
Tacony	Disston Lodge
Wilkes-Barre	Garfield Lodge
Wilkes-Barre	Royal Standard Lodge

Virginia

Richmond	Sir Walter Raleigh Lodge

Wisconsin

| Milwaukee | Heart of Oak Lodge |
| Milwaukee | Acorn Lodge |

Source: St George's Journal, 9:7 (1885).

Appendix 3 Lodges of the Sons of England, 1896

Alberta

Calgary   United Roses Lodge

Assiniboia (Saskatchewan)

Moosomin   King Alfred Lodge
Regina   Empress of the West Lodge

British Columbia

Chilliwack   Chilliwack Lodge
New Westminster   Rose of Columbia Lodge
Vancouver   Wilberforce Lodge
Vancouver   Vancouver Lodge
Victoria   Alexandra Lodge
Victoria   Pride of the Island Lodge

Manitoba

Alexander   Ivy Lodge
Brandon   Brandon Lodge
Carman   Manitoba Lodge
Morden   Anglo-Saxon Lodge
Rathwell   Holly Lodge
Selkirk   Runnymede Lodge
Virden   Sunderland Lodge
Winnipeg   Westward Ho! Lodge
Winnipeg   Neptune Lodge

Winnipeg	Shakespeare Lodge
Winnipeg	Marston Moor Lodge

New Brunswick

Fredericton	Islington Lodge
Moncton	Shaftesbury Lodge
St John	Marlborough Lodge
Stanley	Rose of Stanley Lodge

Nova Scotia

New Glasgow	Kenilworth Lodge
Halifax	Halifax Lodge
Halifax	Chebucto Lodge
Springhill Mines	St Aidans Lodge
Westville	Forest of Dean Lodge

Ontario

Allandale	Kempenfeldt Lodge
Almonte	Nelson Lodge
Arnprior	Severn Lodge
Aurora	Loyalty Lodge
Aylmer	Prince Albert Lodge
Bailieboro	Coventry Lodge
Barrie	Southampton Lodge
Belleville	Oxford Lodge
Belleville	Lydford Lodge
Benmiller	Barnstaple Lodge
Blackstock	Grimsby Lodge
Bowmanville	Wellington Lodge
Bracebridge	Lancaster Lodge
Bracondale	Yarmouth Lodge
Brampton	Brampton Lodge
Brantford	Salisbury Lodge
Brantford	Wolfe Lodge
Brockville	Suffolk Lodge
Burk's Falls	Gainsboro' Lodge
Burlington	Burlington Lodge
Caledon East	Torbay Lodge
Callander	Stockport Lodge
Campbellford	Devonshire Lodge
Cannington	Berkeley Lodge

Canton	Selby Lodge
Carleton Place	Beaconsfield Lodge
Chatham	Thames Lodge
Clinton	Sheffield Lodge
Collingwood	Canterbury Lodge
Cornwall	Victoria Lodge
Deseronto	United Empire Lodge
Elgin	Maple Leaf Lodge
Enfield	Holborn Lodge
Exeter	Plymouth Lodge
Fargo	Rose of Harwick Lodge
Fort William	Guildford Lodge
Fruitland	Rosebery Lodge
Galt	Royal Oak Lodge
Gananoque	Cambria Lodge
Goderich	Liverpool Lodge
Gore Bay	Manitoulin Lodge
Gravenhurst	Dover Lodge
Grimsby	Great Grimsby Lodge
Guelph	Royal City Lodge
Hamilton	Britannia Lodge
Hamilton	Acorn Lodge
Hamilton	Hearts of Oak Lodge
Hamilton	Devon Lodge
Hamilton	Rose of England Lodge
Hamilton	Cornwall Lodge
Hamilton	Osborne Lodge
Hamilton	Hamilton Lodge
Hampton	Darlington Lodge
Huntsville	Croydon Lodge
Ingersoll	Imperial Lodge
Kingston	Leicester Lodge
Lakefield	Exeter Lodge
Lambton Mills	Bradford Lodge
Lindsay	Westminster Lodge
Londesborough	Londesboro' Lodge
London	Chelsea Lodge
London	Trafalgar Lodge
London	British Lion Lodge
London	Kensington Lodge
London	British Oak Lodge
London	Piccadilly Lodge
London	Beresford Lodge
Longford Mills	St Asaph Lodge

Merritton	Union Jack Lodge
Midland	Cromwell Lodge
Milton	Milton Lodge
Mitchell	Mitchell Lodge
Newcastle	Newcastle Lodge
Lodge Newtonville	Newton Lodge
Niagara Falls	Norwich Lodge
North Toronto	Sherwood Lodge
Orangeville	Northampton Lodge
Orillia	Rose of Couchi'ing Lodge
Ormsby	Cumberland Lodge
Orono	Wolverhampton Lodge
Oshawa	Essex Lodge
Ottawa	Derby Lodge
Ottawa	Bowood Lodge
Ottawa	Stanley Lodge
Ottawa	Russell Lodge
Owen Sound	Mistletoe Lodge
Paris	Derbyshire Lodge
Pembroke	Black Prince Lodge
Penetanguishene	Macclesfield Lodge
Peterborough	Landsdowne Lodge
Petrolea	Duke of Cornwall Lodge
Port Hope	Durham Lodge
Port Perry	Old England Lodge
Ridgetown	Lancashire Lodge
Rosseau	Epping Lodge
St Catharines	Victory Lodge
St Thomas	Chester Lodge
St Thomas	Truro Lodge
Sarnia	Bridgewater Lodge
Simcoe	Royal George Lodge
Smiths Falls	Guelph Lodge
Stratford	Queen Victoria Lodge
Sturgeon Falls	Northumberland Lodge
Sudbury	Sudbury Lodge
Thornbury	Ludlow Lodge
Toronto	Albion Lodge
Toronto	Middlesex Lodge
Toronto	Kent Lodge
Toronto	York Lodge
Toronto	Brighton Lodge
Toronto	Somerset Lodge
Toronto	Surrey Lodge

Toronto	Warwick Lodge
Toronto	Manchester Lodge
Toronto	St George Lodge
Toronto	London Lodge
Toronto	Stafford Lodge
Toronto	Windsor Lodge
Toronto	Portsmouth Lodge
Toronto	Norfolk Lodge
Toronto	Richmond Lodge
Toronto	Preston Lodge
Toronto	Birmingham Lodge
Toronto	St Alban's Lodge
Toronto	Rugby Lodge
Toronto	Mercantile Lodge
Toronto	Bristol Lodge
Toronto	Hull Lodge
Toronto	Boston Lodge
Toronto	Chatham Lodge
Toronto	Lichfield Lodge
Toronto	Launceston Lodge
Toronto	Shrewsbury Lodge
Toronto	Clifton Lodge
Toronto	Cheltenham Lodge
Toronto	Hammersmith Lodge
Toronto	Hereford Lodge
Toronto	Commercial Lodge
Toronto Junction	Worcester Lodge
Tyrone	Temple Bar Lodge
Utterson	Burnaby Lodge
Uxbridge	Buckingham Lodge
Welland	Welland Lodge
Weston	Leeds Lodge
Whitby	Sussex Lodge
Windsor	Prince of Wales Lodge
Windsor	Waterloo Lodge
Wingham	Torquay Lodge
Woodstock	Bedford Lodge
Wyoming	Coronation Lodge

Prince Edward Island

Charlottetown	Eton Lodge

Quebec

Capelton	Albert Lodge
Hull	Tennyson Lodge
Lachine	Royal Rose Lodge
Lennoxville	Clarence Lodge
Montreal	Excelsior Lodge
Montreal	Yorkshire Lodge
Montreal	Victoria's Jubilee Lodge
Montreal	Primrose Lodge
Montreal	Denbigh Lodge
Montreal	Britannic Lodge
Montreal	Grovesnor Lodge
Montreal	Monarch Lodge
Montreal	Cardigan Lodge
New Rockland	Fidelity Lodge
Richmond	Enfield Lodge
Sherbrooke	Gloucester Lodge
St Lambert	Lincoln Lodge
Westmount	Westmount Lodge

Source: Subordinate Lodge Directory, *Record*, June 1896, pp. 6–7.

Bibliography

Primary sources

Manuscript collections

Royal Society of St George
Loughton, Essex, RSStG Headquarters.
  Miscellaneous minutes books, rolls, invitations, communications, etc.
Canberra, Australia, National Archives.
  1919/10401/A2487, Royal Society of St George, Resolutions of Meetings, 1919.
  A2/04/2695/0, Prime Minister's Department.
Palmerston North, New Zealand, Mathieson Archive.
  Royal Society of St George, Palmerston North branch, correspondence with Royal Society of St George, Melbourne branch, 1904.
Wellington, Archives New Zealand.
  NZ, AEFZ/W5727/22620/171, Royal Society of St George, miscellaneous correspondence, dinner invitations, magazines, ephemera, 1958–2000; 'Rules', 11 December 1951, Rule 1 (b).
  C344 831, Misc + RSStG, Minutes of the Combined Commonwealth and Kindred Societies, meeting, 3 February 2000, Wellington.

St George's societies (North America)
Baltimore, Maryland Historical Society [MdHS], MS 1881.
Baltimore St George's Society Records.
  Minute Books, 7 vols, 1866–1964.
  Account books, 1890–1912; accounts also included in Minutes, vols 6, 7.
  Members and Dues Books, 1900–50, 1950–.
Charleston, South Carolina, South Carolina Historical Society.
Miscellaneous St George's Society materials, 1813–1977.
Kingston, Ontario, Anglican Diocese of Ontario Archives [ADOA], XM-72, XM-72A, XM-72B.

St George's Society of Kingston Records, 1858–86.
    Minute books with some membership information, accounts, etc.
New York Historical Society.
    BV.A1, Ogden papers, letter book, 1800–01.
    New York Public Library.
St George's Society of New York.
    Programmes, menus for dinners, meetings, etc., 1880–1906.
Ottawa, Library and Archives Canada [LAC].
    MG28-V3, St George's Society of Ottawa records.
    Minute books, 13 vols, 1859–1932.
    Ledgers, 1903–16.
    Miscellaneous correspondence, invitations, membership cards, orders of
    service, magazines.
MG26-G, Laurier papers.
    Letter, invitations to St George's Society dinners, 1908–10.
MG30-D35, Lowe family papers.
    St George's Society ephemera.
    Miscellaneous publications.
Philadelphia, Historical Society of Pennsylvania [HSP].
(Phi) 1733, Sons of St George Archive.
Rules and Constitution, 1772.
Accounts, 1875–98.
Stewards' Books, 4 vols, 1860s–1900s.
Minute Books, 6 vols, 1770s–1880s.
Miscellaneous posts, invitations, etc.
Williams-Skerrett papers.
Including rules of the Albion Society, nineteenth-century Philadelphia.
Sons of St George ephemera, dinners, toasts, menus, etc.
Welsh Society of Philadelphia, Historical Society of Pennsylvania, Wj 502.
Toronto, City of Toronto Archives [CTA].
Fonds 1575, St George's Society of Toronto.
    Series 1093, St. George's Society meeting minutes.
    Series 1094, St. George's Society financial records.
    Series 1095, St. George's Society annual reports and publications.
    Series 1096, Relief programmes.

Sons of England Benefit Society
Moose Jaw Public Library, Archives Department, MJ-6.001.
Moose Jaw, Sons of England Benefit Society, fonds.
    Minutes, accounts, membership rolls, 1904–07.
Ottawa, Archives of Ontario, F 1155 – MU 2864.
Sons of England Benefit Society Records.
    Grand Lodge Minutes, including some accounts and membership rolls,
    1896–1925.
Calgary, Alberta, Glenbow Museum Archive [GMA].
M-1659, Sons of England, United Roses Lodge, No.117.
    Minutes, membership rolls, accounts, 1890–1931.

BD.I.U58A V2, Sons of England, Lodge Calgary Records, Minute Book.
Papers of John Stokoe, 1903–12.
Interview with Edward King in 1959, George Clift King fonds, M 4030 D920.
K52.

Other sources
Belfast, Public Record Office Northern Ireland.
Dufferin Papers, DIO71/H/B/P/155/4, Canada 1872–78 (by kind permission of
Lady Dufferin).
Letters from Sons of England, Canada.
Letters from St George's Society, New York.
London, The National Archives.
NA/FO/37/1182/137 RP no. 20/1965, *Report of the Commission of Enquiry in the
Secret Organizations*, part II, 13-30 [South Africa].
San Antonio, Daughters of the Republic of Texas Library.
Col 883, Leo M.J. Dielmann Papers, Drawings, and Photographs.

Official reports and government papers

1839 (3-II) *Appendix (A.) to report on the affairs of British North America, from
the Earl of Durham, Her Majesty's High Commissioner* ... 1840 [211] [221]
[222] [250] *Canada: Correspondence relative to the affairs of Canada*, part I.
61st Congress, 3d Session, Doc. 756, *Reports of the Emigration Commissioners:
Statistical Review of Immigration, 1820–1910*, vol. 3: *Distribution of
Immigrants, 1850–1900* (Washington, DC, 1911).
106th Congress, 2d Session, Report 106-482, 'Hermann Monument and Hermann
Heights Park'.
1872 [C. 617] *Reports on the present state of Her Majesty's colonial possessions.
Transmitted with the blue books for the year 1870. Part III. North American
colonies; African settlements and St. Helena; Australian colonies and New
Zealand; and the Mediterranean possessions, &c.*
1878-79 [C. 2372] *Eighth annual report of the Local Government Board*, British
Parliamentary Papers.
1892 [C. 6795–XI] *Royal Commission on Labour. Foreign reports. Volume II. The
colonies and the Indian Empire. With an appendix on the migration of labour.*
1906 [Cd. 2979] *Departmental Committee on Agricultural Settlements in British
Colonies. Minutes of evidence taken before the Departmental Committee
appointed to consider Mr. Rider Haggard's report on agricultural settlements
in British colonies, with appendices, analysis, and index.* II, 208, 5490.
*Annual Report of the President and Directors of the Baltimore and Susquehanna
Railroad* (Baltimore, MD, 1828).
Annual Reports of the Bureau of Industries for the Province of Ontario, 1895, parts
I, II and II: *Agricultural* Statistics (Toronto, 1896).
Annual Reports of the Bureau of Industries for the Province of Ontario, 1898, parts
I, II and II: *Agricultural* Statistics, part IV: *Chattel Mortgages* (Toronto, 1899).
Annual Reports of the Bureau of Industries for the Province of Ontario, 1906, part
I: *Agricultural Statistics*, part II: *Chattel Mortgages* (Toronto, 1906).

Bulletin of the Bureau of Labor Statistics of New York, vol. 2 (Albany, 1901).

Bureau of Census, *The Seventh Census of the United States, 1850, Embracing a Statistical View of Each of the States and Territories, Arrange by Counties, Towns, etc. ...* (Washington, DC, 1853).

—— *Population of the United States in 1860: Compiled from the Original Returns of the Eighth Census under the Direction of the Secretary of the Interior* (Washington, DC, 1860).

—— *Ninth Census*, vol. 1: *The Statistics of the Population of the United States Embracing the Tables of Race, Nationality, Sex, Selected Ages, and Occupations ... From the Original Returns of the Ninth Census (June 1, 1870), under the Direction of the Secretary of the Interior* (Washington, DC, 1872).

—— *Statistics of the Population of the United States at the Tenth Census (June 1, 1880), Embracing Extended Tables of Population of States, Counties, and Minor Civil Division, with Distinction of Race, Sec Age, Nativity, and Occupation; together with Summary Tables ...* (Washington, DC, 1880).

—— *Report of the Population of the United States at the Eleventh Census*, part 1 (Washington, DC, 1894).

—— *Census Reports*, vol. 1: *Twelfth Census of the United States*, part 1 (Washington, DC, 1901).

Census of Canada, 1870–71, vol. 1 (Ottawa, 1873).

Census of Canada, 1880–81, vol. 1 (Ottawa, 1882).

Census of Canada, 1890–91, vol. 1 (Ottawa, 1893).

Clipperton, R.C., HM's Consul, USA. 1886 (C.4783) *Commercial*, No. 20 (1886). *Reports by Her Majesty's Representatives abroad, on the System of Co-operation in Foreign Countries*.

Department of National Defence Records, R.G. 24, vol. 2018, Sons of England Lodge Milford, Library and Archives Canada.

Fourth Census of Canada, 1901, vol. 1: *Population* (Ottawa, 1902).

Immigration Commission, *Reports of the Immigration Commission*, 42 vols (Washington, DC, 1910). Vol. 40: *The Immigration Situation in Other Countries: Canada* (1 April 1910), 61st Congress, 2d session, document no. 409 [William P. Dillingham Commission].

Report of the Inspector of Insurance and Registrar of Friendly Societies of Ontario 1900 (Toronto, 1900).

Report of the Inspector of Insurance and Registrar of Friendly Societies of Ontario 1911 (Toronto, 1911).

Reports of the Immigration Commission: Immigrants in Industries, part 17: *Copper Mining and Smelting* [chaired by William P. Dillingham], 1911.

Published primary sources

32nd National Saengerfest N.A.S.B., Indianapolis, June 17–20, 1908. Official Souvenir (Indianapolis, 1908).

The act of incorporation and bye-laws of the St George's Society of Montreal, founded by Englishmen in the year 1834, for the purpose of relieving their brethren in distress (Montreal, 1867).

Albion Society, *Constitution and By-Laws* (Philadelphia, 1856, 1858).

—— *Constitution and By-laws of the Albion Society of Philadelphia: Together with a List of the Officers and Members in the Year 1888, and a Complete List of Members Since the Foundation of the Society* (Philaldephia, PA, 1888).

Bericht über das Festessen zur Feier des 118–jährigen Bestehens der Deutschen Gesellschaft der Stadt New York am 8. März 1902 im Waldorf-Astoria, New York (New York, 1902).

'Biographical Sketch of John Thomson, A.M.', in Ellis Paxson Oberholtzer (ed.), *Philadelphia, A History of the City and its People: A Record of 225 Years*, 4 vols (Philadelphia, 1912), vol. 3, p. 38.

Board of United Charities, *Hand Book of the Benevolent Institutions and Charities of New York for 1876* (New York, 1876).

—— *Hand Book of the Benevolent Institutions and Charities of New York From 1877* (New York, 1877),

By-Laws and Rules of Order of Inverness Camp, No. 54, S.O.S. (Goderich, 1893).

By-Laws of the Canadian Club, with a list of officers and members (New York, 1885).

City of Chicago, *Department of Public Welfare: Social Service Directory* (Chicago, 1915).

Constitution, by-laws and standing rules and orders of the British Columbia St George's Society (Victoria, 1886).

Constitution of the St Andrew's Society of the City of Toronto and Home District of Upper Canada (Toronto, 1836),

Deutsch-Amerikanisches Vereins-Adressbuch fuer das Jahr 1914–15 (Milwaukee, 1914).

Deutsche Gesellschaft der Stadt New York, *Jahresbericht für 1916* (New York, 1917).

'England's Greatness': Anniversary Sermon Delivered to the Members of St George's Society of Ottawa and the Sons of England by Rev. Dr. Herridge (Ottawa, 1899).

Forty-Second Annual Report of the Insurance Commissioner 1907 (Business of 1906), Part III: Fraternal Societies – Twelfth Annual Report (Hartford, 1907).

History of Luzerne, Lackawanna, and Wyoming Counties, Pa; with Illustrations and Biographical Sketches ... (New York, 1880).

Hundertjährige Feier der Incorporation der Deutschen Gesellschaft von Pennsylvanien (Philadelphia, 1882).

Jahrbücher der Deutsch-Amerikanischern Turnerei (New York, 1890).

Jahres-Bericht des Vorortes des Nord-Amerikanischen Turner-Bundes (Milwaukee, 1880).

Jahresbericht des Vororts des Nordamerikanischen Turnerbundes (Indianapolis, 1909).

Jahresbericht und Mitglieder-Liste des Deutschen Liederkranz für das Vereinsjahr 1880–81 (New York, 1881).

Jahresbericht und Mitglieder-Liste des Gesangs-Vereins Deutscher Liederkranz der Stadt New York für das Vereins-Jahr 1905–1906 (New York, 1906).

Jahresbericht und Mitgliederliste des Gesangsvereins Deutscher Liederkranz der Stadt New York für das Vereinsjahr 1915–1916 (New York, 1916).

Library of Congress, *A List of Works Relating to the Germans in the United States* (Washington, DC, 1904).

National Archives and Records Administration, Washington, DC; *Index to New England Naturalization Petitions, 1791–1906 (M1299)*, microfilm serial: M1299, microfilm roll 22, L523.

Neunzehnhundertste Jahresfeier der Schlacht im Teutoburger Walde: Gedenkblätter an das Fest der Deutschen von Californien (San Francisco, 1909).

New York Charities Directory (New York, 1888).

Norman, R.W., *'Our Duties and Opportunities': Annual Sermon by Rev. R. W. Norman* (Montreal, 1877).

North America St George's Union, *Report of the Fifth Annual Convention, held at St George's Hall, Philadelphia, PA, September 12th, 13th and 14th, 1877* (Bridgeport, CT, 1877).

The original painting of Her Majesty, Queen Victoria the First, painted by Mr. Thomas Sully, expressly for 'The Society of the Sons of St. George,' Philadelphia (Philadelphia, 1839).

Praktische Rathschläge und Mittheilungen für deutsche Einwanderer (New York, 1883).

Report of the National Rifle Association of America, 1905 (New York, 1906).

Royal Society of St George, *Annual Report and Year Book 1904* (London, 1904).

—— *Annual Report and Yearbook of the Royal Society of St George* (London, 1906).

St George's Society of Montreal, *The Constitution and By-Laws of the St George's Society* (Montreal, 1855).

St George's Society of New York, annual reports, various.

—— *Constitution of the St George's Society of New York*, contained in *Annual Report for 1897* (New York, 1897).

—— *History of St George's Society of New York, from 1770–1913* (New York, 1913).

St George's Society of Quebec, *Officers and Members with the Reports* (Quebec, 1847).

St George's Society of Toronto, *Charter and By-Laws, with the Report of the Committee for 1858* (Toronto, 1859).

—— *Charter and By-Laws of the St George's Society of Toronto ... to which is added a Report of the Committee for 1862, together with a List of Officers* (Toronto, 1863).

—— *Charter and By-Laws of the St George's Society of Toronto ... to which is added a Report of the Committee for 1863, together with a List of Officers* (Toronto, 1864).

—— *Charter and By-Laws of the St George's Society of Toronto ... to which is added a Report of the Committee for 1864, together with a List of Officers* (Toronto, 1865).

—— *Charter and By-Laws of the St George's Society of Toronto ... to which is added a Report of the Committee for 1865, together with a List of Officers* (Toronto, 1866).

—— *Charter and By-Laws of the St George's Society of Toronto ... to which is added a Report of the Committee for 1866, together with a List of Officers* (Toronto, 1867).

—— *Charter and By-Laws of the St George's Society of Toronto ... to which is added a Report of the Committee for 1867, together with a List of Officers* (Toronto, 1868).

—— *Charter and By-Laws of the St George's Society of Toronto ... to which is added a Report of the Committee for 1869, together with a List of Officers* (Toronto, 1870).

—— *Charter and By-Laws of the St George's Society of Toronto ... to which is added a Report of the Committee for 1870, together with a List of Officers* (Toronto, 1871).

—— *Charter and By-Laws of the St George's Society of Toronto ... to which is added a Report of the Committee for 1871, together with a List of Officers* (Toronto, 1872).

—— *Charter and By-Laws of the St George's Society of Toronto ... to which is added a Report of the Committee for 1872, together with a List of Officers* (Toronto, 1873).

—— *Charter and By-Laws of the St George's Society of Toronto ... to which is added a Report of the Committee for 1873, together with a List of Officers* (Toronto, 1874).

—— *Charter and By-Laws of the St George's Society of Toronto ... to which is added a Report of the Committee for 1874, together with a List of Officers* (Toronto, 1875).

—— *Charter and By-Laws of the St George's Society of Toronto ... to which is added a Report of the Committee for 1875, together with a List of Officers* (Toronto, 1876).

—— *Charter and By-Laws of the St George's Society of Toronto ... to which is added a Report of the Committee for 1876, together with a List of Officers* (Toronto, 1877).

—— *Charter and By-Laws of the St George's Society of Toronto ... to which is added a Report of the Committee for 1877, together with a List of Officers* (Toronto, 1878).

—— *Charter and By-Laws of the St George's Society of Toronto ... to which is added a Report of the Committee for 1879, together with a List of Officers* (Toronto, 1880).

—— *Charter and By-Laws of the St George's Society of Toronto ... to which is added a Report of the Committee for 1880, together with a List of Officers* (Toronto, 1881).

—— *Charter and By-Laws of the St George's Society of Toronto ... to which is added a Report of the Committee for 1881, together with a List of Officers* (Toronto, 1881).

—— *Charter and By-Laws of the St George's Society of Toronto ... to which is added a Report of the Committee for 1882, together with a List of Officers* (Toronto, 1883).

—— *Charter and By-Laws of the St George's Society of Toronto ... to which is added a Report of the Committee for 1883, together with a List of Officers* (Toronto, 1884).

—— *Charter and By-Laws of the St George's Society of Toronto ... to which is added a Report of the Committee for 1884, together with a List of Officers* (Toronto, 1885).

—— *Charter and By-Laws of the St George's Society of Toronto ... to which is added a Report of the Committee for 1885, together with a List of Officers* (Toronto, 1886).

—— *Charter and By-Laws of the St George's Society of Toronto ... to which is added a Report of the Committee for 1886, together with a List of Officers* (Toronto, 1887).

—— *Charter and By-Laws of the St George's Society of Toronto ... to which is added a Report of the Committee for 1887, together with a List of Officers* (Toronto, 1887).

—— *Charter and By-Laws of the St George's Society of Toronto ... to which is added a Report of the Committee for 1888, together with a List of Officers* (Toronto, 1889).

—— *Charter and By-Laws of the St George's Society of Toronto ... to which is added a Report of the Committee for 1889, together with a List of Officers* (Toronto, 1890).

—— *Charter and By-Laws of the St George's Society of Toronto ... to which is added a Report of the Committee for 1890, together with a List of Officers* (Toronto, 1891).

—— *Charter and By-Laws of the St George's Society of Toronto ... to which is added a Report of the Committee for 1891, together with a List of Officers* (Toronto, 1892).

—— *Charter and By-Laws of the St George's Society of Toronto ... to which is added a Report of the Committee for 1892, together with a List of Officers* (Toronto, 1893).

—— *Charter and By-Laws of the St George's Society of Toronto ... to which is added a Report of the Committee for 1893, together with a List of Officers* (Toronto, 1894).

—— *Charter and By-Laws of the St George's Society of Toronto ... to which is added a Report of the Committee for 1894, together with a List of Officers* (Toronto, 1895).

—— *Charter and By-Laws of the St George's Society of Toronto ... to which is added a Report of the Committee for 1895, together with a List of Officers* (Toronto, 1896).

—— *Charter and By-Laws of the St George's Society of Toronto ... to which is added a Report of the Committee for 1896, together with a List of Officers* (Toronto, 1897).

—— *Charter and By-Laws of the St George's Society of Toronto ... to which is added a Report of the Committee for 1897, together with a List of Officers* (Toronto, 1898).

—— *Charter and By-Laws of the St George's Society of Toronto ... to which is added a Report of the Committee for 1898, together with a List of Officers* (Toronto, 1899).

—— *Charter and By-Laws of the St George's Society of Toronto ... to which is added a Report of the Committee for 1899, together with a List of Officers* (Toronto, 1900).

—— *Charter and By-Laws of the St George's Society of Toronto ... to which is added a Report of the Committee for 1900, together with a List of Officers* (Toronto, 1901).

—— *Charter and By-Laws of the St George's Society of Toronto ... to which is added a Report of the Committee for 1901, together with a List of Officers* (Toronto, 1902).

—— *Charter and By-Laws of the St George's Society of Toronto ... to which is added a Report of the Committee for 1902, together with a List of Officers* (Toronto, 1903).

—— *Charter and By-Laws of the St George's Society of Toronto ... to which is added a Report of the Committee for 1904, together with a List of Officers* (Toronto, 1905).

—— *Charter and By-Laws of the St George's Society of Toronto ... to which is added a Report of the Committee for 1905, together with a List of Officers* (Toronto, 1906).

—— *Charter and By-Laws of the St George's Society of Toronto ... to which is added a Report of the Committee for 1906, together with a List of Officers* (Toronto, 1907).

—— *Charter and By-Laws of the St George's Society of Toronto ... to which is added a Report of the Committee for 1907, together with a List of Officers* (Toronto, 1908).

—— *Report of the Committee of the St George's Society of Toronto ...* (Toronto, 1908)

—— *Report of the Committee for 1908 ... together with a list of Officers and Members of the Society* (Toronto, 1909).

—— *Report of the Committee for 1909 ...* (Toronto, 1910).

—— *Report of the Committee for 1910 ...* (Toronto, 1911).

—— *Report of the Committee for 1911 ...* (Toronto, 1912).

—— *Report of the Committee for 1917 ...* (Toronto, 1918).

—— *Report of the Committee for 1918 ...* (Toronto, 1919).

—— *Report of the Committee for 1919 ...* (Toronto, 1920).

—— *Report of the Committee for 1920 ...* (Toronto, 1921).

—— *Report of the Committee for 1921 ...* (Toronto, 1922).

—— *Report of the Committee for 1922 ...* (Toronto, 1923).

—— *Report of the Committee for 1923 ...* (Toronto, 1924).

—— *Report of the Committee for 1924 ...* (Toronto, 1925).

—— *Report of the Committee for 1925 ...* (Toronto, 1926).

—— *Report of the Committee for 1926 ...* (Toronto, 1927).

—— *Report of the Committee for 1930 ...* (Toronto, 1931).

—— *Report of the Committee for 1935 ...* (Toronto, 1936).

—— *Report of the Committee for 1940 ...* (Toronto, 1941).

—— *Revised Constitution and Laws, with a list of officers and members* (Toronto, 1844).

Scots' Charitable Society of Boston, *The Constitution and By-Laws of the Scots' Charitable Society of Boston (Instituted 1657) with a List of Members and Officers, and many Interesting Extracts from the Original Records of the Society* (Cambridge, MA: John Wilson and Son, 1878).

A sketch of how 'the diamond anthem' was sung around the world through the colonies of the empire on the 20th June 1897. Being an extract from the annual report of the supreme grand president of the Sons of England, given at St Catherine's, Canada, 8th March 1898 (Toronto, 1898).

Society of the Sons of St George, *Rules and Constitution of the Society of the Sons of St George* (Philadelphia, 1772).

Sons of England, *The Business Directory of the Sons of England for the Cities of Ottawa and Hull* (Ottawa, 1898).

—— *Business Directory of the Sons of England of Ottawa and Hull Lodges* (Ottawa, 1899).

—— *By-laws of Pride of the Island Lodge, No. 131, Sons of England Benevolent Society: instituted January 15th, 1891, established A.D. 1874, under the supreme jurisdiction of the Grand Lodge of Canada* (Victoria, BC, 1891).

—— *Constitution of the Sons of England Benevolent Society under the Supreme Jurisdiction of the Grand Lodge of Canada* (Belleville, 1889).

—— *Constitution of the Sons of England* (Toronto, 1890).

—— *Constitution of the Sons of England Benevolent Society ... 1892* (Belleville, 1892).

—— *Constitution of the Sons of England Benefit Society under the Supreme Jurisdiction of the Supreme Lodge* (Toronto, 1912).

—— *Diamond Jubilee of Her Majesty Queen Victoria, Sunday, 20th June, 1897: Sons of England Service to be Held in Continuous Succession through the British Colonies around the World Victoria, British Columbia* (n.p., 1897).

—— *The Directory of the Members of the Sons of England for the City of Ottawa and the Ottawa Valley* (n.p., 1899).

—— *Journal of the Proceedings of the Twenty-Fourth Supreme Grand Lodge, Sons of England Benefit Society, held in the City of Windsor, Ontario, Tuesday, Wednesday, Thursday, and Friday, August, 14th, 15th, 16th, and 17th, 1900* (Toronto, 1900).

—— *Journal of the Proceedings of the Twenty-Sixth Session of the Supreme Grand Lodge, Sons of England Benefit Society, held in the City of Winnipeg, Manitoba, Tuesday, Wednesday, Thursday, and Friday, August, 12th, 13th, 14th, and 15th, 1902* (Toronto, 1902).

—— *Journal of the Proceedings of the Twenty-Eighth Session of the Supreme Grand Lodge, Sons of England Benefit Society, held in the City of Chatham, Ontario, Tuesday, Wednesday, Thursday, and Friday, August, 14th, 15th, 16th, and 17th, 1906* (Toronto, 1906).

—— *Journal of the Proceedings of the Thirty-First Session of the Supreme Grand Lodge, Sons of England Benefit Society, held in the City of Niagara Falls, Ont., Tuesday, Wednesday, Thursday, and Friday, August, 13th, 14th, 15th, and 16th, 1912* (Toronto, 1912).

—— *Journal of the Proceedings of the Thirty-Second Session of the Supreme Grand Lodge, Sons of England Benefit Society, held in the City of Niagara Falls, Ont., Tuesday, Wednesday, Thursday, and Friday, August, 10th, 11th, 12th, and 13th, 1914* (Toronto, 1914).

—— *Journal of the Proceedings of the Thirty-Fourth Session of the Supreme Grand Lodge, Sons of England Benefit Society, held in the City of Hamilton, Ontario, Tuesday, Wednesday, Thursday, and Friday, August, 11th, 12th, 13th, and 14th, 1919* (Toronto, 1919).

—— *Journal of the Proceedings of the Thirty-Seventh Session of the Supreme Grand Lodge, Sons of England Benefit Society, held in the City of Calgary,*

Alberta, Tuesday, Wednesday, Thursday, and Friday, August, 11th, 12th, 13th, and 14th, 1925 (Toronto, 1925).

—— *Journal of the Proceedings of the Fortieth Session of the Supreme Grand Lodge, Sons of England Benefit Society, held in the City of Windsor, Ontario, Tuesday, Wednesday, Thursday, and Friday, August, 11th, 12th, 13th, and 14th, 1931* (Toronto, 1931).

—— *Minutes of the Conference of Delegates held at Graham's Town, Cape Colony, November 24 and 25, 1891* (King William's Town, 1891).

—— *Proceedings of Conference held at Grahamstown, October 1888* (Grahamstown, 1888).

—— *Proceedings of the Grand Lodge, 30th October 1876*, vol. 1: 1877–88 (Toronto, 1878?).

—— *Report of First Annual Meeting of the Grand Lodge Sons of England Benevolent Society, South Africa, held in the Town Hall, Port Elizabeth, Thursday, Friday and Saturday, October 21, 22 23, 1892* (King William's Town, 1892).

—— *Report of the Fourth Annual Meeting of the Grand Lodge, held in the St Alban's Lodge Room, Grahamstown, Thursday and Friday, Aug. 8th & 9th, 1895* (King William's Town, 1895).

—— *Report of the Fifth Annual Meeting of the Grand Lodge Sons of England Benevolent Society, South Africa, held in the Jubilee Lodge Room, King William's Town [South Africa], August 20th, 21st and 22nd, 1896* (King William's Town, 1896).

—— *Report of the Sixth Annual Meeting of the Grand Lodge Sons of England Benevolent Society (South Africa). Held in Council Chamber, Town Hall, Port Elizabeth, Wednesday, Thursday and Friday, August 25th, 26th and 27th, 1897* (Port Elizabeth, 1897).

—— *Report of the Tenth Annual Meeting of the Grand Lodge, Sons of England, 1885* (Belleville, 1885).

—— *Report of the Thirteenth Annual Meeting of the Grand Lodge, Sons of England Benevolent Society Grand Lodge, Canada, held in Shaftsbury Hall, Toronto, Ontario, Tuesday, Wednesday, Thursday, and Friday, February 14, 15, 16, and 17, 1888* (Ottawa, 1888).

—— *Report of the Fifteenth Annual Meeting of the Grand Lodge, Sons of England Benevolent Society Grand Lodge, Canada, held in the Orange Hal, Port Hope, Ontario, Tuesday, Wednesday, Thursday, and Friday, February 11, 12, 13, and 14, 1890* (Toronto, 1890).

—— *Report of the Twentieth Annual Meeting of the Supreme Grand Lodge, 1895* (Toronto, 1895).

—— *Report of the Twenty-First Annual Meeting of the Supreme Grand Lodge, Sons of England Benefit Society, Canada, held in the town of Peterborough, Ontario, on Tuesday, Wednesday, Thursday, and Friday, March 10th, 11th, 12th, and 13th, 1896* (Toronto, 1896).

—— *Report of the Twenty-Second Annual Meeting of the Supreme Grand Lodge, Sons of England Benefit Society, Canada, held in the town of Brantford, Ontario, on Tuesday, Wednesday, Thursday, and Friday, March 9th, 10th, 11th, and 12th 1897* (Toronto, 1897).

—— *Report of the Twenty-Third Annual Meeting of the Supreme Grand Lodge, Sons of England Benefit Society, Canada, held in the town of St Catherines, Ontario, on Tuesday, Wednesday, Thursday, and Friday, March 8th, 9th, 10th and 11th 1898* (Toronto, 1898).

—— *Report of the Twenty-Fifth Annual Meeting of the Supreme Grand Lodge, Sons of England Benefit Society, Canada, held in the town of Ottawa, Ontario, on Tuesday, Wednesday, Thursday, and Friday, March 14th, 15th, 16th and 17th 1900* (Toronto, 1900).

—— *Third Annual Meeting of the Grand Lodge, South Africa, Sons of England Benevolent Society, held at Temperance Hall, East London, Thursday, Friday and Saturday, October 25th, 26th and 27th, 1894* (East London, 1894).

Sons of Scotland Benevolent Association, *Constitution of the Grand and Subordinate Camps* (Belleville, 1892).

Woods' Baltimore City Directory, Containing a Corrected Engraved Map of the City, A Business Directory, a Street Directory and Appendix … (Baltimore, 1872).

Zur Feier des Fünfzigjährigen Jubiläums des New York Turn Vereins in der New York Turn-Halle (New York, 1900).

Newspapers

North America
Albany Journal
The Argus
The Argus & Democrat
Baltimore American
Baltimore Gazette
Baltimore Sun
Bangor Whig and Courier (ME)
Boston Daily Globe
Boston Evening Transcript
Brooklyn Eagle
The Caledonian
Calgary Daily Herald
Calgary Weekly Herald
Canadian-American
Charleston Mercury
Chicago Daily Times
Chicago Daily Tribune
Chicago Times
Chicago Tribune
Critic-Record
Daily Cleveland Herald
Daily Critic
Daily Evening Bulletin (San Francisco)
Daily Inter Ocean (Chicago)
Daily Mail and Empire (Toronto)
Daily News (Newport, RI)

Daily Picayune
East African Standard
Edmonton Journal
Elyria Daily Telephone
English-Speaking World
Evening Critic (Washington)
Evening Telegram (St John's, Newfoundland)
Forth Worth Register
Galveston Daily News
Grantham Journal
Hawaiian Gazette
Inter Ocean (Chicago)
Kane Daily Republican
Knoxville Journal
Lethbridge Herald
Little Rock Daily Arkansas Gazetteer
Los Angeles Herald
Los Angeles Times
Lowell Sun
Manitoba Daily Free Press
Manitoba Free Press
Milwaukee Daily Journal
Milwaukee Daily Sentinel
Milwaukee Sentinel
Moose Jaw Signal
Montreal Gazette
Morning Herald (Baltimore)
Morning Leader (Regina)
Newark Daily Advocate
New Castle News
New York Evening Express
New York Evening Times
New York Gazette and Weekly Mercury
New York Gazette and Weekly Post Boy
New York Herald
New York Journal
New York Spectator
New York Times
New Yorker Volkszeitung
News (Frederick, MD)
North Adam Transcript
North American (Philadelphia)
North American and Daily Advertiser
North American and United States Gazette (Philadelphia)
Omaha Daily Herald
Ontario Workman
Oswego Daily Times

Oswego Palladium
Ottawa Citizen
Ottawa Daily Citizen
Petersburg Index and Appeal
Philadelphia Inquirer
Pioneer
Political Register
Poulson's American Advertiser
Poulson's Daily American Advertiser
Quebec Saturday Budget
The Republic: A Monthly Magazine of American Literature, Politics & Art
Rocky Mountains News
Royal Gazette
Saint Paul Globe
Salt Lake City Intermountain and Colorado Catholic
San Francisco Call
Scottish Canadian
Southern Literary Messenger
Springfield Republican
Steubenville Daily Herald
St George's Journal
Syracuse Daily Herald
Syracuse Herald
Syracuse Post Standard
Syracuse Sunday Herald
Toronto Daily Mail
Trenton Evening Standard
Washington Critic
Washington Post
Weekly News and Courier (Charleston)
Wetaskiwin Times
Wisconsin Patriot (Madison)
Wisconsin State Journal

Asia
Ceylon Observer (Colombo)
Madras Mail
North China Herald (Shanghai)
Pioneer (Allahabad)
Singapore Free Press
Singapore Free Press and Mercantile Advertiser
Straits Times (Singapore)

Australia
Brisbane Courier
Camperdown Chronicle
Courier (Hobart)

Herald (Melbourne)
Mercury (Hobart)
South Australian Register (Adelaide)
Sydney Morning Herald
West Australian (Perth)
Western Mail (Perth)

New Zealand
Ashburton Guardian
Clutha Leader (Balclutha)
Colonist (Nelson)
Daily Southern Cross (Auckland)
Evening Post (Wellington)
Mataura Ensign (Gore)
Nelson Examiner and New Zealand Chronicle
Otago Witness (Dunedin)
Poverty Bay Herald (Gisborne)
Star (Auckland)
Star (Christchurch)
Thames Star
Tuapeka Times (Lawrence)
Wellington Independent
West Coast Times (Hokitika)

Africa
Beira Post
Bulawayo Chronicle
Central African Times (Blantyre, Malawi)
Grahamstown Journal
Mafeking Mail
Mafeking Mail and Protectorate Guardian
Rhodesia Herald
Uganda Herald

British and Irish Isles
Aberdeen Weekly Journal
Anglo-American Times
British Daily Whig
The English Race
Essex County Standard
Freeman's Journal
Hampshire Advertiser
Leeds Mercury
Lloyd's Weekly Register
Morning Chronicle
The Times
West Suffolk Gazette, and Eastern Counties Advertiser

PhD theses

Bianchi, Hanael P., 'St George's Day: A Cultural History', unpublished PhD thesis, Catholic University of America, 2011.
Robinson, Lesley C., 'Englishness in England and the "Near Diaspora": Organisation, Influence and Expression, 1880s–1970s', unpublished PhD thesis, University of Ulster, 2014.

Secondary sources

Abraham, Lewis, *Gloria Britan[n]ica and the Universality of Anglo-Saxonism. A Paper Read at the Convention of the North American St George's Union, at Toronto, August, 30, 1883* (Washington, DC, 1883).
Adams, Iestyn, *Brothers across the Ocean: British Foreign Policy and the Origins of the 'Special Relationship' 1900–1905* (London, 2005).
Anderson, Benedict, *Imagined Communities: Reflections on the Origins and Spread of Nationalism* (London, 1983).
Anderson, Virginia DeJohn, 'New England in the Seventeenth Century', in Nicholas Canny (ed.), *The Oxford History of the British Empire*, vol. 1: *The Origins of Empire* (Oxford, 1998, reprinted 2001).
Aranya Fradenburg, L.O., 'Pro Patria Mori', in Kathy Lavezzo (ed.), *Imagining a Medieval English Nation* (Minneapolis, 2004).
Aspinwall, B., 'The Welfare State within the State: The Saint Vincent de Paul Society in Glasgow, 1848–1920', in W.J. Sheils and D. Wood (eds), *Voluntary Religion* (Oxford, 1986).
Bailyn, B., *The Peopling of British North America: An Introduction* (New York, 1986).
—— *Voyagers West: A Passage in the Peopling of America on the Eve of Revolution* (New York, 1966).
—— and Philip D. Morgan, 'Introduction', in Bernard Bailyn and Philip D. Morgan (eds), *Strangers in the Realm: Cultural Margins of the First British Empire* (Chapel Hill, NC, 1991).
Baines, Dudley, *Migration in a Mature Economy: Emigration and Internal Migration in England and Wales 1861–1900* (1985; Cambridge, 2002).
Barenreiter, Josef M., *English Associations of Workingmen* (London, 1889).
Barker, Ada, *Victoria Regina et Imperatrix, June 20, 1897* (London, 1897).
Barnes, Ian and Charles Royster, *The Historical Atlas of the American Revolution* (New York, 2000).
Bartlett, Thomas, '"This famous island set in a Virginian sea": Ireland the British Empire, 1690–1801', in Peter Marshall (ed.), *The Oxford History of the British Empire*, vol. 2 (Oxford, 1998).
Beames, M.R., 'Ribbon Societies: Lower-Class Nationalism in Pre-Famine Ireland', in C.E.H. Philpin (ed.), *Nationalism and Popular Protest in Ireland* (Oxford, 2002).
Beath, Robert B., *Historical Catalogue of the St Andrew's Society of Philadelphia: With Biographical Sketches of Deceased Members* (Philadelphia, 1913).

Beaufoy, Mark, *Tour Through Parts of the United States and Canada* (London, 1862).

Beito, David T., *From Mutual Aid to the Welfare State: Fraternal Society and Social Services, 1890–1967* (Chapel Hill, NC, 2000).

Bek, William G., *The German Settlement Society of Philadelphia and its Colony Hermann, Missouri* (Philadelphia, 1907).

Belchem, J., '"Freedom and friendship to Ireland": Ribbonism in Early Nineteenth-Century Liverpool', *International Review of Social History*, 39:1 (1994), pp. 33–56.

Benjamin, Charles F., *The future relations of the English-speaking communities; an essay read before the eleventh convention of the North American St George's union at Chicago, August 20, 1884* (Washington, DC, 1884).

Berguist, James M., *Daily Life in Immigrant America, 1820–1870* (Westport, CT, 2008).

Berthoff, Rowland, *British Immigrants in Industrial America, 1790–1850* (Cambridge, MA, 1953).

Besant, W., *Autobiography of Sir Walter Besant: With a prefatory note by S. Squire Sprigg* (New York, 1902).

—— 'The Atlantic Union', *The Forum* (October 1900) pp. 245–56.

Bickers, Robert (ed.), *Settlers and Expatriates* (Oxford, 2010).

—— *Britain in China: Community, Culture and Colonialism, 1900–49* (Manchester, 1999).

Blaustein, Richard, *The Thistle and the Brier: Historical Links and Cultural Patterns Between Scotland and Appalachia* (Jefferson, NC, 2003).

—— 'Scottish Americans', in J.H. Brunvand (ed.), *American Folklore: An Encyclopedia* (New York, 1996).

Blewett, Mary H., 'USA: Shifting Landscapes of Class, Culture, Gender, Race and Protest in the American Northeast and South', in Lex Heerma van Voss, Els Hiemstra-Kuperus and Elise van Nederveen Meerkerk (eds), *The Ashgate Companion to the History of Textile Workers, 1650–2000* (London, 2010).

—— *Constant Turmoil: The Politics of Industrial Life in Nineteenth-Century New England* (Amherst, 2000).

Bodnar, John, *The Transplanted: A History of Immigrants in Urban America* (Bloomington, IA, 1985).

Bosse, Georg von, *Das deutsche Element in den Vereinigten Staaten unter besonderer Berücksichtigung seines politischen, ethnischen, sozialen und erzieherischen Einflusses* (New York, 1908).

Bouchier, Nancy B., *For the Love of the Game: Amateur Sport in Small-Town Ontario, 1838–1895* (Kingston and Montreal, 2003).

Boynton, Nathan S., *History of the Knights of the Maccabees: Book of the Ancient Maccabees and Biographical Sketches of the Executive Officers of the Order, 1881 to 1898* (Port Huron, MI, 1892).

Bradburn, Douglas, *The Citizenship Revolution: Politics and the Creation of the American Union* (Charlottesville, VA, 2009).

Brassard, Michèle and Jean Hamelin, 'Tarte, Joseph Israel', in *Dictionary of Canadian Biography*, vol. 13, University of Toronto, http://www.biographi.ca/en/bio.php?id_nbr=7097 (last accessed 20 March 2014).

Breen, T.H., '"The baubles of Britain": The American and Consumer Revolutions of the Eighteenth Century', *Past and Present*, 119 (1988), pp. 74–109.

Briderbaugh, Carl, *Cities in Revolt: Urban Life in America, 1743–1776* (New York, 1955).

—— *Cities in the Wilderness: The First Century of Urban Life in America, 1625–1742* (New York, 1938).

Broehl, Wayne J., *The Molly Maguires* (Cambridge, MA, 1964).

Brown, Ronald C., *Hard-Rock Miners: The Intermountain West, 1860–1920* (College Station, TX, 1979).

Brubaker, R., 'The "Diaspora" Diaspora', *Ethnic and Racial Studies*, 28:1 (2005), pp. 1–19.

Buckner, Phillip, 'Introduction: Canada and the British Empire', in Phillip Buckner (ed.), *Canada and the British Empire* (Oxford, 2008).

Bueltmann, Tanja, *Clubbing Together: Ethnicity, Civility and Formal Sociability in the Scottish Diaspora to 1930* (Liverpool, 2014).

—— '"Gentlemen, I am going to the Old Country": Scottish Roots-Tourists in the Late 19th and Early 20th Centuries', in Mario Varricchio (ed.), *Back to Caledonia: Scottish Return Migration from the 16th Century to the Present* (Edinburgh, 2012).

—— 'Anglo-Saxonism and the Racialization of the English Diaspora', in Tanja Bueltmann, David T. Gleeson and Donald M. MacRaild (eds), *Locating the English Diaspora, 1500–2010* (Liverpool, 2012).

—— *Scottish Ethnicity and the Making of New Zealand Society, 1850–1930* (Edinburgh, 2011).

Bueltmann, Tanja, David T. Gleeson and Donald M. MacRaild, 'Invisible Diaspora? English Ethnicity in the United States before 1920', *Journal of American History*, 33:4 (Summer 2014), pp. 5–30.

—— (eds), *Locating the English Diaspora, 1500–2010* (Liverpool, 2012).

—— 'Introduction: Locating the English Diaspora: Problems, Perspectives and Approaches', in Tanja Bueltmann, David T. Gleeson and Donald M. MacRaild (eds), *Locating the English Diaspora, 1500–2010* (Liverpool, 2012).

Bueltmann, Tanja, Andrew Hinson and Graeme Morton, *The Scottish Diaspora* (Edinburgh, 2013).

Bueltmann, Tanja, and Donald M. MacRaild, 'Globalizing St George: English Associations in the Anglo-world to the 1930s', *Journal of Global History*, 7:1 (2012), pp. 79–105.

Buffum, Este E., and Charles E. Whelan, *Modern Woodmen of America: A History … of the Society from its Inception in 1883 to and Including 1926* (Rock Island, IL, 1927).

Bukowyzck, John J., et al. (eds), *Permeable Border: The Great Lakes Basin as a Transnational Region, c.1650–1990* (Pittsburgh, PA, 2005).

Bulik, Mark, *The Sons of Molly Maguire: The Irish Roots of America's First Labor War* (New York, 2015).

Bullock, Steven C., *Revolutionary Brotherhood: Freemasonry and the Transformation of the American Social Order, 1730–1840* (Chapel Hill, NC, 1996).

Burt, Roger, 'Freemasonry and Business Networking during the Victorian Period', *Economic History Review*, 56 (November 2003), pp. 657–88.

Bush, Julia, *Edwardian Ladies and Imperial Power* (London, 2000).

Butler, Jon, *Becoming America: The Revolution before 1776* (Cambridge, MA, 2001).

Cain, P.J., and A.G. Hopkins, *British Imperialism, 1688–2000* (Abingdon, 1993).

Campbell, John H., *History of the Friendly Sons of St Patrick and of the Hibernian Society for the Relief of Emigrants from Ireland* (Philadelphia, 1892).

Campbell, Mildred, 'Social Origins of Some Early Americans', in James Morton Smith (ed.), *Seventeenth-Century America: Essays in Colonial History* (Chapel Hill, NC, 1959).

—— 'English Emigration on the Eve of the American Revolution', *American Historical Review*, 61:1 (October 1955), pp. 1–20.

Campbell Orr, Clarissa, 'The Feminization of the Monarchy, 1780–1910: Royal Masculinity and Female Empowerment', in Andrzej Olechnowicz (ed.), *The Monarchy and the British Nation, 1780 to the Present* (Cambridge, 2007).

Cannadine, David, *Ornamentalism: How the British Saw their Empire* (London, 2001).

Canny, Nicholas, *Making Ireland British, 1580–1650* (Oxford, 2003).

—— (ed.), *The Oxford History of the British Empire*, vol. 1: *The Origins of Empire* (Oxford, 1998, reprinted 2001).

Capace, Nancy, *Encyclopaedia of Maryland* (Baltimore, 1999).

Carnegie, Andrew, *Triumphant Democracy Or: Fifty Years' March of the Republic* (London, 1886).

Carnes, Mark C., *Secret Ritual and Manhood in Victorian America* (New Haven, CT, 1989).

Carroll, F.M., 'Robert Lansing and the Alaskan Boundary Settlement', *International History Review*, 9:2 (1987), pp. 271–90.

Chamberlain, Muriel E., 'Bulwer (William) Henry Lytton Earle, Baron Dalling and Bulwer (1801–1872)', *Oxford Dictionary of National Biography*, Oxford University Press, 2004; online edn, January 2008, http://www.oxforddnb.com/view/article/3935 (last accessed 5 April 2014).

Chambers, Capt. Ernest J., *The Royal Grenadiers: A Regimental History of the 10th Infantry Regiment of the Active Militia of Canada* (Toronto, 1904).

Chan, Arlene, *The Chinese in Toronto from 1878* (Toronto, 2011).

Clark, Peter, *British Clubs and Societies 1580–1800: The Origins of an Associational World* (Oxford, 2000).

Clarke, Brian P., *Piety and Nationalism: Lay Voluntary Associations and the Creation of an Irish-Catholic Community in Toronto, 1850–1895* (Kingston and Montreal, 1993).

Clawson, Mary Ann, *Constructing Brotherhood: Class, Gender, and Fraternalism* (Princeton, NJ, 1989).

—— 'Nineteenth-Century Women's Auxiliaries and Fraternal Orders', *Signs*, 12:1 (1986), pp. 40–61.

Cmiel, K., *A Home of Another Kind: One Chicago Orphanage and the Tangle of Child Welfare* (Chicago, 1995).

Cohen, Lisbeth, *Making a New Deal: Industrial Workers in Chicago, 1919–39* (New York, 1990).

Cohen, Robin, *Global Diasporas: An Introduction* (revised edn, London, 2008).

Cohn, Raymond L., 'The Occupation of English Immigrants to the United States, 1836–1853', *Journal of Economic History*, 52:2 (1992), pp. 377–87.

Coleman, J. Walter, *The Molly Maguire Riots: Industrial Conflict in the Pennsylvania Coal Region* (1936; paperback, New York, 1969).

Colley, Linda, *Britons: Forging the Nation, 1707–1837* (New Haven, 1992).

Condor, S., 'Unimagined Community? Some Psychological Issues Concerning English National Identity', in G.M. Breakwell and E. Lyons (eds), *Changing European Identities: Social Psychological Analysis of Social Change* (Oxford, 1996).

Conway, Alan, *The Welsh in America: Letters from the Immigrants* (St Paul, MN, 1961).

Cordery, Simon, *British Friendly Societies, 1750–1914* (Basingstoke, 2003).

Corfe, T.H., *Phoenix Murders: Conflict, Compromise and Tragedy in Ireland, 1879–1882* (London, 1968).

Crafts, David, *History of Scranton, Pennsylvania ...* (Dayton, OH, 1891).

Craig, Robert M., *The Architecture of Francis Palmer Smith, Atlanta's Scholar-Architect* (Athens, GA, 2012).

Crossman, Virginia, *Politics, Law and Order in Nineteenth-century Ireland* (Belfast, 1996.

Dalziel, Raewyn, 'Popular Protest in Early New Plymouth: Why Did it Occur?', *New Zealand Journal of History*, 20:1 (1986), pp. 3–26.

Damousi, Joy, *Colonial Voices: A Cultural History of English in Australia, 1840–1940* (Cambridge, 2010).

Davis, Graham, 'The Irish in Britain, 1815–1939', in Andy Bielenberg (ed.), *The Irish Diaspora* (Harlow, 2000).

Deacon, Desley, Penny Russell, and Angela Woollacott (eds), *Transnational Lives: Biographies of Global Modernity, 1700–Present* (Basingstoke, 2010).

Dedering, Tilman, '"Avenge the Lusitania": The Anti-German riots in South Africa in 1915', *Immigrants and Minorities*, 31:3 (2013), pp. 256–88.

Deiler, J. Hanno, *Geschichte der Deutschen Gesellschaft von New Orleans: Festschrift zum Goldenen Jubiläum der Gesellschaft* (New Orleans, 1897).

De Tocqueville, Alexis, *Democracy in America*, 2 vols (New York, 2004).

Dickson, R.J., *Ulster Emigration to Colonial America, 1718–1775* (London, 1966).

Diner, H.R., *Hungering for America: Italian, Irish, and Jewish Foodways in the Age of Migration* (Cambridge, MA, 2001).

Dobson, David, *Scottish Emigration to Colonial America, 1607–1785* (Athens, GA, 1994).

Donaldson, Emily Ann, *The Scottish Highland Games in America* (Gretna, 1986).

Easterby, J.H., *History of the St Andrew's Society of Charleston, South Carolina* (Charleston, 1929).

Ekrich, A. Roger, *Bound for America: The Transportation of British Convicts to the Colonies, 1718–1775* (Oxford, 1987).

Elliott, Bruce S., 'Regional Patterns of English Immigration and Settlement in Upper Canada', in Barbara J. Messamore (ed.), *Canadian Migration Patterns: From Britain and North America* (Ottawa, 2004).

—— 'English', in Paul T. Magocsi (ed.), *Encyclopaedia of Canada's Peoples* (Toronto, 1999).

Emmons, David, *The Butte Irish: Class and Ethnicity in an American Mining Town 1875–1925* (Urbana, 1989).

English, J., 'Empire Day in Britain, 1904–1958', *Historical Journal*, 44:1 (2006), pp. 247–76.

Erickson, Charlotte, *Invisible Immigrants: The Adaptation of English and Scottish Immigrants in Nineteenth-Century America* (Ithaca, NY, 1992).

—— 'Emigration from the British Isles to the USA in 1841, Part II: Who were the English emigrants?', *Population Studies*, 44 (1990), pp. 21–40.

—— 'Emigration from the British Isles to the USA in 1841: Part I: Emigration from the British Isles', *Population Studies*, 43 (1989), pp. 347–67.

—— 'English', in Stephan Thernstrom, Ann Orlov and Oscar Handlin (eds), *Harvard Encyclopaedia of American Ethnic Groups* (2nd edn, Cambridge, MA, 1980).

—— *American Industry and the European Immigrant, 1860–1885* (New York, 1958).

Ernst, Robert, *Immigrant Life in New York, 1825–63* (1949; Syracuse, NY, 1994).

Esslinger, Dean E., 'Immigration through the Port of Baltimore', in M. Mark Stolarik (ed.), *Forgotten Doors: The Other Ports of Entry to the United States* (Philadelphia, 1988).

Fairburn, Miles, *The Ideal Society and its Enemies: Foundations of Modern New Zealand Society, 1850–1900* (Auckland, 1989).

Faust, Albert B., *The German Element in the United States, with Special Reference to its Political, Moral, Social, and Educational Influence*, vol. 2 (Boston, 1909).

Fender, Stephen, *Sea Changes: British Emigration and American Literature* (Cambridge, 1992).

Ferguson Clement, Priscilla, *Welfare and the Poor in the Nineteenth-Century City: Philadelphia, 1800–1854* (London, 1985).

Fielding, S., *Class and Ethnicity: Irish Catholics in England, 1880–1939* (Buckingham, 1992).

Finney, J.M.T., *A Surgeon's Life: The Autobiography of J.M.T. Finney* (1940; Whitefish, MT, 2007).

Fisher, Susan, *Boys and Girls in No Man's Land: English-Canadian Children and the First World War* (Toronto, 2010).

Fitzpatrick, David, 'Exporting Brotherhood: Orangeism in South Australia', *Immigrants and Minorities*, 23:2–3 (2005), pp. 277–310.

Foner, Eric, 'The Land League and Irish America', in Eric Foner (ed.), *Politics and Ideology in the Age of the Civil War* (New York, 1980).

Forster, A. Kristen, *Moral Visions and Material Ambitions: Philadelphia Struggles to Define the Republic, 1776–1836* (Oxford, 2005).

Fowler, Alan, *Lancashire Cotton Operatives and Work, 1900–1950: A Social History of Lancashire Cotton Operatives in the Twentieth Century* (London, 2003).

Francis, Andrew, *'To be Truly British we must be Anti-German': New Zealand, Enemy Aliens and the Great War Experience, 1914–1919* (Oxford, 2012).

Francis, Daniel, *National Dreams: Myths, Memory and Canadian History* (Vancouver, 1997).

Francis, R. Douglas, and Chris Kitzan (eds), *The Prairie West as Promised Land* (Calgary, 2007).

Freke Gould, Robert, *The History of Freemasonry*, 3 vols (London, 1882–87).

Fuller, George N., *A History of the Upper Peninsula of Michigan*, 3 vols (Dayton, OH, 1926).

Galenson, David, '"Middling People" or "Common Sort"? The Social Origins of some Early Americans Re-Examined', *William and Mary Quarterly*, 3rd series, 35 (1978), pp. 499–524.

Gallman, Matthew, *Receiving Erin's Children: Philadelphia, Liverpool and the Irish Famine Migration, 1845-1855* (Raleigh, NC, 2000).

Games, Alison, *Migration and the Origins of the English Atlantic* (Cambridge, MA, 1999).

Gaskill, Malcolm, *Between Two Worlds: How the English Became Americans* (Oxford, 2014).

Gemery, A., 'Emigration from the British Isles to the New World: Inferences from Colonial Populations', *Research in Economic History*, 5 (1980), pp. 179–231.

Gerteis, Joseph, *Class and the Color Line: Interracial Class Coalition in the Knights of Labor* (Durham, NC, 2007).

Gibson, Campbell, 'Population of the 100 Largest Cities and other Urban Places in the United States, 1790–1990', Population Division, United States Bureau of the Census, Washington, DC, Population Division Working Paper no. 27 (1998).

Good, Edwin M., 'William Steinway and Music in New York, 1861–1871', in Michael Saffle and James R. Heintze (eds), *Music and Culture in America, 1861–1918* (Abingdon, 2013).

Gosden, P.H.J.H., *The Friendly Societies in England, 1815–1875* (Manchester, 1961).

Gross, Robert A., 'Giving in America: From Charity to Philanthropy', in Lawrence J. Friedman and Mark D. McGarvie (eds), *Charity, Philanthropy and Civility in American History* (Cambridge, 2003).

Gutman, Herbert G., 'Work, Culture and Society in Industrializing America, 1815–1919', *American Historical Review*, 83:3 (1973), pp. 531–88.

Habermas, J., *The Transformation of the Public Sphere* (Cambridge, MA, 1989).

Hackett Fischer, David, *Albion's Seed: Four British Folkways in America* (New York, 1989).

Hamilton, Douglas J., *Scotland, the Caribbean and the Atlantic World, 1750–1820* (Manchester, 2005).

Handlin, Oscar, *The Uprooted: The Epic Story of the Great Migrations that Made the American People* (Boston, 1951).

Harland-Jacobs, Jessica L., '"Maintaining the Connexion": Orangeism in the British North Atlantic World', *Atlantic Studies*, 5 (April 2008), pp. 27–49.

—— *Builders of Empire: Freemasonry and British Imperialism, 1717–1927* (Chapel Hill, NC, 2007).

—— '"Hands across the Sea": The Masonic Network, British Imperialism, and the North Atlantic World', *Geographical Review*, 89 (1999), pp. 237–53.

Harper, Marjory (ed.), *Emigrant Homecomings: The Return Movement of Emigrants, 1600–2000* (Manchester, 2005).

—— *Emigration from Scotland between the Wars: Opportunity or Exile?* (Manchester, 1998).

—— and Stephen Constantine, *Migration and Empire* (Oxford, 2010).

Harris, Bernard, and Paul Brigden (eds), *Charity and Mutual Aid in Europe and North America since 1800* (London, 2007).

Harris, R.C., G.J. Matthews and R. Louis Gentilcore, *Historical Atlas of Canada: The Land Transformed, 1800–1891* (Toronto, 1987).

Hartmann, George Edward, *The Welsh Society of Philadelphia: History, Charter and By-Laws* (Philadelphia, 1979).

Hastings, Adrian, *The Construction of Nationhood: Ethnicity, Religion and Nationalism* (New York, 1997).

Hastings, Paula, '"Our glorious Anglo-Saxon Race shall ever fill earth's highest place": The Anglo-Saxon and the Construction of Identity in Late-Nineteenth-Century Canada', in R. Douglas Francis (ed.), *Canada and the British World: Culture, Migration and Identity* (Vancouver, 2006).

Hawkins, Freda, *Critical Years in Immigration: Canada and Australia Compared* (Kingston, Ont., 1991).

Hayward, Mary Ellen, and Frank R. Shivers (eds), *The Architecture of Baltimore: An Illustrated History* (Baltimore, 2004).

Hechter, Michael J., *Internal Colonialism: The Celtic Fringe in British National Development, 1536–1966* (Berkeley, 1992).

Heckethorn, C.W., *The Secret Societies of All Ages and Countries*, 2 vols (London, 1897).

Heim, Carol E., 'Structural Changes: Regional and Urban', in Stanley L. Engerman and Robert E. Gallman (eds), *The Cambridge Economic History of the United States* (Cambridge, 2000).

Hempton, David, *Religion and Political Culture in Britain and Ireland: From the Glorious Revolution to the Decline of Empire* (Cambridge, 1996).

—— *Evangelical Protestantism and Ulster Society, 1740–1890* (London, 1992).

—— and Myrtle Hill, 'Did Ulster Presbyterians have a Devotional Revolution?', in James Murphy (ed.), *Evangelicals and Catholics in Nineteenth-Century Ireland* (Dublin, 2005).

Hepburn, A.C., 'The Ancient Order of Hibernians in Irish Politics, 1905–1914', *Cithara*, 10 (1971), pp. 5–18.

Hild, Mathew, *Greenbackers, Knights of Labor, and Populists: Farmer-Labor Insurgency in the Late-Nineteenth-Century South* (Athens, GA, 2010).

Hoerder, Dirk, *Creating Societies: Immigrant Lives in Canada* (Kingston, 1999).

Hoisington, Daniel J., *A German Town: A History of New Ulm, Minnesota* (Roseville, 2004).

Hopkins, Eric, *Working-Class Self-Help in Nineteenth-Century England: Responses to Industrialization* (London, 1995).

Horning, Audrey, *Ireland in the Virginian Sea: Colonialism in the British Atlantic* (Chapel Hill, NC, 2013).

Howard, Ella, *Homeless: Poverty and Place in Urban America* (Philadelphia, 2013).

Hughes, Kyle, and Donald M. MacRaild, *Ribbonism in Ireland and Britain* (Liverpool, forthcoming).

—— 'Anti-Catholicism and Orangeism in Nineteenth-Century England and Scotland: Militant Loyalism in Action', in Allan Blackstock and Frank O'Gorman (eds), *Loyalism and the Formation of the British World* (Woodbridge, 2014).

Hume, David H., 'Empire Day in Ireland, 1896–1962', in Keith Jeffery (ed.), *An Irish Empire?* (Manchester, 1996).

Hunter, R.J., and J.S. Morrill, *Ulster Transformed: Essays on Plantation and Print Culture, c.1590–1641* (Belfast, 2012).

Huntley, Horace, 'Ethnicity and the American Working Class, 1850–1900: Fall River, 1850–1900', in Robert Asher and Charles Stephenson (eds), *Labor Divided: Race and Ethnicity in United States Labor Struggles, 1835–1960* (New York, 1990).

Jack, I. Allen, *History of the St Andrew's Society of St John, New Brunswick, Canada, 1798–1903* (St John, 1903).

Jarvie, G., *Highland Games: The Making of the Myth* (Edinburgh, 1991).

Jenkins, Brian, *The Fenian Problem: Insurgency and Terrorism in a Liberal State, 1858–1874* (Liverpool, 2009).

Jenkins, William, *Between Raid and Rebellion: The Irish in Buffalo and Toronto, 1867–1916* (Kingston, Ont., 2013).

Jenner, Thomas, *Victoria Regina et Imperatrix: A Diamond Jubilee Ode in Sixty Lines* (London, 1897).

Johnson, Joan Marie, *South Carolina Women* (Athens, GA, 2009).

Joyce, William L., *Editors and Ethnicity: A History of the Irish-American Press, 1848–1883* (New York, 1976).

Kazal, Russell A., *Becoming Old Stock: The Paradox of German-American Identity* (Princeton, NJ, 2004).

Kealey, Gregory S., *Toronto Workers Respond to Capitalism, 1867–1892* (Toronto, 1980).

Keil, Hartmut, and John B. Jentz (eds), *German Workers in Chicago: A Documentary History of Working-Class Culture from 1850 to World War 1* (Chicago, 1988).

Kelley, N., and M.J. Trebilcock, *Making the Mosaic: A History of Canadian Immigration Policy* (Toronto, 2010).

Kenny, Kevin, 'Diaspora and Comparison: The Irish as a Case Study', *Journal of American History*, 90:1 (2003), pp. 134–62.

—— *The American Irish: A History* (New York, 2000).

—— *Making Sense of the Molly Maguires* (New York, 1998).

Kerr, John J., and Deryck W. Holdsworth (eds), *Historical Atlas of Canada: Addressing the Twentieth Century, 1891–1961* (Toronto, 1990).

Keshen, Jeffrey A., 'Hopkins, John Castell', in *Dictionary of Canadian Biography*, vol. 15, University of Toronto, http://www.biographi.ca/en/bio/hopkins_john_castell_15E.html (last accessed 13 March 2014).

Kiberd, Declan, *Inventing Ireland: The Literature of the Modern Nation* (London, 1995).

King, Greg, *Twilight of Splendor: The Court of Queen Victoria During her Diamond Jubilee* (London, 2007).

King, John S., *The Early History of the Sons of England Benevolent Society* (Toronto, 1891).

Kleber, John F., *The Encyclopedia of Louisville* (Lexington, 2001).

Kleinberg, Jay, *Widows and Orphans First: The Family Economy and Social Welfare Policy, 1880–1939* (Champaign, IL, 2005).

Knauff, T.C., *A History of the Society of the Sons of St George* (Philadelphia, 1923).

Koebner, Richard, *Imperialism* (Cambridge, 1964).

Kohn, Edward P., *This Kindred People: Canadian–American Relations and the Anglo-Saxon Idea, 1895–1903* (Kingston and Montreal, 2004).

Kraly, E.P. and P. Vogelaar, '"Starting with Spoons": Refugee Migration and Resettlement Programs in Utica, New York', in J.W. Frazier, E.L. Tetley-Fio and N.F. Henry (eds), *Race, Ethnicity, and Place in a Changing America* (Herndon, VA, 2011).

Kraut, Alan, *The Huddled Masses: The Immigrant in American Society, 1880–1920* (2nd edn, Arlington Heights, IL, 2002);

Kurland, Gerald, *Seth Low: The Reformer in an Urban and Industrial Age* (New York, 1971).

Kumar, Krishan, *The Making of English National Identity* (Cambridge, 2003).

Lake, Marilyn, and Henry Reynolds, *Drawing the Global Colour Line* (Cambridge, 2008).

Lambert, John, 'Maintaining a British Way of Life: English Speaking South Africa's Patriotic, Cultural and Charitable Associations', *Historia*, 54:2 (2009), pp. 55–76.

—— '"An unknown people": Reconstructing British South African Identity', *Journal of Imperial and Commonwealth History*, 37:4 (2009), pp. 599–617.

—— 'South African British? Or Dominion South Africans? The Evolution of an Identity in the 1910s and 1920s', *South African Historical Journal*, 43:1 (2000), pp. 197–222.

Landsman, Ned C., *Scotland and its First American Colony, 1683–1764* (Princeton, NJ, 1985).

Laurie, Bruce, *Artisans into Workers: Labour in Nineteenth-Century America* (Champaign, IL, 1997).

Lawrence, Vera B., *Strong on Music: The New York Music Scene in the Days of George Templeton Strong* (Chicago, 1999).

Lee, Antoinette J., *Architects to the Nation: The Rise and Decline of the Supervising Architects Office* (New York, 2000).

Lee Hansen, Marcus, *The Immigrant in American History* (Cambridge, MA, 1940).

Leitch, Gillian I., 'The Importance of Being English: English Ethnic Culture in Montreal, c.1800–1864', in Tanja Bueltmann, David T. Gleeson and Donald M. MacRaild (eds), *Locating the English Diaspora, 1500–2010* (Liverpool, 2012).

Lemon, James T., 'Colonial America in the 18th Century', in Thomas F. McIlwraith and Edward K. Muller (eds), *North America: The Historical Geography of a Changing Continent* (Lanham, MD, 2000).

Lempa, Heikki, *Beyond the Gymnasium: Educating the Middle-Class Bodies in Classical Germany* (Lanham, MD, 2007).

Light, Ivan H., *Ethnic Enterprise in America: Business and Welfare among Chinese, Japanese and Blacks* (Berkeley, CA, 1973).

Lloyd, Amy J., '"The Englishmen here are much disliked": Hostility towards English Immigrants in Early Twentieth-Century Toronto', in Tanja Bueltmann, David T. Gleeson and Donald M. MacRaild (eds), *Locating the English Diaspora, 1500–2010* (Liverpool, 2012).

Lowry, Donal, 'The Crown, Empire Loyalism and the Assimilation of Non-British White Subjects in the British World: An Argument against "Ethnic Determinism"', in Carl Bridge and Kent Fedorowich (eds), *The British World: Diaspora, Culture and Identity* (London, 2003).

Lu, H., *Beyond the Neon Lights: Everyday Shanghai in the Early Twentieth Century* (Berkeley, 2004).

MacCarthy-Morrogh, Michael, *The Munster Plantation: English Migration to Southern Ireland, 1583–1641* (Oxford, 1986).

MacRaild, Donald M., *The Irish Diaspora in Britain, 1750–1939* (2nd edn, Basingstoke, 2010).

—— 'Orangeism in the Atlantic World', in David. T. Gleeson (ed.), *The Irish in the Atlantic World* (Columbia, SC, 2010).

—— *Faith, Fraternity and Fighting: The Orange Order and Irish Migrants in Northern England, c.1850–1906* (Liverpool, 2005).

MacRaild, Donald M., Sylvia Ellis and Stephen Bowman, 'Interdependence Day and Magna Charta: James Hamilton's Public Diplomacy in the Anglo-World, 1907–1940s', *Journal of Transatlantic Studies*, 12:2 (2014), pp. 126–48.

MacRaild, Donald M., and D.A.J. MacPherson, 'Sisters of the Brotherhood: Female Orangeism on Tyneside in the Late 19th and Early 20th Centuries', *Irish Historical Studies*, 34:137 (May 2006), pp. 40–60.

MacRaild, Donald M., and David E. Martin, *Labour in British Society, 1830–1914* (Basingstoke, 2000).

MacRaild, Donald M., and Malcolm Smith, 'Migration and Emigration, 1600–1945', in Liam Kennedy and Philip Ollerenshaw (eds), *Ulster since 1600: Politics, Economy, and Society* (Oxford, 2013).

Magee, Gary B., and Andrew S. Thompson, *Empire and Globalisation: Networks of People, Goods and Capital in the British World, c.1850–1914* (Cambridge, 2010).

Mangan, J.A., '"The Grit of our Foregathers": Invented Traditions, Propaganda and Imperialisms', in John M. MacKenzie (ed.), *Imperialism and Popular Culture* (Manchester, 1986).

Martin, John B., *Call it North Country: The Story of Upper Michigan* (1944; Detroit, MI, 1986).

Matthews, B., and M. Cross, *Whispering Mountains: A History of Lewis, New York* (Honeoye Falls, NY, 2006).

Maxwell, M. Percival, *The Scottish Migration to Ulster in the Reign of James I* (Belfast, 1990).

McCarthy, Kathleen D., 'Women and Political Culture', in Lawrence J. Friedman and Mark D. McGarvie (eds), *Charity, Philanthropy and Civility in American History* (Cambridge, 2003).

McCartin, Joseph A., *Labor's Great War: The Struggle for Industrial Democracy and the Origins of Modern American Labor Relations, 1912–1921* (Raleigh, NC, 1997).

McCaughey, Robert A., *Stand, Columbia: A History of Columbia University* (Columbia, NY, 2013).

McGowan, Mark, *The Waning of the Green: Catholics, the Irish, and Identity in Toronto, 1887–1922* (Kingston and Montreal, 1999).

M'Culloch, John, *A Concise History of the United States, from the Discovery of America till 1795 ...* (Philadelphia, 1795).

Meagher, Timothy J., *Inventing Irish America: Generation, Class and Ethnic Identity in a New England City, 1880–1928* (Notre Dame, IA, 2001).

Menard, Russell R., 'British Migration to the Chesapeake Colonies in the Seventeenth Century', in Lois Green Carr, Philip D. Morgan and Jean B. Russo (eds), *Colonial Chesapeake Society* (Chapel Hill, NC, 2000).

Messamore, Barbara J., 'Canada and Migration: Kinship with the World', in Barbara J. Messamore (ed.), *Canadian Migration Patterns: From Britain and North America* (Ottawa, 2004).

—— (ed.), *Canadian Migration Patterns: From Britain and North America* (Ottawa, 2004).

Metzner, Henry, *A Brief History of the North American Gymnastic Union* (Indianapolis, 1911).

Middleton, David, and Derek Edwards (eds), *Collective Remembering* (London, 1990).

Mirala, Petri, *Freemasonry in Ulster, 1733–1813* (Dublin, 2007).

—— 'Lawful and Unlawful Oaths in Ireland, 1760–1835', in Allan Blackstock and Eoin Magennis (eds), *Politics and Political Culture in Britain and Ireland, 1750–1850: Essays in Tribute to Peter Jupp* (Belfast, 2006).

Mitchell, B.C., *The Paddy Camps: The Irish of Lowell, 1821–61* (1988; Champaign, IL, 2006).

Moffrey, R.W., *A Century of Oddfellowship. Being a Brief Record of the Rise and Progress of the Manchester Unity ...* (Manchester, 1910).

Moore, James R., and John Smith, *Corruption in Urban Politics and Society: Britain, 1780–1950* (London, 2007).

Morgan, Gwenda, and Peter Rushton, *Eighteenth-Century Criminal Transportation: The Formation of the Criminal Atlantic* (Basingstoke, 2004).

Morris, R.J., 'Urban Associations in England and Scotland, 1750–1914: The Formation of the Middle Class or the Formation of a Civil Society?', in Graeme Morton, Boudien de Vries and R.J. Morris (eds), *Civil Society, Associations, and Urban Places: Class, Nation, and Culture in Nineteenth-Century Europe* (Aldershot, 2006).

—— 'Clubs, Societies and Associations', in *The Cambridge Social History of Britain, 1750–1950*, 3 vols (Cambridge, 1993), vol. 3: *Social Agencies and Institutions*.

—— 'Voluntary Societies and British Urban Elites, 1780–1850: An Analysis', *Historical Journal*, 26:1 (1983), pp. 95–118.

—— 'Samuel Smiles and the Genesis of Self-Help', *Historical Journal*, 24 (1981), pp. 89–109.

Morrison, George Austin, *History of the Saint Andrew's Society of the State of New York, 1756–1906* (New York, 1906).

Morrow, Mary Sue, 'Somewhere between Beer and Wagner: The Cultural and Musical Impact of German Männerchöre in New York and New Orleans', in Michael Saffle and James R. Heintze (eds), *Music and Culture in America, 1861–1918* (Abingdon, 2013).

Morton, Desmond, 'Coffin, William Foster (1808–78)', *Dictionary of Canadian Biography*, vol. 10 (1871–1880), http://www.biographi.ca/en/bio/coffin_william_foster_10E.html (last accessed 10 August 2013).

Mosehthal, Hermann, *Geschichte des Vereins Deutscher Liederkranz in New York. Im Auftrag seines 50-jährigen Bestehens am 9. Januar 1897* (New York, 1897).

Murdoch, Alexander, *Scotland and America, c. 1600–c. 1800* (Basingstoke, 2010).

Murdoch, Lydia, *Daily Life of Victorian Women* (Santa Barbara, 2014).

Murphy, James (ed.), *Evangelicals and Catholics in Nineteenth-Century Ireland* (Dublin, 2005).

Murray, Charles A., *Travels in North America during the years 1834, 1835, & 1836, etc.*, 2 vols (London, 1839).

Nash, Gary B., *First City: Philadelphia and the Forging of Historical Memory* (Philadelphia, 2002).

Nau, John F., *The German People of New Orleans* (Leiden, 1954).

Neils Conzen, Kathleen, David A. Gerber, Ewa Morawska, George E., Pozzetta and Rudolph J. Vecoli, 'The Invention of Ethnicity: A View from the U.S.A', *Journal of American Ethnic History*, 12 (Fall 1992), pp. 5–41.

Newman, Gerald, *The Rise of English Nationalism: A Cultural History, 1740–1830* (London, 1987).

Nobles, Greg, 'Class', in *A Companion to Colonial America* (Oxford, 2003).

Noor, Masi, Rupert Brown and Gary Prentice, 'Prospects for Intergroup Conciliation: Social Psychological Indicators of Intergroup Forgiveness and Reparation in Northern Ireland and Chile', in Arie Nadler, Thomas E. Malloy and Jeffrey D. Fisher (eds), *The Social Psychology of Intergroup Reconciliation: From Violent Conflict to Peaceful Co-existence* (New York, 2008).

Nora, Pierre, 'Between Memory and History: Les Lieux de Mémoire', *Representations*, 26 (1989), pp. 7–24.

Nugent, Walter, *Crossings: The Great Transatlantic Migrations, 1870–1914* (Bloomington, 1992).

Ohlmeyer, Jane H., *Making Ireland English: The Irish Aristocracy in the Seventeenth Century* (New Haven, CT, 2012).

—— 'Colonization within Britain and Ireland', in Nicholas Canny (ed.), *The Oxford History of the British Empire*, vol. 1: *The Origins of Empire* (Oxford, 1998, reprinted 2001).

O'Leary, Paul, 'When was Anti-Catholicism? The Case of Nineteenth- and Twentieth-Century Wales', *Journal of Ecclesiastical History*, 56:2 (April 2005), pp. 308–25.

Olton, Charles S., *Artisans for Independence: Philadelphia Mechanics and the American Revolution* (Syracuse, NY, 1975).

O'Neill, Timothy N., 'Miners in Migration: The Case of Nineteenth-Century Irish and Irish-American Copper Miners', in Kevin Kenny (ed.), *New Directions in Irish-American History* (Madison, WI, 2003).

Ortlepp, Anke, *'Auf den, Ihr Schwestern!': Deutschamerikanische Frauenvereine in Milwaukee, Wisconsin, 1844–1914* (Stuttgart, 2004).

Ostendorf, Ann, *Sounds American: National Identity and Music Cultures of the Lower Mississippi River Valley, 1800–1860* (Athens, GA, 2011).

Panayi, P., *The Enemy in Our Midst: Germans in Britain during the First World War* (Oxford, 1991).

Parker, Florence Evelyn, *Care of Aged Persons in the United States* (Washington, DC, 1929).

Parry, Glyn, 'Mythologies of Empire and the First English Diaspora', in Tanja Bueltmann, David T. Gleeson and Donald M. MacRaild (eds), *Locating the English Diaspora, 1500–2010* (Liverpool, 2012).

Patterson, Brad, 'Cousin Jacks, New Chums and Ten Pound Poms: Locating New Zealand's English Diaspora', in Tanja Bueltmann, David T. Gleeson and Donald M. MacRaild (eds), *Locating the English Diaspora, 1500–2010* (Liverpool, 2012).

Peskin, L.A., *Manufacturing Revolution: The Intellectual Origins of Early American Industry* (Baltimore, 2003).

Pfleger, Birte, 'German Immigration to Philadelphia from the Colonial Period through the Twentieth Century', in Ayumi Takenaka and Mary Johnson Osirim (eds), *Global Philadelphia: Immigrant Communities Old and New* (Philadelphia, 2010).

Phillips, Jock and Terry Hearn, *Settlers: New Zealand Immigrants from England, Ireland and Scotland, 1800–1945* (Auckland, 2008).

Pickles, Katie, 'A Link in "the great chain of friendship": The Victoria League in New Zealand', *Journal of Imperial and Commonwealth History*, 33:1 (2005), pp. 29–50,

—— *Female Imperialism and National Identity: Imperial Order Daughters of the Empire* (Manchester, 2002).

Pohlsander, Hans A., *National Monuments and Nationalism in Nineteenth-Century Germany* (Bern, 2008).

Pollard, Sidney, 'The Ethics of the Sheffield Outrages', *Transactions of the Hunter Archaeological Society*, 8:3 (1953–54), pp. 118–39.

Pomfret, Richard, *The Economic Development of Canada* (Abingdon, 2006).

Pope, Peter E., *Fish into Wine: The Newfoundland Plantation in the Seventeenth Century* (Chapel Hill, NC, 2004).

Portes, Alejandro, 'Conclusion: Towards a New World: The Origins and Effects of Transnational Activities', *Ethnic and Racial Studies*, 22:2 (1999), pp. 463–77.

Potter, Fred W., *Forty-Third Annual Insurance Report of the Insurance Superintendent of the State of Illinois, Part III: Casualty and Assessment Insurance and Fraternal Societies* (Springfield, 1911).

Potter, J., 'The Growth of Population in America, 1700–1860', in *Population History: Essays in Historical Demography* (London, 1965).

Potter, Simon, *Broadcasting Empire: The BBC and the British World, 1922–1970* (Oxford, 2012).

—— *News and the British World* (Oxford, 2003).

Pula, James S., 'Ethnic Utica', *Oneida County Historical Society* (Oneida, 2005).

Purvis, Thomas L., *Colonial America to 1763* (New York, 1999).

Radley, A., 'Artefacts, Memory and a Sense of the Past', in D. Middleton and D. Edwards (eds), *Collective Remembering* (London, 1990).

Rappaport, Helen, *Queen Victoria: A Biographical Companion* (Santa Barbara, CA, 2003).

Ray, Celeste, *Ethnicity* (Chapel Hill, NC, 2007).

—— 'Scottish Immigration and Ethnic Organization in the United States', in Celeste Ray (ed.), *Transatlantic Scots* (Tuscaloosa, 2005).

Redmond, Gerald, *The Sporting Scots of Nineteenth-Century Canada* (Toronto, 1982).

Reed, Charles V., *Royal Tourists, Colonial Subjects and the Making of a British World, 1860–1911* (Manchester, 2016).

Reitbergen, Peter, *Europe: A Cultural History* (London, 2005).

Richards, Thomas, *The Commodity Culture of Victorian England: Advertising and Spectacle, 1851–1914* (Stanford, CA, 1991).

Ridge, John T., 'Irish County Societies in New York, 1880–1914', in Ronald H. Bayor and Timothy J. Meagher (eds), *The New York Irish* (Baltimore, 1996).

Riedi, Eliza, 'Women, Gender, and the Promotion of Empire: The Victoria League, 1901–1914', *Historical Journal*, 45:3 (2002), pp. 569–99.

Rittner, Don, *Schenectady: Frontier Village to Colonial City* (Stroud, 2011).

Roberts, Jeffrey, *Imperialism and Music: Britain, 1876–1953* (Manchester, 2002).

Robinson, Lesley C., English Associational Culture in Lancashire and Yorkshire, 1890s-c.1930s', *Northern History*, 51:1 (March 2014), pp. 131–52.

Rockman, Seth, *Scraping By: Wage Labor, Slavery, and Survival in Early Baltimore* (Baltimore, 2010).

Rosen, Robert N., *A Short History of Charleston* (Columbia, 1997).

Ross, Peter, *The Book of Scotia Lodge: Being the History of Scotia Lodge, No. 634* (New York, 1895).

Rush, Anna S., *Bonds of Empire: West Indians and Britishness from Victoria to Decolonization* (Oxford, 2011).

St John, Ian, *Disraeli and the Art of Politics* (London, 2005).

Salinger, Sharon, *Taverns and Drinking in Early America* (Baltimore, 2002).

Sanderson, T. H., 'West, Lionel Sackville Sackville-, second Baron Sackville (1827–1908)', rev. H.C.G. Matthew, *Oxford Dictionary of National Biography*, online edn, October 2006, http://www.oxforddnb.com/view/article/35902 (last accessed 29 August 2013).

Sanford, John L., *History of the St George's Society of Baltimore* (Baltimore, 1929).

Savage-Armstrong, George F., *Victoria, Regina et Imperatrix: A jubilee Song from Ireland, 1887* (London, 1887).

Saxon Mills, J., *The Gathering of the Clans: How the British Dominions and Dependencies have Helped in the War* (London, 1916).

Scharf, J. Thomas and Thompson Westcott, *History of Philadelphia, 1609–1884*, 3 vols (Philadelphia, 1884).

Seeley, J.R., *The Expansion of England: Two Courses of Lectures* (London, 1883; Chicago, 1971).

Seidensticker, Oswald, *Geschichte der Deutschen Gesellschaft von Pennsylvanien, 1764–1917* (Philadelphia, 1917).

Shahrodi, Zofi, 'The Experience of Polish Catholics in the Archdiocese of Toronto, 1905–1935', in Mark McGowan and Brian P. Clarke (eds), *Catholics at the 'Gathering Place': Historical Essays on the Archdiocese of Toronto, 1841–1991* (Toronto, 1993).

Shepperson, Wilbur S., *Emigration and Disenchantment: Portraits of Englishmen Repatriated from the United States* (Norman, OK, 1965).

—— *British Emigration to North America Emigration* (Oxford, 1956).

Short, K.R.M., *Dynamite Wars: Irish American Bombers in Britain* (Dublin, 1979).

Sim, David, *A Union Forever: The Irish Question and US Foreign Relations in the Victorian Age* (Ithaca, NY, 2013).

Smialkowska, Monika, 'An Englishman in New York? Celebrating Shakespeare in America, 1916', in Tanja Bueltmann, David T. Gleeson and Donald M. MacRaild (eds), *Locating the English Diaspora, 1500–2010* (Liverpool, 2012).

—— 'Conscripting Caliban: Shakespeare, America, and the Great War', *Shakespeare*, 7, 2 (2011), pp. 192–207.

Smiles, S., *Thrift: A Book of Domestic Counsel* (London, 1875; London, 1908).

—— *Self-Help; with Illustrations of Conduct and Perseverance* (London, 1886).

Smith, A.E., *Colonists in Bondage: White Servitude and Convict Labor in America, 1607–1776* (Chapel Hill, NC, 1947).

Smith, Andrew, *British Businessmen and Canadian Confederation: Constitution-Making in an Era of Anglo-Globalization* (Montreal and Kingston, 2008).

Smith, Anthony D., *Ethno-Symbolism: A Cultural Approach* (London, 2009).

Smith, Goldwin, *The Schism in the Anglo-Saxon Race: An Address delivered before the Canadian Club of New York* (New York, 1887).

Smout, T.C., Ned Landsman and T.M. Devine, 'Scottish Emigration in the Seventeenth and Eighteenth Centuries', in Nicholas P. Canny (ed.), *Europeans on the Move: Studies in European Migration* (Oxford, 1994).

Spengler, Otto, *Das deutsche Element der Stadt New York: Biographisches Jahrbuch der Deutsch-Amerikaner New Yorks und Umgebung* (New York, 1913).

Steers, J.A., 'The East Coast Floods, January 31–February 1, 1953', *Geographical Journal*, 119 (1954), pp. 163–66.

Steffen, Charles G., *The Mechanics of Baltimore: Workers and Politics in the Age of Revolution, 1763–1812* (Champaign, IL, 1984).

Stelter, Gilbert A., 'The Political Economy of Early Canadian Urban Development', in Gilbert A. Stelter and Alan F.J. Artibise (eds), *The Canadian City: Essays in Urban and Social History* (Ottawa, 1984).

—— 'Political Economy', in Gilbert A. Stelter and Alan F.J. Artibise (eds), *The Canadian City: Essays in Urban and Social History* (Ottawa, 1984).

Stevens, Albert C. (ed.), *The Cyclopedia of Fraternities* (New York, 1899).

Steward, Patrick, and Bryan P. McGovern, *The Fenians: Irish Rebellions in the North American World, 1858–1876* (Knoxville, TN, 2013).

Stortz, Gerald J., 'An Irish Radical in a Tory Town: William O'Brien in Toronto, 1887', *Eire-Ireland*, 19 (1984), pp. 35–58.

Stott, Richard B., *Workers in the Metropolis: Class, Ethnicity and Youth in Antebellum New York* (Ithaca, NY, 1990).

Surridge, K.T., *Managing the South Africa War, 1899–1902* (London, 1998).

Sutton, William R., *Journeymen for Jesus: Evangelical Artisans Confront*

Capitalism in Jacksonian Baltimore (Philadelphia, 1998).

Swingen, Abigail, L., *Competing Visions of Empire: Labor, Slavery, and the Origins of the British Atlantic Empire* (New Haven, CT, 2015).

Tamarkin, Elisa, *Anglophilia: Deference, Devotion, and Antebellum America* (Chicago, 2008).

Tengg, Julius, Carl C. Wurzbach and Emmett Whitsett (eds), *90th Anniversary Harmonia Lodge No. 1 Order of the Sons of Hermann, San Antonio, Texas, July 6, 1951: A Short History from the Documents of Harmonia Lodge No. 1 from 1861 to 1951* (San Antonio, 1951).

Thernstrom, Stephan, Ann Orlov and Oscar Handlin (eds), *Harvard Encyclopaedia of American Ethnic Groups* (2nd edn, Cambridge, MA, 1980).

Thistlethwaite, Frank, 'Migration from Europe Overseas in the Nineteenth and Twentieth Centuries' and 'Postscript', in R.J. Vecoli and S.M. Sinke (eds), *A Century of European Migrations 1830–1930* (Champaign, IL, 1991).

Thomas, Alexander R., *In Gotham's Shadow: Globalization and Community Change in Central New York* (New York, 2003).

Thompson, Peter, '"The friendly glass": Drink and Gentility in Colonial Philadelphia', *The Pennsylvania Magazine of History and Biography*, 113:4 (October 1989), pp. 556–77.

Timpe, Dieter, *Römisch-germanische Begegnungen in der späten Republik und frühen Kaiserzeit: Voraussetzungen – Konfrontationen – Wirkungen* (Munich, 2006).

Trollope, Joanna, *Britannia's Daughters: Women of the British Empire* (London, 1983).

Twining, Thomas, *Travels in America 100 Years Ago* (1894; Bedford, MA, 2007).

Valverde, Mariana, *The Age of Light, Soap, and Water: Moral Reform in English Canada, 1885–1925* (Toronto, 2008).

Van der Linden, Marcel (ed.), *Social Security Mutualism: The Comparative History of Mutual Benefit Societies* (Bern, 1996).

Van Heyningen, E. and P. Merrett, '"The Healing Touch": The Guild of Loyal Women of South Africa, 1900–1912', *South African Historical Journal*, 47 (November 2002), pp. 24–50.

Van Vugt, William E., 'British and British Americans (English, Scots, Scots Irish, and Welsh), to 1870', in Elliott R. Barkan (ed.), *Immigrants in American History: Arrival, Adaptation, and Integration*, 4 vols (Santa Barbara, CA, 2013), vol. 1:1.

—— 'British (English, Scottish, Scots Irish, and Welsh) and British Americans, 1870–1940', in Elliott R. Barkan (ed.), *Immigrants in American History: Arrival, Adaptation, and Integration*, 4 vols (Santa Barbara, CA, 2013), vol. 1:2.

—— 'The Hidden English Diaspora in Nineteenth-century America', in T. Bueltmann, David T. Gleeson, and D.M. MacRaild (eds), *Locating the Hidden Diaspora, 1500–2010* (Liverpool, 2012).

—— *British Immigration to the United States, 1776–1914* (London, 2009).

—— *British Buckeyes: The English, Scots, and Welsh in Ohio* (Kent, OH, 2006).

—— 'English', in Peter Eisenstadt and Laura-Eve Moss (eds), *The Encyclopaedia of New York State* (Syracuse, NY, 2005).

—— *Britain to America: Mid-Nineteenth Century Immigrants to the United*

States (Urbana and Chicago, 1999).

—— 'Prosperity and Industrial Emigration from Britain during the Early 1850s', *Journal of Social History*, 5 (Winter 1988), pp. 390–405.

—— 'Running from Ruin? The Emigration of British Farmers to the USA in the Wake of the Repeal of the Corn Laws', *Economic History Review*, 41 (August 1988), pp. 411–28.

Vertovec, Steven, 'Conceiving and Researching Transnationalism', *Ethnic and Racial Studies*, 22:3 (1999), pp. 447–62.

Vincent, Ted, *The Rise and Fall of American Sport* (Lincoln, 1994).

Volz, Louis, *German Beneficial Union and German Beneficial Union of Pittsburgh* (Pittsburgh, 1917).

Wager, Daniel E., *Our County and its People: Oneida County* (Boston, 1896).

Waller, Robert, *A Sketch of the Origin, Progress and Work of the St George's Society, A.D. 1786–1886* (New York, 1887).

Ward, Paul, *Britishness since 1870* (London, 2004).

Ward, W. Peter, 'Population Growth in Western Canada, 1901–71', in John E. Foster (ed.), *Developing the West* (Edmonton, 1983).

Watson, James, 'English Associationalism in the British Empire: Yorkshire Societies in New Zealand before the First World War', *Britain and the World*, 4 (2011), pp. 84–108.

Webster, Noah, *Sketch of American Policy …* (Hartford, CT, 1785).

Webster, Wendy, 'The Empire Comes Home: Commonwealth Migration to Britain', in Andrew Thompson (ed.), *Britain's Experience of Empire in the Twentieth Century*, Oxford History of the British Empire Companion Series (Oxford, 2012).

—— *Englishness and Empire, 1939–1965* (Oxford, 2007).

Weinbren, Daniel, 'Beneath the All-Seeing Eye: Fraternal Orders and Friendly Societies' Banners in Nineteenth- and Twentieth-Century Britain', *Cultural and Social History*, 2 (2006), pp. 167–91.

Weir, Robert E., *Beyond Labor's Veil: The Culture of the Knights of Labor* (University Park, PA, 2010).

Whatley, Harlan D., *Two Hundred Fifty Years, 1756–2006: The History of the St Andrew's Society of the State of New York* (New York, 2008).

Whelehan, Niall, *The Dynamiters: Irish Nationalism and Political Violence in the Wider World, 1867–1900* (Cambridge, 2012).

Widdis, Randy W., *With Scarcely a Ripple: Anglo-Canadian Migration into the United States and Western Canada, 1880–1920* (Montreal, 1998).

Wiesinger, Gerhard, 'Orden der Hermanns Söhne and Deutscher Orden der Harugari: Two Antinativist Fraternal Orders in the United States', *In Their Own Words*, 3:2 (1986), pp. 135–57.

Williams, J.W., *A Sermon Preached before the St George's Society* (Quebec, 1868).

Williams, Keith, '"A way out of our troubles": The Politics of Empire Settlement, 1900–1922', in Stephen Constantine (ed.), *Emigrants and Empire: British Settlement in the Dominions between the Wars* (Manchester, 1990).

Wittke, Carl, *We Who Built America* (New York, 1939).

Wokeck, Marianne S., *Trade in Strangers: The Beginnings of Mass Migration to*

North America (Philadelphia, 1999).

Wood, William, *The Laws of Athletics* (New York, c.1880).

Wyman, Mark, 'Emigrant Returning: The Evolution of a Tradition', in Marjory Harper (ed.), *Emigrant Homecomings: The Return Movement of Emigrants, 1600–2000* (Manchester, 2005).

—— *Hard Rock Epic: Western Miners and the Industrial Revolution, 1860–1910* (Berkeley, 1979).

Yates, Austin A., *Schenectady County, New York, Its History to the Close of the Nineteenth Century* (New York, 1902).

Yates, Keith L., *An Enduring Heritage: The First One Hundred Years of the North American Benefit Association (formerly Women's Benefit Association)* (Port Huron, MI, 1992).

Young, Robert J.C., 'The Disappearance of the English: Why is there no 'English Diaspora'?', in Tanja Bueltmann, David T. Gleeson and Donald M. MacRaild (eds), *Locating the English Diaspora, 1500–2010* (Liverpool, 2012).

—— *The Idea of English Ethnicity* (New York, 2008).

Zarnowski, Frank, *All Around Men: Heroes of a Forgotten Sport* (Lanham, MD, 2005).

Websites and online sources

Clipson, Addison H., 'The Caledonian Society of Cincinnati', Caledonian Society of Cincinnati, http://www.caledoniansociety.org/societyhistory.html (last accessed 28 May 2015).

Dictionary of Canadian Biography, http://www.biographi.ca (last accessed 18 March 2016).

Oxford Dictionary of National Biography, http://www.oxforddnb.com (last accessed 18 March 2016).

Royal Society of St George – Australia, http://www.royalsocietyofstgeorge.com.au (last accessed 18 March 2016).

St George's Society of New York, http://www.stgeorgessociety.org (last accessed 18 March 2016).

Scots' Charitable Society, Boston, http://scots-charitable.org (last accessed 18 March 2016).

Statistics Canada, 2006 Census of Population, http://www12.statcan.gc.ca/census-recensement/2006/dp-pd/index-eng.cfm (last accessed 26 June 2014).

United States Census Bureau, 2009 American Community Survey, http://www.census.gov/compendia/statab/2012/tables/12s0052.pdf (last accessed 18 June 2015).

United States Census Factfinder, http://factfinder2.census.gov/faces/nav/jsf/pages/searchresults.xhtml?refresh=t (last accessed 20 July 2015).

University of Alberta, Peel's Prairie Provinces online newspaper archive, http://peel.library.ualberta.ca/newspapers/ (last accessed 18 March 2016).

University of Virginia, Historical Census Browser, http://mapserver.lib.virginia.edu (last accessed 5 August 2015).

Index

Lightning Source UK Ltd.
Milton Keynes UK
UKHW021517280319
340081UK00003B/127/P

9 781526 139597